PHONETICS

PHONETICS

REVISED EDITION

An Introduction to the Principles of Phonetic
Science from the Point of View of
English Speech

Claude E. Kantner, Ph.D.

Professor of Dramatic Art and Speech, Ohio University

and

Robert West, Ph.D.

Professor of Speech, Brooklyn College

Cartographer: Harry S. Wise
Medical Director, U.S. Public Health Service Hospital
Tuba City, Arizona

HARPER & BROTHERS   *Publishers*   *New York*

Contents

Section IV.   English Speech Styles in America

Section V.   Phonetic Alphabets

Section VI.   Applied Phonetics

Illustrations

vii

Preface to the First Edition

The material in this book has been developed with two main purposes in mind: First, it has been our aim to lay here a foundation of phonetic principles on the basis of a sound neurophysiological background. Second, we have endeavored to make the subject matter of phonetics more teachable than that frequently presented to the student. By *teachable* we mean not only more palatable but also more understandable. In pursuance of this latter aim, we present herein a somewhat "different" approach to the subject—an approach which, we believe, emphasizes a consistent and logical development of the material.

This book is intended primarily as a text for the introductory course in phonetics as offered by departments of speech in colleges and universities. It is hoped that it will fill the need for a textbook in phonetics written from the point of view of the teacher of speech. It provides ample material for a semester's study. It is particularly adapted to this use, since its primary concern is with fundamental principles. It should give to the beginning student the basic background and material necessary for advanced study or for work in the fields of applied phonetics. It is also our hope that the material will find favor in the eyes of those who are out in the field working in situations where daily use is made of phonetic principles. Specifically, the actor, public speaker or reader, the elementary teacher of reading, the college teacher of public speaking, interpretation, or dramatics, the teacher of speech or English in the secondary schools, the speech correction worker, and the teacher of the deaf should find in this book basic material and guiding principles to aid them in the conduct of their work.

In selecting the material to be included in this book, we have tried to avoid the mere duplication of material already contained in other textbooks of phonetics, the only overlapping with other works in the field being in the foundation material that is common to all introductory works in phonetics. Wherever possible, we have introduced new material or new approaches to old material. At each point where the book touches on material that is treated exhaustively in other texts, we have aimed to present only the general principles involved and to indicate the line of approach, making, at the same time, reference to books that treat the subject in detail. This is especially true of the treatment of the vowels, which ordinarily occupies a large place in textbooks of phonetics. In general, our effort has been to avoid duplicating a mass of material that has already received excellent treatment by other authors and yet to present to our readers a complete and well-balanced treatise.

In the interests of simplicity and teachability, we have made a number of departures from the conventional in material and presentation, but we have endeavored to build upon a scientific foundation and to present the material in a logical manner, so that it can be readily followed and understood by the student.

In the matter of applied phonetics we are fully aware that in each of the several fields of application of phonetic theory an entire book, as large as the present one, could well be written. We have, therefore, covered in special chapters certain of these fields, outlining the rationale of the applications, but leaving to further study and to other texts the practical development of the several fields. We have striven always to keep our book practical, but our conception of the means of accomplishing that end is not to elaborate practical details, but to equip the student with basic information that will be of use to him no matter what field of applied phonetics he may enter.

The subjects of respiration, phonation, and resonance, while undoubtedly of great interest to the phonetician, have been given only cursory treatment, since they seem to belong more properly to the field of voice science. Little has been said concerning local dialects, sectional pronunciations, or foreign sounds, except where such material is useful for illustrative purposes or to round out a point of view presented in the text. It is the belief of the authors that such material is more properly taught in advanced courses after the student has been thoroughly grounded in the fundamental principles of phonetics.

We wish here to call special attention to the two chapters called "The Symbolization of Speech Sounds" and "An Introduction to Phonetics." Both contain important material that is well worth careful consideration. Since some of it may offer difficulties to the student who is just beginning his study of phonetics, we suggest a careful reading of these sections before he begins his consideration of specific speech sounds in Section II, and a restudying of the material after he has made some progress in his understanding of the field.

We wish also to make clear the reasons why certain deviations from the standard symbols of the International Phonetic Alphabet are used in the body of this book. The writers have no quarrel with the International Phonetic Association or its alphabet. This phonetic alphabet is the recognized and standard medium for the symbolization of speech sounds, and its mastery is one of the tasks that the beginning student must undertake. However, certain principles and points of view that the authors believe to be basic are difficult, if not impossible, to present adequately by means of the IPA symbols. We have, then, in order to keep our presentation of these principles clear and consistent, made certain minor changes. It should be clearly understood that these changes are made solely for pedagogical purposes. They are not intended to supplant the International symbols. The phonetician who wishes to communicate his ideas to the profession must use the more universal International Alphabet. We believe that the teacher of phonetics can clarify and systematize his presentation of ideas to the neophyte by making certain changes in symbolization. Having learned the principles involved, it is an easy matter for the beginner to become proficient in the use of the IPA symbols.

One word of caution is necessary. The material in this book is arranged in a definite sequence of ideas. The underlying point of view is, for the most part, carried progressively from chapter to chapter, so that material presented in one portion can be best approached with the perspective given by previous discussions. Although the authors have striven at all times to express their ideas clearly, they do not pretend that the material is always easily assimilated. Consequently, this book does not lend itself readily to skimming, nor can isolated portions be read to the best advantage.

We desire to take this opportunity to thank our many colleagues and former students who have been most liberal with their criticism of the text. We are, likewise, indebted to the College Typing Company of Madison, Wisconsin, for their patience and cooperation in producing the various previous editions of this book, for their work has made it possible for us to put our ideas to that best of all tests—actual classroom use. We are especially anxious to thank Harper & Brothers for their cooperation in bringing to printed form so ambitious a work in phonetics, involving as it does complicated technical problems and expensive manufacturing procedures. This book contains many evidences that the publishers have been willing to break a costly trail that others coming after them may travel more easily. Chief of these evidences is the generous use of specially-cut phonetic types. No previous text has shown as many printed systems of phonograms and diacritics as does this work. We believe the publishers have herein rendered a distinct service, not only to us as authors, but to all scholars in this field. We acknowledge also a special indebtedness to Miss Lousene Rousseau for her painstaking editing of our manuscript.

We wish to thank Dr. Claude M. Wise of Louisiana State University for his scholarly advice in the preparation of the manuscript. It has been a distinct advantage to us to have the benefit of his many years of experience as a teacher in the field of phonetics and as a recognized authority in American dialects. We gladly acknowledge our indebtedness to many friends and coworkers for such merits as this book may possess, but the onus for any errors that may appear must rest on us alone.

ROBERT W. WEST
CLAUDE E. KANTNER

Preface to the Revised Edition

Those readers who are familiar with the first edition of this book will probably notice first of all that the authors are now "conforming" in respect to phonetic symbolization. The symbols used in this revision are quite respectably "conventional." This represents, first of all, an attempt to follow as closely as possible the symbols of the International Phonetic Alphabet for the convenience of those who have learned this system. Secondly, since with only one or two exceptions the symbols correspond to those used in Kenyon and Knott's *Pronouncing Dictionary of American English*, anyone who studies this text can enjoy without difficulty the very real pleasure of checking pronunciations in a phonetic dictionary. Lastly, since this book is admittedly aimed primarily at the speech correction trade, it seemed advisable to conform to the generally prevailing practices in textbooks in this field with, as might be expected, a special attempt to be consistent with the symbols used in the latest edition of *The Rehabilitation of Speech* be West, Ansberry, and Carr.

The authors have, however, continued to indulge themselves in a few idiosyncracies of symbolization in dealing with questions of close transcription and then only for what seemed to them to be good reasons. This conformity was not achieved without certain arguments, misgivings, and regrets which will probably be shared by some of the friends of the earlier edition. The authors still feel that the International Phonetic Alphabet is in some notable respects outdated, inadequate, and lacking in internal consistency. It is proving to be just as difficult to reform in the light of advancing knowledge as is our present written alphabet, and there is some danger that its continued use will impede progress in the development of phonetic science. Contrary considerations are, of course, the need for a common tool that can be used by all students of the subject and the confusion and loss of negotiability that results when different systems are used by different writers.

Conformity in symbolization does not, however, necessarily mean conformity in concepts and principles and the authors have retained nearly all, and expanded some, of the differing points of view that characterized the first edition. These have now been recast within the framework of conventional symbolization—a task that was not always easy—but the general organization of the material and the underlying concepts are essentially the same.

The authors have also taken advantage of this opportunity to correct as many as possible of the errors of both negligence and ignorance that appeared in the first edition. More important still, a number of years of experience in teaching the older version has shown areas of weakness, exposed the problems and misunderstanding that occur most frequently among students, and led to the discovery of better ways of presenting some of the material. As a result of this learning by experience, for which we freely acknowledge our indebtedness to our colleagues and students, numerous changes and additions have been made in the interests of improved teachability. Lastly, much of the practice material in the appendices has been revised to make it more usable for classroom practice and better adapted to the beginning student.

CLAUDE E. KANTNER
ROBERT W. WEST

Foreword

A Word to the Student

The phonetic symbols on the following pages are the tools with which the student must do his work in the field of phonetics. They are as important to him as the plane, the saw, and the hammer are to the carpenter. Start to learn the symbols at once and keep studying them until you have thoroughly mastered them. The task is not as difficult as it first appears, since the majority of the symbols are taken directly from the written alphabet and many are already properly associated with the sounds for which they stand. Note the symbols **p**, **b**, **t**, **d**, **k**, **g**, **f**, **v**, **s**, **z**, **m**, **n**, **l**, **r**, and **h**. Obviously, if the reader's production of these sounds is defective or dialectal in any way, they cannot be considered as representative of the sounds intended by the symbols.

Only through usage can the symbols be learned easily and fixed in the mind firmly. The student is urged to do much transcription of his own and other people's speech. Watch for peculiar pronunciations of words and try to record them in phonetic symbols. Practice reading passages written in phonetic symbols. Work of this sort done early in the course will yield rich returns as the study of the subject progresses.

A word of warning should be included concerning the use of key words in determining the sound values of the symbols associated with the words. Obviously, *they are of value only if the student pronounces the words in the way the writers intended them to be spoken*. For example, the word *vacation* is used to illustrate the **e** sound. Now, if the reader pronounces the word as **vəkeɪʃən** so that the vowel in the first syllable is like the first vowel in *about*, it is apparent that he will get an entirely wrong impression of the

The Phonetic Symbols

STOP PLOSIVES (CONSONANTS)[a]

	Printed Symbol	Key Word	Transcription
1.	p	pay	peɪ
2.	b	bay	beɪ
3.	t	tip	tɪp
4.	d	dip	dɪp
5.	k	call	kɔl
6.	g	gone	gɔn

FRICATIVE CONTINUANTS (CONSONANTS)

	Printed Symbol	Key Word	Transcription
1.	f	fat	fæt
2.	v	vat	væt
3.	θ	thin	θɪn
4.	ð	then	ðɛn
5.	s	sue	su
6.	z	zoo	zu
7.	ʃ	shoe	ʃu
8.	ʒ	vision	vɪʒen

AFFRICATES (CONSONANTS)

	Printed Symbol	Key Word	Transcription
1.	tʃ	church	tʃɜtʃ
2.	dʒ	judge	dʒʌdʒ

GLOTTAL FRICATIVE (CONSONANT)

	Printed Symbol	Key Word	Transcription
1.	h	hat	hæt

NASAL CONTINUANTS

	Printed Symbol	Key Word	Transcription
1.	m	may	meɪ
2.	n	nip	nɪp
3.	ŋ	lung	lʌŋ

VOWEL CONTINUANTS

	Printed Symbol	Key Word	Transcription
1.	i	eat	it
2.	ɪ	it	ɪt
3.	e[b]	vacation	vekeɪʃen
4.	ɛ	pen	pɛn
5.	æ	sat	sæt
6.	ɑ	father	fɑðɚ
7.	ɔ	all	ɔl

[a] This simplified list of the phonetic symbols used to represent the sounds of English speech is adequate for broad transcription, and is adapted to the needs of beginning students. Symbols for foreign sounds and other symbols indicating refinements in the representation of English are introduced from time to time in the text. For a complete list of all the symbols used in this book and the modifying signs used in close transcription, see Chap. 12.

[b] In English, this sound is pronounced as a vowel glide (diphthong) when it occurs in accented syllables. Note, for example, the second syllable in **vekeɪʃen**. It occurs occasionally as a "pure" vowel (with little or no gliding movement) in unaccented syllables if the vowel does not unstress to **ə**.

Printed Symbol	Key Word	Transcription
INTERVOWEL GLIDES (SEMIVOWELS)		
1. w	we	**wi**
2. j	yes	**jɛs**
3. l	law all	**lɔ ɔl**
4. r	rob bar	**rɑb bɑr**
INTERVOWEL GLIDES (DIPHTHONGS)		
1. eɪ[g]	aim	**eɪm**
2. aɪ	high	**haɪ**
3. ɔɪ	boy	**bɔɪ**
4. aʊ	loud	**laʊd**
5. oʊ[h]	open	**oʊpən**

Printed Symbol	Key Word	Transcription (continued)
VOWEL CONTINUANTS		
8. o[c]	notation	**noteɪʃən**
9. ʊ	pull	**pʊl**
10. u	pool	**pul**
11. ʌ ə[d]	above	**əbʌv**
12. ɝ ɚ[e]	worker	**wɝkɚ**[f]

[c] This sound, like the e, is usually pronounced in English as a vowel glide when it occurs in accented syllables as in the words *boat* **bout** and *open* **oʊpən**. It occurs occasionally as a relatively pure vowel in unaccented syllables if the vowel does not unstress to ə. Note, for example, *opinion*, which may be **opɪnjən** or **əpɪnjən**.

[d] This symbol is an exception to the general rule that a phonetic alphabet should have only one symbol for each sound. For our purposes at this point it can be said that ə represents the same sound as ʌ. However, in English this sound occurs so frequently in unaccented syllables that it seems helpful to have a second symbol to represent the unstressed form. In a sense these symbols serve as accent signs. If the reader of phonetic transcription sees the symbol ʌ, he knows that the syllable in which it occurs must be given either a primary or a secondary stress. On the contrary, the use of the ə indicates that the syllable must be unstressed.

[e] The ɚ is another exception to the one symbol per sound rule. Both ɝ and ɚ represent the same basic sound but, as in the case of ʌ and ə, the sound occurs so often in an unstressed form that it seems desirable to have a second symbol. Assuming general American pronunciation (see footnote f), use ɝ if the syllable receives primary or secondary stress and ɚ if it is unstressed.

[f] This transcription represents what is called general American speech, that is, the usual pronunciation of the vowel r in the Midwestern, Northern, and Western sections of the United States. The symbols ɝ and ə would be used to represent the usual pronunciation of this word in Southern England and in parts of Eastern and Southern America, thus, **wɝkə**. The ɝ and ə should be regarded as variants of the same basic sound.

[g] See also e which is considered as a variant of this sound.
[h] See also o which is considered as a variant of this sound.

sound value of the symbol **e**. This difficulty is especially likely to arise in connection with vowels and with foreign sounds. This means that in learning the symbols the student should not rely too much on his own pronunciation of the key words, lest he inadvertently associate a given symbol with the wrong sound. The symbols should be learned under someone versed in phonetics. The non-English sounds should be learned under the supervision of someone who knows both phonetics and the foreign language represented. Key words are excellent memory devices, but *they do not teach the correct sound for the symbol unless the student already has that sound in his habitual pronunciation.*

It is important that the student learn early in the course to associate the symbol with its sound and the sound with its symbol, not only accurately but also quickly and almost automatically. Thus, if he sees the symbol **æ**, he should be able without hesitation to remember and produce the sound it represents. Conversely, if someone utters the sound, the written symbol should come instantly to mind. The beginning student may find it necessary to establish this association through the use of key words. For example, he may have to remember that the symbol **ɛ** stands for the first sound in *ever* and seek to recall the sound by pronouncing the word. This must be regarded only as a learning device and quickly supplanted by a direct and immediate connection between symbol and sound. Otherwise the student's phonetic transcription will always be slow and laborious.

Since phonetic symbols are used to convey information about speech sounds, it is important that they mean approximately the same things to different people in different places and at different times. They are used in analyzing and recording speech and in writing down the results of observation and research. If they are to be of the greatest possible service, they must be kept as standard as possible and the student must make certain that his concepts of the sound represented by a given symbol coincide as nearly as possible with those of other people. To do this, he must through ear training increase his ability to discriminate between sounds and this is achieved only by constant practice in comparing his own speech sounds with those of others.

Footnote *a* on page xviii calls attention to the fact that the symbols given here are for use in broad transcription. Broad transcription means the representation of the sounds that occur in a given portion of speech without any attempt to indicate refinements of pronunciation or subtle differences in sounds. Technically, it is a transcription using one symbol per phoneme—a conception that will be more clear to the student after he has read the discussion on phonemes. Frequently, however, such a gross representation of speech sounds is not satisfactory. Additional symbols and various diacritic markings are needed to indicate delicate shadings of pronunciation. When such symbols are used, we speak of the transcription as "narrow" or "close." In the main, narrow transcription is employed to indicate which of the various members of a sound phoneme was used by a given speaker. As an example, we may say that the representation of *cat* as **kæt** is a broad transcription. However, if we write it as **kæ̃ᵊt**, we indicate that a particular speaker nasalized the **æ** sound and spoke the word with an off-glide **ə** between the **æ** and the **t**. The beginning student will use the broad form for his early transcriptions. Special symbols and signs for close transcriptions are introduced in the text as occasion demands, especially in Section II, which contains detailed discussions of the separate speech sounds. Problems arising in narrow transcription are described and illustrated in some detail in Chapter 12. For the convenience of the student the complete phonetic alphabet, including signs for close transcription, is given in that chapter. The transcriptions in this book are in the broad form except when some point of distinction is being illustrated. In such cases, the particular sound or sounds under discussion are usually written in the narrow form while the rest of the word or sentence is represented in broad transcription.

The authors have had no intention of writing a prescriptive text laying down rules for correct pronunciation. Nevertheless, the writer of a textbook in phonetics is faced with the necessity of deciding what pronunciation to indicate when transcribing his illustrative material. In this book, many of the illustrations exemplify special forms of pronunciation or dialectal speech. When such is not the case, the transcriptions are based on the pronunciation given in Webster's unabridged *New International Dictionary*. In instances in which the dictionary does not indicate clearly the pronunciation, because of sectional variations, the so-called general American dialect[1] is followed. Needless to say, this is in no way a claim to superiority on the part of the general American speech. The writers feel that in order to avoid confusion a textbook of phonetics should adhere rather closely to one of the major American dialects. They have chosen the general American, partly because they are best acquainted with it, and partly because they feel that it will be the most serviceable to the majority of their readers. Neither is it to be assumed that the words and phrases given in phonetic transcription are intended as guides to the "proper" pronunciation. They are intended only as illustrations, not examples to be followed. In fact, many instances can be found in which the same word is given variant pronunciations. Unless otherwise indicated, the writers have endeavored to transcribe their illustrations in what they consider to be good general American speech but they are in no way interested in setting up standards of pronunciation, either general American or otherwise.

---

[1] See Chap. 16.

An Introduction to the Study of Phonetics

Chapter 1 The Symbolization of Speech Sounds

Definition

In a sense, phonetics may justly be called a study of symbols. The process we call speech is essentially a system of symbolization that has been built up to make negotiable from one individual to another his concept of certain objects, qualities, acts, ideas, or relationships. Speech uses as its medium of transmission sound waves that are set up in various parts of the speech mechanism. This mechanism is capable of producing a large number of sounds that are within the auditory range. A relatively small number of these sounds become stereotyped in their production and serve, by the common consent of those speaking the language, as units in the formation of the acoustic symbols we call words. These units we may properly call speech sounds.

The sounds represented by the symbols **k**, **æ**, and **t**, for example, are produced by the speech mechanism, received by the auditory mechanism, stereotyped in their production, and used as units in the formation of auditory symbols, i.e., words. Thus they qualify as speech sounds. This particular combination of speech sounds serves, when it impinges upon the auditory mechanism of someone using the same set of symbols, to call forth an image of a small furry animal with a long tail. We may further qualify our definition of a speech sound by saying that it ought to be a single sound, that is, a sound that, in terms of the fundamental movements involved in its production, is incapable of further division.

Ordinarily speech sounds do not carry meaning when used alone. They are to be regarded as units that are combined to form the words we use in speech as auditory symbols. However, some speech sounds do have meaning when used individually. Among these we may note ʃ meaning "be quiet," s expressing disapproval, m indicating uncertainty, aɪ the personal pronoun, and æ, ɑ, ɔ, and oʊ which, when spoken with the proper inflection, indicate various emotional attitudes such as disgust, fear, disapproval, surprise, and disbelief.

Out of all the sounds that can be produced by the speech mechanism, only a few are used in the formation of the auditory symbols that constitute speech. Naturally, in the development of different languages somewhat different sounds will be selected for this purpose, different combinations of these sounds may be used, or the same combinations may become symbols representing different meanings.

For those who like categorical definitions, the writers present the following: On the perceptual side, a speech sound is a time order of acoustic events so stereotyped in its symbolic semantic uses that any significant portion of it will engender a perception of the whole. From the standpoint of production, a speech sound is a sound within the auditory range, produced by the speech mechanism, stereotyped in its production so that it is usually produced in approximately the same manner, and used as a unit in the formation of symbols which have come by association to be connected with certain objects, qualities, acts, ideas, or relationships in such a manner that these symbols convey meaning when they impinge upon the auditory mechanism of anyone using the same set of symbols. From the standpoint of physics, a speech sound is a series of physical vibrations produced by the speech mechanism, lying within the auditory range and having symbolic significance in the process of communication.

Thus we may say that our spoken language is in reality a series of auditory symbols that can be further broken up into symbol units or speech sounds. These symbol units are composed of physical vibrations known as sound waves in the atmosphere. The producing mechanism is that part of the body known as the speech mechanism. The receiving mechanism is the auditory mechanism, using this term in a broad sense to include not only the ear, but also the higher auditory centers in the brain.

The Relationship of the Written Alphabet to Speech

So far as we know, spoken language has always preceded writing. Except in pictographic or ideographic languages, the written alphabet, as it develops, is an attempt to symbolize visually speech sounds that have already been in the language for a long time. This is certainly true of the alphabet that we use to write the English language. In the sixth century the progenitor of our English language had no alphabet. There existed only the very cumbersome runic writing which was a religious form. It was at this time that Christian missionaries began to use characters of the Latin alphabet to represent native speech sounds. Thus, in the fore-runner of our English alphabet each character stood more or less accurately for a given sound according to the phonetic knowledge of the missionaries. The written alphabet is then, in reality, a series of visual symbols which stand for corresponding auditory symbols, which, in turn, symbolize objects, ideas, or relationships.

Phonetic Alphabets

We have mentioned previously that when the Roman alphabet was first used to represent the speech sounds of the ancestor of our English language, it is probable that there was a closer correspondence between the letters of the alphabet and the sounds of the language. Although no such language exists, it is possible to imagine an ideal situation in which each letter in the written alphabet stands for a sound and each sound in the spoken language has a letter to represent it. Such an alphabet is called a phonetic alphabet and the characters of which it is composed are phonetic symbols. In a phonetic alphabet we expect complete consistency between written symbols and sounds; that is, each symbol must always represent the same sound and that one sound only, and each sound must be represented by only one symbol. Hungarian and Spanish approximate this ideal situation, which means that the spelling of these languages serves as a rather reliable guide to pronunciation and that the reverse is also true.

Representation of sounds by the Roman alphabet was probably very inaccurate even at the beginning, and it has grown increasingly so with the passage of time. At the present time any student of speech knows that the letters on a page of writing fall far short of representing the sounds. This means that the auditory symbol units or speech sounds have changed at a vastly more rapid pace than the visual symbols. Thus, the speech sounds as they are produced from individual to individual, year to year, and generation to generation vary more *in their production* than do the corresponding letters of the alphabet. The reason for this is largely a matter of the permanence of the two types of symbols. It is evident that the auditory symbols, that is to say, the sound waves themselves, have no permanency. They are gone the instant they are produced and, up to the invention of recording apparatus, could be retained only in memory. The visual symbols, on the other hand, are as permanent as the materials out of which and on which they are recorded. This explains in part why the spoken language has changed so radically since the sixth century that we would be unable to understand the language of that time if we heard it, whereas the alphabet used to record the language, even though changed in many respects, is still essentially the same.

In this connection it is interesting to note the influence of the invention of the printing press with movable metal type in Europe in the middle of the fifteenth century. Before that time, when "manuscripts" were literally and laboriously written by hand, changes in the form of the letters and in the spelling of words were much more likely to occur. It is safe to say that as printed materials and the ability to read them have become increasingly widespread, the rate of change in the written language has slowed down correspondingly. Until very recent times there has been no comparable influence to check the rate of change in spoken language. Nearly all of the development of recording on cylinders, discs, and tapes and of radio, talking pictures, and television has taken place within the last forty years. It seems clear that these media for distributing widely and preserving, more or less permanently, the spoken word are already tending to "homogenize" our American English and will work increasingly in the future to slow down the rate of change.

The Necessity for Using Phonetic Symbols in the Study of Phonetics

The above discussion enables us to understand why the study of phonetics begins with either the construction of a phonetic alphabet or the learning of one previously constructed by others. Perhaps, however, the student who is shortly to be faced with the task of learning these symbols and of using them in transcription is not yet convinced of their necessity. A single illustration should suffice to emphasize their value. Note the sounds represented by the letter *a* in the following words: *Aaron, at, ably, above, alms,* and *awe.* Note also the spellings of the sound **i** in the words l*i*ter, b*ea*t, Ph*oe*nix, p*eo*ple, d*ee*p, k*ey*, qu*ay* and bel*ie*f. The consonant ʃ also has various spellings in the words pa*ss*ion, *sh*ip, an*x*ious, auc*t*ion, *ch*agrin, *s*ugar, con*sc*ious, and *sch*ist. Now try to write out some instructions on the pronunciation of these sounds for the benefit of some real or imaginary foreign friend who does not understand our English sound system. It is evident that this would be about as difficult as trying to introduce a large number of people to each other without knowing their names. True, one could point at them, or describe their appearance, or compare them with someone else whose name he did know, but the process would be clumsy, time-consuming, and inaccurate. It is difficult to think, talk, or write about speech sounds without some symbol or name that will stand for each one. As a matter of fact, it is practically impossible to record observations made in the field of phonetics in such a way that the reader can understand them without resorting to phonetic symbols.

The question naturally arises as to why one cannot use the system already developed for use in the dictionaries and thus avoid the necessity of learning a new set of symbols. We need not consider the implied assumption that the dictionary markings have been learned, and the fact that different publishers of dictionaries use many somewhat different systems. The question partially answers itself if we consider the exact nature of the dictionary symbols. They are basically an attempt to represent speech sounds within the framework of a written alphabet which is essentially unphonetic. Since the letters of the alphabet are not sufficient in themselves, they are supplemented by certain arbitrary signs called diacritical markings.[1] In this connection we should recall that the minimum number of symbols needed in our phonetic alphabet for purposes of broad transcription of American speech is at least thirty-six, whereas there are but twenty-six letters in the written alphabet. Additional confusion arises from the fact that the so-called vowels of the written alphabet (*a, e, i, o, u,* and sometimes *y* and *w*) are pronounced in from three to eight different ways and that most of the consonants have more than one pronunciation. Consequently, we find Webster listing eight diacritical markings for *a* as follows: å, ă, à, ä, ā, â, ă, and á. It is doubtful if the average reader will be able to recall offhand the sound values of all of these markings. Webster's newest unabridged dictionary uses sixty-six symbols altogether, without making any finer distinctions between sounds that can be made with the symbols of the phonetic alphabet presented in the early pages of this book. Obviously there must be considerable overlapping among the dictionary markings. These markings serve their purpose in the dictionaries reasonably well, because they are always accompanied by key words. However, they are ill-adapted to the classroom, the laboratory, and the professional journal since they are unnecessarily complicated, difficult to remember, and confusing in use.

Problems in Constructing a Phonetic Alphabet

We have previously defined a phonetic alphabet as one in which there is a symbol for each sound in the language. Putting it another way, each sound is always represented by one and the same symbol. In contrast to the dictionary system, a phonetic alphabet uses diacritical markings only as *modifying signs* to indicate nuances of pronunciation, not to differentiate the basic sounds, or phonemes, as we shall later call them, of a language.

Since English is still a partially phonetic language, the process of constructing a phonetic alphabet is essentially one of revising our present written alphabet so that there will be separate characters to represent each sound. Although other types of symbols could be and have been used, the interests of economy in expense

---

[1] For a more complete discussion of diacritical markings and an exposition of the systems used by three standard dictionaries, see Chap. 19.

as well as in learning dictate the use of the regular letters of our alphabet with whatever changes and additions are necessary. This means first that typewriters and linotype machines, etc., already have most of the symbols available for use, and, second, that the student starts out with a good share of the alphabet already learned. This double use of the letters of the alphabet can, however, be confusing unless the student keeps clearly in mind the distinction between the *name* of the letter and the *sound* represented by that same letter when it is used as a phonetic symbol. This distinction is illustrated in the following sentence: The letter *s* (naming the letter) is pronounced as **s** (producing the sound) in the word *some* which is pronounced **sʌm**.

A number of phonetic systems have been devised from time to time, some of which have been discarded for various reasons. While these are outside the scope of this discussion, the student will find it interesting to investigate some of these older phonetic alphabets in books dealing with the history of the subject.[2]

Devising a set of symbols to represent the sounds used in speech is by no means simple. Without going into detail, we may enumerate three of the major difficulties involved: (1) the problem of finding what sounds are present in a given language, avoiding both unnecessarily fine distinctions and gross overlapping; (2) the problem of finding symbols to represent these sounds that will be readily comprehensible and easily available in type, and (3) the problem of devising a system that will be neither too elaborate for practical use nor too abbreviated for accurate speech representation. Except for the availability of the symbols on typewriters and in standard print, these problems have been largely solved for us by phoneticians. The problem of finding additional symbols is worthy of special mention, since an understanding of the origin or form of these new symbols will often aid in learning them more rapidly.

We have already listed fifteen symbols taken from the written alphabet that have the same sound value customarily given them in English. Four vowels and one glide sound are represented by regular printed letters in the alphabet [i, e, o, u, and j] which have

---

[2] See Alexander G. Bell, *The Mechanism of Speech*, Funk and Wagnalls Co., 1916; and Henry Sweet, *A Primer of Phonetics*, 3rd ed., Oxford University Press, 1906. Chap. 18 also contains some related material.

been assigned arbitrary yet logical values. Two more symbols, [ɪ and ʊ] are derived from small forms of capital letters. ɑ is a written *a*, ɛ is a modified form of the Greek letter epsilon, ɜ is a reversed epsilon, and ɝ is a reversed epsilon with a curl at the top. ɔ is an open *o*, ʌ is an upside down *v*, ə is an inverted *e*, and æ is formed by combining lower case *a* and *e*. Of the remaining consonant symbols that are unfamiliar, θ is the Greek letter theta; ð is an old English form of *th*; ʃ and ʒ are elongated forms of *s* and *z*; and ŋ is an *n* with a tail.

The International Phonetic Alphabet

It is not surprising that every set of symbols yet devised has had its imperfections. The most satisfactory and widely used system at the present time is the International Phonetic Alphabet (IPA) as developed by the International Phonetic Association. As indicated by its name, this alphabet includes symbols not only for English sounds, but also for all modern European languages, as well as for some others. That even the IPA has its imperfections is shown by the fact that practically every writer in the field of English phonetics has seen fit to make some changes in it to meet the needs of his presentation. It is, however, the one common vehicle for the exchange of ideas in the phonetic world. It is more widely used than any other set of symbols, with the exception of the diacritic markings used in the dictionaries. For these reasons, the student of phonetics must learn, and be able to use, the IPA symbols.

Mention should also be made here of the alphabet used by the American Dialect Society in recording and preserving speech in local communities throughout the United States for the Dialect Atlas Survey. This alphabet is basically the same as the IPA. A few changes have been made, and a number of new symbols and modifying signs have been added in order to meet the need for a very narrow form of transcription in recording the niceties of dialect speech.

The Phonetic Alphabet Used in This Book

The alphabet presented in the front of this book is essentially that of the International Phonetic Association. It contains the symbols necessary for a broad transcription of English speech. The student in speech pathology and correction will find the symbols used here to be the same as those in *The Rehabilitation of Speech* by West, Ansberry, and Carr.[3] With two exceptions, they are also similar to those used in *A Pronouncing Dictionary of American English* by Kenyon and Knott.[4] The authors of this phonetic dictionary make no distinction between the **o** and the **ou** or the **e** and the **eɪ**, using the symbols **o** and **e** to represent all varieties of these sounds. The present writers believe that this distinction should be made because of its importance in the correction of most foreign accents and in the acquiring of a foreign language. The use of both symbols is, admittedly, a form of close transcription and the use of either (but preferably **ou** in English) as a broad transcription symbol is justified. On the other hand, both of the previously mentioned books make a distinction between the **ju** in *use* **juz** and the **ɪu** in *beauty* **bɪutɪ**, whereas in this text these are considered as close transcription forms and **ju** is used for both in broad transcription.

The writers have introduced and used in the body of this text a few changes from the conventional representation of IPA. It is our conviction that changes in the International Phonetic Alphabet should not be made at random, or indeed at all, unless they are definitely warranted. We feel, however, that the changes here introduced are justified in the interests of teachability in that they make the material easier to assimilate and retain. The International Phonetic Alphabet is discussed in detail in Chapter 18.

Sample Transcriptions

The following transcriptions illustrate a broad transcription of English speech in the General American dialect. A slow and rather careful manner of reading is assumed. The symbols for broad transcription as presented in the early pages of this book are used. The transcription follows:

ðə lɔrd ɪz maɪ ʃɛpəd aɪ ʃæl nɑt wɑnt
hi meɪkɪθ mi tu laɪ daʊn ɪn grin pæstʃəz

---

[3] 3rd ed., Harper & Brothers, 1957.
[4] G. & C. Merriam Co., 1953.

hi lidɪθ mi bɪsaɪd ðə stɪl watɚz
hi rɪstoʊrɪθ maɪ soʊl
hi lidɪθ mi ɪn ðə pæðz əv raɪtʃəsnɪs
fɔr hɪz neɪmz seɪk
jeɪ ðoʊ aɪ wɔk θru ðə vælɪ əv ðə ʃædoʊ əv
     dɛθ
aɪ wɪl fɪr noʊ ivəl fɔr ðaʊ ɑrt wɪθ mi
ðaɪ rad ænd ðaɪ stæf ðeɪ kʌmfɚt mi
ðaʊ prɪpɛrɪst ə teɪbəl bɪfoʊr mi
ɪn ðə prɛzənts əv maɪn ɛnɪmiz
ðaʊ ənɔɪntɪst maɪ hɛd wɪθ ɔɪl
maɪ kʌp rʌnɪθ oʊvɚ
ʃʊrlɪ gʊdnɪs ænd mɝsɪ ʃæl fɑloʊ mi ɔl ðə deɪz
     əv maɪ laɪf
ænd aɪ wɪl dwɛl ɪn ðə haʊs əv ðə lɔrd
     fɔrɛvɚ

Chapter 2 Basic Principles in the Study of Phonetics

The Purpose of This Section

It is our aim in this chapter to introduce the reader to the science of phonetics. In addition to defining the field of phonetics and its spheres of usefulness, we hope to lay down some basic considerations to be kept in mind in the study of this subject, to enumerate with brief comments various approaches to the study, and to discuss with some detail one such approach. This chapter will also include a discussion of the various problems connected with the study of phonetics.

This material should serve to illustrate the connections between phonetics and other branches of speech study, particularly speech science. It should also prepare the student for a further study of the subject by giving him a general background in the field.

Definition of Phonetics

Broadly speaking, phonetics is the study of speech sounds. Such a study includes the consideration of the symbolic nature of speech sounds, the way in which speech sounds are produced by the speech mechanism, the physical and psychological problems connected with the perception of these sounds by the auditory mechanism, and, lastly, the varying usage and variant pronunciation of these sounds in different parts of a given country or of the

13

world. Usually the study involves the devising and use of a set of symbols to represent these sounds.

Care must be taken to distinguish between phonetics proper and applied phonetics. As indicated above, phonetics proper is the scientific study of speech sounds from the standpoints of their production, reception, and symbolic use. Phonetics as a study has broad applications, but it is not accurate to call these applications phonetics. Thus, the use of phonetics in the correction of defective speech or in the teaching of a standard speech is not to be considered as a study of phonetics proper, but rather as applied phonetics.

As indicated above, phonetic principles may have many applications: (1) to studies in other branches of general linguistics, i.e., morphology, etymology, dialect studies, etc.; (2) in the field of speech correction; (3) in speech science, speech psychology, and other informational speech courses; (4) in such practice speech courses as interpretation, voice training, general speech, etc.; (5) in dramatics, i.e., the teaching of stage speech or of a given dialect for use in a play; and (6) general application to the teaching of pronunciation by means of dictionaries, workbooks, etc.

Allied Fields

It is obvious that the study of phonetics draws heavily upon other related fields. Anatomy, neurology, and physiology contribute material on the structure and functioning of the speech mechanism. Information covering the nature of sound in general and of speech sounds in particular is drawn from the field of physics. Psychology helps us to understand the symbolic nature of speech sounds. Needless to say, phonetics is also closely related to other phases of speech study, especially speech science. Dialect studies and foreign language studies, together with studies of sound changes, bring in also such related fields as geography, history, and sociology. Phonetics is a branch of general linguistics and is thus related to studies in etymology, morphology, and orthoepy.

The technical study of phonetics in the laboratory also requires a wide range of technical skill in, and knowledge of, different fields. Such projects as the phonographic recording of speech sounds, making x-ray pictures of the mechanism in action, making palatograms, photographing the vocal and articulatory mechanism during the production of speech, and the analysis of the sound waves present in speech sounds are examples of the work done in the phonetics laboratory.

Some Basic Considerations in the Study of Phonetics

With this general introduction, we may proceed now to lay down several general principles that are basic in the study of phonetics. This is an attempt, not to summarize the whole field of phonetics or even all of its important phases, but rather to formulate and state some broad general principles that will serve as foundation stones, or, perhaps better still, as points of departure, for students undertaking a study of phonetics. There are six such principles to be enumerated. Lack of space forbids a lengthy discussion of each one, but the broad applications of each are indicated. It will be noted that some of the statements are broad enough to apply to other phases of speech study while others have ramifications into the fields of applied phonetics.

1. *Speech sounds are produced by portions of the vegetative system.* This statement indicates that the study of phonetics will be concerned in one of its aspects with contracting and conducting tissues —muscles and nerves. It will involve a neurological and anatomical study of the various structures that make up the speech mechanism and of the action of these structures in the production of speech sounds. It means also that the nature of the sounds produced will be restricted and governed by the laws and limitations governing muscle movement and the conduction of nerve impulses. Also involved are the implications of the fact that the structures that produce these sounds have other vital functions, which take precedence over speech.[1]

2. *Speech sounds are received by the auditory mechanism.* These speech sounds so produced are received and interpreted by the auditory mechanism together with its associated higher centers in the brain. This implies the consideration of speech sounds as acoustic phenomena and involves such problems as the following: the physics of sound in general; the anatomy and functioning of

---

[1] See Chap. 3 for a more complete discussion of this statement.

the auditory mechanism, its limitations and possibilities; auditory range, carrying power, ability to distinguish between sounds, pitch, volume, resonance, and pressure patterns; and the effect of hearing on sound changes, the learning of speech sounds, and the development of speech defects.

3. *Speech sounds are symbol units.* These speech sounds become stereotyped and serve as units in the formation of symbols that, by usage and common consent of those using the symbols, become associated with certain objects, qualities, acts, ideas, and relationships. This statement has been discussed elsewhere and needs no further elaboration here.

4. *Speech sounds are learned.* Speech is an acquired, not an inherited, trait, and each child learns anew the auditory symbols used by those about him. Moreover, the ability to develop and use any very complicated set of symbols seems to be limited to the human race. This statement, once the subject of dispute but now a truism, has an important application to any phase of speech that has to do with the acquiring of speech habits or the reeducation of those habits, for example the learning of speech by children, the teaching of foreign language, and the correction of dialects.

5. *Speech sounds are influenced by forces that work to produce variation.* There are forces in operation that work to produce a great deal of variation in the way in which any given speech sound is produced and, to a lesser extent, in its acoustic effect. This variation occurs in the speech of any one individual when he makes a certain sound at different times. It occurs also in different individuals subject apparently to the same environment. It occurs in different sections of a country or in different countries where the same language is spoken with varying dialects. The forces that act to produce this variation may be enumerated as follows: the inability of the neuromuscular mechanism to repeat a movement after an absolutely exact pattern; the influence of the position of the body as a whole upon the functioning of the speech mechanism and on the production of the sounds; the variation in structure from one individual to another; the influence of neighboring sounds; and the tendency of an individual to produce a sound as he hears it. This last point, which is very important, means that, in the absence of training, speech sounds will vary according to variation in hearing and this variation will grow more pronounced

in districts lacking widespread intercommunication. Obviously all this has an important bearing on the way in which speech sounds are produced, on the origins of dialects, and on the studies of such dialects.

6. *Speech sounds are influenced by forces that work to prevent variation.* There are also in operation forces that work to prevent change and to keep speech in general, and speech sounds in particular, static. If it were not for such forces it is possible that only those who live in close proximity would be able to communicate with each other, and speech in isolated districts would become unrecognizable to nonresidents at a much faster rate than it does at present. One of these stabilizing forces in the physiological tendency of the organism to follow the line of least resistance —in other words, to form habits whereby movements or acts are repeated time after time in a similar, if not exactly identical, fashion. This is essentially a matter of laying down neural patterns or neurograms in the nervous system for the production of each sound. These patterns become more stereotyped with each repetition, and as they become more stereotyped they become more difficult to change. The similarity of movement is not absolute, but there are definite limits to the probable variation.

Furthermore, while speech mechanisms and auditory mechanisms differ in different individuals, they are alike in their broader aspects. Thus, given mechanisms with no actual pathologies, the variations in a sound that occur as the result of differences in structure are usually minor, and they do not affect greatly the fundamental nature of the sound.

A third force operating to check change has its basis in the perceptual side of the problem. Since these sound units combine to form symbols that serve to stir up meanings, it follows that they lose their value if they are no longer recognized by the listener as the sound the speaker intended to use. In other words, the amount of variation in the production of any given speech sound, if that sound is to remain serviceable, is limited by the ability of those who hear the sound to recognize it as the symbol the speaker thought he was using. Thus, other factors remaining equal, the greater the intercommunication among the residents in a given geographical area, the stronger will be the forces working toward stabilization of the language.

The Phoneme Theory [2]

The two sets of forces discussed above, the one working to produce change and the other resisting change, form the basis for a discussion of the phoneme theory. Perhaps the term "sound family" is the most adequate simple interpretation of the term *phoneme*; it implies a group of sounds that are closely related to each other in some way yet by no means identical. Let us take the usual sound of the letter *t*, symbol **t**, for an example. We have stated that it is theoretically impossible for anyone to make two *t* sounds *exactly* alike. Even for practical purposes, the *t* may vary greatly as it is pronounced by one individual in different combinations or by different individuals. It is well known that *t* can be produced with the tongue tip placed anywhere from behind the lower front teeth, to the edges of the upper front teeth, and as far back on the hard palate as the tongue can reach by curling upwards and backwards. On the other hand, these variations are limited, first, by the physiological tendency of the mechanism to stereotype the movements, and, second, by the fact that the resulting sound must still be recognized acoustically as a *t* or it loses its symbolic value. But within these limits, there is considerable variation. The symbol **t**, then, obviously does not stand for a single distinct sound which is an entity in itself. It is, rather, a general symbol standing for any one of a series of *t* sounds. Such

[2] The beginning student may wish to supplement this discussion with additional reading in John S. Kenyon, *American Pronunciation*, 10th ed., George Wahr, 1950, "Introduction"; Charles K. Thomas, *An Introduction to the Phonetics of American English*, Ronald Press, 1947, Chap. 1; Claude Merton Wise, *Applied Phonetics*, Prentice-Hall, Inc., 1957, pp. 74–79. Those who wish to study the phoneme in more detail should consult the following sources: Leonard Bloomfield, *Language*, Henry Holt and Company, 1933, Chaps. 5 and 6; M. Swadesh, "The Phonemic Principle," *Language*, June, 1934; W. Freeman Twadell, "On Defining the Phoneme," *Language Monographs*, March, 1935; M. J. Andrade, "Some Questions of Fact and Policy Concerning Phonemes," *Language*, January–March, 1936; *Proceedings of the Second International Phonetic Congress of Phonetic Sciences*, Cambridge University Press, 1935 (contains numerous addresses dealing with the phoneme); H. A. Gleason, *An Introduction to Descriptive Linguistics*, Henry Holt and Company, 1955, Chaps. 12 and 13; Kenneth Pike, *Phonemics; A Technique for Reducing Language to Writing*, University of Michigan Press, 1947; Kenneth Pike, "On the Phoneme Status of English Diphthongs," *Language*, April–June, 1947; G. W. Trager, "The Phoneme 'T': A Study in Theory and Method," *American Speech*, October, 1942; and G. W. Trager, "What Conditions Limit Variance in a Phoneme?" *American Speech*, September, 1934.

a family of sounds is called a phoneme. The phoneme theory is simply an attempt to take account of the variation in the production of any given speech sound and to place limits on that variation. These limits of variation are governed, as noted previously, by the recognizability of the sound as a *t*. If those who hear the sound perceive it as a *t*, then it is within the *t* phoneme for those individuals and in terms of that particular phonetic and situational context. We cannot, however, generalize from any single example. The accidental or occasional misinterpretation of a sound does not establish it as belonging or not belonging in a given phoneme. A particular variety of sound may be said to be within the *t* phoneme of an individual if he usually or consistently perceives that type of sound as a *t* in his interpretation of what is said. Thus, if a listener fails under certain special conditions to notice any difference between the use of a glottal stop **ʔ** and a **t** in words such as *battle* **bætl̩ bæʔl̩**, this does not necessarily mean that the **ʔ** belongs in his phoneme family of *t* sounds. If, however, he consistently substitutes **ʔ** for **t** in such words without awareness of the difference or hears the sound in the speech of others with equal unawareness, we would say that *for this individual* the **ʔ** is a variant of the *t* phoneme.

On the basis of the discussion thus far, we can list briefly some of the basic principles that are embodied in the general concept of the phoneme being presented here:

1. Any speech sound is composed of a variety of auditory characteristics.

2. These auditory characteristics vary considerably from one utterance to another, one individual to another, and one dialect of a language to another.

3. In the perception of the sound and the subsequent interpretation of its symbolic significance, many of these differences are not significant (nondistinctive); that is, their presence or absence does not alter the final interpretation of the meaning of what was said.[3]

---

[3] There are, of course, many nuances of meaning, some of which may be affected by so-called nondistinctive features. The statement applies to the rather gross semantic meanings carried by the speech sounds when they are used as symbol units.

4. By the same token, some of the auditory characteristics are significant or distinctive; that is, they enable us to perceive and identify the sound as belonging in a certain classification (phoneme).

5. All the members of a phoneme family are presumably (this remains to be fully proven in the laboratory) characterized by the same or similar distinctive feature or features.

6. The distinctive features of each phoneme, **t**, **k**, and **p** for example, must (presumably) be different from those for every other phoneme so that when we hear **tap** we not only recognize the first sound as belonging to the **t** phoneme but we also know that it is not a member of the **k** phoneme as in **kap** or the **p** phoneme as in **pap**.

7. Phonemic identification is, then, a psychological process of perceiving, recognizing, and classifying. The process of classification is an act of association that is, for the adult user of the language, as automatic as the motor act of sound production. The final determinant in phonemic identification is meaning, that is, how this particular speech sound or symbol unit (sometimes called allophone) fits into the larger symbolic patterns of sounds (words) that we use in communication.

8. In one sense the physical "reality" of the phoneme may be said to lie in the nerve impulses, contracting muscles, and sound waves that are part of the production of the sound. It seems probable, however, that the real essence of the phoneme lies in the act of perception rather than of production. In a very real sense the laboratory cannot tell us what a phoneme is; it can only describe the characteristics of a sound that someone has perceived and reported as belonging to a certain classification, i.e., phoneme family.

9. It may, thus, very well be that the only phoneme that can be said to exist in reality is to be observed *in situ* only in the single utterance of a sound in a meaningful sequence and its subsequent perception and classification by a single individual. Anything beyond this is an abstraction or generalization. Thus, we say that sounds similar to this one are usually heard by individual *A* as belonging to the **t** phoneme. Obviously, we are generalizing on widely different levels when we speak of a sound as belonging in a certain phoneme for individual *A*, the Pennsylvania Dutch,

general American speech, American English, and the English language.

It is not to be supposed, however, that in listening to speech we consciously analyze the continuous flow of language into its separate symbol units and make mental note of the phonemes used. The process of breaking speech down into phonemes is highly artificial so far as the layman is concerned. We can say that the layman recognizes at least two types of variations in speech sounds: (1) He may recognize that the sounds used by another individual are defective or distorted—that they differ somewhat from the ones he uses. He notes the distortions, but recognizes the sounds as his own; that is, they fall within his own phonemes. (2) The layman may note that the sounds used by another individual are quite different from the ones he uses in the same combinations. They are not merely distortions of his own sounds; they are different sounds. They may be sounds with which he is familiar in other combinations or sounds quite foreign to him, but they are not the ones he, himself, would have used. They lie in different phonemes.

We should note here that a change of phonemes does not necessarily cause a misinterpretation of the meaning. The Middle Westerner who pronounces *penny* as **pɛnɪ** may understand the Southerner who says **pɪnɪ**, but again be aware of a difference that goes beyond mere distortion. Thus, even the layman who probably has never heard the word *phoneme* may be aware of phonemic changes without losing the meaning of what is said.

On the other hand, phonemic changes do frequently result in misinterpretation of meaning. For example, one Middle Western farmer who is accustomed to saying, "My father is in the barn" **maɪ fɑðɚ ɪz ɪn ðə bɑrn** might misunderstand completely another Middle Western farmer of German extraction who said **maɪ fɑɡɚ ɪs ɪn ɡə bɑrn.**[4]

We have discussed the phoneme as a psychological phenomenon having to do with the recognition of variations in the production of speech. The degrees of awareness of variation and their relation to the phoneme concept may be classified as follows: (1) If the listener is unaware of any difference in the speech of a second person, then, *for him*, his own phonemes have been used.

---

[4] For an explanation of the modifier **ʀ**, see page 217.

(2) If the listener is aware of a difference but thinks of the sound as a distorted or defective utterance of the same one he would have used, then it is still within his own phoneme. (3) If, on the other hand, the listener observes that the speaker has used a quite different sound, then, even though he may still understand the meaning, a different phoneme has been used. (4) If the listener misunderstands the meaning because of a difference in the sounds used, we may also say that, so far as the listener is concerned, the speaker has employed another phoneme. We have previously illustrated differences in pronunciation that may seem to the listener to involve different phonemes. As an example of a distortion not felt to be in a different phoneme, note the difference between the pronunciation of *cat* in an ordinary fashion as **kæt** and then definitely nasalized, as **kæ̃t**.[5] Similarly, a listener whose own *s* is produced normally might be aware of distortion in a speaker whose *s* is "spread" because of wide spaces between the upper front teeth, but still recognize it as an *s* sound. If, however, the spread *s* was so distorted that the listener misunderstood and heard **ʃɪp** when the speaker meant **sɪp**, then the *s* of the speaker is outside the listener's own *s* phoneme, and falls rather within his *sh* phoneme.

It seems to follow that individuals will vary considerably in their awareness of phonemes and phonemic variants and, to a lesser extent, in the number of functional phonemes they may have in their own speech. For example if we consider American English as a whole, we conclude that it contains an **æ** phoneme and an **ɑ** phoneme and that, for the great majority of speakers, the **a**[6] is heard as a variant of either or both of these two sounds. Some speakers use the **a** unconsciously in their own speech as a variant of **æ** and some as a variant of **ɑ**, yet there are others for whom **a** is a separate phoneme that is distinct from either of the other two. These individuals use **a** consistently in a certain class of words. For them, *ant* and *cant* are **ænt** and **kænt** but *aunt* and *can't* are **ant** and **kant**. A similar example can be found in the **ɒ** sound which lies between **ɑ** and **ɔ**.

The point being illustrated here is that a sound which may be a

---

[5] For an explanation of the modifier ~ , see page 217.

[6] See page 77 for a discussion of the **a** sound. This is a close transcription symbol representing a sound between **æ** and **ɑ**.

phoneme for an individual may not be for his local group and a sound that may be phonemic in a given dialect may not be in the language as a whole. Finally, the phonemes for any given language are never exactly equivalent to, and often vary widely from, those of another language. Basically the differences are of two types. One language will contain certain phonemes that are not to be found in a second language and the second language will have phonemes that are not present in the first. More important to one who tries to learn a foreign language, the phonemes that are present in both languages rarely overlap each other with any degree of exactness. Frequently the number and nature of the variants for a phoneme in one language, are markedly different from those for the "same" phoneme in another language The grosser differences caused by the presence or absence of phonemes are usually more easily overcome than are the minor variations that exist between comparable phonemes. Evidence for this last statement is to be heard daily in the speech of those who have learned to speak a foreign language imperfectly.

It follows, of course, that two languages will have different sets of phonemes to a much greater extent than two individuals or two sections of a country speaking the same language. Thus the Italian language has an ŋ sound but no phoneme, because this sound is always heard as a variant of the **n**. In some words, the French language employs a sound close our æ, but it is regarded as a part of the **a** phoneme. Several Romance languages do not have separate **i** and **ɪ** phonemes but have instead a single phoneme that appears to lie between the two. Zipf[7] makes the interesting observation that in the speech of North China a voiceless plosive, such as **k**, is one phoneme when followed by a puff of air (aspirated) and another when this puff is absent (unaspirated). That is, in that language, there are two **k** phonemes, and the listener has to be aware of this difference or he may misinterpret meaning. In English both types of *k* are used, but without any difference in symbolic significance, hence they are variants of one phoneme. Despite these differences, however, two related languages are more similar in their gross aspects at least than they are different.

In our attempt to evolve a practical working definition of a

[7] George K. Zipf, *The Psycho-Biology of Language*, Houghton Mifflin Company, 1935, p. 56.

phoneme, we have stressed two concepts: *variation* in the production of speech sounds, and *awareness* of these variations by individuals who hear them. Although simple definitions are likely to be misleading, we may say that the concept of a phoneme is present whenever an individual becomes aware of a variation in the production of a given speech sound that is divergent enough to make him feel that the speaker has used a different sound from the one he, himself, would have used. This statement has three implications: (1) The phoneme concept is present in all individuals who have speech even though they may not have the vocabulary for expressing the concept. (2) A phoneme exists only by comparison; it is not a static entity, but a fluctuating awareness of differences. (3) Different individuals may have different sets of phonemes.

We should remind ourselves at this point that the phoneme theory is primarily a utilitarian concept that arises of necessity from the very nature of spoken language. Speech employs sounds that are constantly varying. Since these sounds are used as symbols, it is imperative that limits be set on this variation, because symbols are by nature arbitrary signs that can have meaning only when mutually agreed upon and recognized. These symbols may vary in any direction and to any extent just so long as they are still recognized as the intended symbol and are not confused with some other symbol or not recognized at all. We need the phoneme concept to keep us aware of these variations and to help us reconcile the fact that speech sounds do vary with the equally obvious fact that they are usable as symbols in communication.

The most widely accepted test for determining whether or not a given sound is phonemic for an individual, a group or a language is to compare it with other sounds in otherwise identical words to see if the meaning changes.[8] As a simple example, if we have a series of words such as **sæt, pæt, gæt, fæt, væt, mæt, næt,** and

---

[8] In Chap. II of his book, *The Psycho-Biology of Language*, George K. Zipf defines the phoneme as "the smallest unit of distinctive significance." He goes on to say, "Two sounds of a language may be considered either as identical or as appertaining to the same phoneme, if a substitution of one for the other throughout the entire language will not lead to the confusion of meaning of a single word." See also H. A. Gleason, *An Introduction to Descriptive Linguistics*, Henry Holt and Company, 1955, Chaps. 12 and 13.

ðæt, that are identical except for the difference in the initial sound, we note that in each case this difference changes the meaning of the word. Furthermore, if we try out another sound t, we again have a word that differs in meaning from all of the rest. This leads us to suspect that s, p, g, f, v, m, n, and ð are all phonemic in English, and more exhaustive tests of the same type would confirm this observation. Note, however, that the meaning does not change if in saying kæt we use the kind of k we make in *key*, or in *coo* or in *skip*. This indicates that for us these different *k*'s (see page 167) are members of one phoneme.

In a similar fashion the changes in meaning between sit, sɪt, sɛt, sæt, sɑt, and sɔt are preliminary proof that the vowels i, ɪ, ɛ, æ, ɑ, and ɔ are separate phonemes. Using this method, the reader can test his own speech to determine whether or not such sounds as hw and a are phonemic for him or members of the w and æ phonemes—this on the assumption that he can both produce and hear these sounds properly.

We may summarize this discussion by saying that the phoneme theory is to be regarded as a practical concept designed to explain the variation of the speech sounds that form the basic units of a language. Since the limits imposed upon this variation must ultimately be based on individual perception, each individual has his own set of phonemes, and the phonemes of a language are to be thought of as a generalized cross-section of the phonemes used by the speakers of that language. We need to remember, also, that the phonetic alphabet is really a phonemic alphabet; that is to say, it provides one symbol for each observed phoneme in the language. Although we often use the terms interchangeably, we should understand that the term *speech sound* means any single utterance of one of the symbol units of speech, whereas the word *phoneme* includes all of the variants of a given sound that are recognized as that particular symbol. Speech sounds can be measured and analyzed, a phoneme cannot. In broad transcription we write in terms of these sound families, or phonemes. In narrow transcription we attempt to record some of the variants within the phoneme.

Approaches to the Study of Phonetics

The student who takes up the study of phonetics is soon faced with the task of classifying speech sounds—a task frequently made unnecessarily confusing and burdensome, because of failure to recognize that it can be approached from at least three distinct angles. The ordinary classification is sometimes confusing to the beginner because it uses all three approaches in a haphazard manner, and the resulting mixture of terminology is bewildering. In order to lessen this confusion and to lay the foundation for an orderly presentation, the writers preface their own classification by listing these three approaches and noting the terminology applicable to each:

1. *The acoustic approach.* In the first place, the study of speech sounds can be approached from the standpoint of the effect produced by these sounds upon the auditory mechanism. This is an acoustic approach. Such a study is chiefly concerned with problems of pitch, volume, resonance, pressure patterns, duration, etc. —that is to say, acoustic problems. Under such a scheme, speech sounds are classified on the basis of their acoustic effect and in terms that apply to auditory sensation. All sounds are first divided into vowels, semivowels, diphthongs, and consonants. For the vowels, there is no clear-cut acoustic classification, although such terms as *stressed, unstressed, long, short, weak, strong, more or less sonant, more or less resonant, high pitch,* and *low pitch* are auditory terms or adjectives used to indicate the type of sound. Similarly the words *tense* and *lax,* although they really should be used to indicate the degree of muscle tension, have been used so often to describe sound quality that they are now almost auditory terms.

With the consonants, there is a fairly complete set of terms to describe the sounds according to this approach. All consonants are first separated into *sonants* and *surds.* These two main classifications are further subdivided by such terms as *sibilants* **s, z,** etc., *fricatives* **ʃ, θ, f, ʒ,** etc., *affricatives* **tʃ, ts, dz,** etc. *plosives* **p, d, k,** etc., *nasals* **m, n, ŋ,** etc: and *liquids* **l, r, w,** etc. The words *rolled, trilled, scraped, clicks, aspirated, whispered, silent, voiceless,* and *voiced,* etc., are also auditory terms used frequently.

2. *The placement or position approach.* A second approach to the study of phonetics is what we may call the position or placement approach. Such an approach takes up the study of speech sounds from the standpoint of the position of the articulatory mechanism when the sounds are produced. Specifically, the investigator wishes to know the position of the tongue, soft palate, mandible,

and lips for the production of every speech sound. X-ray and palatographic studies are examples of research using this type of approach. The placement approach involves a study of anatomy in order to determine the nature of the structures making up the speech mechanism and the positions that these structures are capable of taking.

There are in the literature a large number of terms dealing with speech sounds that designate placement or are descriptive of position. Vowels, for example, are divided into *front, mid,* and *back* vowels. The front vowels are subdivided into *high front, mid front,* and *low front,* and similarly for the mid and back vowels. In addition the terms *close, half-close, half-open, open, narrow,* and *broad,* are used to describe vowel sounds. For the consonants this placement terminology is even more abundant. The terms *bilabial, labiodental, dental, alveolar, retroflex, palato-alveolar, palatal, velar, uvular, pharyngeal, glottal, linguadental, linguarugal, lingua-palatal,* and *linguavelar* are all used to describe positions of the articulatory mechanism.

3. *The kinesiologic approach.* Still a third approach to the study of phonetics is the kinesiologic, or movement, approach. It is closely related to the study of positions discussed above and usually goes hand in hand with it. There is, however, a different emphasis. Here the investigator wishes to know, not only the position that the speech mechanism was in when the sound was made, but also what movements of the mechanism were necessary to produce that position. If the study be carried even further, it involves the determination of the muscles in contraction to produce those movements and the nerve centers and paths by which the activating impulses reached the muscles. There are relatively few terms that apply strictly to a kinesiologic approach. The words *continuant, stop,* and *glide,* however, are descriptive of movement rather than of position or acoustic effect.

Overlapping of the Various Approaches

As has been suggested before, no one approach is usually followed consistently or used solely as the basis for a classification of speech sounds. Each approach has its contribution to make to the field, and the student's understanding of phonetics cannot be well rounded if any one of them is left out of consideration. There is some danger that the student will become confused by the apparent conflict in terminology. For example, the sound **s** might correctly be referred to as a surd continuant, a voiceless continuant fricative, a sibilant, or a whispered linguadental continuant. It could also be called a voiceless, linguadental, continuant fricative. Given this name *linguadental* represents the placement approach, *continuant* the movement approach, and *fricative* the acoustic approach. This apparent confusion is easily overcome if the student remembers that the terminology is drawn from three different sources and studies each term carefully.

In the present book it is our aim in Section II, Kinesiologic Phonetics, to present primarily a movement approach. This is impossible, however, without also taking into consideration the position taken by the speech mechanism for the production of each sound, thus involving indirectly the placement approach. Section III, Phonetic Metamorphology, embodies the application of phonetic principles to the problem of sound changes. Chapter 14, Acoustic Changes, is written from the auditory approach, while Chapter 15, Physiologic Changes, involves largely a kinesiologic approach.

Problems in the Study of Phonetics

A number of problems arise in the very beginning of an attempt to study the speech sounds of a language. It will perhaps be advantageous if we take up at this time some of the more pertinent of these problems and discuss them briefly. This should serve to give an additional insight into the field of phonetics and to prepare the student for a better appreciation of the material that follows. Eight such problems are discussed in the following pages.

1. *The problem of determining the speech sounds present in a given language.* Fortunately, the average student who takes up the study of a language, either native or foreign, is not faced with this task. It has already been done for him by competent authorities and he is, so to speak, handed the speech sounds on a platter. The sounds of English, for example, have been studied by phoneticians and language experts over a long period of time, so that for us the problem of determining these sounds is largely already solved. Suppose, however, that the student were a research worker studying a totally unknown African dialect. It is obvious that his

first task in learning the language would involve learning the sounds of that language. (Many people, it should be noted, learn to speak a language without having any conception of the separate sounds that make up the language.) Our research worker would then have the task of analyzing the speech into its separate components, that is, speech sounds. This would involve an intensive study of the language, using the acoustic and placement approaches to break it up into its phoneme units.

2. *Problems arising from the variation in the way a given individual produces the same speech sound at different times.* It has been demonstrated experimentally time and again that such variations exist and that no speech sound is produced twice in exactly the same way, even by the same individual. We have already mentioned the possibility of producing the *t* sound by different adjustments, but even when the individual attempts to use exactly the same movement, there is still some variation. For example, two palatograms of the sound **t** made under what appear to be exactly the same conditions and with a special effort to produce precisely similar sounds, will always show some, and often considerable, variation. This variation is present in all speech sounds and is especially noticeable in the vowel sounds. It is customary to describe a certain position for each of the sounds of speech. But if so much variation exists, and if any sound can be, and apparently is, made in a number of different ways but never in exactly the same way, the question naturally arises as to whether anything is to be gained by a study of the movements made in producing those sounds. There are several reasons for an affirmative answer to this question.

The variations that occur in the speech of any one individual are due largely to three causes. First, from a theoretical standpoint, an exact repetition of a movement made by a living, changing organism is an impossibility. However, we may justifiably dismiss such variations as being too minute to make any practical difference. Such differences are more than offset by the counteracting tendency of the mechanism to follow the line of least resistance and stereotype the movements. Some variation will always exist but any attempt to assume that the movements involved in the production of speech sounds are of a haphazard and hit-and-miss nature is in direct contradiction to all of our knowledge concerning habit formation and the laws governing muscular contraction and the conduction of nerve impulses.

In the second place, variations in movement occur as the result of adjustments made by the articulatory mechanism in compensation for changes in the relations between various parts of the speech mechanism as a whole. For example, speaking with the head bent forward necessarily demands a different muscular adjustment than speaking with the head bent backward or to one or the other side. For this reason, there will always be some variation in movement when the same sound is produced under different structural conditions.

Lastly, the influence of neighboring sounds causes variation in the way a given sound is produced. It is obvious that the nature and extent of a given movement will depend in large degree upon the point at which the movement begins and ends. Again using the sound **t** as an example, we note that in each of the four words, *cut*, *kit*, *list*, and *lint*, there is a sound that is recognized acoustically as a **t**. Yet in each of these words the movement begins from a different position, i.e., the positions of **ʌ**, **ɪ**, **s**, and **n**, respectively. Carried to its logical conclusion, this observation means that there are as many slightly varying movements for the production of the sound **t** as there are combinations of that sound with other sounds in the languages.

It will be seen at once that all this points to an almost unlimited number of minute variations or movements. An attempt to analyze all of these variations would present a task impossible of achievement. However, the crux of the situation lies in the fact that there is always a fundamental movement that remains essentially the same. An analogy may be drawn from the movements in writing in which all three of the conditions mentioned above that produce variation are likewise present. It is possible to form the letters of the alphabet in any number of ways, but in ordinary writing these movements tend to become fixed and stereotyped so that we can recognize without difficulty the handwriting of a friend, while experts in the subject can identify writing that has been carefully disguised. Variations always exist but they are comparatively slight, and the movements always tend toward standardization.

In terms of muscle movements the situation may be summarized thus: The general direction of the movement and the muscles that produce it remain essentially the same. The variation is a matter of *difference in the degree of muscle movement* and *not of type*. This is equivalent to saying that all of the members of a given phoneme are produced by the same fundamental type of movement. One or two exceptions to this statement will be noticed later. The term *speech sound*, as used in this study, should be taken as referring to the typical member of the corresponding phoneme. Likewise, in the section on Kinesiologic Phonetics the movements described for a given sound are the fundamental movements requisite to the production of a typical member of that phoneme.

We may conclude then that an analysis of the typical movements occurring during the production of speech sounds is of value, and that general descriptions of these movements can be made that will be applicable to all normal speech.

3. *Problems arising from the variation in the way speech sounds are produced by different individuals and in different sections of the country.* Still another problem of variation that arises in connection with the study of speech sounds is the difference in the way various individuals produce a given speech sound. This variation is often especially pronounced in different sections of the country. In general, these variations are due to three causes: differences in the structure of the speech mechanism, differences in the way individuals hear the various sounds, and those purely local or sectional differences that arise in communities where speech develops along tangents different from those in other sections. It should be remembered that the variations existing in dialects are often not caused by differences in the way the sounds themselves are produced, but rather by the substitution of one sound for another, and also the broadness of the phoneme in one section as against another.

We have mentioned that in any one individual variation in the production of sounds is held in check by two factors, one an acoustic factor that operates because of the necessity of keeping the sounds within their respective phonemes, the other a physiological one that operates because of the tendency of the mechanism to stereotype movements. In differences between individuals, however, it is obvious that only the acoustic factor is in operation. This serves to keep the production of sounds similar in different individuals only in so far as a given acoustic effect can be produced by only one adjustment of the mechanism. That this factor is only rather loosely binding can be easily demonstrated by experimenting a little with the making of the same sound (acoustically) by different adjustments. It will soon be seen that almost any sound can be produced in different ways and still remain acoustically about the same. This points to a greater degree of variation among individuals than in one individual.

Even taking into consideration all of these factors, we are, however, still safe in assuming that the movements by which one individual produces a given sound are fundamentally the same as those of another individual. Differences in structure will sometimes force a different adjustment but the structures are fundamentally alike. The same principle holds here that applies to variations within the individual, namely, that the variations are usually of degree rather than of kind.

If the above is true, it would seem worth while to study the movements involved in the production of speech sounds, not with the idea that the results can be applied in detail to all individuals, but rather with the understanding that these are typical movements that give the essential factors in the production of the sound under consideration.

4. *Problems involved in the consideration of a given speech sound as it is produced in isolation versus that same sound when present in continuous speech.* In our study of phonetics, we sometimes lose sight of the fundamental fact that speech is not a series of isolated sounds, but a smooth-flowing continuous affair in which, wherever possible, sounds are blended together and the muscular process made continuous from one sound to another. This principle, inherent in the physiological mechanism, is again a matter of conserving energy and saving time. The student can demonstrate this easily for himself by taking a sheet of paper, placing on it a broken series of a dozen or so dots, and then drawing a line that will hit each dot accurately, at the same time stopping at each dot, as in Fig. 1. Now put down the same dots and with one sweeping movement draw a line that will come at least reasonably close to each of the dots, as in Fig. 2. It is obvious that the second movement is much easier and faster. Just as it takes more power to start and stop a car than to keep it going once it is started, so the

speech mechanism finds it easier to make a continuous movement than a series of stops and starts. It is obvious, also, that the continuous type of movement is less accurate than the other—that is,

Fig. I. Schematic illustration of slow and careful speech.

there is a tendency to approach in the general direction of the dots but it is more difficult to hit them exactly.

We are here introduced to two principles that wage eternal warfare in a language, i.e., the necessity of keeping a speech sound within its phoneme versus the strong physiological tendency of the mechanism to smooth out the movements and eliminate

Fig. 2. Schematic illustration of normal continuous speech.

breaks. The first is essential, but the second is easier. If we are to communicate by sound symbols, we must have certain distinguishable symbol units, but the physiological mechanism constantly seeks to destroy the integrity of these units by leveling them down. Academicians in general, and speech teachers in particular, do valiant battle for the integrity of the phoneme and against slovenly, inarticulate speech. Their battle cries are, "speak distinctly," "don't slur those consonants," "pronounce those final *t*'s and *d*'s," "don't drawl those vowels," "don't mumble," etc., etc. Meanwhile, shopgirls and factory hands and indeed many students go blithely on with such time and energy-saving tele- scopings of the language as **lɛzgoʊ** *let's go*, **dʒit-tʃɛt** *did you eat yet*, and **hɑjə** *how are you*. All of which is simply a way of dramati- zing the problem of those who seek to inculcate in their students a desire for a clear-cut articulation and a distinct, understandable speech.

It is evident that the task of analyzing the movements in con- tinuous speech is impossible of achievement. This means that the study of phonetics will perforce be largely a study of speech sounds in isolation, because at present most of our methods and apparatus are adapted only to the study of sounds in isolation. However, refinements in the techniques of motion picture photography, together with the availability of subjects with facial injuries leaving openings that have made it possible to get much clearer interior views of the articulatory mechanism in action have added greatly to our knowledge of the moving stream of speech.[9] Similar valuable information of the auditory blending of speech sounds in continuous speech has resulted from the development of the sound spectograph[10] and similar instruments.

It is also evident that the movements for the production of a given speech sound in isolation are somewhat different from those for that same sound in connected speech. Two factors are respon- sible for this: the tendency of the mechanism to smooth out movements, and the fact that the mechanism is constantly be- ginning the movement for a given sound from the position of the preceding sound and ending it by going to the position of the following sound. Read again the discussion regarding the *t* sound

[9] (1) "Movements of the Tongue in Speech," International Film Bureau, 1948. Fourteen minutes, sound, partly color. May be rented for $7.50. Cat. No. 612.78; (2) "Articulatory Movements in the Production of English Speech Sounds—Part 1: Consonants," Veterans Administration, 1953. Twenty-five minutes, sound and color. May be rented, LC card FiE 54–5; (3) "Articulatory Movements in the Production of English Speech Sounds—Part 2: Vowels and Glides," Veterans Administration, 1954. Twenty-six minutes, sound and color. May be rented, LC card FiE 54-398.

[10] See Ralph K. Potter, George A. Kopp, and Harriet C. Green, *Visible Speech*, D. Van Nostrand Co., 1947.

on page 18. When *t* is pronounced in isolation, the mechanism starts from a resting position and returns to it when the sound is finished. When the *t* is pronounced in the word *little* lɪtl̩, however, the movement is from the ɪ position to the **t** and from the **t** to the l̩ position.[11]

These two factors will produce a large number of minor variations, especially in the way in which the movement begins and ends, but they will not influence the main movement required to any great extent. In the pages that follow, we shall for the most part be considering speech sounds in isolation. However, we should never lose sight of the fact that speech is a continuous process in which these isolated movements are welded into a relatively smooth-flowing whole.

5. *The problem of determining the movements involved in the production of speech sounds.* The problems that have been discussed so far have had to do mainly with factors that work to cause variation in the way in which a given speech sound is produced. We come now to a consideration of the difficulties involved and the methods employed in a study to determine the movements that occur when such a speech sound is produced. Four methods of investigation have been found useful in such studies.

a. Subjective analysis. In using this method the investigator makes a certain sound or assumes the position necessary for its production and then seeks to determine the position and movements of the articulatory mechanism by an analysis of the sensations resulting from this activity. This method is essentially subjective and for this reason its accuracy is open to question. Its great disadvantage lies in the fact that sensations from this region are often not clearly localized. However, such a study does aid materially in analyzing movements that are otherwise difficult to observe and when used in conjunction with other methods may yield much useful information.

b. Direct observation. Much is to be gained by direct observation of the movements that occur during the production of a given sound. Movements and positions of the lips and mandible can be studied accurately by this method. Movements of the tongue, soft palate, and pharyngeal walls can also be observed either directly

---

[11] See Chap. 12. The vertical bar under the symbol indicates that the *l* sound is here serving as the vowel in the second syllable.

or with the aid of a mirror. Direct observations of these parts, however, is not so satisfactory, since they are more or less hidden from view, especially during the articulation of certain sounds. In observing movements inside the mouth cavity, care must be taken to avoid disrupting the ordinary relationships existing between the various parts of the articulatory mechanisms during the production of the sound under consideration. For example, holding the mouth wide open in order to obtain a clearer view of the tongue may force that organ to make adjustments resulting in movements different from those that would occur in ordinary speech. Many movements are at best so slight or so completely hidden from view as to be incapable of direct observation. Within these limitations, however, this method of study is both fruitful and reliable.

c. Palatographic studies. Studies of this type employ a hard rubber or metal plate formed to fit the roof of the mouth in a manner similar to the mounting for a set of false upper teeth. This artificial palate is moistened, dusted with a fine white powder (calcium carbonate is very satisfactory) and placed in position. If the sound to be studied is then made and the plate removed, movements in which the tongue makes contact with the roof of the mouth will be indicated by a removal of the powder from the artificial palate and a corresponding deposit on the tongue. Obviously, care must be taken to avoid any movements other than those made in producing the sound. The presence of the plate results, at first, in a feeling of clumsiness and probably in some distortion of movement, but with a little practice these difficulties are easily overcome. Such studies yield interesting and accurate data, but their application is limited to movements in which the tongue makes a contact with some part of that portion of the roof of the mouth covered by the artificial palate. Thus there are a number of sounds that cannot be studied at all by this method and, in the case of those that can, one cannot be quite certain that there were not other important movements that were not registered on the plate.

d. X-ray studies. The application of x-ray photography to the analysis of speech sounds has yielded valuable information. It has been used extensively, especially in earlier studies of the vowels.[12]

---

[12] See especially in this connection: G. Oscar Russell, *The Vowel*, Ohio State University Press, 1928, and *Speech and Voice*, The Macmillan Company, 1931.

In essence, such a study involves making an x-ray picture of the articulatory mechanism during the production of the sound under consideration and analyzing this picture to determine the positions taken by the various structures. Usually a lateral view is taken. A marker of some sort must be employed to make visible such soft structures as the tongue and soft palate. A gold chain, gold leaf, or some adhesive compound containing barium is employed. There is, of course, always the possibility that these materials when placed on the tongue may cause a distortion of its normal movements. Another disadvantage lies in the fact that the view obtained is limited to one perspective, namely that of a sagittal section through the midline. For example, if the marker used is a gold chain running along the midline of the tongue, the resulting x-ray picture will show the position of that organ only at its midline— not such movements as narrowing or broadening of the tongue and depression or elevation of its sides.

It will be seen from the above discussion that each of the four methods of studying speech sounds has both advantages and disadvantages. An analysis based on any one method would certainly contain many inaccuracies. Each method is more valuable when its results are checked and interpreted in the light of results obtained from other approaches. In the analyses that follow, information has been drawn from every possible source and every method utilized that would aid in the formation of a composite picture of the movements and positions of the articulatory mechanism during the production of the sounds analyzed.

6. *The problem of distinguishing between essential and accessory movements.* Still another problem that arises in such a study is that of determining which movements are essential to a given sound in contrast to those that are merely accessory in their nature. Many of the movements in the total speech process are accidental or transitional in nature. Some may be characteristic of, and peculiar to, the individual as, for example, the eversion of one side of the lips in the production of a "lateral" s which may be normal acoustically even though defective in its manner of production. Others may be generally characteristic of the sound but not indispensable as, for example, the lip rounding that often accompanies ʃ. Note the variation in the production of ʃ in *shoe* and *she.*

In the present study we have followed the policy of describing the movements that are essential to the production of the sound. A movement may be regarded as essential to the normal production of a sound if the inability to make that movement results in an inability to make the sound or in the production of the sound by an adjustment markedly different from the one typically used.

7. *The problem of determining the muscles and nerves that function in the production of speech sounds.* Even when the movements of the mechanism are determined and those that are nonessential eliminated, the picture is still incomplete without an analysis of the muscles and nerves that function in the production of these movements. This brings phonetics into the fields of anatomy and neurology. Such a study is the logical completion of the analysis of speech sounds, but it is perhaps a little too involved for the beginning student. It would begin with an analysis of the muscles of the articulatory mechanism and a study of their nerve supply, followed by a determination of the movements that the muscles are capable of making and the effect of these movements on the structures upon which they act. This information, coupled with information about the movements necessary to the production of each speech sound, would provide the basis for determining the muscles and nerves involved in each sound. The muscles and nerves involved in the production of speech can be studied in any standard textbook of anatomy [13] or in certain books in the field of speech science.[14]

8. *The problem of selecting a point of departure for a description of the movements involved in the production of a given sound.* We have stated that any description of the movements involved in the production of speech sounds must of necessity deal largely with these sounds in isolation. However, even though sounds are considered in isolation, there still remains the necessity for some fixed point that will serve as a basis of comparison in describing the movements that follow. It seems advisable, therefore, to designate some arbitrary position of the articulatory mechanism

---

[13] D. J. Cunningham, *Textbook of Anatomy*, 6th ed., Oxford University Press, 1931; Henry Gray, *Anatomy of the Human Body*, 23rd ed., Lea and Febiger, 1936; or any standard textbook on anatomy.

[14] L. S. Judson and A. T. Weaver, *Voice Science*, F. S. Crofts, 1941, Chap. XI; G. W. Gray and C. M. Wise, *The Bases of Speech*, 3rd ed., Harper & Brothers, 1959, Chap. IV.

as the fixed point at which all movements to be described will begin and end. For this purpose, we have chosen the position prevailing in normal, quiet respiration. This position will be described in detail later.[15] This is, practically speaking, the resting position of the speech mechanism, insofar as any living mechanism can reach a resting state. It will be referred to hereafter as the "neutral position." An analysis of any given sound will include, therefore, a description of the movements of the mechanism from the time it leaves the neutral position to the termination of the sound.

9. *The problem of determining the acoustic characteristics of speech sounds.* So far we have been primarily concerned with problems connected with positions and movements of the articulators. Speech sounds are, however, in the last analysis auditory phenomena and the study of their acoustic characteristics is an important field in itself. Modern equipment for recording and analyzing sound has made it possible to determine more accurately than ever before the auditory components of speech. Each sound can be described in terms of the frequencies present and the distribution of energy among these frequencies.

Just as some of the movements of speech are extraneous, so it has long been known that many of the frequencies present in a given speech sound are not essential to its recognition or even to its perception as a "normal" speech sound. The ability to analyze accurately all of the characteristics of a sound has also opened the way to the determination of its essential characteristics. There are, in general, two ways of approaching this problem. One is to "filter" out certain frequencies and combinations of frequencies from recorded samples of speech sounds until by a process of elimination the essential elements for recognition or undistorted perception have been found. The other is to "manufacture" speech synthetically by producing and combining frequencies known to be present, again for the purpose of discovering which are essential.

The determination of the essential acoustic characteristics of speech sounds is, of course, of great practical value in the construction of any equipment designed to transmit sound and it seems clear that the production of synthetic speech will also have commercial possibilities.

[15] See Chap. 4.

Chapter 3   A Brief Review of the
Speech Mechanism

Introductory Statement

Since the kinesiologic approach to the study of speech sounds demands of the student a certain technical knowledge of the speech mechanism, a brief review of the structures making up this mechanism is here presented to acquaint the student with the structures and their functions and to familiarize him with the terminology of the subject. This discussion will not, however, provide an adequate background to students who are unfamiliar with the material treated. Such students may wish to read more extensively in books that treat the subject in detail.[1]

All English speech sounds normally produced have one factor in common: the utilization of the moving column of air furnished by the expiratory phase of the process of respiration. As this column of air passes through the larynx it may be set into vibration by the action of the vocal folds when the glottal edges are approximated, or it may be allowed to pass through a relatively unrestricted aperture. Thus the action of the laryngeal mechanism forms the basis for a division of all sounds into two main groups: voiced sounds, i.e., those formed from a stream of air that has previously been set into vibration in the larynx; and voiceless

[1] See, for example, G. W. Gray and C. M. Wise, *The Bases of Speech*, 3rd ed., Harper & Brothers, 1959; or L. S. Judson and A. T. Weaver, *Voice Science*, F. S. Crofts, 1941; or Jon Eisenson, *Basic Speech*, The Macmillan Company, 1950.

sounds, i.e., those formed from a column of air that has been allowed to pass through a relatively unrestricted glottal opening, in other words, nonvibrated.

This vibrated or nonvibrated column of air leaves the larynx to enter the pharyngeal cavity. From the pharyngeal cavity proper it may enter the nasopharynx and nasal chambers or pass through the faucial orifice into the oral cavity, or it may divide, part passing into each cavity. It finally leaves the body through either the oral (lips) or nasal (nostrils) orifice or both. These various cavities act as resonating chambers that distribute the energy of the laryngeal tone among its various overtones and thus give the voice its distinctive quality. ·

In the course of its outward passage this column of air may be subjected to an almost unlimited number of modifications produced by different adjustments of the articulatory mechanism. Many, though not necessarily all, of these alterations in the outflowing stream of air result in physical vibrations which are interpreted as sound. All sounds so produced are potential auditory symbols, but only a part of them are stereotyped as to production and symbolic significance and used as speech sounds.

This introduction lays the groundwork for a division of the speech mechanism into four main parts: the power mechanism, the vibrator mechanism, the resonator mechanism, and the articulatory mechanism. Let us hasten to say that this division is largely for the purposes of description and that the speech mechanism functions as a whole and not in four parts. Furthermore there is considerable overlapping in both structure and function. For the purpose of this study we are most interested in the articulatory mechanism. We may now proceed to a brief discussion of these four mechanisms with particular emphasis on the last.

The Power Mechanism

The power mechanism for speech is the same as that employed in the vital process of respiration. Respiration, as the layman uses the term, means the act of getting air in and out of the lungs. Technically the term refers to the basic function which involves the exchange of gases that occurs when a living organism takes in oxygen and gives off carbon dioxide. This exchange of gases takes place at two points: internally between the blood stream and the tissues of the body, and externally between the blood stream and the air contained in the alveoli. The former is called internal, and the latter external, respiration. The term is used broadly in this book to refer to the whole process of breathing.

The power mechanism is formed by the parts of the walls and contents of the thorax concerned in the respiratory process. The thorax, commonly called the chest, includes the whole middle section of the body between the neck and the abdomen. The bony framework of the chest is referred to as the thoracic cage. The thoracic cage is bounded superiorly by the clavicles or collar bones; posteriorly, by the upper part of the spinal column and the posterior portions of the ribs; anteriorly, by the sternum, or breast bone, and the anterior portions of the ribs; laterally, by the middle portions of the ribs; and inferiorly, by the diaphragm. This bony cage is covered with various muscles and tissues that serve to form an airtight cavity, the thoracic cavity. This cavity is separated from the abdominal cavity by the diaphragm, which is a muscular and tendonous sheet attaching to all the inner walls of the body cavity and acting as an important muscle in breathing. The thoracic cavity contains the lungs which are the essential organs of breathing, and also the heart, the thymus gland and a number of major blood vessels and nerves. The lungs are two in number, one on each side of the thoracic cavity, which, under normal conditions, is completely filled by them and the other organs. Each lung is covered by a membrane and subdivided internally into an almost infinite number of air tracts, roughly similar to a tree upside down and minus the roots. The largest of the passageways is the trachea, a cartilaginous air tube running from the lower border of the larynx to approximately the notch between the two collar bones. The trachea bifurcates to form the bronchi and these, in turn, subdivide into bronchioles and then continue to branch out until each air passage ends in the almost invisible alveolar sacs. By means of the trachea, the air passages in the lungs are connected with the larynx and pharynx, through the latter of which the air stream may pass out into the nasal chambers to exit through the nostrils, or into the oral cavity to exit through the mouth.

Inhalation, the drawing of air into the lungs, and exhalation, the driving of air out of the lungs, are accomplished by changes of pressure within the thoracic cavity. In inhalation, the muscles surrounding the thoracic cage, especially the diaphragm, act to increase the size of the chest cavity, thus decreasing the pressure therein, and drawing air into the lungs. We are not here concerned with a detailed enumeration of the muscles that produce this action. Suffice it to say that the breathing process brings into play a large number of the trunk muscles. This is particularly true of forced or labored inhalation. The diaphragm and the muscles immediately surrounding the thoracic cage are most important, but muscles of the back, neck, and even of the pelvic region play more or less important roles. The number of accessory muscles brought into play and the degree of the muscular contraction determines the force of the inhalation. These muscles act to increase the size of the thoracic cavity in all of its diameters, i.e., anteroposteriorly, laterally, and vertically.

In quiet breathing exhalation is accomplished largely by the relaxation of the muscles active in inhalation, plus the elastic recoil of the tissues themselves. This decreases the size of the cavity and forces air out of the lungs. In controlled breathing, as in speech, the muscles that are antagonistic in action to the inspiratory muscles come into play to control the rate and force of exhalation. Control of the ascent of the diaphragm by action of the abdominal muscles is one important factor in giving the type of speed and power control necessary to speech. Except for the elastic recoil of their own tissues, the lungs play a purely passive role in breathing. They expand as the thoracic cavity enlarges and decrease in size as it contracts.

In this brief review of the power mechanism, we have seen that its primary biological function is to provide a way for the human organism to take in oxygen and eliminate carbon dioxide. Secondarily, it also produces a controlled column of moving air that furnishes the motive power for speech, thus providing the energy that runs the vibrator which is about to be described. Though it employs essentially the same muscles, breathing for speech purposes is controlled from brain centers other than those used in ordinary respiration. Breathing for speech shows other characteristic differences from ordinary breathing. In breathing for life purposes, inhalation and exhalation occupy about the same period of time; inhalation is an active muscular process while exhalation, unless forced, is largely passive. In breathing for speech, the inspiratory phase is speeded up and the expiratory phase lengthened. At the same time exhalation becomes an active muscular process controlled in force and rate. Other differences have to do with the volume of air breathed and with the rhythm of breathing.

The Vibrator Mechanism

Given a source of energy, it is evident that the next step in the production of speech is the formation of sound vibrations that can later be formed into the symbol units of speech. The mechanism that produces these vibrations is the larynx. The larynx, or voice box, is essentially an enlargement at the upper end of the trachea to form a valvular mechanism by means of which the outflowing air stream can be partially or entirely cut off. It is thus a continuation of the air passage from the lungs. It is located in the anterior portion of the neck and opens superiorly into the pharynx. Behind the larynx at its lower end is the esophagus, which is the food tube to the stomach. The esophagus opens superiorly into the laryngopharynx. The laryngopharynx is that portion of the pharynx that lies behind the upper part of the larynx.

The vocal folds form the valve itself. They are two strips of voluntary muscle with elastic tissue edges, running anteroposteriorly across the diameter of the larynx. The anterior attachment of the muscles is located slightly below the notch in the thyroid cartilage, which forms the protrusion called the "Adam's apple." The attachments are contiguous in front; when open, the folds spread in a "V" formation to their attachments on the arytenoid cartilages at the back of the larynx. The larynx itself has a semisolid framework of cartilages, ligaments, and tissues. A number of muscles acting upon this framework permit the vocal folds to be opened or closed and tensed or relaxed.

Like the other structures of the speech mechanism, the larynx has various vital functions. Through its control over the amount of air leaving the lungs and the pressure at which it leaves, it influences the circulation of the blood through the lungs and the amount of carbon dioxide eliminated. By complete closure of the vocal folds, air can be impounded under pressure within the lungs, thus giving the muscles of the thorax firmer attachments from which to work and increasing the strength of their pull. This "thorax fixation" function of the larynx is important in many bodily activities, particularly those requiring strong exertion of the thoracic muscles or a compressor action of the abdominal muscles. The larynx also plays an important part in the process of directing food and drink into the laryngopharynx and esophagus and preventing the passage of foreign substances into the air tract.

Apart from their biological function, however, the vocal folds play an important role in the speech process, since it is through their activity that sound waves are produced. From the speech standpoint, the vocal folds are capable of taking four important general positions: (1) A wide open position which allows the air column to escape with no appreciable noise; (2) a partially closed position which can also be called the whisper position, since the vocal folds are close enough together to produce the friction noises characteristic of whispering; (3) the phonating position, involves a very rapid alternate closing and partial opening of the vocal folds in such a manner that the air column is allowed to escape in the rhythmical puffs of air that produce the sound waves typical of speech; (4) the vocal folds are held in the closed position, completely stopping the passage of the air stream. If at the same time the muscles active in controlled exhalation are brought into play, it is possible to put the air column below the vocal folds under considerable pressure. This last position is also called the "glottal stop position."

We are not here interested in a detailed description of the muscles controlling the vibrator mechanism nor in the exact manner in which the vocal folds function. Suffice it to say that the larynx, through its glottal valve, the vocal folds, utilizes the energy in the outflowing column of air furnished by the power mechanism to produce the sound waves that form the basis of speech.

The Resonator Mechanism

The sound waves produced at the vocal folds are still far from being the finished product that we hear in speech. It is the resonators that give the characteristic quality to the voice (Fig. 3). The problem of resonance is very complex and cannot be treated in detail in this book. Essentially, however, these resonating cavities select certain of the complex series of frequencies present in the laryngeal tone and act to concentrate the energy represented by these frequencies instead of allowing it to be dissipated. The cavities contribute no energy to the sound waves—they merely act to conserve and concentrate energy already present in the laryngeal tone.

There are two general types of resonators, the cavity type and the sounding board type. The piano uses the sounding board type of resonator. This type can also be represented by placing a tuning fork which has been struck on a table or desk. Horns use the cavity type. Both types of resonance are present in the speech mechanism. The sounding board type is illustrated by the chest walls, the bones of the head, the hard palate, etc. Cavity resonance is produced in the cavities of the larynx, pharynx, nose, and mouth. Of the four, the nasal and laryngeal chambers are relatively fixed in their form and consequently exert a rather constant influence. The pharyngeal and oral cavities, on the other hand, are subject to wide variations in shape, size, and orifice and thus have variable effects on the sound quality. The pharynx is divided into three parts: the laryngopharynx, which has been mentioned previously, the oropharynx, which opens into the mouth cavity, and the nasopharynx, which lies behind the soft palate and connects with the nasal cavities. It is generally, though not universally, agreed that the sinuses play little or no part as resonators. It is a matter in dispute as to just what and how much effect the subglottal cavities (i.e., those of the larynx below the vocal folds, the trachea, and the air spaces in the lungs) have on resonance.

The resonance factor is especially important in the case of vowels, since it is the chief factor that distinguishes one from another.

The Articulatory Mechanism

The resonated laryngeal tone described above is still not speech. Without the action of the articulatory mechanism (Fig. 3) there would be possible only a sound of variable pitch, volume, and quality—a sound that could be either continuous or interrupted by glottal action. It is obvious that a language built upon this basis would be essentially a series of vowel tones like the whine of a dog and would be quite inadequate to express other than emotional meanings. It is the function of the articulatory mechanism to break up and modify this laryngeal tone and to create new sounds within the mechanism itself. Strictly speaking,

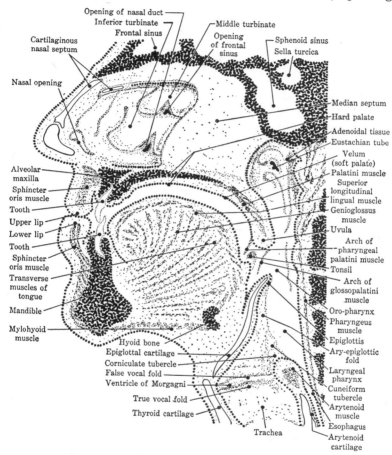

Fig. 3. Sagittal section of the head and neck.

the verb *articulate* means to join together. Actually this mechanism not only articulates, but also separates and molds, the sounds delivered to it by the vibrator and resonator mechanisms. In addition it creates new sounds within itself by utilizing the energy supplied by the power mechanism in such a way as to produce within the oral cavity friction noises that are independent of the laryngeal tone. Because of this, the articulatory mechanism assumes considerable importance to the student of phonetics. We may properly begin our review of this mechanism with a description of its parts.

We have already had occasion to speak of the mouth cavity (also called the oral or buccal cavity) as one of the important resonators. It is within this cavity that articulation takes place. In fact, the articulatory mechanism could be described as composed of the walls of, and the structures within, the oral cavity. This includes the tongue, lips, teeth, mandible or lower jaw, cheeks, faucial pillars, hard palate, the velum or soft palate, and the muscles composing or acting upon these structures. The hyoid bone, because of its influence on the movements of the articulator mechanism proper, is an important associated structure.

The posterior boundary of the oral cavity is the soft palate and the anterior pillars, or fauces. These are not articulatory structures *per se*. Rather, they form, together with the muscular walls of the pharynx, a two-way valve system by means of which the out-flowing column of air can be shunted into either the oral or the nasal cavity or both. The velum, the muscular curtain that can be seen in the back of the mouth, is the most important structure in this valvular action. It terminates in a small pencil-like structure called the uvula. Anteriorly it is continuous with the hard or bony palate which forms the rest of the roof of the mouth. When the soft palate hangs relaxed and the oral cavity is closed at some point, the air stream is directed into the nasal chambers and out through the nostrils. On the other hand, certain muscles serve to draw the soft palate upward and backward at the same time that the pharyngeal walls are being drawn forward so that the port into the nasopharynx is closed and the air stream is forced into the mouth cavity.

The fauces are two pairs of muscular bundles that lie antero-posteriorly on either side of the tonsils. The anterior fauces or pillars arise from the root of the tongue, the posterior ones from the pharyngeal wall. Both arch upward to terminate in the soft palate. The former is sometimes called the glossopalatine arch, the latter the pharyngopalatine arch. The anterior pillars mark the dividing line between the oral and pharyngeal cavities and the opening between them is the posterior or faucial orifice. The lateral walls of the oral cavity are formed by the inner surfaces of the cheeks, while the roof is formed by the hard palate and a limited portion of the soft palate. The lips and teeth form the anterior boundary. The lips are muscular bundles running, for the most part, in a circular direction and forming the anterior oral or bi-labial orifice. The floor of the cavity is formed by the tongue itself and by the mylohyoid muscle, a very important tongue muscle running from the hyoid bone to the base of the tongue.

The cavity contains of course the tongue and teeth. The teeth not only play a prominent part in the formation of certain sounds, but they serve also as useful landmarks in describing the position taken by the tongue in the production of other sounds. Attention should be drawn to the alveolar or rugal ridge, which borders the line of upper teeth and breaks the otherwise smooth curve of the dome of the hard palate.

The tongue is by far the most important articulatory structure. Five pairs of extrinsic and four pairs of intrinsic muscles enter into its makeup. Aside from its nerves, blood vessels, connecting and covering tissue, glands and taste buds, it is entirely muscular and thus capable of a wide variety of movements. For descriptive purposes in phonetics we divide the tongue arbitrarily into parts as follows: the tip, the extreme forward edge, especially when the tongue is pointed; the blade, which includes the tip—the whole front part; the dorsum, the upper surface, which is divided into a front portion that lies under the hard palate and a back portion that lies opposite the velum; and the root or radix, a term applied to the most posterior part of the tongue, where it attaches to the surrounding structures. In a position of rest, with the jaw closed, the tongue almost completely fills the mouth cavity. It would be difficult to overestimate the importance of the tongue in articulation. Its ability to perform finely coördinated movements rapidly is essential to fluent speech.

We can complete our description of the articulatory mechanism by mentioning a few remaining structures. The mandible, or lower jaw, is capable of movement in three directions: up and down, laterally, and forward and back. The up and down movement, the most important for speech, serves to regulate the size of the opening between the teeth and at the same time to influence the size and shape of the bilabial orifice and the oral cavity. The hyoid bone and the suprahyoid muscles are accessory structures in the articulatory mechanism, since they coöperate to a large extent in its action. The infrahyoid and the extrinsic laryngeal muscles support to a lesser extent the action of parts of the mechanism. The facial muscles, especially those controlling the action of the cheeks and the corners of the mouth, are also important.

The structures just described "articulate" the sound produced by the vibrator and reinforced by the resonator mechanisms. They are important in speech, but they also have important biological functions. As a group they function in the food-getting activities, chewing, and swallowing. Many of them also take part in such important reflex actions as coughing, sneezing, hiccoughing, regurgitation, etc. When these vital functions come into conflict with language activities, it is speech that suffers.

It can readily be seen that the division of the speech mechanism into four separate parts is largely arbitrary. There is much overlapping both in structure and function. The so-called vibrator mechanism, for example, functions in part as a resonator. The resonator and articulatory mechanisms overlap even more. The mouth cavity serves at the same time as one of the most important resonating chambers and as the locus of articulation. The tongue is the most important organ in changing the shape and size of the oral cavity for purposes of resonance and it is likewise the chief articulator of the consonants. Speech is to be viewed, not as the combined result of the separate action of four mechanisms, but rather as the result of the unit functioning of one large system that operates in a coördinated and synchronized manner. We now turn our attention to the coördinating system that directs and standardizes the activity of the speech mechanism.

The Coördinating System

From our description of the speech mechanism it is evident that speech is a complicated process, brought about by activities of a large portion of the body structure—activities that involve the use of large and small muscle groups in both sequential and overlapping action. Moreover, these activities require the subordination of the more basic vital functions of the structures used. The nervous system controlling these activities is equally complicated.

In terms of function, we may speak of four phases of the activity of this coördinating and supervising system: the motor or activating system, the sensory or reporting system, the auditory or monitoring system, and the associating or integrating system. We must understand again that these functions do not exist independently of each other, the division merely being convenient for descriptive purposes. It represents general types of functions that can be observed in operation and that can be said to be indispensable to the normal functioning of the speech mechanism.

The motor system includes that portion of the voluntary nervous system directly concerned in the transmission of motor impulses to the muscles of the speech mechanism. These motor impulses activate the muscles to contraction, and speech is built upon the contractions so produced. The motor system begins in the precentral convolution of the frontal lobe on both sides of the brain, in the part of the cortex called the voluntary motor area. From cell bodies located in the gray matter of this area nerve fibers pass through various structures of the brain to terminate at points of junction in the portions of the lower brain and spinal cord from which the cranial and spinal nerves that take part in speech arise. The bundle of fibers is variously designated as the voluntary motor system, the upper motor neurone system, and the pyramidal system. Most of these upper motor neurones cross to the opposite side of the brain before terminating, but a small portion of those that synapse with motor neurones in the cranial nerves terminate on the same side. In each case the termination is a point of synapse with cell bodies of motor nerve fibers, called lower motor neurones, that run in certain of the cranial nerves (trigeminal, facial, glossopharyngeal, vagus, spinal accessory, and hypoglossal) and in some of the upper spinal nerves. These lower motor neurones carry motor impulses directly to the muscles of the speech mechanism. This motor system, acting in conjunction with other important brain structures, particularly the striate bodies, thalamus, medulla, and cerebellum, is the immediate activator of the muscles that take part in speech.

All of the cranial and spinal nerves that function in the motor system carry also sensory neurones that report back to the brain the sensations arising as a result of the movement of the speech mechanism. These reports are of two types, one known as general sensation and comprising in this case mostly touch and pressure, the other called muscle sense or kinæsthesia. The latter type is probably the more important, since it indicates the nature and extent of the movement in muscles and joints. All of these sensory reports pass by various pathways to the opposite side of the brain where they terminate in a general sensory area in the parietal lobe, at which point they are said to "enter consciousness." We may speak of this part of the coördinating system as the sensory or reporting system. It supplies the means of knowing what has taken place and thus furnishes the basis for repetitions or modifications of the movement. It plays an important part in the coördinating process, since without it there would be no means of knowing how a given movement had been made and hence no basis for habituating it.

Up to this point we have discussed a system for producing movement and one for reporting the nature of the movements so made. The auditory system can be regarded as a system that tests by comparison the suitability of the sounds produced by such movements. The hearing mechanism receives sound waves and transforms them into nerve impulses that pass along the auditory nerve (eighth cranial) to the auditory sensory areas in the temporal lobes of the brain, where they reach consciousness. This system makes it possible for the individual to hear the speech sounds used by those about him and likewise to hear those that he himself produces. This forms the basis for a comparison and makes it possible for him to set up standards by which to judge his own speech products. The hearing mechanism thus serves as a monitoring system by means of which standards are set up, comparisons made, and speech sounds checked and modified until they conform to the standard.

The associating or integrating system is the central link in the coördinating system. Speech, we have learned, is symbolic, and it uses auditory symbols. These symbols are meaningful only when they have become connected through experience with meanings. This process, called association, resides in the auditory association area in the temporal lobe. Similar connections between visual symbols and their meanings are made in the visual association area in the occipital lobe. Thus one associative function is to tie up with meaning the symbols used in written and spoken language.

A somewhat different type of associative function, called motor association, resides in Broca's area in the frontal lobe. Broadly speaking, this area may be said to associate the speech symbol with the motor activities that lead to its production. Among other things, it provides what we may call the motor patterns for speech. More picturesquely, it contains the blueprints from which the motor system builds the finished product, speech. The nature, sequence, and timing of the movements that produce speech are laid down in this area when learned, and it is from here that the motor system receives its impulse to action. Motor association is the keystone of the coördinating system, since it bridges the gap between the motor system on the one hand and the sensory system, the auditory system, and auditory association on the other. The associative system as a whole makes possible the symbolic nature of speech by connecting the sound symbol with its meaning and with the pattern of muscle movements necessary to produce it.

In this chapter we have shown that the speech mechanism can be divided into four units, distinct functionally but overlapping structurally: the power mechanism, the vibrator mechanism, the resonator mechanism, and the articulatory mechanism. These various functions and structures are coördinated through the activity of the voluntary nervous system—a coördination made possible by four types of activity carried on by the nervous system: (1) motor activity that provides the stimuli that cause muscles to contract; (2) sensory reporting that gives information as to how the movements were produced; (3) auditory monitoring that makes possible the setting up of, and conformance to, speech standards; and (4) the associative function that ties up the auditory symbol with its meaning and with the motor pattern necessary to produce it.

SECTION II
Kinesiologic Phonetics

Chapter 4 Introduction

In this section we take up the detailed study of specific speech sounds and the way in which they are connected in continuous speech. The approach is primarily kinesiologic. It is our purpose to describe a typical member of each phoneme as to its position and the movements of the articulatory mechanism necessary to its production. Our main interest is in the sounds of English speech, although certain foreign sounds are mentioned occasionally in order to aid in the understanding of an English sound or to clarify some phonetic principle. Although acoustic considerations are discussed in Chapter 14, it is not possible to exclude all such material from this section. Acoustic terms are used frequently and acoustic phenomena are occasionally mentioned in connection with the description of a sound in order to tie up the movements with the auditory results.

An attempt has been made to develop and present this material in such a way as to make it seem logical and to make clear the phonetic principles involved. Consequently the treatment is somewhat different from that given in other texts. Some worth while contributions to the study of phonetics have been omitted from this section because they have been treated copiously in other texts. Usually references are given which cover the omitted matter, and the student is urged to make liberal use of these suggested readings in order to broaden and increase his understanding of the field.

A Classification of Speech Sounds

On the basis of the types of movements involved all speech sounds may be placed in one of three divisions: continuants, stops, and glides. These three types of sounds may be further subdivided on an acoustic basis as follows:

Continuants: vowels
               fricative consonants
               nasals

Stops: plosive consonants

Glides: intervowel

These categories may be defined as follows: A *continuant* is a speech sound in which the speech mechanism first takes the position typical of the sound and then, for all practical purposes, is held fixed during the period of the production of the sound. If the opening through which the air stream exits is relatively open so that friction noises are not set up around the orifice, and if the stream of air is vibrant, the resulting sound is a *vowel*. Example: **a**. If the orifice is relatively small and friction noises are set up by the outflowing air stream the sound is a *continuant consonant*. Examples: **s** and **z**. If the oral cavity is blocked at some point and the vibrant air stream allowed to exit through the nasal cavities, the resulting sound is a *nasal continuant*. Example: **m**.

A *stop sound* is one in which the articulatory mechanism moves to or from a certain position that momentarily blocks completely the exit of the air stream through the oral cavity. Either the movement to the closed position or the movement from it, or both together, may call forth recognition of the sound. Example: **t**.

A *glide* is a sound produced by an uninterrupted movement of the articulatory mechanism from the position of one sound to that of another. Glides may occur between vowel or vowel-like sounds.

Additional Definitions

The following definitions of terms common in the field of phonetics are offered here as an aid to the student in reading this and other books on the subject:

Terms Referring to Parts of the Speech Mechanism

MAXILLARY. Pertaining to the upper jaw.

MANDIBULAR. Pertaining to the lower jaw.

LABIAL. Pertaining to the lips.

LINGUAL. Pertaining to the tongue.

DENTAL. Pertaining to the teeth.

RUGAL or PREPALATAL. Pertaining to the upper gum ridge.

ALVEOLAR. Pertaining to either the upper or lower gum ridge.

PALATAL. Pertaining to the hard palate.

VELAR. Pertaining to the soft palate.

UVULAR. Pertaining to the uvula, the pencil-like projection on the middle of the lower border of the velum.

ORAL or BUCCAL. Pertaining to the mouth cavity.

FAUCIAL. Pertaining to the narrow passage from the mouth cavity to the pharynx.

FAUCIAL ARCHES. The arches formed by the pillars of the fauces.

ANTERIOR PILLARS. The linguapalatal muscles.

POSTERIOR PILLARS. The pharyngopalatal muscles.

PHARYNGEAL. Pertaining to the pharynx, the cavity immediately behind the oral cavity and separated from it by the velum and the anterior pillars. The cavity is often subdivided into the NASOPHARYNX, the portion behind the soft palate; the OROPHARYNX, the portion behind the faucial arch; and the LARYNGOPHARYNX, the portion behind the larynx.

NASAL. Pertaining to the nasal cavity. Also used to indicate a quality of sound.

GLOTTAL. Pertaining to the glottis, the space between the vocal folds.

Terms Used to Describe Consonants

SIBILANT. Descriptive of friction noises emitted through a very narrow orifice. s is a sibilant sound.

AIR BLADE. Descriptive of friction noises emitted through an orifice that is wide horizontally and narrow vertically. f is accompanied by air blade vibrations.

ROLLED or TRILLED. Signifying the rapid fluttering of some part of the articulatory mechanism as for example the tip of the tongue, the uvula, or the lips. Example: trilled *r* *ř*. The modifier ˇ indicates a trilled sound.

ONE-TAP TRILL. A sound made with a single quick tap of the tongue tip against the teeth, rugal ridge, or anterior hard palate. Also called FLAPPED. Example: one-tap trill *r* symbol ɾ.

SCRAPES. A term applied to fricative sounds produced by the back of the tongue acting in conjunction with the velum or posterior pharyngeal wall.

LIQUIDS. An older term used to designate the sounds **l**, **r**, **w**, **j**.

LONG CONSONANT. A term applying to a consonant that is held long enough in its production to give the effect of doubling the sound without actually repeating the movements necessary to make it. Example: *this city* **ðɪsːɪtɪ̩**, *come Mary* **kʌmːɛrɪ̩**, *cat tail* **kætːeɪl**. The modifier ː indicates lengthening.

AFFRICATE. A term used to designate a sound combination in which a fricative follows a plosive, both sounds being made in the same organic position. Example: **tʃ**.

ASPIRATION, UNASPIRATION. These terms are usually applied to plosive consonants. An aspirated plosive is one that is followed by a puff of unvoiced air. Example: **p** as in *pat*. An unaspirated plosive is one in which no such puff of air is present. Example: **b** as in *bat*.

FORTIS, LENIS. These terms mean strong and weak, respectively. They refer to the degree of muscular tension present in the articulatory mechanism and the amount of breath pressure during the production of consonants. They are commonly used in describing plosive sounds. Examples: fortis **p** as in *pay*, lenis **p** as in *upper*.

Terms Used to Describe Vowels

PURE VOWEL. One made with relatively no movement of the speech mechanism during its production. Opposite in meaning to diphthong or glide.

ORAL VOWEL. One delivered through the oral cavity.

NASAL or NASALIZED VOWEL. One delivered in part through the nasal cavity.

FRONT, MID or CENTRAL, BACK. These terms refer to the portion of the tongue showing the point of highest arching in the production of a given vowel. Examples: front vowel **i**, central vowel **ɝ**, back vowel **u**.

HIGH, MID, LOW. Terms descriptive of the degree of arching of the tongue. Thus **i** is a high front vowel. **ɛ** a mid front vowel and **æ** a low front vowel.

CLOSE, OPEN, HALF CLOSE, HALF OPEN. Terms designating the relative size of the opening between the jaws.

ROUNDED, SPREAD. Terms referring to the position of the lips in the production of vowels. **u** is a lip rounded sound in contrast to **i** for which the lips are spread.

RAISED, LOWERED. A vowel is said to be raised when it is made with the tongue arched higher than is typical for that sound, yet not enough higher to place it in another phoneme. For a lowered vowel, the situation is reversed.

ADVANCED or FRONTED. A vowel is said to be advanced or fronted when the point of highest arching is farther forward on the tongue than is typical for that sound, but not enough so to place the sound in a different phoneme.

RETRACTED or BACKED. A vowel made with the point of highest arching farther back on the tongue than is typical.

LONG, SHORT. These terms refer to the duration of a vowel. Thus **i** is normally a longer vowel than **ɪ**. Also, a given vowel such as **ɑ** may be lengthened in certain combinations. Note the Eastern pronunciations, *father* **fɑðə** and *farther* **fɑːðə**.

TENSE, LAX. Terms referring to the amount of tension in the articulatory muscles. **i** is sometimes described as tense, **ɪ** as lax.

SONORITY. A term descriptive of loudness or carrying power in a speech sound.

Miscellaneous Terms

VOICED or SONANT, VOICELESS or SURD. During the production of a voiced or sonant sound the vocal folds are closed to the point of phonation. Example: **v**. During the production of a voiceless or surd sound the vocal folds are not in vibration. Example: **f**.

SPEECH NOISES. A term indicating the friction sounds that accompany speech; used in contrast to speech tones which result from laryngeal vibrations.

CENTRAL EMISSION. A sound is said to be centrally emitted when the orifice through which the air stream flows is centrally located in respect to the tongue and the mouth cavity. All mouth-delivered English sounds except the varieties of *l* are centrally emitted.

LATERAL EMISSION. Sounds in which the air stream is emitted through a lateral orifice formed along one or both sides of the tongue. **l** is laterally emitted.

RETROFLEX. A term used to describe sounds for which the tip of the tongue is curled upwards and backwards farther than is typical for the sound.

NASALIZATION. The production of a sound that should normally be free from nasal resonance with some accompanying nasality. To be distinguished from the term *nasal sound* which designates a sound normally emitted through the nose.

STRESSED, UNSTRESSED. Terms referring to degree of emphasis placed on a given speech element. Changes in emphasis may result from changes in pitch, duration, or force. We usually speak of stressed or unstressed vowels and syllables but the terms can be applied to consonants as well.

TRANSITIONAL SOUND. One that occurs accidentally as the result of the movement from the position of one speech sound to that of another. Examples: the **p** in *something* **sʌmpθɪŋ**, and the **t** in *fence* **fɛnts**.

GUTTURAL. Refers to sounds made far back in the mouth or pharynx. Also used to describe a sound quality, as a guttural tone.

SYLLABLE. A unit of speech containing a peak of sonority and divided from other such peaks by a hiatus or a weakening of sonority.

SYLLABIC CONSONANTS. Certain sounds, ordinarily considered as consonants, may upon occasion form syllables by themselves without an accompanying vowel. The sounds that are not usually syllabic in English, but may become so, are **m** and **n**. Examples: *chasm* **kæzm̩** and *button* **bʌtn̩**. The sounds **l** and **r** are also given by many phoneticians as sounds that may become syllabic. In this book they are treated as glide sounds that may, if pronounced as continuants, become true vowels, either stressed or unstressed. Thus the syllabic (unstressed vowel) form of **r** is written as ɚ and not ɻ. However, since there is no special symbol for the vowel *l* and since this sound occurs only in unstressed syllables, it is usually written as **l̩**.

The Neutral Position

We have mentioned previously the need for some landmark or position of the mechanism to use as a constant factor in describing

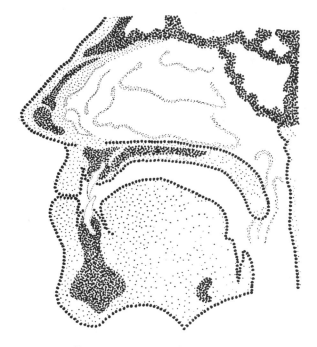

Fig. 4. The neutral position.

speech sounds. We have chosen for this purpose the position of the speech mechanism in ordinary quiet respiration. This we have called the neutral position (Fig. 4).

The neutral position may be described as follows: The vocal folds are open, permitting the free passage of air. The exact extent of the opening varies with changes in the force of respiration, but the vocal folds are never closed to the point that friction noises are set up as the air stream passes through the glottis. The port into the nasopharynx is open, the soft palate hanging relaxed and pendant. The tongue lies passively in the floor of the mouth, its dorsal surface convex from end to end and from side to side. The tip and sides of the tongue lie in loose contact with the inner surfaces of all the lower teeth, thus filling completely the lower part of the mouth cavity. The medium fissure produces a slight depression running along the midline from front to back. The external oral orifice is closed, the upper and lower lips meeting in a light contact. The line of junction is usually approximately horizontal, with perhaps a slight upward turn at the middle and a little downward turn at the two sides. The amount of red lip margin showing and the external appearance of the two lips varies in different individuals. The mandible is depressed slightly by the force of gravity, thus bringing the upper edges of the lower incisors about on a level with, and slightly posterior to, the lower edges of the corresponding teeth of the maxilla. With the mandible in this position the mouth cavity is practically obliterated by the tongue, the dorsal surface of which reaches almost to the hard and soft palates. The larynx and hyoid bone are in resting positions, these positions being determined by the counterbalancing effect of the tonic contractions of the antagonistic muscles that control their movements. In fact, all of the muscles of the speech mechanism may be described as in a position of rest, i.e., the position which results when the muscles are reacting only to the impulses necessary to maintain muscle tonus.

Although the neutral position described above was chosen more or less arbitrarily, there are good reasons why it was the logical choice. In the first place, as mentioned previously it represents the normal resting state of the speech mechanism. The muscles controlling the mechanism approach relaxation more nearly than in any other position that could be described. It is a relatively stable position and the one assumed by the mechanism between periods of activity. From a physiological standpoint it is thus the logical choice for our study.

In the second place, a number of speech sounds are produced by relatively slight changes of this neutral position, as for example the consonant sounds **m**, **b**, **p**, **v**, **f**, and the neutral vowel **ʌ** (see

Figs. 65, 53, 33, and 7). All of these sounds will be described in detail later; for the present we may simply say that another reason for the choice of the neutral position described above is that it is closely related to a number of important English speech sounds and thus furnishes an excellent starting point for the analyses that follow.

Although probably unnecessary, it might be well to add one last word of caution in order to avoid any possible misunderstanding. It must not be thought that ordinary speech is a series of isolated sounds with the articulatory mechanism starting from and returning to the neutral position for the production of each sound. On the contrary, speech is the result of a series of movements, each of which is not only built upon the preceding movement, but is also modified somewhat by the nature of the movement to follow. The concept of the neutral position and its use in the analysis of isolated speech sounds is an arbitrary method of study made advisable by the fact that it offers the most suitable approach to the problems we are attempting to solve. Our procedure in the description of speech sounds will therefore be to specify for each the modifications of the neutral position that are necessary to produce the sound.

The Resonated Laryngeal Tone as the Acoustic Basis of Speech

From a physiological standpoint the whisper is perhaps the basis of speech, since it is the type of sound that is produced with the least expenditures of effort, requiring only a partial closure of the vocal folds. From an acoustic standpoint, however, such whisper sounds are so lacking in carrying power and flexibility that they would make a very poor basis for a language. We may safely say that the laryngeal tone set up in the vibrator mechanism and resonated in the resonating cavities is the acoustic basis of speech.

It is easily seen that only one change in the neutral position is necessary to produce a laryngeal tone—an approximation to the point of phonation by the vocal folds. If this is done in conjunction with the action of the power mechanism, the rest of the speech mechanism remaining in the neutral position, a humming through the nasal cavities resembling the sound **m** will be produced. It is but a short step from this activity to the production of the vowel sounds. Note that we have begun here with the neutral position and made one modification, an approximation of the vocal folds, to produce a resonated laryngeal tone. With this as a point of departure, we are now ready to consider the further modifications of the neutral position necessary to produce the various vowel sounds.

Chapter 5   The Vowels

General Remarks

In terms of movement, the vowel sounds are continuants. By this we mean that the speech mechanism assumes the position for the vowel and holds it with relatively little movement for a measurable fraction of a second while the sound is produced. Assuming the position for a vowel sound means essentially shaping the resonators in such a way as to produce the desired acoustic effect. Although the periods of time involved are small, continuants are characterized by these brief periods of holding. By contrast, the glide sounds are produced while the mechanism is *in movement* and their identifying characteristics are the result of this movement.

No continuant sound, and this is especially true of the vowels, is ever made through an absolutely fixed position that does not waver even so much as a piston in an automobile engine. The speech mechanism is made of flesh and blood, not steel, and its "tolerance" is not to be compared with the one ten-thousandths of an inch considered acceptable for some machine parts. More important still, there is in most phonetic contexts a movement to the vowel from some other sound and from the vowel to another sound. Hence, the period of even relative stability of position tends to be short and to fall in the middle of the duration of the vowel. For this reason we define a *pure* vowel as one in which the mechanism is held *relatively* stable in contrast to the glides in which the movement is the essence of the sound.

So long as the fluctuation is within the phoneme for the vowel in question or the natural result of the transition between sounds, we consider the sound a continuant. However, when the extent of the movement is great enough that we are aware of a transition from one vowel or vowel-like position to another, we call the resulting sound a glide. Thus the ɔ in *gauze* gɔz is a continuant even though it is affected somewhat by the preceding g and the following z, but the ɔɪ in bɔɪ is a glide (diphthong) because there is uninterrupted movement from one vowel position to another.

From an acoustic point of view, the vowels are characterized by voicing, absence of friction noises, and resonance. Although vowel sounds can be whispered, they are normally produced with the vocal folds in vibration, which means that a fundamental tone in the low frequency range is present. In contrast to the consonants, the openings through which the vowel sounds are produced are large enough that no noticeable friction noises are produced and, in the negative sense, this lack of friction is characteristic of the vowels.

By far the most important acoustic characteristic, however, is the pattern of overtones or resonance frequencies that is the essence of each vowel sound. All vowels, per se, have resonance but each vowel also has its own distinctive pattern of resonance that is the result of the number, frequencies and energy distribution of the overtones that are present. It is by means of these differences in the overall pattern of resonance that we are able to hear and discriminate one vowel from another. These changing resonance patterns are produced by altering the shape and size of the resonators, principally the pharyngeal and oral cavities, and by varying the size and shape of the discharging orifice.

Our descriptions of these resonators in terms of a placement approach are usually rather general and confined to an attempt to indicate the gross positions of the lips, jaws, and tongue. In describing the lip positions, we say that the orifice is either *spread* (elongated from side to side), or *rounded*, or *neutral*. Jaw positions are described in terms of the distance between the upper and lower jaws as *open, half-open* or *half-close*, and *close*. In relation to tongue position the terms *front, central*, and *back* refer to the location on a horizontal plane of the point of greatest arching of the tongue and the words *high*, *mid*, and *low* describe the extent of the arching on a vertical plane.

Two additional characteristics of vowel sounds need to be introduced at this point, namely length and tension. Differences in duration and in degree of tension are not ordinarily phonemic in English; that is to say, they do not make a distinctive difference in meaning between one phonemic unit and another. They do, however, serve at times to convey some of the nuances of meaning that we are constantly deriving from speech as we interpret changes in these factors together with those in pitch, quality, stress, and rate. Moreover, noticeable differences in length and tension do occur between regional dialects and between one language and another, and they are often important in determining whether or not one "speaks like a native." Thus anyone interested in the study of dialects or foreign languages or in the correction of dialectal speech needs to be aware of these aspects of vowel production.

The matter of vowel length or duration, sometimes called "vowel quantity," is rather complicated. We need to remember first that these terms are not equivalent to customary dictionary definitions when certain vowels are described as "long" or "short," e.g., short *a* (ă) and long *a* (ā). Here the words refer not so much to duration as to a change in the character of the sound, in this case from æ to eɪ respectively. As used in the study of phonetics vowel duration means the actual length of time occupied by the utterance of a given vowel. In the second place, we need to keep clearly in mind that there are two aspects of vowel duration: (1) certain vowels are characterized by the fact that they are typically and rather consistently shorter than certain other vowels; and (2) all vowels vary greatly in duration, depending upon the context in which they are used, the dialect spoken, the mood of the speaker at the moment, and the amount of stress used.

Concerning the first of these aspects of vowel duration we can say that the vowels i, a, ɑ, ɔ, u, ɜ, and ɝ are usually relatively long as compared with the vowels ɪ, e, ɛ, æ, o, ɒ, ʊ, ʌ, and l. In any specific utterance, of course, a vowel described as short might actually be longer than one described as long. However, as they are typically pronounced in connected speech, the vowels in the first group are characterized by relatively greater length and those in the second are usually shorter in duration. Variations in vowel duration as a result of context, stress, and other factors is more difficult to reduce to specific statements. John S. Kenyon[1] lists four rules that apply to the factor of stress in relation to phonetic context: (1) "The same vowel, if stressed, is longer when final or before a voiced consonant than it is before a voiceless consonant"; (2) "The same vowel, if stressed, is longer when final or before a final consonant than it is when followed by an unaccented syllable"; (3) "The same vowel, if stressed, is longer when followed by a sonorant **m, n, ŋ, l** plus a voiced consonant than it is when followed by a sonorant plus a voiceless consonant"; and (4) "The same vowel becomes longer or shorter as its stress is increased or decreased."[2]

Certain vowels are also produced with the musculature somewhat more tense than is customarily the case with other vowels. In this connection, tension refers to the relative degree of contraction or relaxation occurring in the articulatory mechanism, particularly in the muscles of the tongue and secondarily in those of the lips and jaw. Here again we need to be careful to use the terms *relatively tense* or *relatively lax*, recognizing that variations occur depending upon specific circumstances. Three general observations can be made in connection with the factor of tension: (1) Differences in tension are more distinct and observable among the high front and high back vowels and considerably less so, if not insignificant, among the others. Thus we can say with some assurance that **i, e, u**, and **o** are usually relatively tense and that **ɪ, ɛ, ʊ**, and **ɔ** are typically relatively lax. (2) Such differences in tension seem to be more characteristic of English than of some other languages which tend in general toward more tense vowels and which lack the relatively relaxed sounds that occur in English. (3) Any vowel can of course be produced with the musculature more tense than usual, often with undesirable acoustic results.

The movements involved in the production of vowel sounds are subject to even more variation than those for consonants. However, the variations within any one individual, and even those from one individual to another, are not so great as to constitute essential differences in the nature of the movement. Strictly speaking, it is

---

[1] *American Pronunciation*, 10th ed., George Wahr, 1950, pp. 60–63.
[2] For a more detailed discussion of vowel duration see Webster's *New International Dictionary*, 2nd ed., 1934, par. 49, p. xxxi.

inaccurate to say that exactly the same sound can be produced by
a variety of methods. It is more correct to say that each variation
in movement produces a slightly different sound, but that as long
as the sound remains in the phoneme under consideration we are
not ordinarily conscious of the differences.

Vowel phonemes are delimited by auditory judgment more than
by the nature or extent of the movement; hence resonance, pitch,
and duration are important factors. Consonant sounds are much
more definite as to position, but there is no sharp dividing line between vowels and consonants. For example, the sounds **m**, **n**, and
ŋ have several vowel characteristics and **l**, **r**, **w**, and **j** are often
classified as semivowels, although they are not so defined in this
book. One distinction between consonants and vowels is made on an
acoustic basis. Each sound except the nasals is delivered through
an oral orifice of a certain size, and it would be possible to arrange
these sounds in order from **s**, the one with the smallest orifice, to **ɑ**,
the one with the largest opening. As long as the opening is small
enough that friction noises are produced by it when the air stream
passes through, the sound is by definition a consonant. When the
opening becomes large enough that friction noises are not produced the sound is classified as a vowel. Looked at in this way, it
is evident that in the middle of the series of orifices there will
be some that will be on the borderline between the vowel and consonant ranges. The corresponding borderline sounds are difficult
to classify, since they have both vowels and consonant qualities.

The number of vowel phonemes to be differentiated depends
upon the fineness of the distinctions made. The number is limited
by the auditory mechanism and not by the neuromuscular
mechanism. The speech mechanism is capable of producing an
almost unlimited number of slightly varying vowel tones but *the
number of these sounds that can be used in speech for symbolic
purposes is limited by the ability of the auditory mechanism to
recognize them as separate sounds when they are employed in the
communicative process.* Note the connection between this statement and the phoneme theory previously discussed. In English,
we have at least ten[3] distinctive vowel phonemes; they are

[3] **e** and **o** are not included in this number since they are considered as belonging more properly to a group of glide phonemes that is to be discussed in a
later chapter. **ɜ** is considered as a member of the same phoneme as **ɝ**.

described in succeeding pages. Although some twenty-five vowel symbols are presented and described in this chapter, this need not be confusing. Two symbols represent "pure vowel" forms of glide sounds that are counted later among the glide phonemes; in two other instances there are separate symbols for the stressed and unstressed forms of the phoneme; three symbols represent variant forms of certain phonemes, one represents the vowel *l* which is a variant of the glide or consonantal *l* phoneme, and the remaining seven represent non-English vowels. The basic vowel phonemes in English are: **i, ɪ, ɛ, æ, ɑ, ɔ, ʊ, u, ʌ**, and **ɝ**.

The procedure in each case is to describe the typical movements of the jaw, lips, and tongue that occur when these sounds are pronounced in isolation. All descriptions are made in comparison with the neutral position.

It has long been customary to present the vowel system of a language in some sort of diagram, which aims to represent more or less accurately the position of the tongue for each of the vowels placed in the picture. Various shapes have been used for this diagram, including triangles, parallelograms, and parabolas. The vowel diagram that has enjoyed the most popularity in recent years is reproduced here in its conventional shape.

In this drawing the position **i** represent the highest and farthest forward and **a** the lowest and farthest back points of arching of the *front* of the tongue in the normal production of English vowels. Similarly, **u** represents the highest and most retracted and **ɑ** the

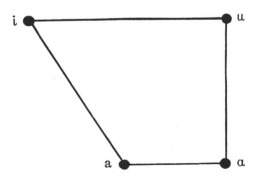

Fig. 5. The conventional vowel diagram. See also Figs. 12 and 19.

lowest and most forward point of arching of the back of the tongue. Other vowels are then put in their proper places on the diagram in accordance with their tongue positions. The central vowels occupy the middle part of the figure. This scheme of representation, while graphic, has its disadvantages in that it implies much too definite positions for the various vowels. Even if the diagram is presented with reservations, still the very definiteness of the picture tends to make one visualize the vowels as occupying fixed and unvarying positions. This is definitely not the case.

Nevertheless, since there are advantages to a pictorial representation of the vowel system, the writers include such a diagram

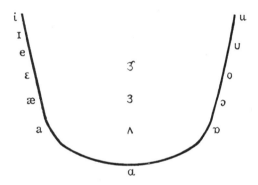

Fig. 6. A schematic vowel diagram.

(Fig. 6), which is essentially the vowel parallelogram with the corners smoothed into curves. An attempt has been made to make the drawing seem less definite in an effort to avoid the danger of reading too much into the diagram as a picture of actual tongue positions. The vowel ɬ is omitted because it cannot be represented with any accuracy in a picture of this type.

It must be emphasized again that this diagram is not intended to represent exactly the tongue positions for the various vowels. In so far as it is physiologically schematic at all, it is representative of *types* of position and *directions* of movement. The neutral vowel position is represented by ʌ, a central vowel. From this position the front vowel series (Fig. 8), **a** to **i**, develops as the front of the tongue arches progressively higher and farther forward. The back vowel series (Fig. 9) from ɒ to u involves, in general, an upward and backward movement of the back of the tongue. For the central vowels (Fig. 10), ʌ to ɝ, the central portion of the tongue arches successively higher. The position for ɑ is extremely variable but with most people it is probably a central vowel characterized by a tongue placement flatter than the neutral position. It is so presented in this diagram.

Two modifications of the neutral position that remain constant for all the vowels may be mentioned here in order to avoid repetition. The first, closure of the vocal folds to the point of phonation, has already been mentioned. The second is the closure of the port into the nasopharynx. There seems to be some question as to whether the closure of the soft palate is always complete, or whether in some cases it may remain partially open. For our purposes we are safe in assuming that the integrity of all the English vowels depends upon the ability to elevate the soft palate and draw forward the pharyngeal walls so that the opening into the nasopharynx is almost if not completely closed. The continuant nature of each of the vowels is also assumed.

Each vowel described in the succeeding pages is given a descriptive name based on the tongue, lip, and jaw positions and, if relevant, the factors of length and tension previously discussed. To avoid repetition the words *voiced, continuant, orally emitted vowel* which should properly accompany each description have been omitted.

The Neutral Vowel ʌ as in "Up" ʌp

Low central, half-open, neutral, relatively lax, relatively short

This is called the neutral vowel because it is the vowel that is made most easily from the neutral position. ʌ is produced by dropping the mandible to half-open [4] position and directing the voiced air stream through the oral cavity by means of a palatal closure (Fig. 7). The opening of the bilabial orifice is neutral in shape and follows passively the depression of the lower jaw. No movement of the tongue is necessary for this sound although a slight upward arching of the central portion is typical of the neutral position. At times the arching is probably somewhat back of the

---

[4] In comparison with ɑ, which is typically the most open of the vowels.

central portion of the tongue, but the British variety of ʌ is made with the tongue actively depressed so that to the American ear it resembles the ɑ sound.

Many phoneticians regard ʌ as the stressed form of ə or vice versa. They regard the two sounds as identical in position, the

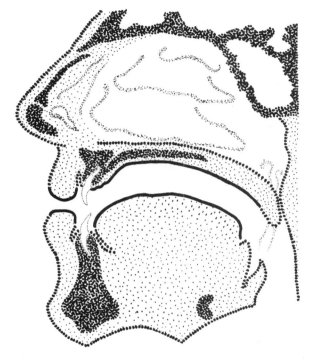

Fig. 7. The position for the neutral vowel, ʌ.

difference being entirely a matter of stress. Other phoneticians describe a slight difference in the tongue position for the stressed ʌ as opposed to the unstressed ə, ə having a slightly higher and perhaps slightly farther forward tongue position. It seems to the writers that neither of these conceptions quite gives the entire picture, though both are partially true. Consequently a full discussion of ə is given later. (See page 92.)

The position for ʌ is not fixed and hence it cannot serve as an absolute standard of reference. Like other vowels, and perhaps even more so than some, ʌ varies in different combinations and with different individuals. The variation away from a strictly neutral position is usually in the direction of a slight arching and retraction of the central portion of the tongue. However, if the vocal folds are in vibration, the soft palate closed, and the jaw dropped slightly, the result will be a sound like ʌ, and it is probable that most people actually produce ʌ in this way, with little or no active movement of the tongue. For all practical purposes we can speak of ʌ as the neutral vowel. It is chosen as the starting point for this discussion of the vowels because it so closely approximates the neutral position and because it can be used conveniently to mark the beginning of the three series of tongue movements that include all English vowels except ļ, which needs to be described separately.

Up to this point we have described the position of the vowel ʌ and indicated the general directions of the movements from this neutral tongue position for the formation of the remaining vowels. We may resume our description of specific vowels by taking up next the ɑ sound.[5]

ɑ as in "Father" fɑðɚ
Low central (or low back), open, neutral, relatively long, relatively lax

Lips: Open wide and neutral in shape. The bilabial orifice is formed almost entirely by the depression of the mandible. The sound can be produced without any activity on the part of the lips. Ordinarily the lips are open wider for ɑ than for any other sound.

Mandible: Open wide. The mandible is depressed farther for ɑ than for any other sound.

Tongue: From the neutral position the tongue is usually somewhat lowered, lying approximately flat in the floor of the mouth cavity. We have mentioned previously that the tongue position for ɑ is variable. The variations are usually in the direction of a retraction of the whole tongue and a slight elevation of its back

---

[5] Appendix A provides words and phrases for transcription practice on each of the sounds in the order in which they are presented.

portion. For most people, however, **ɑ** is a central vowel made with the tongue relatively flat in the mouth. Thus it is the lowest of the central vowel series. Its tongue position is similar to that for the neutral vowel **ʌ**, except for a certain amount of active flattening. The two sounds are likewise close together acoustically, the difference being largely due to the increased size of the oral resonator and bilabial orifice for **ɑ**. The most important essential for **ɑ** seems to be a large unobstructed resonator in the oral cavity with a large orifice. **ɑ** is frequently placed in vowel diagrams as the first of the back vowel series, and it should be recognized that the sound is often made with the back of the tongue slightly raised, thus making it part of this series.

a as in "Class" klas[6]
Low front, neutral, relatively lax, relatively long

This sound is the lowest of the front vowel series. Acoustically it lies between **æ** and **ɑ**. It is approximately the sound of *a* in French *la*.[7] The position for this sound frequently forms the starting point for such glides as **aɪ** in *high* **haɪ** and **aʊ** as in *allow* **əlaʊ**.[8] It is also used frequently as a compromise between **æ** and **ɑ** in such words as *after, shaft, bath, fast*, etc. This use is fairly common in the East and appears to be spreading elsewhere.

Lips: Open widely but not spread. Although the lip muscles may play a slight role in opening the orifice, this is accomplished mainly by depression of the mandible. This sound could be produced without any activity of the lips. The lip position is the first of a series for the front vowels in which the general direction of the movement is toward closing and spreading.

Mandible: An "open" sound; the lower jaw is depressed farther for this sound than for any of the front vowels. The jaw movement for the rest of the series is toward the closed position.

Tongue: The tongue position varies for this sound. As usually made, **a** belongs with the front vowels and should be placed at the

---

[6] This word is also pronounced as **klæs** and **klɑs**.

[7] The special symbol **ɐ** is sometimes used to represent this sound when it occurs finally in Spanish and Italian. It is slightly unstressed with something of the quality of schwa.

[8] **ɑ** is even more commonly used as the starting point for such glides, especially in Middle Western speech. The exact vowel used as starting point is subject to a great deal of sectional and individual variation.

beginning of the first series of movements. The tongue as a whole is drawn slightly forward and upward from the ᴀ position. The tip of the tongue is flattened and raised slightly so that it lies in contact with the lower front teeth. The dorsal surface of the forepart of the tongue is somewhat concave from side to side, whereas the remaining portion is convex. The central portion of the tongue is arched upward toward the hard palate. The point of greatest elevation is toward the posterior third of the hard palate, but the elevation is not pronounced. a is the lowest and farthest back of the front vowels. The next vowel in the forward series is æ. With some speakers, a is produced so that it is closer to ɑ both in sound and in movement than it is to æ.

Those who are unfamiliar with the a sound, and thus have difficulty in producing and hearing it, can practice either by attempting to isolate the first element in the glide aɪ as in *eye* or by alternately pronouncing æ and ɑ and then attempting to produce a sound about halfway between the two. If this proves difficult, the device of increasing the differences in position and acoustic effect between æ and ɑ by raising the tongue position for æ and exaggerating the wide-open position for ɑ may help in establishing the first awareness of an in-between sound.

æ as in "At" æt
Low front, open, neutral, relatively lax

Lips: The initial opening of the lips is probably due to an active contraction of the muscles concerned in this movement. Beyond that, the lips follow passively the depression of the mandible. The orifice is similar in shape to that for a and slightly smaller in size. Typically there is a very slight retraction of the angles of the mouth, although this movement is not essential.

Mandible: The mandible is depressed slightly less than for **a**.

Tongue: The tongue movement continues the upward and forward movements begun for **a**. The tongue is drawn a little farther forward and elevated a little higher. The sides of the tongue are in contact with the inner borders of the upper molars and with a small strip of the corresponding lateral portions of the hard palate. The forward movement of the tongue has the effect of increasing the size of the back cavity formed between the back of the tongue and the soft palate. In addition, there may be a slight depression of the back of the tongue.

æ is normally produced as a relatively open and relaxed sound with no great elevation of the front of the tongue. However, it seems to be more subject than most vowels to an unpleasant distortion which usually arises from raising the tongue position and tensing the musculature, often with accompanying nasalization. In close transcription, this effect can be represented by ˔ for the raised tongue position and ~ for the nasality, thus æ̃˔.

ɛ as in "Ever" ɛvɚ
Mid-front, half-open, spread, relatively lax, relatively short

Lips: Open to form an orifice similar to that for æ but narrower in its vertical extent and with a definite retraction of the angles of the mouth.

Mandible: The depression is noticeably less than for æ.

Tongue: The central elevation remains about the same as for æ. However, the front of the tongue moves upward and forward from the æ position, while the back moves forward and slightly down. The tip of the tongue is spread and concave from side to side, as in **a**. The sides of the tongue are in contact with the molar teeth and the corresponding lateral portions of the hard palate as in **a**. So far as movements from the neutral position are concerned, ɛ is essentially a continuation of the same movements that were begun with **a** and continued in æ.

A vowel with a sound somewhere between æ and ɛ is heard frequently in such words as *air, carry, Mary, hair,* etc. Many speakers feel that they do not say either **kærɪ** or **kɛrɪ**. In broad transcription, the student should choose the sound that seems to be nearest to his own pronunciation. In narrow transcription such in-between sounds can be represented by a raised æ or a lowered ɛ, thus: **kæˑrɪ** or **kɛˬrɪ**.

e as in "Vacation" vekeɪʃən
Mid-front, half-close, spread, relatively tense, relatively short

Lips: The angles of the mouth are retracted to form an orifice slightly smaller than that for ɛ.

Mandible: Slightly more closed than for ε.

Tongue: In producing this sound, the tongue continues its upward and forward movement from the position for the neutral vowel ʌ. The back of the tongue is drawn still farther forward and downward. The central portion of the tongue arches higher toward the hard palate and the point of highest elevation is anterior to that for ε. The front of the tongue is drawn still higher forward and upward. It is still slightly concave from side to side. The sides of the tongue are now in contact with the teeth and corresponding lateral portions of the hard palate, as far forward as the second premolars. The sides of the forepart of the tongue touch the upper teeth as far forward as the canines. Typically, the tongue muscles as a whole are more tense for e and more lax for ε.

As noted previously, when this sound is given either primary or secondary stress in English it tends strongly to become the glide eɪ which may be regarded as the typical form of the phoneme. Something approaching a short, continuant e is heard when the sound is retained in unaccented syllables. (See the word list in Appendix A for examples.) The distinction between e and eɪ is particularly important for those attempting to master a foreign language, especially the Romance languages, and in the correction of foreign accent. Unlike English, many other languages use the short, relatively pure e.

ɪ as in "It" ɪt

High front, close, spread, relatively lax, relatively short

Lips: Spread to form an orifice slightly smaller vertically and more retracted at the angles of the mouth than for e.

Mandible: Noticeably less open than for e. The teeth are almost together.

Tongue: The back of the tongue remains practically the same as for ε. The arching of the central portion of the tongue is also similar to that for ε, except that the point of highest elevation is farther forward. The front of the tongue is also raised higher for ɪ than ε. The contact of the sides of the tongue with the hard palate extends forward about as far as the first premolars.

This sound is difficult for many foreigners whose language does not contain a similar ɪ phoneme. This is especially true of the Romance languages. In speaking English, a sound similar to the nearest phoneme in the native language is substituted, and this is usually either a sound like our i or one approximately halfway between i and ɪ. In either case those who work with problems of foreign accent will find that instructing the speaker to lower his tongue position slightly is often not enough to obtain a good ɪ. There are also important differences in length and tension (see the discussion of these factors on pages 69–70 of this chapter) between i and ɪ. Better results will often be obtained if the speaker is also instructed to relax the tongue muscles and shorten the duration of the sound.

One problem concerning the transcription of the ɪ sound in a certain class of words arises so frequently that it deserves a special mention at this point. Many students hear the final vowel of words ending in *y* such as *city*, *mighty*, *likely*, *body*, etc., as an i and question the recommended use of ɪ in transcription. There are two good reasons why the question arises. The first is that the sound does resemble i and frequently seems to be so much of an in-between sound that some writers suggest the use of a special symbol ɨ to resolve the argument. This symbol is useful in illustrating the idea, but there seems to be little point in the regular use of a narrow transcription symbol in what is otherwise broad transcription and in a situation where close transcription is neither possible nor profitable.

The second reason is that when the student is asked to transcribe a sentence he almost invariably slows down his rate of speaking and articulates considerably more distinctly than usual. The result is usually an undeniable i. The question, however, is what happens when these words are spoken casually and rapidly as in ordinary speech. The answer seems to be twofold: (1) When the sound is spoken rapidly in an unstressed syllable, it becomes almost impossible to identify it as either i or ɪ and the argument becomes somewhat pointless; (2) In so far as it is possible to determine, the sound appears to be closer to ɪ. Thus in broad transcription when an admittedly somewhat arbitrary choice has to be made between i and ɪ, it seems preferable to use the ɪ as more generally characteristic of casual speech.

i as in "Eat" it
High front, close, spread, relatively tense, relatively long

Lips: Open to form an orifice elongated from side to side and narrow in its vertical extent—slightly narrower than that for ɪ.

Mandible: Closed slightly more than for ɪ.

Tongue: This is the highest of the front vowel series (Fig. 8 and Fig. 13). The whole front of the tongue is elevated farther than it

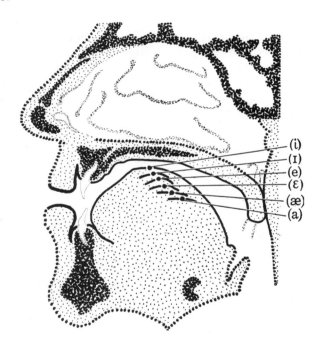

Fig. 8. The front-vowel series.

has been elevated for any previous vowel. The arching is greater, with the tongue almost touching the hard palate. The point of the highest elevation is farther forward, somewhat anterior to the central portion of the hard palate. The contact made by the sides of the tongue with the lateral portions of the hard palate is similar to that for ɪ except that it extends farther centrally, thus leaving only a narrow central orifice for the passage of the air stream. The forward and downward movement of the back of the tongue is considerably greater for **i** than for **ɪ**. In these front vowels, however, it is the movement of the front of the tongue that is important. We may assume that the positions taken by the back of the tongue are largely the results of its passive following of the movements of the front. Whatever their cause, these movements serve to form a posterior mouth cavity that increases in size at the same time that the anterior mouth cavity is decreasing. It is thought that the ratio in size between these two cavities formed by the elevation of the central portion of the tongue is important in determining the acoustic quality of the various front vowels. The vowel **i** is sometimes characterized as tense in contrast to **ɪ** which is called lax. This difference can be readily felt by placing the finger under the lower jaw just back of the bone and producing the two sounds alternately.

ɒ as in "Not" nɒt
Low back, open, slightly round, relatively lax, relatively short

The key word *not* is frequently pronounced as **nɑt** in this country and hence cannot be relied upon by many speakers to provide an example of the **ɒ** sound. **ɒ** is not phonemic in the language as a whole although it may be in the speech of some individuals. It occurs as a variant of both the **ɑ** and the **ɔ** phonemes. Other typical words in which the sound *may* be used are *watch, forest, hospital, nod, mock, soft, foreign*, etc. It is used regularly in England, frequently in the Eastern part of this country and occasionally in other sections. Although it is not indigenous in general American speech, it is usually easy to find individual examples once the ear has been trained to discriminate the sound from **ɑ** and **ɔ**. Sometimes examples can be found by asking a number of people to pronounce such pairs of words as *don-dawn, hock-hawk, cot-caught, yon-yawn*, etc. Many individuals will pronounce the first word in each pair with a readily identifiable **ɑ** and the second with an **ɔ**. On the other hand, some speakers will make little if any distinction between the two sounds and in these instances the sound that is used will probably, *though not necessarily*, be an in-between sound resembling **ɒ**.

Those needing to learn to produce the sound should start by pronouncing alternately **a** and **ɔ**, making an effort to widen the difference between the two by exaggerating the openness of the first and the lip rounding of the second. After learning to feel and hear the differences the student should attempt to produce a third sound falling somewhere between the two. Repeated efforts will usually improve both the ability to discriminate between the three sounds and the ability to produce something resembling an **ɒ** at will. Good results are often obtained by leaving the tongue in approximately the position for **a** and making sure that the jaw is noticeably closer and the lips definitely rounded.

Lips: The bilabial orifice is considerably smaller than that for **a** and there is noticeable, though not pronounced, lip rounding.

Mandible: Open noticeably less than for the **a** sound.

Tongue: **ɒ** can be considered as the first sound in the back vowel series, in the sense that there is typically a slight elevation of the back of the tongue which is not always true for **a**. The tongue position is between those for **a** and **ɔ**, being usually closer to that for **a**. The front and central portions lie relatively flat in the mouth or are slightly depressed and retracted.

ɔ as in "Law" lɔ
Mid-back, half-open, rounded, relatively tense, relatively long

Lips: Open widely, but definitely rounded with the angles of the mouth drawn medially and some protrusion of the lips.

Mandible: Relatively open, but somewhat closer than for **ɒ**.

Tongue: In assuming the position for **ɔ**, the movements of the tongue show a continuation of the backward and upward movements from the neutral position. The whole tongue is further retracted, and the forepart shows an additional depression. The back of the tongue, on the other hand, shows an additional elevation and retraction.

o as in "Obey" o̧beɪ
Mid-back, half-close, rounded, relatively tense, relatively short

This sound is a variant of the **ou** phoneme. The relatively continuant (unglided) form of the vowel is common in other languages but can be found in English only when the sound occurs in lightly stressed syllables. Common examples are such words as *opinion, obedience, annotate, shadowing, window, potato,* etc. In each case, including the key word used above, the assumption is that the sound is pronounced with an identifiable **o** quality and

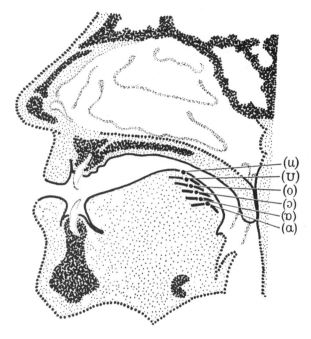

Fig. 9. The back-vowel series. **a** is here shown with the back-vowel series. It is sometimes, though probably not typically, so produced.

not unstressed to **ə** or sometimes **ʊ**. If the syllable in which the sound occurs receives either primary or secondary stress it will be pronounced as a glide, the extent of the gliding movement varying considerably, depending upon the degree of stress and the phonetic context.

Lips: Definitely rounded and with considerable protrusion.

Mandible: Considerably closer than for ɔ.

Tongue: In comparison with ɔ the front of the tongue is still further depressed while the back shows an additional elevation and retraction toward the soft palate.

ʊ as in "Book" bʊk
High back, close, rounded, relatively lax, relatively short

Lips: Marked rounding and protrusion, with the orifice considerably smaller than for o.

Mandible: Nearly closed, with only a small opening between the teeth.

Tongue: The tongue position is generally described as slightly higher and more retracted in the back than for o with a corresponding depression and retraction of the front portion. However, there is evidence that the position for ʊ may represent a break in the series of upward and backward movements for the back vowels. Trevino and Parmenter [9] in reporting on their x-ray study of vowel positions, compare o and ʊ as follows: "Although the height of the tongue is about the same for both vowels, in the ʊ the back part of the tongue has moved forward and the front is much higher."

u as in "Boot" but
High back, close, rounded, relatively tense, relatively long

Lips: Marked rounding and protrusion. The orifice is smaller than for ʊ.

Mandible: Nearly closed with an opening between the teeth that is similar to that for ʊ or slightly smaller.

Tongue: The sound is the highest of the back vowels. The front of the tongue is depressed and retracted beyond the position for any vowel yet considered. The back of the tongue is elevated and retracted until only a narrow orifice is left between it and the soft palate. This position represents the limit of upward and backward movements for this series of vowels. It will be observed that for this series it is the movement of the back of the tongue that is

---

[9] "Vowel Positions as Shown by X-Ray," *The Quarterly Journal of Speech* (vol. XVII, no. 3), June, 1932.

important. The front of the tongue retracts and lowers more or less passively as it follows the movements of the back.

ɜ as in "Early" ɜlɪ
Mid-central, half-open, neutral or slightly round, relatively tense, relatively long

The key word given above, or any other that might be used as a sample, assumes the typical pronunciation of this sound in British speech or in the so-called "standard" Southern and Eastern speech, although the sounds used in these three varieties of English are not quite identical. The ɜ is a variant of the ɝ phoneme, speaking from the point of view of American English, in which the ɝ occurs much more frequently and appears to be gaining in usage. If we look at English as a world language we might want to reverse the statement and describe ɝ as a variant of the ɜ phoneme, since the latter is probably more prevalent in other countries. Those who use ɜ when the vowel is stressed as in *work* **wɜk** and *shirk* **ʃɜk** usually use ə for the unstressed form of the sound, as in the second syllables of *worker* **wɜkə** and *shirker* **ʃɜkə**.

This sound is one of the central vowels and belongs to the third series mentioned at the beginning of this discussion. There are four vowels in this central series if we include ɑ, which is probably produced with some active flattening of the tongue. The second in the series, ʌ, is made in the neutral position; ɜ is produced with some active elevation of the central portion of the tongue and ɝ with considerable central arching.

Lips: Neutral in position with an opening similar to that for ʌ or with a slight rounding.

Mandible: Somewhat less depressed than for ʌ.

Tongue: Ordinarily the whole of the tongue, including both front and back, is raised slightly from the neutral position, with an additional elevation of the central portion. The tip of the tongue is spread and lies behind the lower front teeth. Palatograms show the sides of the tongue in contact with the teeth and corresponding lateral portions of the hard palate as far forward as the second premolars, leaving a wide central orifice for the passage of the air stream.

ɝ as in "Early" ɝlɪ

Mid-central, half-close, neutral or slightly round, relatively
tense, relatively long

This symbol represents the sound of the *r* vowel that is typical of Midwestern, Northern, and Western speech. Those who use this sound in stressed positions use approximately the same sound in unstressed syllables. The special symbol ɚ has been developed to represent the unstressed form since it occurs so frequently, thus **wɝkɚ** and **ʃɝkɚ**. This means that for practical purposes we have two symbols representing the same sound. Use ɝ when the syllable in which it occurs is given primary or secondary stress and ɚ when it is unstressed.

Lips: A bilabial orifice similar to that for ɜ is used in the production of this sound. It is, however, slightly smaller and there may be a little more rounding of the lips.

Mandible: Somewhat less open than for ɜ but noticeably more open than for the high front and high back vowels.

Tongue: The tongue position for ɝ varies in individuals (Figs. 15 and 16). Typically the sound is produced by a slight retraction of the whole tongue and a decided elevation of its central portion, thus making it the highest of the central vowel series. This position is usually considered the "correct" position for the sound, since the vowel so produced is judged as more "pleasant" acoustically than some other varieties of ɝ. Another variety of ɝ is produced by a decided retraction of the whole tongue and a bunching and elevation of the front of the tongue. The amount of elevation may vary considerably, and in some instances the front of the tongue may be curled backward toward the hard palate. This latter position produces the so-called "burred" *r* which is usually considered an unpleasant sound. It is this variety of the ɝ phoneme in Middle Western speech that is usually found most objectionable by those living in other sections of the country. As we shall see later, the *r* phoneme contains many varieties of sounds, usually considered as consonants. ɝ, however, because it is a continuant sound of some length, and because it is produced through an orifice large enough to prevent the formation of friction noises, is generally grouped with the vowels and called a vowelized *r*.

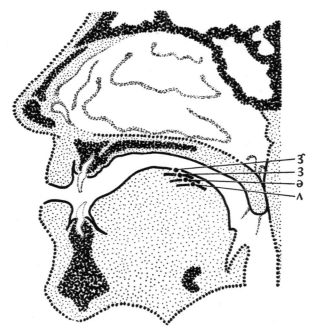

Fig. 10. The central-vowel series. The position
for ə is purely arbitrary. See the discussion of
schwa vowels in the succeeding pages. The ɑ
has been omitted in this picture.

l̩ as in "Title" taɪtl̩ and "Buckle" bʌkl̩

We have mentioned previously that the vowelized form of the *l*
sound does not fit into any of the three series of movements
described above. This is because the sound is emitted laterally. It
is the only sound in English that is correctly produced in this
manner. It occurs most commonly in a consonantal, or, as we
shall prefer to call it later, a glide form. It is, however, frequently
syllabic—that is, it forms a separate syllable by itself.

If we define vowels and consonants from a linguistic point of
view, we can say that every syllable must contain a vowel and that
only vowels can form syllables by themselves without the presence
of any other sound. Conversely, a consonant is a sound that must

be accompanied by a vowel to make a syllable. The vowel (or diphthong) provides the peak of sonority that is said to characterize each syllable. From this point of view, the *l* sound behaves like a consonant most of the time—that is, it requires an accompanying vowel to form a syllable as in *lily* lɪlɪ. However, in a word such as *title*, it is possible to produce the *l* without any other sound between it and the **t**. This is done by leaving the tongue tip in the *t* position and dropping the sides to permit the normal lateral emission of the *l*. This we call a syllabic *l*. It is a continuant rather than a glide and it is here serving as the vowel in the second syllable. A syllabic or vowel *l* is represented by placing a vertical bar under the symbol, thus, **taɪtl̩**.

The reader should be cautioned that the *l* is truly syllabic only if there is no other sound between it and the preceding consonant. If, in the example given, the tongue is pulled completely away from the *t* position, there will be an intervening sound which in this case might be represented as **taɪtəl** or **taɪtɪl**. This is another way of saying that a true syllabic sound can only occur following a homorganic sound, that is, one made in essentially the same position. The homorganic sounds of **l** are **t, d, n**, and also **k** and **g** if we use what is later described as a back *l*.

On the other hand, if we define vowels on an acoustic basis (see page 68), syllabic *l* has all the qualifications. It is a continuant sound and is characterized by voicing, resonance and absence of friction. Note that the glide *l* also has all of these characteristics except that it is not a continuant. The occasional friction that may seem to accompany some *l* sounds is caused by the preceding or following consonant as in the words *slide* **slaɪd** and *clay* **kleɪ**. The sound of *l*, like that of *r*, is subject to considerable variation, but it is customary to distinguish only two main varieties. They are also called front *l* and back *l*, respectively, in terms of the position of the tongue for their production (Figs. 17 and 18).

Lips: The lips are opened slightly to produce a bilabial orifice similar to, but smaller than, that for ʌ.

Mandible: Depression is variable but limited.

Tongue: For front *l* the tongue is drawn forward and the tip elevated so that it is in contact with the alveolar ridge behind the upper incisors, while the sides of the forepart touch the inner borders of the canines and premolars. The sides of the back of the tongue are depressed so that they do not lie in contact with the teeth. The dorsum of the tongue is elevated somewhat in its central portion but the posterior part is approximately in the neutral position, or it may be slightly depressed. The movements of the tongue block the central part of the mouth cavity so that the air stream is emitted laterally on both sides; that is, it is forced out between the upper and lower molars, to pass outward between the cheeks and the alveolar ridges, finally emerging from the bilabial orifice.

In narrow transcription, a modifying sign consisting of a bar drawn through the symbol is used to represent a back *l*, thus, ɫ or ł. The symbols without the modifying sign are then assumed to represent front *l*'s. In broad transcription, the symbols l and ḷ represent all varieties.

Practically the only difference between front *l* and back *l* is in the position of the tongue. The contact of the tip of the tongue is farther posterior for ł than for ḷ. The middle of the tongue is convex for ḷ, whereas for ł it is slightly concave and the back of the tongue is elevated toward the **u** position. In fact, when the sound follows a **k** or a **g** the ł may be made around the back of the tongue while the tip is depressed. Another variety of *l* is made with the tip of the tongue behind the lower front teeth while the forepart rolls up and forward to make a contact behind the upper front teeth. We may correctly think of a series of *l* sounds produced through a corresponding series of tongue positions and discharging lateral orifices. These vary from front to back with ḷ representing those made farther forward and ł those made farther back. The position of the vowel *l* will be determined largely by that of the preceding sound. Preceding sounds made with the front of the tongue tend to pull the ḷ forward, whereas back sounds cause it to be formed farther back.

The *l* vowels described thus far are typical sounds that are present in everyone's speech, variation between front and back varieties depending upon the influence of neighboring sounds. In addition we should mention the clear or extremely fronted *l* and the dark or retracted *l*. Clear *l* occurs regularly in Southern and Eastern speech in certain positions. This sound is made with the tongue tip far enough forward that it comes in contact with the upper front teeth. Dark *l* is more common among Middle

Westerners. As its name indicates, it is made with the tongue retracted beyond the typical position for a back *l*. Dark *l* is closely related to, and often confused with, **o**, whereas clear *l* has more of an ɪ resonance. Vowelized *l* seldom occurs in English except in unstressed syllables. This is probably why the phonetic alphabet does not have a special symbol for the vowel *l* corresponding to the symbol ɝ for the vowel *r*. However, such words as *milk* and *bulk* are occasionally pronounced in such a way that the only vowel present seems to be a sort of stressed *l*, thus: **mḷk** and **bḷk**.

The Schwa[10] Vowels ə as in "About" əbaʊt, "Battalion" bətæljən, "Telephone" tələfoun

We have previously discussed sixteen vowel sounds that are members of thirteen phonemes. Each sound is subject to some variation but the variation is relatively limited and the sounds are easy to distinguish. The ə symbol, on the contrary, stands for many gradations of sounds. It serves, as it were, as the dumping ground for all of the variations caused by unstressing in each of the vowel phonemes, wherever these sounds have strayed so far from their own sound families that they are no longer recognized as belonging to them.

The need for such a symbol grows out of two very important and related characteristics of English that set it apart from most other languages. The first is a tendency toward sharp differences in stress among different syllables in the same word and among different words in a sentence. As an example, pronounce the word *constitutionality* ˌkɑn stə ˌtju ʃən ˈæl ə tɪ casually and note the marked differences in stress given to the various syllables. Now say a group of words such as "page one in the book on the top of the shelf" and notice how the words *page*, *one*, *book*, *top*, and *shelf* are heavily stressed in relation to the others, which are passed over quickly and lightly.

These marked differences in emphasis are typical of English. There are all degrees of stress but for practical purposes we can talk in terms of four gradations: primary stress, secondary stress, light stress, and unstressed. In phonetic transcription primary

[10] This is a German word of Hebrew origin. It has somewhat the same general meaning in German as in English and it has been used by a number of English and American phoneticians.

stress is shown by placing an accent mark above and in front of the syllable. Secondary is indicated when the mark is below and in front of the syllable. Syllables that are only lightly stressed or unstressed are not marked. In *constitutionality*, the first and third syllables are given secondary stress, the fifth receives the primary stress, the last is lightly stressed, and the remainder are unstressed.

The second characteristic that sets English apart is the result of the first. There is a strong tendency in English for vowels in unstressed and lightly stressed syllables to lose their original identities and become ə.

As an example of both of these factors note the following pairs of words:

battle **bætḷ**	battalion **bətæljən**
con'tract **'kɑntrækt**	contract' **kən'trækt**
able **eɪbəl**	ability **əbɪlətɪ**
illustration **ɪləs'treɪʃən**	illustrative **ɪ'lʌstrətɪv,**
define **dɪ'faɪn**	definition **,dɛfə'nɪʃən**
reality **ri'ælətɪ**	realize **'riəlaɪz**

In each of the pairs, the vowel in question has one value in the stressed syllable and another in the unstressed position. Thus in *battle* the first vowel is definitely æ. However, in *battalion* the sound is unstressed and it becomes a *schwa* vowel. Now this unstressed æ will vary greatly in its pronunciation by different individuals. In some cases the sound of the first vowel in *battalion* will be very near to the æ itself, in others it will be made practically in the ʌ or neutral position, and there will be all shades of gradation between these two extremes. However, we can safely say that no one can place the accent definitely on the second syllable of the word and still produce a clear-cut æ in the first. We may define unstressing, then, as the tendency of vowels in unaccented positions to migrate toward the neutral position. Notice the word *toward*. The migration may reach the neutral position or it may stop anywhere along the line. Referring once more to the above list of words, note that there may be considerable difference between the schwa vowels in the words *battalion*, *contract'*, *ability*, and

illus'trative. They all have this one element in common, that what
were once (in stressed syllables) clear-cut vowels or glides, i.e., æ,
ɑ, eɪ, and eɪ, respectively, have migrated toward the neutral position. Let us give a few other illustrations. *Milk* is sometimes pronounced **mɪlk** and sometimes **mɪək.** *Better* may be either **bɛtɚ**
or **bɛtə.** Note the unstressed sounds in *telephone, capable, potato,
vegetable,* etc.

We are now ready to make some general statements concerning
the schwa vowels. First, we may say that any of the vowels
described above may move toward the neutral position to such an
extent that they are no longer clear-cut representatives of their
own phonemes but have become schwa vowels. Second, the ə
symbol represents an unusually wide variety of sounds because of
the fact that it tends to retain some of the acoustic "coloring" of
the original vowel (Fig. 11).

It should now be clear why this section was headed "the schwa
vowels" and also why we have not been willing to call ə the unstressed equivalent of ʌ. The vowel ʌ is, in a sense, a stressed
schwa, if this is not too much of a paradox. It is the schwa made
nearest to the neutral position and stressed. However, ʌ occurs
frequently as a relatively stable vowel in its own right and can
be considered as a phoneme lying near the neutral position with
ə as one of its variants. The vowel ə, on the other hand, has no
typical position. It represents a tendency rather than a position,
a tendency of vowels to lose their identity by moving toward the
neutral position. Perhaps Fig. 11 will serve to clarify this whole
discussion.

We have reproduced here, with slight modifications, the vowel
diagram given earlier in these pages. The circles around the vowels
indicate that these symbols represent sounds that are subject to
considerable variation. The *l* sound has been arbitrarily placed in
the drawing for the sake of completeness, but it must be remembered that its position on the diagram is in no way indicative
of its tongue position, nor is it possible to represent pictorially the
lateral emission of the sound. The large egg-shaped area surrounding the neutral vowel ʌ represents the schwa vowel area.
The lines drawn from the various vowel phoneme areas indicate
graphically the tendency of all these sounds to approach the schwa

area when they occur in unstressed positions. Since ʌ is already in the neutral position, it perforce becomes one of the schwas whenever it is unstressed. In English, unstressing is generally in the direction of the schwa vowel area, though it may upon occasion be in other directions, even to the extent of reversing the trend. The main pull is that of physiological inertia, which tends to make the mechanism return to the neutral position. However, other forces are also in operation, probably the chief one being

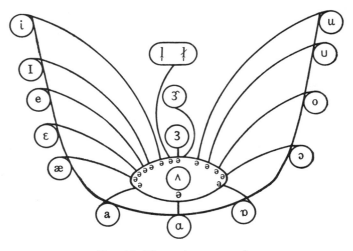

Fig. 11. The schwa vowels.

the influence exerted by neighboring sounds. What finally happens to the unstressed vowel will be the result of the sum of these various forces.

We may now speak briefly of the problems involved in symbolizing these schwa vowels. One of these is knowing just when a given vowel in its movement toward a central position leaves its own phoneme and enters the schwa area. There is no rule to determine this and the only test is an acoustic one. For example, the word *amplitude* in the writer's speech is unquestionably **æmplətɪud**. Some, however, pronounce it more carefully as **æmplɪtjud** and others as **æmplɪtjud**. Now, if the unstressed sound is unmistakably ə or ɪ or i there will be little difficulty in deciding upon the proper transcription. Even so, the lightly stressed sounds represented by ɪ or i are obviously quite different from the sounds of these symbols in such words as *fit* **fɪt** and *street* **strit**. There will also be times when it will be very difficult to decide whether the sound has unstressed all of the way to ə or should still be thought of as an ɪ or an i.

This leads us to the conclusion that our representation of unstressed vowels would be more exact if we had a modifying sign to be used in close transcription to indicate a sound midway between any given vowel and a schwa. The writers suggest, and have used in this book, a dot placed under the vowel to indicate partial unstressing. This affords three refinements of distinction in approaching this problem of symbolization. Thus in a given word such as *address*, if the pronunciation of the first vowel is definitely **æ**, we would write **ædrɛs**. This would indicate considerable stress on both syllables, since both **æ** and **ɛ** are represented as receiving full vowel value. But if the first vowel is definitely unstressed to a schwa vowel, we can write it as **ədrɛs**. This implies that the stress is on the second syllable. However, if the first vowel is neither **æ** nor **ə**, but something in between, we write **æ̣drɛs**. In this case the vowel has started its migration toward the schwa vowel area but has gone only part way. It has some of the characteristics of **æ** and some of **ə**, yet to use either of these symbols is a misrepresentation. The use of the dot in this manner to indicate partial unstressing is logical, and is so employed in the *Century Dictionary*.

Even though there is a strong tendency for unstressed vowels to become ə this does not always happen and there are regional differences. The tendency is strongest in general American speech, less strong in Southern and Eastern speech, and considerably less strong in British speech. As we have just noted, any vowel may unstress to a weak form of itself and the glides **ou** and **eɪ** may become **o** and **e**. In addition, the vowel **u** may unstress to **ʊ** rather than ə and the vowels **i**, **e**, and **ɛ** may become **ɪ**. Thus *repeat* may be heard as **rị̣pit**, **rɪpit**, or **rəpit**; *subject* may be **sʌbdʒẹkt** or more likely **sʌbdʒɪkt** or possibly **sʌbdʒəkt**; *office* may be **ɔfịs** or **ɔfəs** and *lettuce* may be **lɛtụs** or **lɛtəs**.

Summary of the Vowel Sounds of English

General Remarks

Several general observations may be made on the basis of this survey of the positions taken by the articulatory mechanism in the production of the various vowel sounds. In the first place, it should be noted that the exact movements of the tongue are still difficult to describe, even with the aid of all the information obtained from studies by x-rays, palatograms, and direct observation. Such descriptions must be more or less general, partly because of the variation that exists, and partly because the movements are exceedingly difficult to view in their entirety. The gross movements have been described above but there may be fine gradations of movement which our present technique does not uncover. Furthermore, other factors besides movement are important in giving the vowels their characteristic quality. Some of the differences between vowels may be partly or largely a difference in duration. The degree of tenseness or laxness of the tongue and of the muscular walls of the mouth cavity and pharynx also influences vowel quality.

In the second place, it is difficult to lay down specific minimum essentials for the production of a given vowel, since the factors involved are apparently relative rather than absolute. A change in the position of the front of the tongue may be compensated for by an adjustment of the back of the tongue, or a difference in the amount of depression of the mandible may be offset to a certain extent by a difference in the position of the lips, etc. One can only say that certain movements usually accompany the production of a given vowel, and that, while the general nature of the movement may be essential and remain a constant factor, it is subject to many variations.

Finally, it seems evident that many of the vowels are produced by essentially the same type of movement and involve substantially the same muscles in different degrees of contraction. As mentioned previously, this section has been limited to a consideration of the movements of the lips, mandible, and tongue. Our next step will be to summarize, as far as these structures are concerned, the general requirements of the vowel sounds.

Lip Movements (Fig. 12)

Vowels ʌ, ɑ, a, æ, ḷ, ə, and, with most speakers, ɜ and ɝ. What might be called a passive bilabial orifice is formed for these sounds. No special movement other than that of opening is required. Usually the initial part of the opening movement is produced by an active contraction of the depressors of the lower lip and the elevators of the upper lip, but for the most part the

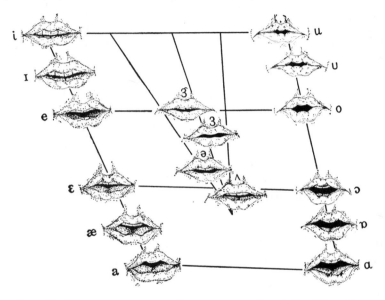

Fig. 12. The lip positions for the vowels of English. The vowels are here arranged on the conventional vowel diagram. ə is pictured as if it were a stable vowel in its typical position.

opening is effected as the lower lip follows passively the depression of the mandible.

Vowels i, ɪ, e, and ɛ: In addition to the opening movement various degrees of spreading accompany these sounds. This involves a retraction of the angles of the mouth so as to produce an orifice enlongated from side to side and relatively narrow in its vertical extent.

Vowels ɒ, ɔ, o, ʊ, u, and with some speakers ɜ and ɝ: In
ıddition to the opening movement these sounds are typically
accompanied by various degrees of protrusion and rounding of
the lips.

Movements of the Mandible

The mandible is depressed in varying degrees for all vowels
made normally. The amount of depression for any given vowel

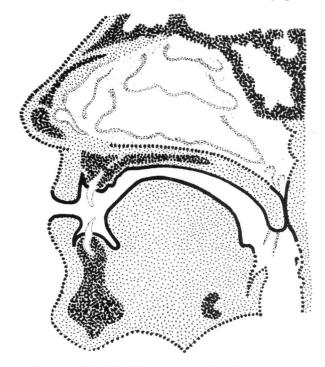

Fig. 13. The position for i.

may vary within wide limits without seriously affecting the
character of the sound. The mandible is depressed to the greatest
extent for the vowel ɑ. It closes progressively for the front vowel
series ending in i and the back vowel series ending in u. The
openings for ɜ and ɝ are approximately the same or slightly
smaller than for ʌ.

Tongue Movements

Vowels **a, æ, ɛ, e, ɪ**, and **i**: The essential movements of the tongue involved in the production of these sounds are as follows: forward movement of the whole tongue; depression of the back of the tongue; elevation of the tip and forepart of the tongue, and an

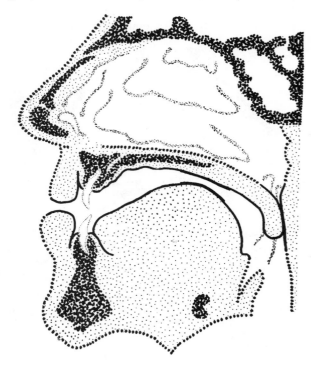

Fig. 14. The position for **u**.

additional arching upward of the central portion of the tongue. The point of highest elevation moves successively anterior for the various sounds in the order given from **a** to **i**.

Vowels **ɒ, ɔ, o, ʊ**, and **u**: The production of these sounds depends upon the ability of the individual to execute the following tongue movements: retraction of the whole tongue, elevation of the back of the tongue, and depression of the front of the tongue. These three general movements are essential to all the sounds, while the relative extent of the various movements determines the particular sound that will be produced.

Vowels ɑ, ʌ, ɜ, and ɝ: ʌ has been described as the neutral vowel since it is made in or close to the neutral position. Typically it is probably made with a slight raising of the central portion of the tongue, whereas for ɑ the tongue is flattened. With ɜ and ɝ

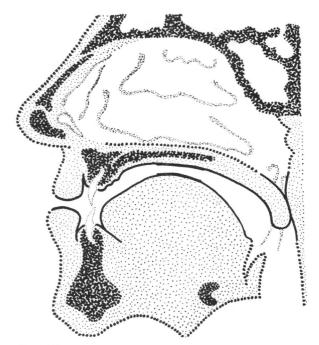

Fig. 15. A typical position for ɝ. See also Fig. 16.

the essential movement is a definite elevation of the central part of the tongue. This elevation may be accompanied by a non-essential drawing forward or retraction of the whole tongue. As indicated above ɝ may also be made with the tip of the tongue elevated and retracted.

The vowels ḷ to ḭ: The essential movement for these sounds is an elevation of some portion of the tongue to form an occlusion with the hard palate at the midline, at the same time that the sides of the tongue are depressed, allowing the air stream to escape laterally.

The Five Key Vowel Positions (Figs. 7 and 13–18)

Five vowel positions are important because they indicate types of tongue movement and because they represent extremes of

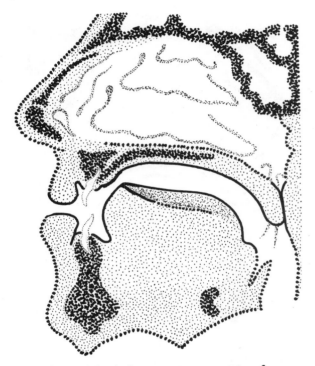

Fig. 16. A high front tongue position for ɝ.

movement in certain directions. We have called the vowels made in these positions *key vowels*. They are ʌ, the vowel made in or nearest the neutral position (see Fig. 7); i, the vowel representing the usual limit of the movement toward a high front position; u, the vowel representing the usual limit of the movement toward a high back position; ɝ, representing the limit of the movement toward a high central position; and ḷ, the high central laterally emitted vowel. We will have occasion to refer to these five key vowel positions again, especially in discussing glide sounds.

The Cardinal Vowel System

The English phonetician Daniel Jones is the originator of a system of standard vowels called the "Cardinal Vowels." [11] It

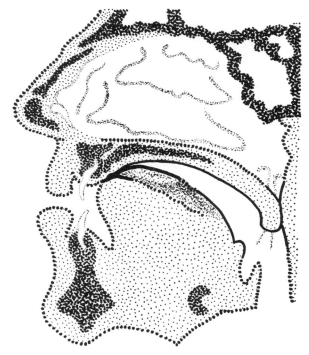

Fig. 17. A typical position for ḷ.

should be clearly understood that these vowels are not intended to represent vowels actually used in speech (although in some instances they do approximate vowels present in certain languages),

---

[11] See Daniel Jones, *An Outline of English Phonetics*, 6th ed., E. P. Dutton & Co., 1940, pp. 31–38. The writers have based their discussion of the cardinal vowels upon the description given by Jones in this book. See also Ida C. Ward, *The Phonetics of English*, D. Appleton-Century Company, 1929, pp. 52–59.

nor are they meant to serve as models in a system of standard speech. The Cardinal Vowel system grew out of a desire for a standard of measurement to facilitate the analysis and description of the vowels used in a given language or by a given speaker.

There are eight primary cardinal vowels, established arbitrarily as follows: cardinal **i**[12] is the highest and farthest front vowel

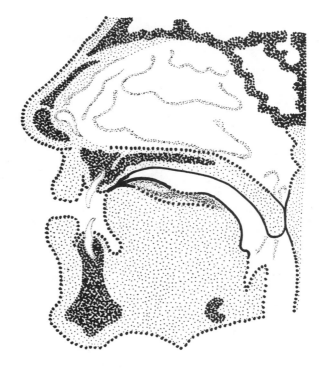

Fig. 18. A typical position for **i**.

sound that can be made, the lips being spread. Cardinal **ɑ** is made with the tongue lowered and retracted as far as possible, the lips being unrounded. Cardinal vowels **e**, **ε**, and **a** are front vowels

[12] Note that the symbols are the same as those for vowels in regular usage. Care must be taken in speaking and writing to add the word "cardinal" whenever a cardinal vowel is intended.

chosen to form a uniform *acoustic* sequence between cardinal **i** and cardinal **a**. The cardinal vowels **ɔ**, **o**, and **u** are back vowels that continue the equidistant series up to the highest and most retracted back sound that will still be a vowel.

After these eight cardinal vowels had been selected and standardized in this manner, x-ray photographs were made of their production. The resulting pictures form the basis of the cardinal

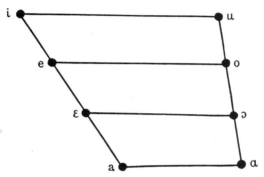

Fig. 19. The cardinal vowel diagram. Only the primary cardinal vowels are shown here.

vowel diagram (Fig. 19). The cardinal vowels have also been recorded by Jones and these records are available[13] for purposes of study and comparison.

The reader is warned that the cardinal vowels cannot be learned adequately by means of written descriptions or x-ray pictures of tongue positions. They must be learned "by ear," preferably under the tutelage of some one thoroughly acquainted with them, or, if this is not possible, from the cardinal vowel records. After the cardinal vowels have been mastered they can be used as standard points of reference in describing any vowel in any language.[14] For example, the typical English **i** is lowered and retracted from the position for cardinal **i**, whereas

[13] No. DAJO 1–2, distributed by the Linguaphone Institute, 30 Rockefeller Plaza, New York.

[14] See Ida C. Ward, *The Phonetics of English*, pp. 60–108, for examples of such comparisons.

the sound of **i** in the French word *si* is very close to the cardinal vowel.

Daniel Jones, in some explanatory notes published by the Linguaphone Institute and written to accompany the recording of the cardinal vowels, explains their purpose and function as follows:

> The principle is to describe the qualities of unknown vowels by their relation to those of known vowels. As has been shown above, the vowels of any particular language cannot be used for this purpose. It has therefore been found necessary to choose a standard set of vowels for reference—a scale of vowels which can be used in the same way as a scale of degrees enables us to specify temperatures. The vowels of such a scale are called *cardinal vowels*. They are chosen on a scientific basis and are independent of the vowels of any language.

The system of cardinal vowels is thus essentially an attempt to meet the very real need for a standard of measurement that will make it possible to describe and compare vowels more specifically and objectively. Although modern equipment for the analysis of sound has provided a much more accurate way of measuring and describing vowels in the laboratory, there is still a need for some such method of comparison that can be used conveniently in the classroom and for survey studies.

Symmetrical and Asymmetrical Vowels

We have previously observed that the front vowels of English are characterized by various degrees of lip spreading, ranging from the bilabial orifice for **i**, which is spread horizontally and narrowed vertically to a considerable degree, to the orifice for **a**, which is usually neither spread nor rounded, but neutral. Similarly the back vowels in English are characterized by various degrees of lip rounding. Such a vowel system, in which front vowels are spread and back vowels are rounded, is said to be a symmetrical system. Conversely, a vowel system that contains rounded front vowels or spread back vowels is said to be asymmetrical. Individual vowels are also spoken of as symmetrical or asymmetrical depending upon their conformance to this system. The symmetrical and asymmetrical pairs for the front and back vowels are given in the columns below:

Front Vowels		Back Vowels	
Symmetrical (Spread)	Asymmetrical (Rounded)	Symmetrical (Rounded)	Asymmetrical (Spread)
i	y	u	ɯ
ɪ	ʏ	ʊ	ʊ̲
e	ɸ	o	ɣ
ɛ	œ		

The asymmetrical vowel **y** is formed by making an **i** with the lips rounded, **ʏ** is rounded **ɪ**, **ɯ** is spread **u**, etc. Although English formerly contained asymmetrical vowels,[15] they no longer exist except in accidental situations. In some languages they occur regularly as separate phonemes. For examples, German uses **y**, **ʏ**, **ɸ**, and **œ** and French has **y**, **ɸ**, and **œ**.[16]

Nasal Vowels

Any vowel sound can be nasalized by lowering the soft palate and allowing a part of the air stream to exit through the nose. In French, however, four vowels are regularly nasalized when they occur in certain situations. These vowels are **ã**, **õ**, **ɛ̃**, and **œ̃**. Examples: *quand* **kã**, *dans* **dã**, *garçon* **garsõ**, *sont* **sõ**, *bien* **bijɛ̃**, *fin* **fɛ̃**, *un* **œ̃**, and *chacun* **ʃakœ̃**. There is considerable difference between the acoustic effect of these nasal vowels in French and the same sounds as nasalized by a careless American speaker. The difference is difficult to analyze. It may consist of differences in duration, tension and degree of nasality, the French nasals being usually shorter, more tense, and seemingly more completely nasal.

A View of the Remaining Speech Sounds as Methods of Initiating or Terminating Vowels

In this discussion we first considered the neutral position of the speech mechanism and the minor modifications of that position

[15] John S. Kenyon, *American Pronunciation*, 10th ed., George Wahr, 1950, p. 63.

[16] Some phoneticians add to the foregoing list ʌ and ɑ as the unrounded forms of ɔ and ɒ respectively, thus making ʌ and ɑ asymmetrical vowels. While this adds to the completeness of the system, it seems to stretch unduly the physiological facts in the case.

necessary to produce the neutral vowel ʌ. We next pointed out how further modifications of the neutral position, involving movements in three general directions, produce the four types of vowels: front, back, central, and laterally emitted. We have discussed each of these vowels in some detail. Lastly, we have spoken of the tendency of all of these vowels to move toward the neutral position when they occur in unstressed syllables, thus producing the group of schwa vowels symbolized by ə. These vowel sounds, all of them symbol units, form the basic material out of which speech is made.

Clearly, however, a speech limited to the vowel sounds would be quite inadequate to carry the complex meanings that modern language is called upon to convey. There are two chief reasons for this inadequacy: first, there are not enough symbol units upon which to base a complicated language; and second, the vowels are difficult to join together if their integrity as separate symbol units is to be retained. It was thus inevitable that other types of speech sounds would arise to remedy these two deficiencies. It is an interesting as well as clarifying approach to the remaining speech sounds if we consider them simply as methods of initiating and terminating these basic vowel sounds. *This approach is the basis for the order of presentation of the remaining material in this section.* We will discuss, in order, the various methods by which these vowel sounds are started and stopped or otherwise modified. Some of these methods will result in sounds that are symbol units. Others will produce transitional sounds usually present in speech but without symbolic significance. We turn our attention first to modifications of the vowel sounds produced by the action of the laryngeal mechanism.

Chapter 6 Laryngeal Modifications
of the Vowels

It seems logical to start a discussion of the methods of initiating and terminating vowels by considering those modifications of vowel tones that can be produced in the larynx. In discussing the vibrator mechanism we described four type positions that the vocal folds are capable of taking: open, closed to the whisper position,[1] closed to the point of phonation, and completely closed. These positions are the basis of three methods of approaching and terminating vowel tones.

The Glottal Fricative Approach or Termination, Symbol h as in "Hat" hæt

If, with the articulatory mechanism set in the position for **a**, the vocal folds pass from the open position through the whisper position simultaneously with the exit of the air stream, the vowel will be preceded by the escape of a certain amount of unvoiced air accompanied by friction noises. The result is written phonetically as **h**. This is the glottal fricative or *h*-approach. It has its basis in the fact that there is a certain range in the approximating movements of the vocal folds where they are close enough to produce friction noises but not voice. In this approach, the articulatory

---

[1] Other factors enter into the production of the whisper, but we have limited our discussion here to the action of the vocal folds which is the important factor in producing what we think of as an *h*.

mechanism is always preset for the vowel. It is the breath impulse and the whisper vibrations preceding the vowel that give the effect of **h**. Compare for example *at hat, eat heat,* and *it hit.* The prominence of **h** depends upon two factors[2]—the air pressure below the glottis and the speed of the glottal closure. An increase in subglottal pressure or a decrease in the speed of closure serves to make the sound more prominent. This means that a series of *h*'s can be produced, varying all the way from one that is barely perceptible to one that is greatly exaggerated. This is readily demonstrated by observing how easy it is to vary the duration and amplitude of the *h*-approach.

There are, then, as many positions of the articulatory mechanism for **h** as there are sounds that can be approached by this method. In the words *heat, hit, hat, hot, hut, hoot,* and *hurt*—**hit, hɪt, hæt, hɔt, hʌt, hut,** and **hɜt**—the *h* is produced through seven different positions. **h** has no articulatory position of its own; it always takes the position of the succeeding vowel. It follows that any attempt to produce an *h* in isolation will succeed only in producing the voiceless analogue of some vowel or vowel-like sound. One can, however, distinguish a voiceless **ɑ** from a voiceless **hɑ**. This would indicate that there is more to **h** than simply the friction noises set up when the vocal folds pass through the whisper position. This factor is largely the breath impulse, i.e., the escape of a large amount of air when the vocal folds pass from the open to the whisper position. **h** is not a voiceless vowel. It is the acoustic result of the change from an open position of the vocal folds to a much closer one, usually one that actually produces sound vibrations.

Although **h**[3] has been and still is considered by some writers as

---

[2] This is true only in so far as the vocal folds are concerned. It may be that supraglottal constriction also plays a part in increasing the prominence of the **h**.

[3] Some phoneticians describe also a so-called voiced *h*, IPA symbol **ɦ**. This sound is said to occur under certain conditions between two vowels as in *ah ah* which might be **afiɑ** or **ɑɦɑ**. Physiologically, a voiced *h* is a paradox, but the effect of *h* might be given acoustically by a diminution of the volume of a vowel almost to the point of hiatus, followed by a rather rapid increase in volume. Also, it may be that the sound described as a voiced *h* is a regular **h** made with so little breath pressure and so rapid a closure of the glottis that the sound is barely perceptible. Thus, when the words *see him* **si hɪm** are spoken more and more rapidly, it becomes increasingly difficult to decide whether or not the *h* is present. Eventually, the pronunciation becomes **sim**. In connection with our

a distinct sound, it is now generally recognized that it is not a sound entity in itself, but merely a method of approaching other sounds. It is, however, a symbol unit; its presence or absence in certain combinations changes the meaning of the symbol. Thus *eight* has a different meaning from *hate*, *ail* from *hail*, and *ill* from *hill*.

There is also a glottal fricative termination to vowel sounds in which the movements described above occur in reverse. That is, at the completion of the production of a vowel, the vocal folds pass from the vibrating position back to the open position, with the result that friction noises are again set up. This glottal fricative termination is not acoustically significant unless it is exaggerated. It has no symbolic meaning. It is interesting to note that when recordings of sound combinations such as **tɑ**, **pɑ**, etc., are played in reverse, the results often sound much like **hɑt** and **hɑp**, although the *h*-ending is not observable when the record is played in the normal sequence. This would seem to indicate that we use the glottal fricative termination to vowels more frequently than we would think. It might also indicate that we are psychologically set to hear initial *h*'s because they carry meaning, but we fail to hear the final ones because they have no significance. There is of course also the possibility that an initial *h* is actually physiologically easier to hear than a final one.

We should mention also instances in which the **h** occurs between vowels as in *a hail storm*, *go home*, etc. Here the **h** serves to link the two vowels, and could be considered either as a glottal fricative termination to the first vowel or a glottal fricative approach to the second. In the examples given it seems more reasonable to think of the **h** as a method of approach to the second vowel.

The Glottal Vibratory Approach or Termination (No Special Symbol)

We have said that if the vocal folds pass from an open to a vibrating position during the passage of the air stream an *h* will be produced. On the other hand, if the air stream is arrested momentarily while the vocal folds are moving into the vibrating position,

---

discussion of laryngeal modifications, it is interesting to note the various ways in which these two words can be linked by laryngeal action. They are **si hɪm, si ʔɪm, si ɪm, si əm, si m̩ː,** and **sim.**

voicing will begin simultaneously with the outward passage of air, without any preliminary breath impulse. We have called this manner of initiating vowels the glottal vibratory approach. It has no special symbol. In transcription, if no other symbol precedes that for the initial vowel, it is assumed that the glottal vibratory approach is indicated.

The essential difference between glottal fricative and glottal vibratory approaches is, then, a matter of the timing of the movements of the vocal folds in relation to the movements of the outflowing column of air. If this column is already in motion when the vocal folds move to the vibrating position, an **h** results; if it does not begin to move until the folds are already in position, the tone is initiated without the preliminary puff of air that characterizes the fricative approach. A laryngoscopic study [4] of the action of the vocal folds indicates that the glottal vibratory approach is usually accomplished by bringing the folds together before the air stream starts and then releasing the contact just enough so that when the air stream starts vibration can be initiated immediately, without any definite explosion and without any escape of unvoiced air.

The glottal vibratory termination operates according to the same principles. If at the close of phonation the air stream is checked at the instant the vocal bands open, there is no acoustic effect. This is the glottal vibratory termination. On the other hand, if the stream of air continues to flow during the opening movement, the glottal fricative termination results. We have commented previously that what appears to be a glottal vibratory *ending* is usually heard as a glottal fricative *approach* when a record of the sound is played in reverse. The glottal vibratory termination is probably used infrequently. Normally it is indistinguishable from the fricative termination.

The Glottal Plosive Approach or Termination, Symbol ?

In the glottal plosive approach the air stream is dammed up momentarily below the glottis by a complete closure of the vocal folds. The glottis is then opened quickly, allowing the air stream

[4] Research done by R. W. West in the laboratories of the Speech Department at the University of Wisconsin.

to escape suddenly and producing an explosive effect. This is the glottal explosive approach to a vowel sound. The intensity of the sound can be varied by increasing or decreasing the amount of air pressure exerted on the closed glottis just before its opening. When used as a method of termination, the vocal folds move from the vibrating to a completely closed position, thus stopping suddenly the voiced air stream. This is the glottal implosive termination. The glottal explosive approach to a vowel thus implies damming up the air stream below the glottis before the vowel is begun. The implosive termination implies a similar damming up of the air stream immediately following the vowel. In both approach and termination it is the quickness of the glottal movement, plus the amount of pressure built up by the respiratory mechanism, that gives the plosive quality to the sound.

This method of approach and termination is sometimes called the "glottal stop." It is not phonemic[5] in English and is not ordinarily represented except in close transcription. It appears much more frequently in some languages than others, particularly in Scotch and German. In English it is frequently substituted for other sounds, especially the plosives, in both dialectal and defective speech. Thus, *gentlemen, little, buckle, button, bottle, didn't*, and *couldn't* may become **dʒɛnʔl̩mən, lɪʔl̩, bʌʔl̩, bʌʔn̩, bɑʔl̩, dɪʔn̩t**, and **kuʔnt**. Dialectically the substitution seems to be characteristic of a substandard variety of "big city" speech, the most notable examples being the Cockney dialect in London and the Brooklyn accent. It also appears in other large cities. The use of **ʔ** in such words as *didn't, couldn't, shouldn't,* and *wouldn't* seems to occur anywhere in the country, though infrequently, and to be more related to a general carelessness in articulation than to a dialectal tendency.

The use of **ʔ** is also common in cleft palate speech and in other cases of organic damage to the soft palate that occurred in early childhood before the learning of speech. Such individuals are unable to create sufficient air pressure in the mouth cavity for the proper formation of plosive sounds and some of them learn to substitute a glottal stop which they can make easily and with the proper explosive character. The substitution is more likely to occur for the voiceless plosives, since these require greater air

[5] Except possibly in one instance—the difference between **m̩:hm̩** and **ʔm̩ʔm̩**.

pressure than their voiced counterparts. It is interesting to note that the tongue will sometimes go through the articulatory movement for **t** or **k** to such an extent that it requires close observation to reveal that the explosive sound is actually being made at the vocal folds.

Although it is not so generally recognized, the sound also occurs rather frequently in cultivated speech where it is used before initial vowels to add emphasis or between vowels as a method of transition, rather than as a substitute for a plosive consonant. Normally a less explosive form of the glottal stop is used. As an example of the use of the **ʔ** for emphasis, read aloud the sentence, "He's always in trouble" with strong emphasis on the word *always*. You will probably find that you started the initial **ɔ** in this word with a glottal stop, thus, **hiz ʔɔlwɪz ɪn trʌbəl**. Other examples may be found in imperative statements such as "Answer me!" **ʔænsɚ mi** or when strong contrast is desired as in *"over* not *under"* **ʔouvɚ nat ʔʌndɚ**. In general we can say that whenever we wish to put strong emphasis on a word that begins with an accented vowel, there will be a tendency to use the glottal stop approach.

The glottal stop is also used as one of the four ways of making the transition between adjacent vowel sounds when they must be spoken in rather rapid succession. Such combinations usually occur in sentences between words such as *he entered, he even, who opened, I eyed,* or in compounded words such as *Joanne, overall, however,* and in words with prefixes such as *coöperate, coördinate, reunion,* and *reinstate.*

Assuming that the basic articulatory movements between adjoining vowels are not changed by the introduction of an extraneous consonant, the four types of transition in terms of laryngeal action are the following:

1. If the vocal folds are kept in continuous vibration during the changing of the articulators from the position for the first vowel to that of the second, an intervowel glide will be produced. (See Chapter 7.) Examples: **hiʲɛntɚd, huʷoupənd, ouvɚʳɔl,** and **hauʷɛvɚ**.

This is the method most commonly used under conditions of ordinary stress and when the movement is from the position of one of the higher front, central, or back vowels to a lower vowel.

2. The vocal folds may be closed briefly while a slight pressure is built up and then opened to the vibrating position, thus producing a glottal stop. This type of transition is more likely to occur: (a) When the two vowels are the same as in **hiʔivən** and **lɔʔɔfɪsɚ**, or (b) when the movement is from a lower to a higher vowel as in **lɔʔivən** or **mɑʔoupənd**, or (c) when the meaning requires stress on the second vowel as in **dɪd hi ʔɛvɚ** or **hi ʔɔlwɪz**.

3. The vocal folds may open briefly and close again to the vibrating position thus producing an intervocalic **h**. This method is rarely used unless the *h* is already present in the spelling. Examples: **bihɛd, haɪhaʊs, laɪklɪhʊd**, and **əhɔɪ**.

4. The fourth method is to insert a soundless hiatus between the two vowels by momentarily stopping the breath stream or by reducing the breath pressure to the point where the transition becomes for all practical purposes inaudible, the vocal folds being held in readiness for vibration and the articulatory mechanism making the change in position during the hiatus. The effect of this action might be represented phonetically as **hi-ivən, hu-oupənd** with the dash indicating a brief cessation of sound. This method is probably rarely used in ordinary speech because it requires a slowing down of the movements and a considerable degree of conscious control.

We should mention here the possibility that the strength of the explosion in the glottal explosive attack may be so greatly reduced that the acoustic effect is largely lost. This is done by making the complete closure of the vocal folds a rapid one, and perhaps by retarding at the same time the outward flow of the air stream by the action of the muscles of respiration. If, then, the vocal folds open again quickly to the point of phonation before much pressure has been built up below the glottis, the resulting sound may be very similar, acoustically, to the glottal vibratory approach. To put it more simply, a rapid glottal stop movement may sound much the same as the glottal vibratory approach. It is probable that we actually initiate many vowels in this way. This supposition is borne out by the results of playing records in reverse. Thus words beginning in vowels, for example *alm, apple, are*, may, when recorded and played in reverse, appear to end with a glottal stop. This would indicate that we do frequently, though by no means always, approach initial vowels with a light glottal stop.

Summary of the Laryngeal Modifications

Vowel sounds may be initiated in various ways by modifications of the action of the vibrator mechanism. A closure of the vocal folds while the air stream is in motion results in the glottal fricative approach. The glottal vibratory approach occurs when the folds are placed in the vibrating position before the flow of air begins. A complete closure of the vocal folds, followed by a rapid opening after air pressure has been built up beneath them, produces the glottal plosive approach. Only one of these approaches serves as a phoneme in the language, namely, **h**. Each of these approaches is paralleled by a corresponding method of terminating vowel sounds.

Chapter 7   Intervowel Glides

Introductory Statement

One important means of modifying vowel sounds and of getting from one vowel to another is the glide type of movement. We have already defined the glide sound as one in which the mechanism moves without interruption from the position of one sound to that of another. While such gliding movements undoubtedly occur also in connected speech between consonant sounds and between nasal sounds, we are here concerned with those that take place between vowels. An intervowel glide may be defined as one in which the movement proceeds without interruption and with continuous voicing from the position of one vowel or vowel-like sound to that of another.

In the succeeding pages we shall frequently describe glide sounds as beginning or ending in certain vowel positions. Such statements are always to be interpreted as meaning "approximately in the position indicated." The origins and terminations of these glides, particularly when unstressed, vary even more than do the positions for the vowels themselves. The essential characteristic of the vowel glide is the movement. If the position of the articulatory mechanism is held stable at the beginning or end of the glide or at any point in between, a continuant sound will be produced that may or may not be a standard vowel but will always be a vowel-like tone. The acoustic effect of the glide results from the movement, i.e., from the changing pattern of resonance.

Some of the glides so produced are standardized and phonemic. By this we mean that the points of origin and termination are conventional in the language and the particular pattern of movement with its accompanying pattern of changing resonance is a distinctive determinant of meaning. For example, the glide ɔɪ, in which the vowels ɔ and ɪ serve as the origin and termination respectively, is a phonemic unit that is separate and distinct from either ɔ or ɪ when these sounds are used alone. Thus the word *toil* tɔɪl means something quite different from either *tall* tɔl or *till* tɪl. Again, ɑʊ is a different phoneme from either ɑ or ʊ, as is shown by the words *cod* kɑd, *could* kʊd, and *cowed* kɑʊd.[1] Individual examples of glide sounds may appropriately be called *diaphones*, literally "through a sound." The term *diaphoneme* could then be used to refer to all of the variants of a given glide sound. This usage would be parallel to the use of *phone*, meaning any given speech sound, and *phoneme*, meaning a cluster of related variants. The word diaphone is suggested as a substitute for diphthong because the literal meaning (two sounds) of the latter term is at variance with the physiological and linguistic facts and because it is conventionally used to refer to only a small number of one type of intervowel glides.

It should be understood that many diaphones are not diaphonemic. Rather they are intervowel glides that are dialectal or transitional in nature. Examples of the latter have already been noted in such words as *coöperate* kouʷɑpɚeɪt, *he entered* hiʲɛntɚd, etc. Other examples may be found in the so called schwa glides that are discussed later in this chapter. There are many nonphonemic dialectal glides such as the use of bɜɪd for bɜd, lɔo for lɔ, hæɪd for hæd, puʷl for pul, etc. While this chapter is primarily concerned with the intervowel glides that are phonemic we shall note in passing some of the nonphonemic forms.

General Characteristics of Diaphonemes

When we study carefully the intervowel glides that are phonemic we discover that they all have certain characteristics in common.

---

[1] The use of the **a** in the glide **aʊ** is quite arbitrary and conventional. For many speakers the actual glide is more accurately represented by **ɑʊ**.

These occur with so few exceptions as to warrant the laying down of three general rules:

1. In every phonemic intervowel glide one of the positions, either origin or termination, will be stressed and relatively definite in sound and stable in position; the other will be unstressed, indefinite, and relatively unstable. In other words, such glides do not show even approximately equal stress throughout. Two adjacent vowels can be pronounced with nearly equal stress by using one or another of the transition devices discussed in Chapter 6, but the result is two independent vowels, not an intervowel glide. Such glides will always be characterized by *changing* stress in one or another of two patterns. The glide may start with heavy stress and fade away as it progresses or it may start with a very light stress that becomes progressively stronger until the glide terminates. Glides characterized by increasing sonority may be called "crescendo." **wɑ** may be cited as a typical example. Progressively decreasing sonority is illustrated by the glide **ɑʊ** which we may call "diminuendo."

2. The stressed portion of the glide may be any vowel in the language. This rule holds true whether the glide is crescendo or diminuendo in nature. However, as we shall see later, there are certain exceptions to this general statement. While it is literally true that any vowel *may* be used for the stressed portion of the glide, in actual practice only certain vowels can be used as the starting point for standard (diaphonemic) diminuendo glides in the group usually called diphthongs.

3. The position of the unstressed indefinite vowel will always be in or near one of four key vowel positions: **u, i, ɝ, or l**. *This statement is not to be construed as meaning that the unstressed origin or termination will be one of these vowels with its specific acoustic and positional characteristics.* Rather, the key vowels are used to indicate the observed fact that all phonemic intervowel glides begin or end in either a general high front area which includes **i** and **ɪ**, or a general high back area which includes **u** and **ʊ**, or a general high central area which includes all varieties of **ɝ**, or in the general position of any of the laterally delivered *l* vowels. Moreover, it will always be the unstressed portion of the glide that begins or ends in one of these general positions. The very fact that

the sound is always unstressed means that the position will be indefinite and variable.

Receding and Approaching Glides

We have already noted that in every glide movement one of the positions will be stressed and the other unstressed. This fact provides the basis for dividing all glides into two main types in terms of the general nature of the movement. If the origin of the glide is stressed and the movement is away from this position we can classify it as *receding*. If the termination is stressed and the movement is toward that position the glide is of the *approaching* type. Receding and approaching are, thus, kinesiologic terms describing the direction of the movement in relation to the stressed vowel. Thus **au** is a receding glide because the movement is away from the position for the stressed **a** and **wɑ** is an approaching glide since the mechanism moves toward the position for the stressed **ɑ**. (**w** is sometimes classified as a consonant. See the discussion of approaching intervowel glides on page 54.) We have already described these same glides in acoustic terms as diminuendo and crescendo respectively.

We can also describe glide sounds in terms of what happens at the oral orifice through which the sound is discharged. For **au** the orifice formed by the lips and jaw changes from more open to more closed, whereas the reverse is true for **wɑ**. From this point of view **au** is a *closing* and **wɑ** an *opening* glide. In terms of the direction of the tongue movement these same glides may be classified as *rising* or *falling*. For **au** the tongue is moving from a lower to a higher position—that is, rising. **wɑ** is a falling type of glide because the tongue moves from a higher to a lower position. All intervowel glides may, then, also be described as either opening or closing and rising or falling, *except those that occur between key vowels*.

In summary, all intervowel glides can be classified in two primary categories in terms of the general direction of the movement in relation to the stressed vowel as either receding **au** or approaching **wɑ**. With the exceptions noted above, all receding glides are also diminuendo in terms of sonority, closing in terms of the discharging orifice and rising in terms of the movement of the tongue. Contrariwise, all approaching glides are crescendo, opening and falling.

These two types of glides are illustrated in Figs. 20 and 21. In Fig. 20 we assume that a receding glide starts at the definite **a** position and moves in the general direction of **u**. Now this movement could end at **ɒ**, **ɔ**, or **o**, but in the English language it usually continues to **ʊ** or **u**. The termination is indefinite but tends to sound more like **ʊ** because of the rapidly decreasing sonority toward the end of the glide. The relative definiteness of the point of

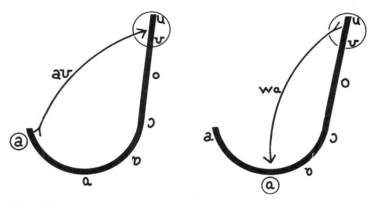

Fig. 20. Receding glides.   Fig. 21. Approaching glides.

origin and indefiniteness of the point of termination is indicated by the small circle around **a** and the larger one surrounding both **u** and **ʊ**.

In Fig. 21 an approaching glide is represented with the movement in the opposite direction. In this case the movement begins in the general high back area and proceeds with increasing sonority to the position for **a**. In theory this glide could begin at **o** or **ɔ** and proceed to **a** but such combinations occur very rarely in the language and never with phonemic significance. If there is to be a glide movement approaching **a** from the direction of the high back vowels, the origin of that movement will almost certainly be somewhere in the **u–ʊ** area.

The Description and Symbolization of Diaphonemes

From the point of view of placement a glide sound can only be described in terms of the positions for the origin and termination of the movement. A rather complete descriptive name for **au** from the movement, acoustic and placement points of view would be as follows: a voiced, resonant, receding, closing, rising, diminuendo, intervowel glide starting from the low front position for **a** and ending in the high back key vowel position. However, since the voicing and resonance are implicit in the word "intervowel" and since all receding movements are likewise diminuendo, closing and rising, we can compress this somewhat to read as follows: a receding intervowel glide beginning in the position for the low front vowel **a** and ending in the high back key vowel position. **wɑ** would then be described as an approaching (crescendo, opening and falling) intervowel glide beginning in the high back key vowel position and ending in the low central position for **ɑ**.

Intervowel glides are also symbolized in terms of their origins and terminations. It may, however, avoid confusion if we note that the two symbols, one representing the beginning of the movement and the other the end, are not of equal value. In other words, they do not have the same significance. The symbolization of the stressed portion of the glide is relatively narrow in contrast to the broader transcription of the unstressed portion. For example, in **au** and **wɑ** the symbols **a** and **ɑ** represent more limited and sharply defined positions, whereas **u** and **w** indicate a more general and indefinite position. To put it another way, the symbol **ɑ** in **wɑtɚ** has about the same value as it does in **ɑmz**, but the sound represented by **u** in **au** is by no means equivalent to its value in **fut**. In **au** the symbol **u** represents the indefinite unstressed ending of the glide just as **w** represents the indefinite unstressed beginning of **wɑ**, a fact that becomes much clearer if we write the first glide as **aw** to show its relationship to **wɑ**.

Receding Intervowel Glides

Receding glides can be divided into four groups according to the key vowel area in which they terminate. These groups are as follows:

1. *Termination in the high front vowel area.* There are three

standard glides of the receding type that move toward the high front vowel area. (See Fig. 22.) These are **eɪ** as in *play* **pleɪ, aɪ** as in *high* **haɪ**, and **ɔɪ** as in *boy* **bɔɪ**. In each case the indefinite termination is symbolized by the **ɪ**. Two of these glides frequently occur in a shortened or unglided form, although for different reasons. Mention has already been made of the fact that the **eɪ** is the typical member in English of the diaphoneme that also includes **e**. In this case the unglided form is the result of unstressing. The glide **aɪ** is also heard frequently as a relatively continuant **a**

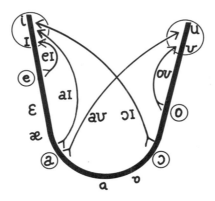

Fig. 22. Standard receding glides
ending in the high front or high
back key vowel positions.

and sometimes as **ɑ** in such words as *high* **ha** and *my* **ma**, etc., but the loss or reduction of the glide is here dialectal rather than a matter of stress.

In theory any of the remaining vowels could serve as a starting point for a receding glide to the high front position. Only these three, however, are phonemic and accepted as standard speech forms. Other substandard glides do occur dialectally such as **ɛɪ** in *flesh* **flɛɪʃ**, **æɪ** in *sad* **sæɪd**, **ʌɪ** or **ɜɪ** as in *bird* **bʌɪd** or **bɜɪd**.

2. *Termination in the high back key vowel position.* There are two standard glides that move toward the high back vowel position. (See Fig. 22.) They are **aʊ** as in *ounce* **aʊns** and **oʊ** as in *boat* **boʊt**. Both have been previously discussed. **ɑʊ** is to be

considered as an acceptable variant of **aʊ**, but **æʊ** is regarded as an undesirable form. **oʊ** has already been described as a typical member of a diaphoneme that includes **o** in unstressed positions.

Substandard glides ending in the high back vowel position that occur in various dialects are **ɛʊ** as in *house* **hɛʊs** and *don't* **dɛʊnt**, **ʌʊ** as in *house* **hʌʊs**, **ɔʊ** or **ɔo** as in *walk* **wɔʊk** or **wɔok**.

3. *Termination in the high central key vowel area*[2] (receding *r* glides). The receding glides discussed thus far have been those that are commonly called diphthongs. If now we produce a similar glide sound beginning in, for example, the **a** position and ending in approximately the position for **ɝ**, the result will be a receding diminuendo glide resembling in every way the conventional diphthongs **eɪ**, **aɪ**, **ɔɪ**, **aʊ**, and **oʊ**. There is, it is true, a difference in symbolization in that we usually write such a glide as **ar** rather than as **aɝ** or **aɚ**. Note that the origin **a** is stressed and that the termination in the general area of the midcentral key vowel **ɝ** is unstressed and indefinite. The glide is also voiced and characterized by a changing resonance pattern and the absence of friction noises.

The symbol **r**, then, represents the glide movement up to the **ɝ** position and its indefinite termination in this general area. There is perhaps some inconsistency in using the so-called "consonantal" symbol **r** to represent the termination of this glide when the regular vowel symbols **ɪ** and **ʊ** are used to indicate the same kind of endings in the high front and high back positions. Some writers have in fact advocated representing these receding *r* glides with a vowel symbol, either **aɝ** or **aɚ**. There are, however, two reasons for preferring the **ar**, although the choice is admittedly somewhat arbitrary: **ar** is the form more commonly used by writers in the field of phonetics; and **ar** seems to suggest more effectively the gliding movement and the indefinite termination which are the essence of the sound, whereas **aɚ** implies and emphasizes a continuant ending to the glide. When the glide occurs in such words as *car*, *fear*, *air*, etc., there is often some prolongation of the final sound. This is especially true if the words

---

[2] The student should remember that all of the illustrative words used in this section are usually pronounced in Southern and Eastern speech with schwa glides or lengthened vowels thus: **kɛə**, **hɪə**, **kɑ:**, **fɔ:m**.

are spoken slowly and carefully. We can, if we wish, represent this prolongation in narrow transcription by writing **kɑr³**, **fir³**, and **ɛr³** or **kɑrɪ**, **firɪ**, and **ɛrɪ**. However, the **ɚ** effect is not essential and it is somewhat reduced when the glide is followed by a voiced consonant as in *card* **kɑrd** and *cared* **kɛrd** and *beard* **bɪrd** and absent for all practical purposes when followed by a voiceless consonant as in *cart* **kɑrt** and *sort* **sɔrt**. For purposes of broad transcription the **r** is recommended as a more appropriate symbol to represent the termination of the glide.

The examples given above serve to illustrate the fact that **ɑr** is only a typical sample of receding *r* glides of a diphthongal type that can start, in theory at least, from any vowel in the language. In practice **ir**, **ɪr**, **ɛr**, **ær**, **ɑr**, and **ɔr** glides are very common. Note also such multiple-vowel glides as **eɪr**, **aɪr**, **aʊr**, and **oʊr**.

4. *Termination in the lateral key vowel area* (receding *l* glides). A receding type of movement from the **ɑ** position to that for the lateral vowel **ḷ** will produce another receding or diphthongal type of glide symbolized by **ɑl**. These receding *l* glides may likewise start from any vowel position as is indicated by such common words as *eel* **il**, *ill* **ɪl**, *elbow* **ɛlboʊ**, *Alps* **ælps**, *doll* **dɑl**, *all* **ɔl**, *full* **fʊl**, *pool* **pul**, *dull* **dʌl**, and *pearl* **pɝl**. Multiple-vowel glides occur in such words as *ail* **eɪl**, *I'll* **aɪl**, *oil* **ɔɪl**, *owl* **aʊl**, and *old* **oʊld**.

Many of the words listed above end with the *l* glide. If these words are pronounced slowly, a slight continuant vowel **ḷ** will probably be produced following the glide. This is similar to the continuant **ɚ** that we have already noted when the *r* glide is final; like **ɚ**, it tends to be reduced slightly when the *l* is followed by a voiced consonant as in *field* **fild** and to disappear when followed by a voiceless consonant as in *felt* **fɛlt**.

There are, as we have seen, many intervowel glides of the receding diminuendo type and these include the five that are usually called diphthongs. Some are phonemic and others are variants that occur either dialectally or under the influence of phonetic context. All have certain characteristics in common: voicing, resonance, movement away from the stressed vowel, decreasing sonority, decreasing size of orifice, rising tongue move-ment (except for those glides between key vowel positions), and an indefinite termination in one of the key vowel areas. If the ending is in the high front or the high back vowel positions, the termination is symbolized by ɪ and ʊ, respectively, and the origin is limited to a few standard vowel positions. When the glides end in the high central or lateral vowel positions, the terminations are symbolized by r and l and the origin may be, with a few practical limitations, any vowel or receding vowel glide in the language. Glides ending in any of the four key vowel areas may under certain conditions be continued for a brief period in the terminating position, thus producing continuant vowels generally equivalent to i, u, ɝ, or ḷ. However, these continuants if present are usually disregarded in broad transcription, since the glide movement is considered to be the essence of this type of sound.

We turn now to a consideration of the approaching intervowel glides which begin, rather than end, in the key vowel positions and which have characteristics that are in general the reverse of those described for the receding glides.

Approaching Intervowel Glides

The approaching glides that have phonemic significance may also be divided into four groups in terms of the origin of the movement. The termination may be any vowel in the language. The four groups are:

1. *Origin in the high back key vowel position* (approaching *w* glides as in *we* **wi**, *wet* **wɛt**, and *woo* **wu**. This glide results when the articulatory mechanism moves from a vowel position that is approximately that of **u** to some other vowel. This is the **w** usually described in textbooks of phonetics. It is often considered as a voiced continuant. From our point of view there is no such thing as a separate **w** sound; what we ordinarily call **w** always occurs as part of a vowel glide. If there is any question as to the true glide nature of the movement that produces the **w** the student should try the simple expedient of producing it as a continuant. Take the word *waft* **waft**, for example, and fix the articulatory mechanism in the position from which the **w** starts. If a continuant is then produced, the result will not be what we ordinarily call the **w** sound, but rather a continuant vowel that will be very close to **u**. The acoustic effect of **w** is given only

when the mechanism begins moving toward the position of the following vowel. The glide nature of **w** is further indicated by the fact that if **wɑ** is recorded and then reproduced backwards the result will be heard as a sound very similar to **ɑʊ**. Similarly, if **ɑʊ** is recorded and the record played backwards the sound is heard as **wɑ**. This seems to indicate that what we have here is essentially a movement from one point to another. If the movement goes in one direction it produces one acoustic effect; reversed, it gives another. Yet we have been accustomed to thinking of **wɑ** as a combination of a consonant and a vowel and of **ɑʊ** as a diphthong made by combining two vowels.

We wish to stress again the fact that the position from which these approaching **w** glides start need not be exactly the position of the vowel **u** when produced alone. There are glide families (diaphonemes) just as there are phonemes. The most variable part of a glide is the unstressed position. The two fundamental factors in the production of **u** are likewise present in the approaching **w** glide. These two factors are the high back tongue position and the protruded, rounded lip position. When an approaching **w** glide is produced, the tongue moves from its high back position to that of the following vowel at the same time that the lips make a similar movement. There are thus two opening orifices, one formed by the lips and the other by the back of the tongue and the posterior hard palate and velum. It is interesting to note in passing that the acoustic effect of **w** is still retained when the tongue movement is eliminated. The tongue can be held flat in the mouth with a tongue depressor or pencil and a very clear **w** effect produced by a simple opening of the bilabial orifice. It is difficult to hold the lips fixed while the tongue alone moves from its position for **u** to that for some other vowel, but so far as this can be done the results seem to indicate that the tongue movement alone is not enough to produce the effect of **w**. We are then led to the conclusion that in approaching **w** glide the one essential factor is the opening of the bilabial orifice. The opening of the back tongue orifice is usually simultaneous with the opening of the lips, simply because the lip and tongue positions are closely associated in the production of **u**. The size of the initial bilabial orifice will be determined somewhat by the following vowel. In the word *woo* [**wu**], for example, in order to give the effect of **w** the movement must start from the lip position of a very close **u**, while in glides such as **woᴜ**, **wɔ**, and **wɑ** the initial lip orifice is often larger.

It should be noted also that a movement from the position of any of the high back vowels to that of some other vowel tends to give somewhat the effect of **w**. Thus the combinations **ᴜ-a**, **o-ɛ**, **o-i**, and **ɔ-e** all sound somewhat like **w** if pronounced rapidly with the stress on the last vowel. A **w** occurs because the essential lip opening movement is present in each case. We have mentioned previously that glides like these do not remain in the language. They soon become definite **w** glides.

There is then a fundamental difference between these glide sounds, of which **w** is a typical example, and all other sounds. A vowel such as **u** is a continuant. It is the perceptual result of the voiced air stream exiting through a certain relatively fixed position. The essential factor is the *position* of the articulatory mechanism. **w**, on the other hand, is the perceptual result of a *movement* occurring in a certain *temporal* relationship, both factors being essential. What we call a **w** is not perceived unless there is a movement involving an opening bilabial orifice occurring within certain time limits. If the movement is too slow the **w** disappears. Other glide sounds involve the same principle.

With this understanding of the nature of **w** we can predict that it will occur frequently as a transitional sound resulting accidentally from the linking of two juxtaposed vowels where the movement from one to the other is of the **w** type. Note such words as *February*, *going*, *duel*, *Noel*, *eventual*, *pool*, *school*.

Phoneticians who consider **w** as a consonant also describe **hw** as a separate sound and another phoneme distinct from either **h** or **w**. It is sometimes symbolized by **ʍ** and sometimes by **ʰw**. It is conventionally described as a voiceless *w*. The writers feel that the sound is more accurately described as an *h*-approach to a **w** glide. This means that the vocal folds, instead of being closed to phonation at the instant the glide begins, do not close until it is partially under way, thus giving a glottal fricative approach. This is illustrated by the words *who* **hu** and *what* **ʰwɑt**.[3] In the first,

---

[3] We have mentioned that there is a basic difference between an *h*-approach to a **w** glide and an *h*-approach to a vowel. The difference lies in the action of the articulatory mechanism. In the former the articulatory mechanism is in movement; in the latter it is relatively stationary. In broad transcription the one

the *h*-approach takes place while the articulatory mechanism is held fixed in the **u** position; in the second, it occurs while the mechanism is in movement from the **u** position to that of **ɑ**. The first is a glottal fricative approach to a continuant vowel, the second a glottal fricative approach to an intervowel glide. The fundamental principle is exactly the same in both instances.

We should point out also that in the *h*-approach to a **w** glide the vocal folds may close to phonation at any point in the movement. Consequently the unvoiced portion of the glide may vary. The vocal folds may take hold almost at the beginning of the movement, in which case there will be very little of the *h*-approach. Again, they may not close to phonation until the mechanism has almost left the **u** position with the result that the **w** will seem mostly unvoiced.

When an approaching **w** glide is preceded by an aspirated voiceless plosive consonant, as in *twice* **tʰwaɪs** and *quick* **kʰwɪk**, the first part of the glide is unvoiced because of the puff of air that follows these plosives in English.[4] In terms of movement the articulatory mechanism gets started in the **w** glide before the vocal folds have closed to phonation following the production of the voiceless plosive. Such examples are to be considered as another variation of the glottal fricative approach to an intervowel glide.

The appearance or nonappearance of the **ɦ** in a **w** glide is then dependent upon the factor of timing in the action of the vocal folds. If the vocal folds close to phonation before, or at the very instant of, the beginning of the glide movement, a **w** glide results. If the closing of the vocal folds is delayed momentarily until the glide is under way, the result is an *h*-approach to a **w** glide. Note such pairs of words as *watt what, witch which, wen when, wear where*, etc.

2. *Origin in the high front key vowel position* (approaching *j* glides as in *yes* **jɛs** and *union* **junjən**. There are approaching **j** glides that are similar in nature to the **w** glides. When the movement begins at or near the position for **i** and proceeds with increasing

---

symbol **h** can be used to represent both types. In close transcription the writers suggest that the symbol **h** should be used to indicate a glottal fricative approach to a continuant, as in *house* **haʊs**, and **ɦ** to represent a glottal fricative approach when the articulatory mechanism is in movement, as in *what* **ɦwɑt**.

[4] See also page 159.

stress to that of some other vowel, we have an approaching **j** glide as in *yes* **jɛs**, *ye* **ji**, *onion* **ʌnjən**, *yam* **jæm**, *yard* **jɑrd**, etc.

Like **w**, **j** has been considered as a separate consonant sound when it forms the origin of a glide, but as a part of a diphthong ending in **ɪ** when it is the termination. The essential nature of both the **w** and the **j** sounds may be illustrated by pronouncing rapidly, with continuous voicing, **iuiuiuiu**. The opening of the linguapalatal orifice in going from **i** to **u** results automatically in the **j** sound, while the enlargement of the bilabial orifice in going from **u** to **i** produces **w**. The result is **ijuwijuwijuwiju**.

The size of the linguapalatal orifice at the beginning of the glide may vary. The articulatory position will be essentially that of **i**. It may be very lax and open when the glide is from **i** to some open vowel like **ɑ**, or it may be close as in *ye* **ji**. In the latter case the initial position will be more like that of cardinal **i**, or it may even start from the position of the voiced linguapalatal fricative **ʝ**.[5]

A glide **ɪʊ** which is closely related to **ju** is sometimes listed[6] as a separate sound and discussed in conjunction with the diphthongs. It is then used to represent the pronunciation of such words as *student* **stɪʊdənt**, *new* **nɪʊ**, and *tune* **tɪʊn** when these words are pronounced with a vowel glide. (Note, however, that these same words are often pronounced with a continuant **u** as the vowel, thus: **studənt**, **nu**, and **tun**.) The present writers question the inclusion of **ɪʊ** as comparable with the other diphthongs, since it seems to differ considerably in its acoustic and movement patterns. In fact, although there are slight differences in stress, it seems to belong more properly among the approaching type of glides. It is here regarded as a variant of **ju** to be used in close transcription when we wish to indicate a somewhat shortened form of the glide that begins in a lower tongue position more like that for **ɪ**. The use of **ʊ** to indicate the ending of the glide in such words as *new* is conventional but probably not very accurate. It usually ends more nearly in the position of **u**.

The glottal fricative approach to these **j** glides is symbolized by **ɦj** in close transcription or **hj** in the broad form. It is present in such words as *huge* **ɦjudʒ**, *human* **ɦjumən**, and *cute* **kʰjut**.

<hr/>

[5] See page 153.
[6] See John S. Kenyon and Thomas A. Knott, *A Pronouncing Dictionary of American English*, G. & C. Merriam Co., 1953.

The principles here are the same as those applying to the *h*-approach to the **w** glides. The closure of the vocal folds is delayed for a fraction of a second after the articulatory mechanism has begun its glide movement with the result that the first part of the glide is unvoiced. This glottal fricative approach to a **j** glide is to be distinguished from the voiceless linguapalatal fricative **ç**[7] which is made through approximately the same position. In the former the articulatory mechanism is in movement while the vocal folds are closing; in the latter it is held fixed with the vocal folds open.

3. *Origin in the high central key vowel position*[8] (approaching *r* glides as in *read* **rid**, *rod* **rɑd**, and *rude* **rud**). In approaching *r* glides the movement is from the **ɜ˞** position to that of some other vowel or vowel glide. Crescendo-type glides are formed with practically every other vowel and with receding glides. Examples: *reed* **rid**, *rid* **rɪd**, *red* **rɛd**, *radish* **rædɪʃ**, *rod* **rɑd**, *raw* **rɔ**, *rural* **rʊrəl**, *rue* **ru**, *raid* **reɪd**, *ride* **raɪd**, *roil* **rɔɪl**, *rowdy* **raʊdɪ**, and *road* **roʊd**.

The **r** sound is not always considered as a glide. Yet it seems evident that the *r* that occurs before and after vowels is definitely a glide sound. In the word *rod*, for example, if the articulatory mechanism is set in position for the beginning of this word and held there while a continuant is produced, the result is a vowel-like sound that is either **ɜ˞** or something close to it. This sound can be continued indefinitely, but the **r** we hear in *rod* does not occur until the mechanism begins to move away from the **ɜ˞** position. This procedure would produce something like **ɜ˞** . . . **rɑd**. This **r**, then, is the acoustic effect of moving away from the **ɜ˞** position. We have already pointed out that in the word *are*, on the other hand, the **r** is the acoustic effect of moving to the **ɜ˞** position. In words like *merry* **mɛrɪ** and *Erie* **ɪrɪ** both types are present, with the movement to the **ɜ˞** forming the end of the first syllable and the movement away from this position the beginning of the second. In *furry* **fɜ˞rɪ** the mechanism is held in the **ɜ˞** position long enough to give the effect of a continuant and then moved on to the **ɪ** position, thus producing a glide *r*.

[7] See page 155.
[8] For a complete discussion of the *r* phoneme, see page 168. See page 88 for the discussion of **ɜ˞**.

There is no reason why there could not be an *h*-approach to approaching **r** glides just as there is in the case of **w** and **j**. However, such an approach is not used in modern English. We could, for instance, have correlative words like *rot* **rɑt** and *rhat* **hrɑt** just as we have *watt* **wɑt** and *what* **hwɑt**, and *you* **ju** and *hue* **hju**. There are plenty of *rh* spellings in the language but in no case is the *h*-attack used in pronunciation, as it often is in the *wh* words. Note the words: *rhapsody, rheumatism, rhinoceros, rhythm,* etc. The nearest approach to the **hr** sound comes in words like *try* **tʰrɑɪ** and *cry* **kʰrɑɪ** in which the first part of the **r** glide is unvoiced because of the influence of the preceding voiceless plosive.

4. *Origin in the lateral key vowel position* (approaching *l* glides as in *let* **lɛt** and *law* **lɔ**). A receding *l* glide is the acoustic effect of a movement from the continuant **l** [9] position to that of any other vowel or consonant. As in the case of **w**, **j**, and **r**, these glides occur in conjunction with nearly any other vowel or receding vowel glide in the language. Some illustrative words are *lead* **lid**, *lid* **lɪd**, *led* **lɛd**, *lad* **læd**, *laud* **lɔd**, *lewd* **lud**, *laid* **leɪd**, *lied* **lɑɪd**, and *loud* **lɑʊd**. In words such as *lily* **lɪlɪ**, *Nellie* **nɛlɪ**, and *Alice* [10] **ælɪs**, both receding and approaching *l* glides occur as a result of the movement to and from the **l** position.

In theory at least a glottal fricative approach would result in **hl** combinations similar to **hw** and **hj**. Although a word like **hlɑt** or **hlu** could be pronounced as easily as **hwɑt** and **hju**, we do not use the *h*-approach to an *l* glide in English. The nearest equivalent will be found in words like *clown* **kʰlɑʊn** in which the release of air after the **k** forms a kind of **hl** combination. The Welsh *l* which is represented in English by the double *l* spelling at the beginning of proper names such as *Llewellyn* is closely akin to **hl**.

The **l** position which serves as the point of origin and termination for the approaching and receding *l* glide may vary just as

---

[9] See page 89 for a description of this sound.

[10] When glides such as the **lɪ** in the second syllables of *lily, Nellie,* and *Alice* and the **rɪ** in *merry* occur in unaccented syllables, they seem to contradict the general rule for approaching glides, namely, that the origin in the key vowel position will always be unstressed and the termination stressed. Note, however, that even though the entire syllable is unstressed in relation to the accented syllable, there is still a slight difference in stress within the glide, with the emphasis falling on the **ɪ**.

does the vowel from **l̩** to **l̩**. The *l* glides are not usually accompanied by perceptible friction noises unless the friction is carried over into the **l** from a preceding voiceless plosive or fricative consonant, as for example in the words *clay* **kleɪ** and *slay* **sleɪ**.

The tongue position for the *l*, as either a vowel or a glide, is influenced among all speakers by the associated vowels or consonants. Thus the *l* in *buckle* **bʌkl̩** is made with the point of elevation of the tongue farther back than is the case in *battle* **bætl̩**[11] because of the influence of positions for the preceding plosives. Similarly the *l*'s in *mill* and *leap* are produced farther forward than those in *lull*. We should point out here that the so-called "lightness" or "clearness" of an *l* is not entirely dependent upon the position of the forepart of the tongue. In other words, the terms "front *l*" and "light *l*" are not exactly synonymous. A little experimentation will demonstrate that it is possible to keep the tip of the tongue on the upper teeth and produce *l*'s of varying degrees of lightness and darkness.[12] Some of these variations in position are shown in Figs. 23–30.

Two factors other than the point of highest elevation of the tongue play a part in determining the degree of lightness or darkness of an *l*. One of these is the amount of lip spreading. An increase in lip spreading appears to produce a lighter variety of *l*. The other, and most important, factor is the position of the remainder of the tongue. The back of the tongue needs to be flattened and lowered for a very clear *l*, whereas darker varieties are produced with the back of the tongue raised, even when the tip is elevated to the upper teeth or rugal ridge.

Such factors as these probably account for the dialectal differences in the *l* sound that exist in addition to the variations produced by the influence of adjacent sounds. Southern speech frequently employs a lighter *l* than is typical in such words as

[11] The words can also be pronounced as **bʌkəl** and **bætəl**, in which case the *l*'s will still be influenced by the positions for **k** and **t**, although to a lesser extent.

[12] The Dialect Atlas Survey uses a series of modifying signs to indicate various degrees of lightness and darkness in an *l*. We need note here only one of these, the symbol, **l̩**, for a very light *l*. Attention should also be called to the IPA symbol **ʎ** (an inverted *y*), as in the Spanish *Villa* **biʎa**. It occurs also in Italian. The sound is apparently a light *l* made with the tongue-tip behind the lower teeth and followed closely by a **j** glide.

Fig. 29. Palato-gram showing the starting position for the glide læ.

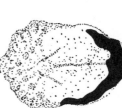

Fig. 27. Palatogram of ʝ or l—uni-lateral release.

Fig. 25. Palatogram of ʝ or l—bilateral release. This shows an unusual type of bilateral orifice.

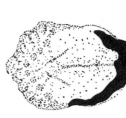

Fig. 23. Palatogram of ʝ or ɫ—bilateral release.

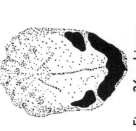

Fig. 30. Lingua-gram showing the starting position for the glide læ.

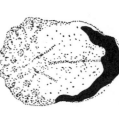

Fig. 28. Lingua-gram of ʝ or l—unilateral release.

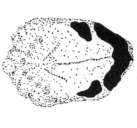

Fig. 26. Lingua-gram of ʝ or l—bilateral release.

Fig. 24. Lingua-gram of ʝ or ɫ—bilateral release.

Alice, lily, and *till,* whereas Midwestern speech is often characterized by an overdark *l* in words like *pool, school,* and *mule.*

The Schwa Glides—to and from the Position for the Neutral Vowel ʌ

All of the intervowel glides involving the neutral key vowel position are nonphonemic, which is to say that their use does not make a difference in the meaning of what is said—with the occasional exception of isolated pairs of words. They differ in this respect from the other key vowels which, as we have seen, are frequently phonemic. It is for this reason that the neutral vowel glides are discussed separately in this section. Since the general rule that the key vowel position will always be unstressed in intervowel glides seems to apply also to ʌ, the indefinite origin or termination can be represented by ə. Hence these glides are called receding and approaching schwa glides.

The schwa glides are for the most part either characteristic of dialectal speech patterns or the result of the factors of phonetic context in relation to the timing of the movements of the speech mechanism. The Southerner's *here* **hɪə** and the Middle Westerner's *school* **skuʷəl** are examples of dialectal patterns. The influence of phonetic context can be illustrated by the ə glides that may occur in *mob* **mᵊɑᵊb**. It should be understood that all vowels are influenced by their neighboring sounds when the articulation is continuous. The beginning of the vowel is changed according to the nature of the sound that precedes it and the ending by the character of the sound that follows. These contextual changes in vowel structure are acoustically analyzable and sometimes perceptible. Ordinarily, however, we are not conscious of any differences between the ɑ in *mob* and that in *shock* because our hearing patterns, like our articulatory habits, have become stereotyped in terms of whole words and phrases.

This means that, although this section is concerned only with the ə glides, others do occur. An ɪ glide, for example, can sometimes be heard when a vowel precedes or follows a tongue-tip consonant such as **s, z, ʃ, ʒ, tʃ,** and **dʒ.** Pronounce the following words slowly and note the extent to which the ɪ shown in the transcription seems to occur: *saw* **sɪɔ,** *zoo* **zɪu,** *flesh* **flɛɪʃ,** *measure* **mɛɪʒɚ,** *chop* **tʃɪɑp,** and *judge* **dʒɪʌɪdʒ.**

1. *Receding schwa glides* as in *Noah* **noᵁə**, *boa* **boᵁə**, *and in Eastern and Southern speech, ear* **ɪə**, *wear* **wɛə**, *oar* **oᵁə**, *poor* **pʊə**, *etc.* These glides, which have often been called "off-glides," are here called schwa glides signifying that there is a glide from the position of some accented vowel into the schwa area, although it need not necessarily reach the actual neutral position. The ə is always unstressed and indefinite in position. Any final vowel may end with a schwa glide. Such glides occur most frequently, however, in the East and South, where a receding glide is used instead of the receding *r* glide so common in the Middle West in words such as *oar, ear, are*, etc. A partial schwa glide is also often present in the Eastern and Southern pronunciation of those words in which the *r* is preceded by a vowel and followed by a consonant. Thus *hard, form*, and *horde* may be either **hɑːd, fɔːm**, and **hoᵁːd** or **hɑəd, fɔəm**, and **howəd**. These receding schwa glides occur because of the tendency of the articulatory mechanism to return to the neutral position. Note also the tendency toward schwa glides in such words as *sob* **sɑəb**, *fool* **fuəl**, *film* **fɪləm**, *elm* **ɛləm**, etc.

2. *Approaching schwa glides.* Approaching schwa glides are much less common than receding. An incipient schwa glide occurs following consonants made with the tongue in the neutral position —**p, b, f, v, m**, etc. Because the tongue is in the neutral position in making these consonants, it goes through that position on its way to the following vowel. Thus in the words *by, pie, my, vie, fie*, etc., there is usually a slight ə glide between the initial consonant and the vowel so that these words would be written phonetically in close transcription as **bəaɪ, pəaɪ, məaɪ, vəaɪ**, and **fəaɪ**.

The prominence of the approaching ə glide is determined by three factors: the degree of voicing present in the initial consonant, the speed of the transition between the initial consonant and the following vowel, and the timing of the tongue movements. The glide is thus more prominent following a voiced than an unvoiced sound. Again, the earlier the voicing begins after an initial unvoiced consonant, the more prominent the glide. If the transition movement is slow the ə glide becomes more noticeable. If the tongue remains in the neutral position until after the formation of the initial consonant and then moves to the position of the following vowel, an ə glide will be definitely present. However, if the tongue is preset in the position of the vowel before or during the production of the initial consonant there will be no ə glide.

Multiple-Vowel Glides

Up to this point we have confined our discussion, if not our illustrations, to glides that involve only two vowel positions. It is obvious that many glide movements involve more than two vowels. Three-vowel glides occur in such words as *rice* **rais**, *pail* **peil**, *goal* **goul**, etc. Such examples could be multiplied indefinitely. Some words are produced by a continuous glide movement from the beginning to the end. Note for example *railway* **reilwei**, *laurel* **lɔrəl**, *early* **ɝlɪ**, *hourly* **aurlɪ**, and *orally* **ourəlɪ**. Such words involve no new principles beyond those already mentioned in connection with two-vowel glides.

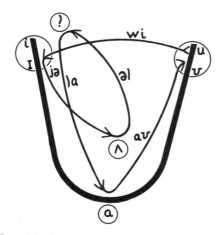

Fig. 31. Schematic representation of the multiple-vowel glides in **wiᶨəlɑu**.

Fig. 31 represents schematically the complete movement of the articulatory mechanism in the multiple-vowel glide *we allow* **wiᶨəlɑu**. A description of this glide will review much of the material presented in this chapter. With the vocal folds in vibration and the soft palate closed, the articulatory mechanism starts its movement from the high back key vowel position and

progresses to the high front position for the vowel **i**, thus producing the approaching crescendo glide **wi**. A slight **j** glide occurs
as the mechanism moves away from the **i** position, and the continuation of this movement to the position for the neutral key vowel
ʌ results in the receding schwa glide **iʲə**. The glide continues to
the lateral key vowel position producing **əl** and moves on with
increasing sonority to the position for the low central vowel **ɑ**,
forming the approaching glide **lɑ**. Finally, the receding glide **ɑʊ** is
formed as the movement continues with decreasing stress to its
termination in the high back position.

Glides Between Key Vowel Positions

Although the discussion thus far has been largely concerned
with glides between one of the key vowels and some other vowel
position, some of the examples used have illustrated the fact that
there are also numerous glides between two key vowel positions.
These glides fall into the same general categories of approaching
and crescendo **wi** and receding diminuendo **ɝl**, but it has already
been pointed out that the descriptions of the discharging orifice as
opening or closing and of the tongue position as rising or falling
cannot be applied, since the movement is from one relatively high
and close position to another.

If we consider only the key vowels **i**, **u**, **ɝ**, and **ḷ**, there will be
six possible combinations of positions: **i** and **u**, **i** and **ɝ**, **u** and **ɝ**,
i and **ḷ**, **ɝ** and **ḷ**, and **u** and **ḷ**. A closer examination of all of the
possible glides formed by movements in either direction between
the two vowels in each of these six pairs reveals some interesting
differences that justify two generalizations. The first is that all of
the glides between the two vowels in the first three pairs, regardless of the direction of movement, will be approaching glides with
the stress on the termination. Note, for example, **wi**, **ju**, **jɝ**, **ri**,
wɝ, and **ru**. The second generalization is that in any glides between two key vowels, one of which is **ḷ** (see the last three pairs
above), the **ḷ** position will always be unstressed. Thus we have
iḷ and **li**, **ɝl** and **lɝ**, and **uḷ** and **lu**. This is, of course, simply
a reflection of the fact that English does not use a stressed
vowel **ḷ**.

Glides Within Key Vowel Positions

It may seem contradictory to speak of glides that occur within a given key vowel position, but it is necessary to account for such evident glides as **wu**, **ji**, **rɝ**, and a theoretical **lḷ**. The explanation is, of course, that the movement which must take place is made possible by starting the glide in a higher, closer position than is normal for the key vowel; thus the origin in **wu** is probably close to the position for the bilabial fricative β (see page 141) and this permits a short glide to **u** which may at the same time be made with a slightly lower tongue position and a more open orifice than usual. The same principle can be used to explain **ji**, **rɝ**, and **lḷ**.

Transition

Following our description of the vowel sounds, we began our consideration of the remaining speech sounds as methods of initiating, connecting, and terminating these vowels. We have thus far discussed two general methods: first, the various methods of initiating and terminating vowels that result from the action of the laryngeal valve, and second, the intervowel glide as a method of connecting vowels. We are now ready to consider a third important method of modifying vowels. These vowel sounds may be initiated, connected, or terminated by sounds, other than the vowels themselves, set up in the oral cavity as a result of further modifications of the outflowing air stream by the articulatory mechanism. These are essentially the consonants. In our discussion we have grouped these sounds under the general heading "Oral Modifications."

Chapter 8 Oral Modifications of the
Vowels : The Consonants

Introductory Statement

We have already defined vowels as speech sounds in which the voiced air stream is emitted through a relatively large opening in the oral cavity. In such vowel sounds friction noises are absent or of negligible importance. We come now to a consideration of a second group of speech sounds formed by further modifications of the oral cavity—the consonants. They provide the most frequently used method of beginning, connecting, and ending vowels.

The word *consonant* is an acoustic term indicating that these sounds are accompanied by certain friction noises. In terms of movement consonants are either continuants or stops. A continuant consonant is a speech sound produced by forcing the air stream through an opening in the oral cavity small enough to produce friction noises. For all practical purposes, the articulatory mechanism is held fixed during the production of the sound. These consonants may be voiced, that is, made with the vocal folds closed to the point of vibration; or voiceless, that is, made with the vocal folds open. *Vibrated* and *sonant* are synonyms for *voiced*. *Surd*, *breathed*, and *whispered* are sometimes used to mean *unvoiced*. With any given position of the articulatory mechanism, it is thus possible to produce two sounds that will be analogues of each other—one voiced and the other voiceless. The voiced, continuant consonants that are phonemic in English are **v, ð, z**, and **ʒ**. Their voiceless analogues in the same order are **f, θ, s**, and **ʃ**. Some phoneticians also list **w, j, l,** and **r** as continuant consonants. These sounds have been classified as vowel glides in this discussion.

The stop sounds are produced by stopping the air stream at some point in the oral cavity, thus building up a slight pressure and then releasing it suddenly. Acoustically these sounds are plosives. They have two phases. The first is an implosive phase during which the articulatory mechanism is moving to the closed position and pressure is being built up within the oral cavity. Typically the mechanism is held in this position for a very brief period with a resulting further increase in pressure. In the second, or explosive, phase the mechanism moves rapidly from the closed position and the imprisoned air is emitted explosively. The voiced stop sounds in English are **b, d,** and **g.** Their voiceless analogues are **p, t,** and **k.**

With this introduction, we are ready to discuss each consonant in some detail. They are presented in three groups, the first two of which are in terms of type of movement, that is, continuants or stops. Since the *r* phoneme has many variants it is treated separately in the third group. Within each group the individual sounds are presented in order from front to back in terms of the place of articulation. Although no attempt is made to introduce all foreign language sounds or to make a definitive comparison of the sound systems of English and other languages, some foreign sounds are described. This is done primarily to supplement our understanding of English phonetics and secondarily to acquaint the reader with some of the non-English sounds that are important in the correction of foreign accent.

Continuant Consonants

β as in "Havana" haβana (Spanish) (Voiced Bilabial Fricative Continuant)

Although closely related to the vowel **u** and the glide **w,** the β is to be distinguished from both. Like **u,** it is a continuant but the lip orifice is much smaller and definite friction noises are present. A good approximation of the sound can be produced by prolonging the starting position for the glide **wu.** (See Fig. 32.) This is the sound of the Greek letter *beta* which we pronounce **beta.** It is present in German, Spanish, and other languages but it is not phonemic in English and probably rarely occurs even accidentally. Note also its similarity to **b** and **v**. It would be difficult for all of these related lip sounds to be used phonemically in one language because they are not sufficiently distinguishable from each other. For example, if a language contained words with different meanings pronounced **wɑt**, **hwɑt**, **βɑt**, **vɑt**, and **bɑt** there would be considerable confusion.

ɸ as in "Pfennig" ɸɛnɪç (German) (Voiceless Bilabial Fricative Continuant)

The ɸ is the voiceless counterpart of β. With the vocal folds open and the soft palate closed, the air stream is forced out through a very small opening between the lips with accompanying

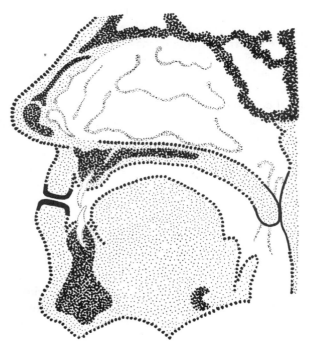

Fig. 32. The position for β and ɸ. This position can also be used as the point of origin for close **w** glides as in **wu**.

friction noises. It is approximately the sound in classic Greek of the letter *phi* which we pronounce as **faɪ**. It is related both acoustically and in position to **hw**, **p**, and **f**; in fact the key word given above is sometimes pronounced as **pɸɛnɪç** or **fɛnɪç**. The sound occurs frequently in German and occasionally in Spanish, where it is a variant of the **β**. It is nonphonemic in English, but is produced incidentally as a substitute for **f** in such words as *campfire*, *comfort*, and *camphor*. In theory these words should be pronounced as **kæmpfaɪr**, **kʌmpfət**, and **kæmpfə** but in practice there is a strong tendency to avoid shifting the articulatory mechanism from a bilabial to a labiodental position by making both sounds in the same place. Thus the words become **kæmpɸaɪr**, **kʌmpɸət**, and **kæmpɸə**. However, it is also possible to make both sounds in the labiodental position, in which case the closure for the *p* sound is made between the upper lip and lower teeth and the air pressure is released directly into the position for the continuant *f*. Note also that the *ph* spelling is pronounced as *f* in English when there is no syllable break between the two letters as in the words *diphthong* **dɪfθɔŋ** and *philosophy* **fɪlasəfɪ**.

v as in "Vat" væt (Voiced Labiodental Fricative Continuant)[1]

This sound is the result of the passage of the outflowing air stream through the articulatory mechanism after it has assumed the position characteristic of the sound. This position is brought about by four modifications of the neutral position: approximation of the vocal folds, closure of the port into the nasopharynx, depression of the mandible to the position for. the neutral vowel **ʌ**, and a loose contact between the lower lip and the upper incisors.

Ordinarily these movements occur practically simultaneously. The exact time order is not important so long as the articulatory mechanism is placed in position before, and held there relatively fixed during, the emission of the voiced air stream.

No movement of the tongue from the neutral position is required. It may lie in the neutral position or it may assume any

---

[1] Although the descriptive names of the various consonants have been drawn largely from John S. Kenyon's *American Pronunciation*, 10th ed., George Wahr, 1950, the writers have introduced a number of modifications in his terminology.

position not actually blocking the flow of air through the oral cavity.

The amount of depression of the mandible is variable, but some downward movement is required in order to make room for the action of the lower lip. There may conceivably be some retraction

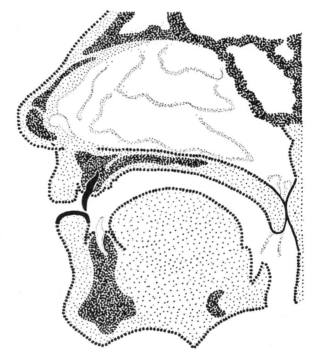

Fig. 33. The position for v and f.

of the mandible, but this movement is not essential and probably seldom occurs.

With the mandible depressed, the partial labiodental closure of the oral orifice is effected by an elevation and drawing inward of the lower lip so that it touches lightly the upper incisors. At the same time, the angles of the mouth are drawn slightly laterally. While this loose contact between the lower lip and the upper incisors is essential, the exact point of contact on the red-lip margin is not important. Ordinarily there is only a relatively slight inward movement of the lower lip, so that the contact is made on its inner border. The upper lip may move passively but its own fibers are not in contraction.

Thus this sound involves essentially the deflection of a voiced column of air into the oral cavity, the external orifice of which has been previously fixed so that the air stream can escape only through a narrow opening between the lower lip and upper teeth. As a result of the narrowness of this opening there is some increase in the air pressure within the mouth cavity. Acoustically, this sound is the result of low-frequency laryngeal vibrations plus high-frequency friction noises produced by the passage of air through the narrow labiodental orifice. The sound is a continuant; that is, it can be produced without change of position as long as there is an outflowing column of air.

f as in "Fat" fæt (Voiceless Labiodental Fricative Continuant)

This sound may be described as identical with **v** except that the vocal folds are not approximated. Thus the only acoustic elements present in this sound are the high-frequency vibrations resulting from the passage of the air stream through the narrow labiodental orifice.[2]

ð as in "Then" ðɛn (Voiced Linguadental Fricative Continuant)

The position of the articulatory mechanism for **ð** may be described as follows: the vocal folds are approximated; the port into the nasopharynx is closed; the mandible is depressed about halfway to the position of the neutral vowel **ʌ**; the lips are everted so as to form an orifice similar to that for **z** but slightly larger; and the sides of the tongue are elevated so that they lie in contact with the inner borders of the upper teeth and with the alveolar ridges, leaving a wide central cavity for the passage of the air stream. The tip of the tongue is flattened, elevated, and protruded so that its inferior surface rests on the lower teeth, while the tip of its dorsal surface is in light contact with the lower edges of the upper teeth (Figs. 34–36).

[2] The IPA uses the symbols **F** and **ʋ**, representing a lax **f** and a lax **v**. F and ʋ are made with a labiodental contact so lax that the friction noises are greatly reduced, if not absent. The sounds are used in German.

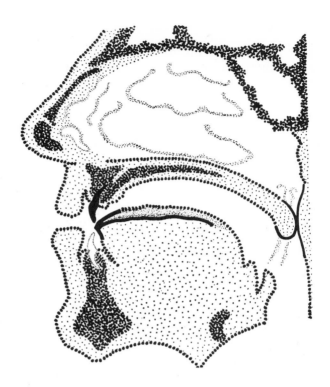

Fig. 34. A typical position for ð and θ. See also
Figs. 35–38.

Fig. 35. Palatogram of a
typical ð.

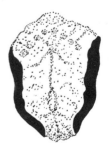

Fig. 36. Linguagram of a
typical ð.

The sound results from the passage of the voiced air stream through a wide but extremely shallow orifice formed between the flattened tip of the tongue and the lower edges of the upper teeth. The friction noises produced at this linguadental orifice, plus the laryngeal tone, make up the acoustic characteristics of this sound.

Variations arise in the movements of the lip, jaw, and tongue. The lips must be open, but the size and shape of the opening may vary within rather wide limits. The mandible must be depressed far enough to make room for the action of the tongue described

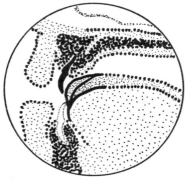

Fig. 37. Tongue blade ð or θ. The tip of the tongue lies behind the lower teeth.

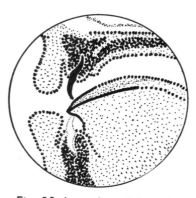

Fig. 38. Interdental ð or θ.

above, but the movement may go some distance beyond this point without distorting the sound. The tongue may be protruded between the teeth for varying distances, just so long as there is a narrow orifice between the tip of the tongue and the upper teeth. This is the so-called "interdental" *th*. In general the movements are those described above, although the interdental *th* is fairly common. (See also Figs. 37 and 38.)

θ as in "Thin" θɪn (Voiceless Linguadental Fricative Continuant)

This sound is the voiceless analogue of ð. The vocal folds are not approximated and the friction noises are increased because of the greater volume of air passing into the oral cavity. The movements made in producing the sound are the same as those for ð.[3]

z as in "Zebra" Zibrə (Voiced Lingua-Alveolar Fricative Continuant)

The z position is brought about by the following modifications of the neutral position: the vocal folds are approximated, the port into the nasopharynx is closed, both lips are everted slightly so as to produce a small orifice, and the entire tongue is flattened and elevated (Figs. 39–41). Its sides lie in contact with the inner borders of the upper teeth and with the alveolar ridge as far forward as the second incisors. The dorsum of the tongue makes an extensive but variable contact with the hard palate, leaving only a narrow central cavity for the passage of the air stream. The tip of the tongue is flattened, elevated, and drawn forward so that it makes a complete contact with the alveolar ridge of the maxilla immediately behind the incisor teeth, except for a small orifice formed along the median fissure of the tongue. This orifice permits the escape of a minute stream of air which is directed downward and then outward in such a manner as to pass over the cutting edge of one of the lower incisors. Usually the air stream is delivered centrally—that is, close to the midline. It is the passage of the air stream against the cutting edge of some lower tooth that produces the high-frequency hissing sound that, along with the laryngeal tone, is characteristic of z.

The movements described above are typical of the z sound as it is made by most individuals. The sound is, however, subject to many variations. There are but three absolute essentials: the production of a laryngeal tone, the deflection of the air stream into the oral cavity, and the exit of this voiced air stream through a narrow orifice and against the cutting edge of some tooth.

[3] θ and ð do not occur in German, French, and Italian; in fact, the sounds are almost peculiar to English and are lacking in nearly all modern languages. They are a constant source of difficulty for foreigners who try to learn English. Usually dental t and d are substituted by foreigners for θ and ð, respectively. Castillian Spanish has θ, although the sound seems to have come into the language as an affectation, in imitation of a popular lisp. Castillian also has a variety of ð which seems to be an affricate combination, ꭰð, with the d lightly exploded. (The modifier ˍ indicates that the sound under consideration is made dentally.) It is sometimes represented by the special symbol đ. Colonial Spanish has no θ, but has a ð that resembles the English sound.

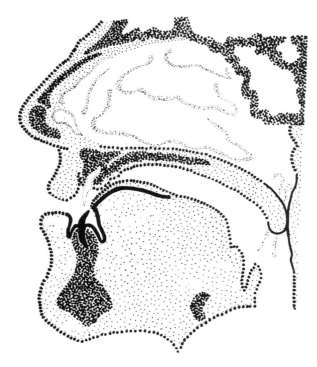

Fig. 39. A typical position for z and s.

Fig. 40. Palatogram of a
typical s.

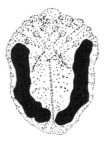

Fig. 41. Linguagram of a
typical s.

The bilabial orifice must be open, and this opening is probably always effected by an active movement of the lips themselves. The amount and nature of the opening are variable factors. Typically the shape of the orifice is roughly that of an elongated oval, flattened on the lower side.

Apparently no one position of the mandible is essential to the sound. It can easily be demonstrated that the sound can be made with the mandible in various degrees of depression, but in ordinary articulation the movement is very slight and probably not essential.

The movements of the tongue are the most variable of all. For any one individual, the movements are usually approximately the

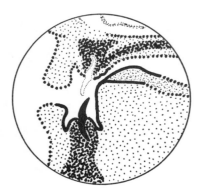 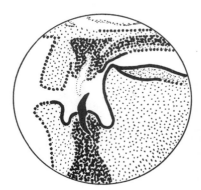

Fig. 42. The position for a   Fig. 43. The position for a
      linguarugal s.   retroflex s.

same, except as they vary due to the influence of neighboring sounds, but there is considerable variation from one individual to another. The tongue is a very adaptable organ and adjusts itself readily within rather wide limits to conditions within the mouth cavity. In different individuals the formation of the teeth is the chief variable factor affecting the production of z. Since we are interested in the average or typical movements in the articulation of the sound, we shall not concern ourselves here with a description of all the possible variations. The variety of z's (and s's) is due to individual, rather than regional, differences.

One common variation existing in many individuals and apparently unrelated to any anomaly of teeth formation might well be mentioned. These individuals place the tip of the tongue against

the inner borders of the lower teeth, while the blade is rolled upward, making about the same contacts as those described above.
Acoustically, the sound is identical with that produced in the so-
called normal manner. Figs. 42 and 43 illustrate two variations of
the typical positions for z and s.

s as in "Sun" sʌn (Voiceless Lingua-Alveolar Fricative Continuant)

s is a voiceless sound, which means that in its production the
vocal folds are not approximated. Otherwise the sound may be
described as exactly similar to z. The discussion of the essential,
as opposed to the variable, factors in the production of z is equally
applicable to s.

ʒ as in "Vision" vɪʒən (Voiced Linguapalatal Fricative Continuant)

Starting from the neutral position the following movements are
required to bring the mechanism into the position for ʒ: the vocal
folds are approximated; the port into the nasopharynx is closed;
the lips are open and protruded slightly so as to form a small,
elongated, oval-shaped, orifice; and the sides of the tongue are
elevated so that they come in contact with the inner borders of the
upper teeth, the alveolar ridges, and a variable portion of the hard
palate as far forward as the first premolar teeth, leaving a wide
central passage for the passage of the air stream. The tip of the
tongue is flattened, elevated, and drawn forward in the direction
of the anterior hard palate just posterior to the alveolar ridge. As
a result, the sides of the flattened tip are in contact with the inner
borders of the teeth and the corresponding gums at approximately
the point between the canine and the first premolar. The contact
continues centrally on the anterior hard palate for a short distance,
leaving a wide but relatively shallow orifice between the tip of the
tongue and the palate. The voiced air stream passes through this
orifice and out between the lips and teeth (Figs. 44–46).
    It will be noted that this sound is very similar to z, except that
for ʒ the linguapalatal orifice is much wider and slightly farther
back on the hard palate, while the bilabial orifice is more rounded
and protruded.
    The mandible remains in approximately the neutral position,

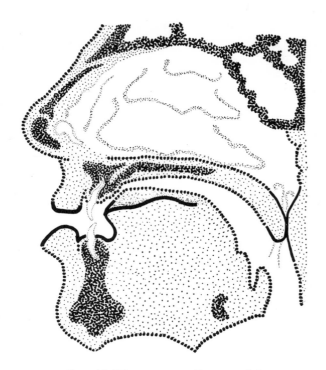

Fig. 44. The position for ʒ and ʃ.

Fig. 45. Palatogram of ʒ.

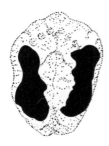

Fig. 46. Linguagram of ʒ.

although in some individuals it may be slightly depressed. Although the ʒ can be made with the lips in almost any position, a certain amount of lip rounding almost invariably accompanies its production and seems to add a characteristic resonance caused by the formation of a small cavity between the lips and the teeth. The amount of rounding and protrusion of the lips varies with different individuals. It also varies under the influence of adjacent sounds. Note the difference in lip position for the ʒ sounds in *beige* and *rouge*. The movements of the tongue may vary somewhat, but they remain essentially as described above.

ʃ as in "Sheep" ʃip (Voiceless Linguapalatal Fricative Continuant)

This sound is the voiceless analogue of ʒ. Like all the voiceless continuant fricatives, the friction noises are accentuated by the increased volume of air entering the oral cavity as a result of the fact that the vocal folds are not closed.

ʝ as in "Fille" fiʝ (French)[4] (Voiced Lingua Anterior-palatal Fricative Continuant)

The symbol ʝ represents a sound similar to ʒ in nature but different in tongue position. If we divide the hard palate into approximate halves, the ʝ is made toward the back of the anterior section. The position for ʝ can be located approximately by making an **i** sound so close that friction noises are set up. The same effect can be obtained by placing the articulatory mechanism in the position for the beginning of the glide **ji** and then making a continuant through this position instead of allowing the mechanism to glide on to the **i** (Figs. 47–49).

ʝ is not present in English. The glide **j** is very common but the continuant ʝ is not used. Some books on phonetics use the one symbol, **j**, to represent both the glide and the continuant sound made around this linguapalatal position. The ʝ is a special symbol adopted in this book to use in close transcription to indicate the difference between the continuant, the glide **j**, and the glottal fricative approach **hj**.

---

[4] When a non-English key word is given it is to be assumed that the sound does not occur regularly in English. However, it is not to be assumed that the sound is limited to the language chosen for the example.

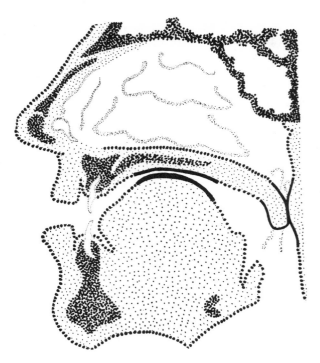

Fig. 47. The position for ɹ and ç. This position can also be the starting point for **j** and **ɦj** glides and the point of termination for **j** glides.

Fig. 48. Palatogram of ɹ.

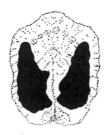

Fig. 49. Linguagram of ɹ.

ç as in "*Licht*" lıçt (German) (Voiceless Lingua Anterior-palatal Fricative Continuant)

This sound is the voiceless analogue of ɹ and is usually known in German as the *ich laut*. It is produced through the same position as ɹ. This sound does not occur in English, our nearest approach to it being the glottal fricative approach to a j glide. Thus if we take the word *huge* hjudʒ and prolong the first stage of the glide as a continuant, we will produce a very passable ç.

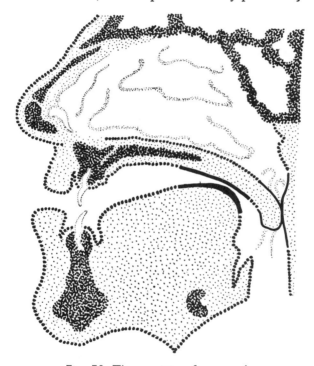

Fig. 50. The position for γ and χ.

γ as in "*Rogar*" řoyař (Spanish) (Voiced Lingua Posterior-palatal Fricative Continuant)

This sound (see Figs. 50–52) is also a foreign sound. The position for it is approximately that of our English **g** as in *go* **goʊ**, to be described a little later. The distinction between the two sounds is that **g** is emitted explosively following a complete stoppage of the air stream, whereas γ is a fricative continuant.[5]

x as in "*Bach*" **bɑx** (German) (Voiceless Lingua Posterior-palatal Fricative Continuant)

The **x** is the voiceless analogue of γ. It is also called in German the *ach laut*. It is made through the same position as γ but with the vocal folds open. This sound differs in its production from ç in the same way that γ differs from ʝ. See the table on page 168.

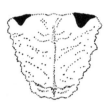   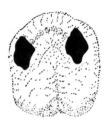

Fig. 51. Palatogram of γ. Note the small size of the contact between the dorsum of the tongue and the hard palate. The tongue may or may not come in contact with the hard palate in making this sound.

Fig. 52. Linguagram of γ.

The Plosive Consonants

b as in "Bat" **bæt** (Voiced Bilabial Stop Plosive)

The production of this sound is the result of a series of movements occurring in a certain time order. Starting from the neutral position, these movements may be described as follows: The vocal folds are approximated and the port into the nasopharynx closed, these two movements occurring almost simultaneously. The voiced air stream is thus directed into the oral cavity, and since the lips are still in the neutral position, i.e., closed, this results in

---

[5] The sound is very similar to the linguavelar fricative *r*, ʁ (see page 177). Confusion is avoided in Spanish, since this language has only front tongue *r*'s. In German, which has ʁ commonly and γ dialectally, confusion is lessened by the fact that γ is used for *g* and is always intervocalic.

a brief period of rising pressure within the mouth cavity (Fig. 53). This increase in pressure is usually resisted by a slight increase in the firmness of contact between the two lips. In lax utterance there may be no more bracing of the lips than that present in the neutral position, while in vigorous articulation the lips are firmly approximated and the buccinator or cheek muscles may contract

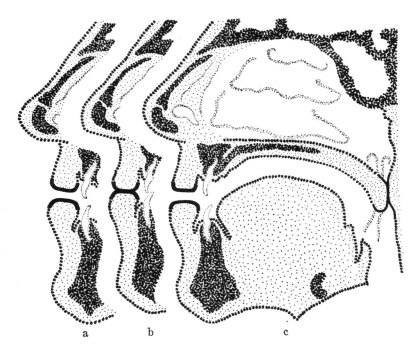

a   b   c

Fig. 53. The position for **b** and **p**. (a) Closing bilabial orifice; (b) position during implosion; (c) opening bilabial orifice immediately after explosion.

slightly. Both these factors serve to resist, and the latter to increase, the rising pressure.

The next step in the production of the sound is the sudden opening of the oral orifice, permitting an explosive emission of the dammed-up air stream. This may be effected in a number of ways: (1) the mandible may be depressed and the lips opened passively as a result of this movement, (2) the mandible may be held relatively fixed and the oral orifice opened by an elevation of the upper lip and a depression of the lower lip, or (3) both of these movements may occur together. The amount of depression of the mandible and eversion of the lips is variable, the essential factor being a sudden separation of the lips. The manner of separation and the extent of the movement are not important. In the ordinary production of this sound, this separation is effected by a slight depression of the mandible (5–10 mm. from the neutral position) occurring simultaneously with a moderate eversion of both lips. Note, however, that the air pressure can also be released through the nasal cavities by a lowering of the velum, as in *cabman* **kæbmæn**.

We may then summarize the events occurring in the ordinary production of **b** in isolation as follows: (1) approximation of the vocal folds; (2) closure of the port into the nasopharynx; (3) a period of rising pressure within the mouth cavity; (4) slight increase in the firmness of contact between the two lips; and (5) sudden release of the impounded air, effected by a depression of the mandible and a moderate eversion of both lips, or by a dropping of the velum, the lips remaining in contact.

It will be seen that this sound can be readily divided into two parts: the time interval between the approximation of the vocal folds and opening of the oral orifice, and the interval from the opening of the lips to the completion of the sound. The first is the period of implosion or rising internal pressure, the second the period of explosion or falling pressure. We sometimes speak also of a third period between these two—a period of holding or "plosion," in which the mechanism is held fixed momentarily, just preceding the explosive phase of the sound. Unless the breath stream is also held momentarily, this period of plosion results in additional air pressure within the oral cavity. The period of plosion is lengthened, both for emphasis and to show double plosive consonants, as in *cab boy* **kæbːɔɪ** and *tubbed* **tʌbːd**.

The auditory perception of either the implosive or explosive phase is accepted as standing for the whole sound. Thus in the word *tub-full* **tʌbfʊl** only the implosive phase of the *b* is heard, the explosion being modified to the sound **f**. In the word *but* **bæt** the explosion is the important factor. The approximation of the vocal folds and the opening of the oral orifice occur so nearly simultaneously that there is practically no acoustic effect from the implosive period. In each of these examples only one part of the sound is actually heard, yet this is sufficient to cause a perception of the whole sound. In a word like *cabby* **kæbɪ**, on the other hand, both implosive and explosive phases are present.

One more comment needs to be made relative to the sound **b**. It will be noted that when the whole sound is pronounced in isolation, the articulatory mechanism ends in position for the neutral vowel **ʌ**. As a matter of fact, it is more accurate to say that the tongue does not leave the neutral position during the production of the sound. Thus in some pronunciations, when the articulatory mechanism goes from the position of **b** to that of some vowel, there will be a tendency to introduce an approaching **ə** glide.

p as in "Pat" pæt (Voiceless Bilabial Stop Plosive)

The movements involved in the production of this sound are, with one exception, exactly similar to those for the **b**. The difference lies in the fact that in the articulation of **p** the vocal folds are not approximated. The air stream passes through a relatively unrestricted glottal opening, thus producing a voiceless sound.

This means that no sound vibrations are produced during the implosive portion of the sound. When produced in isolation the implosive period has no acoustic effect whatever. When only the implosive element of the sound is present in a word, as in *captain* **kæptən**, the sound of **p** as a whole is perceived because of the acoustic effect produced by the cessation of the voiced element in the preceding vowel plus the accompanying closure of the lips. In **p**, as in **b**, the tongue remains in the neutral position. When only the explosive element of the sound is present, as in *pat* **pæt**, the presence of the **p** is recognized by the acoustic effect of the sudden opening of the lips plus the short puff of unvoiced air that is emitted before the vocal folds are approximated in the production of the following vowel. In close phonetic transcription, this puff of air following a voiceless plosive is represented by **h**, since it is made with the vocal folds open. This

h sound is similar in principle to the glottal fricative approach to **w** and **j** (see page 129), in that it is made with the articulatory mechanism in motion. It serves here both as a way of releasing the pressure in the plosive sound and as an approach to the following vowel. In close transcription *pat* would be written as **pʰæt**.[6] The movements of the articulatory mechanism necessary for the production of the sound **p** are the same as those previously described for **b**.

We have now had occasion to mention all but one of the speech sounds whose production revolves about the lips. These sounds include a vowel, a glide, a plosive, a nasal, and a continuant fricative. The bilabial nasal sound **m** is to be discussed later. We may summarize as follows these speech sounds in which the action of the lips plays an important part:

Type of Sound	*Voiced*	*Voiceless, or h-Approach*
Continuant vowel (plus tongue factor)	**u**	**hu**
Glide, intervowel (plus tongue factor)	**w**	**hw**
Continuant fricative	**β**	**ɸ**
Stop plosive	**b**	**p**
Continuant nasal (plus velar factor)	**m**	

Although these are all lip sounds they are not all produced through exactly the same position, the size of the bilabial orifice varying from an opening large enough for a vowel to a complete stop. The sounds are distinguished from each other, then, by two factors: the size of the bilabial orifice and the type of movement employed. In only one sound, **u**, does the tongue play a necessary part. The labiodentals, **f**, **v**, **ɱ**, **F**, **ʋ** are closely associated sounds.

---

[6] This puff of air following voiceless plosives is a characteristic of English not found in most languages. Consequently foreigners almost always experience difficulty in learning the English plosives. The term *aspirated* is used to designate the presence of this puff of air following plosive sounds and *unaspirated* to indicate its absence. These concepts are discussed in detail on page 269. In general, voiceless plosives in English are aspirated, but there are exceptions. These are summarized on page 271.

No one language uses all of these sounds as phonemes although seven are phonemic in English if we include the labiodentals. Nearly all of them occur incidentally in most languages as transitional sounds under the influence of related sounds in context.

d as in "Day" deɪ (Voiced Lingua-alveolar Stop Plosive)

Like the other plosives, this sound may be divided into implosive and explosive periods. Starting from the neutral position, the movements occurring in the implosive period are as follows:

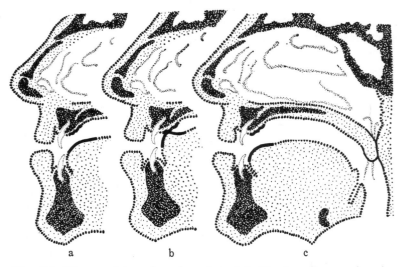

a   b   c

Fig. 54. The position for **d** and **t**. (a) Closing lingua-alveolar orifice; (b) position during plosion; (c) opening lingua-alveolar orifice immediately after explosion.

approximation of the vocal folds, closure of the port into the nasopharynx, slight elevation of the upper and depression of the lower lip, depression of the mandible to a point about halfway to the position for the neutral vowel ʌ, and elevation of the tip and sides of the tongue so that a contact is made with some portion of the mouth in such a manner as to block completely the outward passage of the voiced air stream (Fig. 54).

All of these movements occur practically simultaneously. The amount of depression of the mandible is variable but some depression is essential to the production of an undistorted sound. An opening of the lips is also essential. For the most part this orifice opens passively as a result of the depression of the mandible, but there is in addition some active eversion of the lips themselves. This active lip movement is not essential but it is probably always present.

The movements of the tongue may vary considerably so long as the air stream is completely blocked by a contact between the tongue and some portion of the anterior hard palate. Ordinarily this is brought about by a broadening of the whole tongue and an elevation of the tip so as to make a contact on the alveolar ridge just posterior to the upper front teeth. At the same time, the whole dorsum of the tongue is raised somewhat, especially at the sides, which are elevated so as to lie in close contact with the inner borders of the teeth and with the alveolar ridge as far back as the last molars. This results in the formation of a relatively small cavity between the central portion of the tongue and the hard palate. This cavity is closed completely on both sides and in front so that the exit of the voiced air stream is momentarily blocked during the implosive period of the sound. The position for implosion may be held briefly to produce a period of plosion.

The explosive phase of the sound begins with a rapid depression of the anterior part of the tongue, thus allowing a sudden escape of the dammed-up air stream.[7] At the same time there is usually, though not necessarily, a further depression of the mandible to about the position of the neutral vowel ʌ. After the initial explosion, which is produced primarily by the tip of the tongue, the rest of that organ returns to the neutral position or goes to the position of the following sound.

When the sound is pronounced in isolation, the tongue returns to the neutral position and we hear an ə after the sound, thus, **də**. Either the implosive or the explosive phase is sufficient to call forth recognition of the whole sound. Note the words *gadfly* **gædflaɪ**, *down* **daʊn** and *caddy* **kædɪ**.

The so-called dental *d*, **d̪**, (see Fig. 55) is formed by a pre-

---

[7] The sound may also be exploded laterally by releasing the contact made by the sides of the tongue, as in *saddle* **sædl̩**, or it can be exploded nasally by lowering the velum, as in *sadden* **sædn̩**.

cisely similar action except that the contact made by the tongue is farther forward and lower—that is, on the inner and lower edges of the upper front teeth. The dental *d* is standard in Spanish, French, and Italian. Our nearest approximation to it in English occurs when **d** is preceded or followed by **z**. The **z** tends to pull the **d** farther forward and make it almost, if not entirely, dental. Note the words *lads* **lædz** and *raised* **reɪzd**. The sound can also be made with the tip of the tongue behind the lower front teeth, in which case the blade makes the contact for the explosion.

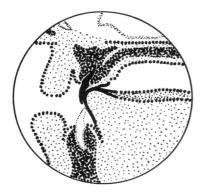 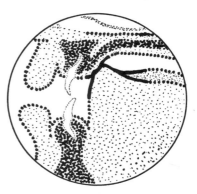

Fig. 55. Implosive position for dental *d* and *t*, ḏ and ṭ.

Fig. 56. Implosive position for retroflex *d* and *t*, ḍ and ṭ.

There is also a retroflex variety of *d*, symbol **ḍ** (see Fig. 56), in which the occlusion is made on the anterior hard palate.

t as in "Tell" tɛl (Voiceless Lingua-alveolar Stop Plosive) [8]

The movements occurring in the formation of the **t** are exactly the same as those for **d**, except that the vocal folds are not approximated. Thus **t** is a voiceless sound. All discussion pertaining to **d** is equally applicable to **t**. **t**, like **p**, is usually followed in English by a voiceless puff of air which we represent by the symbol **ʰ**. Exceptions to this statement are given on page 270.

[8] The English **t** presents special problems for most foreigners. There are three differences between the typical English **t** and the sound as pronounced by many foreigners: (1) English **t** is articulated on the rugal ridge, whereas most languages use a dental *t*; (2) English **t** is aspirated, and many foreigners make the sound unaspirated; and (3) English **t** is usually articulated less vigorously

g as in "Go" **gou** (Voiced Linguavelar Stop Plosive)

This sound is likewise a plosive. It differs from **b** or **d** in that to obtain the acoustic effect of **g** the air stream must be blocked by an elevation of the back of the tongue in such a manner as to form an air-tight contact with the velum and the posterior hard palate (Fig. 57). We have noted that **b** involves a closure of the lips and **d** a closure formed between the tongue and the rugal ridge or

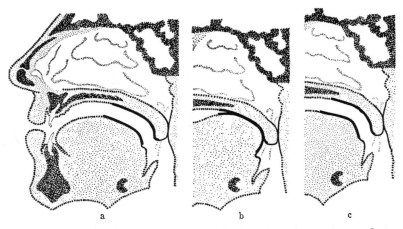

a   b   c

Fig. 57. The position for **g** and **k**. (a) Closing linguavelar orifice; (b) position during implosion; (c) opening linguavelar orifice immediately after explosion.

anterior hard palate. The third plosive, **g**, involves a contact formed between the back of the tongue and the posterior hard palate, including part of the velum.

The acoustic differences between **d** and **g** are probably due largely to the differences in the type of surface from which the

than the foreign varieties of the sound. Of the three, the matter of dentality in the foreign sound seems to be least important. A typical English **t** can be produced dentally, in fact is produced dentally many times by native speakers. The sound will not be typical in most contexts, however, if it is too vigorously articulated or if it is unaspirated. A dental *t* is nevertheless a handicap, since most foreigners do not have the θ and the presence of a dental *t* makes θ doubly difficult to use habitually.

explosion takes place and the size of the cavity into which the puff of air is emitted. Thus **d** explodes into a small front cavity. The explosion occurs as the tongue pulls away from the hard palate which is, in the main, a firm unyielding structure. **g**, on the other hand, explodes into a large cavity and the explosion takes place from the soft palate and from the other soft cushionlike structures that form the posterior walls of the mouth cavity. In the first

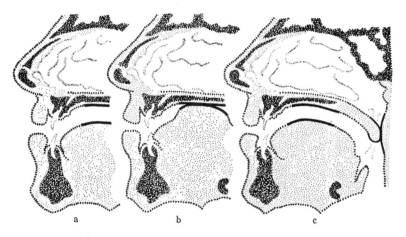

a   b   c

Fig. 58. The position for ʒ and **c**. (a) Closing linguapalatal orifice; (b) position during implosion; (c) opening linguapalatal orifice immediately after explosion.

sound the explosion takes place as the air stream is emitted between the tongue and a relatively hard surface; in the second the air stream passes between the tongue and a soft yielding structure. This fact may account for most of the acoustic differences between the two sounds.

The point of occlusion for **g** on the velum and hard palate may vary. Ordinarily we distinguish but two *g* positions, one at each end of the series. The front *g*, symbol ʒ, marks the forward end of the series, i.e., the point farthest forward at which the tongue can still make a tight contact without involving the tip or blade (see Fig. 58). This is the sound as in *gear* ʒɪr, *geese* ʒis, etc. The front *g* is used regularly following or preceding the front vowels.

The back *g*, symbol **g**, marks the other end of the series, i.e., the point of greatest elevation and retraction of the back of the tongue to make a closure. Between **ʒ** and **g**, there is a whole series of sounds, the exact positions of which are determined by the nature of the preceding or following vowel. In ordinary broad transcription the one symbol **g** is used to represent all of the sounds in the *g* series. In close transcription we can use **ʒ** to designate a front *g* and **g** for one formed farther back.

The position for **g** when it occurs in isolation may be described as follows: the vocal folds are approximated, the port into the nasopharynx is closed, the mandible is depressed to approximately the position of the vowel **ʌ**, both lips are slightly everted to form an orifice similar to that for **ʌ**, and the back of the tongue is elevated and retracted so that it establishes an air-tight contact with the velum and anterior fauces. The sides of the back of the tongue are in contact with the molar teeth. The whole tongue is elevated somewhat but the tip and sides of the forepart remain behind the lower front teeth.

Like other plosives, **g** has an implosive phase in which the voiced air stream is dammed up behind this closed position. This implosive phase may be prolonged to form a period of plosion. The last phase of the sound is the explosive period, in which the pressure is suddenly released. This release is effected as the tongue moves away from its point of contact into the position for the following sound. The explosion may occur laterally as in *wiggle* **wɪgḷ**, or through the nasal cavities as in *signal* **sɪgnəl**.

If, with the tongue in the position for **g**, the sound is emitted as a fricative instead of a plosive, the result will be the voiced lingua-velar fricative sound, symbolized by **γ**.

The articulatory position for **ʒ** is similar to that for **g**, except for the position of the tongue. For **ʒ** the whole tongue, especially the back, is drawn forward so that its sides are in contact with the inner borders of the upper teeth and the corresponding lateral portions of the hard palate as far forward as the first premolars or canines. The forepart of the tongue is flattened and rests on the lower front teeth. The back of the tongue is still in contact with the soft palate but considerably farther forward.

ʒ is also a plosive. If a fricative is made in the same position, it is represented by the symbol **ʝ**.

The general discussion relative to the acoustic nature of the bilabial and lingua-alveolar plosives is also applicable to these back plosive sounds.

k as in "Car" kar (Voiceless, Linguavelar Stop Plosive)

This plosive sound may be described as the voiceless analogue of **g**. The voiceless fricative sound made through the same position is the German *ach laut* symbolized by **x**. **k** is usually aspirated in English, except in such words as *scan, skate, skim*, etc. See page 269 for additional information on aspiration.

The front *k*, symbol **c**, is the voiceless analogue of the front *g*, **ɟ**. It occurs in such words as *key* **ci**, *kin* **cɪn**, etc. If a fricative sound is made in approximately the same position as that for **c**, it becomes the German *ich laut*, symbol **ç**.

The one symbol, **k**, is commonly used to represent all of the series of *k*'s from front to back, **c** being used only in close transcription. The fricatives **x** and **ç**, made in the back and front positions respectively, are foreign sounds occurring only accidentally in English.

From time to time we have described various sounds that employ what we have called an anterior linguapalatal orifice, and other sounds produced with a posterior linguapalatal or linguavelar orifice. The posterior linguapalatal orifice is formed between the back of the tongue and hard palate and velum. The anterior linguapalatal orifice is formed between the forepart of the tongue and the anterior hard palate. The tip of the tongue must remain down in this latter position, the orifice being formed by an arching upward of the anterior portion of the dorsum of the tongue. If the tip of the tongue comes into play, the **t** and **d** or some variety of **ʃ** or **s** will be formed. Through each of these general positions the anterior linguapalatal and the posterior linguapalatal, we can produce five different types of sounds, i.e., a vowel, a glide, a continuant fricative, a plosive, and a nasal, each of which may have either an unvoiced analogue or a glottal fricative approach. The nasal sounds are to be discussed later, but we include them here for the sake of completeness. The following chart shows the various sounds that can be made in these two positions:

| | Anterior Lingua-palatal Position | | Posterior Lingua-palatal Position | |
	Voiced	*Voiceless or h- Approach*	*Voiced*	*Voiceless or h- Approach*
Vowel	i	hi	u	hu
Glide	j	ɦj	w	ɦw
Continuant				
Fricative	ʝ	ç	ɣ	x
Plosive	ɟ	c	g	k
Nasal	ɲ	—	ŋ	—

In terms of the English language, the broad transcription symbols that represent phonemes in the table above are **i**, **u**, **j**, **w**, **k**, **g**, and **h**. All of the rest are close transcription symbols (again from the point of view of English) representing either English variants or foreign sounds. One of these, **ʝ**, is a special symbol used by the authors to point out the distinction between the continuant fricative and the glide **j**, both of which are made in the same general position. The remainder are all regular symbols in the International Phonetic Alphabet that are here used with their conventional significance.

The vowel **u** involves an additional lip factor, and the nasal sounds require an opening of the soft palate. This outline is not to be interpreted as meaning that the various sounds listed are made in an exactly similar position. It is intended rather to show in a general way how different types of sounds are made through these two fundamental positions. The reader will note that all of the sounds listed except the continuant fricatives are used in English. For some reason our language has not developed these particular fricative sounds as separate phonemes, although they may occur accidentally.

The *r* Phoneme

No sound in the English language is more variable than the *r*. There are a great variety of *r* sounds, some of which are scarcely recognizable as an **r**. We have already had occasion to mention the glide *r* and the vowel *r*. It seems best to attempt to draw together in one place all of the discussion pertaining to the *r* sounds.

We are not concerned here with the sectional problem of the inclusion or omission of the *r* in certain combinations. We are, however, concerned with the variable pronunciations of the sound when it does occur.

r is a sound that, even more than *t*, *k*, and *l*, is influenced by neighboring sounds. We will not be far wrong if we think of *r* as being dragged all over the mouth cavity by the various sounds with which it happens to be associated. This means that different sounds that we recognize as *r* are sometimes produced by fundamentally different movements. It is doubtful if we should speak of an *r* phoneme in the usual sense of the word. These various *r* sounds are only loosely bound together into one large phoneme. For some of the sounds the movements are of the same type; for others there may be a similar underlying acoustic factor in each case. Some of the *r* sounds, however, are so divergent that probably only their spelling causes them to be considered as *r*'s. There are listed below nine general types of *r* sound. All are made with the soft palate closed. All *r*'s are voiced sounds, although, as explained below, some members of the phoneme are partially unvoiced under certain conditions.

The Rolled or Trilled Tongue-Tip r, Symbol ř

This *r* is made by a rapid succession of taps of the tip of the tongue against the upper teeth or teeth ridge (Fig. 59). It is not used in American English, but it does occur in some of the dialects of British English, as well as in some foreign languages.

The Semirolled or One-Tap r, Symbol ɾ

This sound is made by a single tap of the tongue against the teeth ridge (Fig. 59). It is very common in British English, and is sometimes used as a linking *r* in American speech.

The Fricative r, Symbol ɹ

This *r* is characterized by the friction noises that are produced by the passage of the air stream through a narrow orifice formed between the tip of the tongue and the anterior hard palate (Fig. 60). The movements occurring in the production of the ɹ in isolation may be described as follows: approximation of the vocal folds; closure of the port into the nasopharynx; depression of the mandible to a position similar to that for the sound **d**; slight eversion of both lips; and a forward movement of the whole tongue, a flattening of its forepart, and an elevation of the tip toward the anterior hard palate. The sides of the tongue lie in contact with the inner borders of the upper teeth as far forward as the

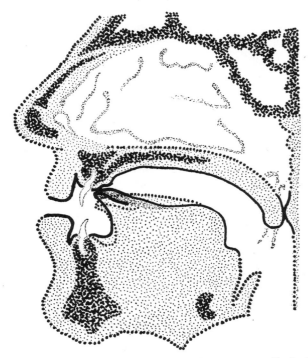

Fig. 59. The position for the trilled and one-tap trill *r*'s, *ř* and *ɾ*.

first premolars. The lateral portions of the dorsum of the tongue are in contact with the corresponding parts of the hard palate. The tongue position for this sound is similar to that for an alveolar *d*, except that the tip of the tongue is not in actual contact with the anterior hard palate. In addition, the tip is retracted somewhat and curled back slightly so as to leave a narrow orifice for the passage of the air stream.

ɹ differs from z and ʒ in that the two latter sounds are made farther forward and their characteristic friction noises are produced mainly as the air stream passes over the teeth. The friction noises that accompany this type of *r* are most apparent when the sound follows a voiceless tongue-tip consonant as in words

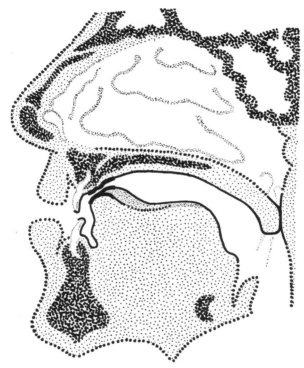

Fig. 60. The position for the fricative *r*, ɹ.

such as *try* tɹaɪ, *thrive* θɹaɪv, and *shrive* θɹaɪv. The fricative *r* tends to occur whenever the sound follows or precedes one of the linguadental or lingua-alveolar consonants, that is, **d, ð, z, ʒ**, and their voiceless analogues. These sounds all involve a movement of the tip of the tongue and are accompanied by definite friction noises. When one of them is followed or preceded by *r*, we tend to make the *r* as nearly as possible in the position of the accompanying sound. The easiest way to produce an *r* from the **d** position, for example, is to drop the tip of the tongue just far enough to produce the explosion of the **d** and then follow this by a slight retraction and curling upward of the tongue-tip to reach the **ɹ** position. If the **d** follows the **ɹ**, the principle works in reverse. The formation of an *r* following or preceding **z**, **ð**, or **ʒ** follows similar lines. In each case some of the friction noises of the accompanying sound are carried over to the **ɹ**, and in addition the orifice for **ɹ** is narrow enough to produce friction noises of its own.

Although the tongue position described above is typical of **ɹ**, it is subject to variations in different individuals and in combination with different sounds. As a matter of fact, in a word like *dry* **dɹaɪ** the tongue scarcely remains in the **ɹ** position long enough to justify calling the sound a continuant. It seems rather that the effect of the *r* is given as the articulatory mechanism goes through the **ɹ** position on its way from the **d** position to the **aɪ**. The **ɹ** can be produced as a continuant when it is pronounced in isolation, but it is not ordinarily so made. We may more accurately think of **ɹ** as a fricative variety of the glide *r* that was discussed on page 131.

Strictly speaking **ɹ** has no voiceless analogue. It is very nearly voiceless, however, when it occurs in combination with a voiceless consonant, as in *try* **tɹaɪ**. In such combination the voicing is not begun until the tongue has passed from the position of the initial consonant to the **ɹ** position and is ready to start the movement to the position for **a**. Thus all but the very last portion of the glide is unvoiced. If, however, that very last portion is not voiced, the acoustic effect of the **ɹ** is so reduced that it is scarcely noticed.

The Vowelized *r*, Symbol ɝ

This is the general American vowel *r*, previously discussed on page 88. In unstressed syllables it is represented by **ɚ**. We need not repeat the description of the movements made in producing this sound. It is a continuant made through a position sufficiently open to avert the formation of friction noises and hence is classified as a vowel (Figs. 15 and 16).

The Glide r, Symbol **r**

This is the sound that we have described on page 131 as the glide *r*. The symbol is used to indicate a glide movement to or from the ɝ position. There are other types of *r*'s that are essentially glide sounds. We have, however, used this *r* that occurs before and after vowels as a typical and unmistakable glide. We need not describe the movements for it any further than to say that it will be either from the position of ɝ to some other vowel or vice versa. This *r* is not usually accompanied by friction noises, since the glide starts from a relatively open position. It is possible, however, to make the vowel ɝ through such a narrow opening that friction noises are set up around the orifice, thus giving it some of the quality of a continuant consonant. If the ɝ is so produced, glides to or from that position will likewise be partially fricative in nature.

In broad transcription, if any one symbol is to be used to represent all of the *r* sounds (except the vowel forms) it should be **r**. In close transcription the various symbols given in this discussion can be used as they fit most appropriately.

The Inverted or Retroflex r, Symbol **ɽ**

This *r* is simply a variation of the ones just described, and its position is the same except that the tip of the tongue is curled upward and backward toward the posterior hard palate (Fig. 61). It is thus a further modification of the ɝ position. There may be various degrees of retroflexing present in normal speech, although the retroflexing of ɝ and **r** is sometimes considered as one of the undesirable features of Middle Western speech. Needless to say, the inverted position may be used in producing a vowelized form of the sound or as the point of origin in termination for glide movements. Retroflexing is symbolized by adding an upward curl to the right of the conventional symbol, thus, **ɽ**.

The Back r, Symbol **я**[9]

We have noted previously that the *r* tends to be formed by the front of the tongue if it is in the neighborhood of any of the

[9] The symbol was devised by the authors to help teach the principle that we have in English a back-tongue fricative *r* that is similar in nature to the generally recognized front-tongue variety.

linguadental or linguapalatal sounds, and by the mid-portion of the tongue when it is associated with vowels. It seems logical to suppose that an *r* might also be made with the back of the tongue when it is connected with some of the back sounds. This is often the case (Fig. 62). The Я ordinarily occurs before or after **g** or **k**. It is a voiced sound but tends to be partially unvoiced when in combination with **k**. Just as the position for *g* may vary all the way

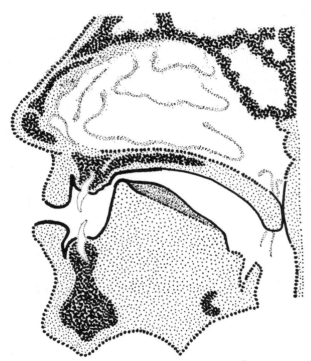

Fig. 61. The position for the retroflex *r*, ʈ.

from **g** to ʒ, so may the position of the discharging orifice for the Я vary through the same range of movements. While the Я sound can be made initially, it usually occurs only in combination with **g** and ʒ or **k** and **c**.

In the production of Я the mandible is depressed slightly farther, and the bilabial orifice is somewhat larger, than is the case

in the *r* sounds previously described. Otherwise, the main difference lies in the action of the tongue. The whole tongue is drawn
backward and elevated, the front being elevated very little or not
at all. Thus it is the back of the tongue that projects up into the
mouth cavity in such a way as to produce the characteristic *r*
resonance.

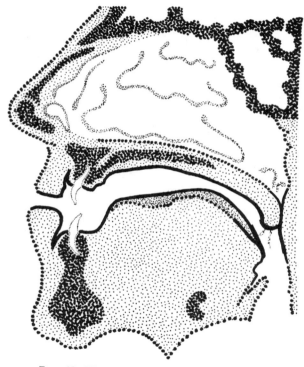

Fig. 62. The position for the back *r*, **Я**.

It is not safe to say that every *r* following or preceding a *g* or *k*
will be a back **Я**, because it is possible to use another type of *r* in
these combinations. In general, however, most of us will tend to
pronounce words like *grape* **gЯeɪp** and *crate* **kЯeɪt** with a back-
tongue *r*. This sound is usually pronounced as a glide and not as
a continuant.

The Uvular Rolled *r*, Symbol Ř

This *r* does not occur in English but it does in several languages, notably German and French. As its name indicates, it is produced by raising the back of the tongue up toward the soft palate in such a way that the outward passage of the air stream causes the uvula

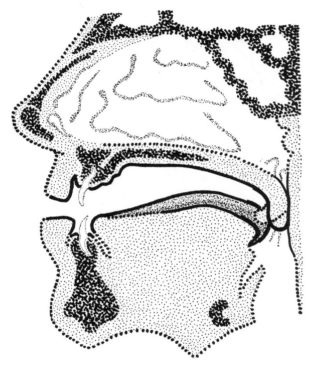

Fig. 63. The position for the uvular trilled and the one-tap uvular trill *r*'s, Ř, and R.

to flutter (Fig. 63). The symbol **R**, without the trill sign, ˘, is used to indicate the one tap, or flapped, form of the sound.

The Velar Fricative *r*, Symbol ʁ

This sound likewise does not occur in English, though it does in German. It is similar to the uvular rolled Ř, except that the ʁ depends upon definite friction noises set up by the passage of the air stream between the back of the tongue and the velum (Fig. 64). The ʁ probably represents also an extreme form of the back-tongue ʀ mentioned just above. It is essentially a less vigorous form

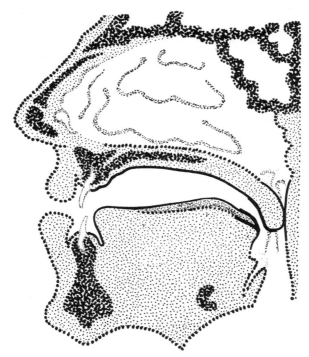

Fig. 64. The position for the velar fricative r, ʁ.

of the uvular *r*, the acoustic effect being that of a scrape instead of a flutter. The **R** and **ʁ** are frequently interchangeable in German.[10]

Summary of the *r* Sounds

A review of the *r*'s discussed in these pages will show that they fall into three main groups:[11] (1) the tongue-tip *r*'s ř, ɾ, and ɹ;

[10] The IPA contains the additional symbol χ, representing a voiceless form of ʁ.

[11] Some writers describe also a labial trilled *r*.

(2) the mid-tongue *r*'s ɚ, **r**, and their retroflexed forms; and (3) the back-tongue *r*'s Я, Ř, and Ƃ.

All of these sounds are grouped together into one large phoneme that is held together partly by a common spelling in the written language and partly by a common acoustic factor. It is probable that in all except ɚ the movement from the position of the sound to the following vowel is more important in giving the effect of the *r* than is the position from which the *r* starts. This is especially true of ɹ, **r**, and Я, in which the acoustic effect of the *r* is primarily the result of movement from their respective positions or to them. A continuant made in the same positions will also give the effect of the *r*, but in actual speech the mechanism is not held fixed in one position long enough to produce a definite continuant, except in the case of the continuant vowel ɚ.

Summary of the Consonants

We have now finished our discussion of the consonant sounds as oral modifications of the vowel sounds. Along with the laryngeal modifications and the intervowel glides they are methods of initiating, connecting, and terminating vowels. In order to clarify this conception, let us note, as an example, the words *satisfy* **sætɪsfaɪ**. Four vowel positions are involved, **æ**, **ɪ**, **a**, and **ɪ**. We might represent the vowel basis of the word as **æ-ɪ-a-ɪ**. The word begins with the articulatory mechanism closed to the position for **s**; the mechanism then opens to form **æ**, closes again to the **t** position, opens to form the **ɪ**, closes again for the **s**, and opens once more for the **a** which is glided to the **ɪ** position. We may well look at the consonants simply as methods of approaching or terminating vowel sounds.

We are now ready to consider the last general method of modifying the vowels, i.e., the nasal sounds.

Chapter 9 Nasal Modifications of the Vowels

Certain sounds in English are produced with the soft palate hanging relaxed and the port into the nasopharynx open. These sounds, the nasals, are continuants. They have, as a group, two essentials: (1) the oral cavity must be closed off at some point so that the vocal tone may not be emitted through the mouth; (2) the soft palate must be open so that the tone can be directed through the nasal cavities. In discussing the consonant sounds we pointed out that it was necessary for the soft palate to be closed in the production of fricatives, plosives, and sibilants in order to direct the air stream into the mouth cavity and to close off the nasal cavities, thus making possible the creation of sufficient mouth pressure for proper formation of the sounds. In the production of the vowels and nasals, however, the soft palate has a different function, i.e., to make available an additional resonance chamber and to change the coupling between resonance chambers.[1]

---

[1] We are discussing in this chapter only the action of the velum as it operates to produce certain definite nasal sounds. We should also mention the possibility of nasalizing any or all of the speech sounds discussed in the preceding pages, that is, producing them with the port into the nasopharynx partially open. In French, vowels in certain positions are normally produced with considerable attendant nasality. We have previously pointed out that there is evidence to indicate that in English some normal speakers produce vowels with the soft palate slightly open. However, whenever this nasalization of either vowels or consonants becomes conspicuous, it is regarded as defective or as evidence of an undesirable form of dialectal speech.

The individual acoustic properties of the nasal sounds depend upon the place of the stoppage of the oral cavity, which serves in these sounds as a cul-de-sac resonator. The difference between one nasal sound and another depends upon how much of the oral cavity is serving in this manner.

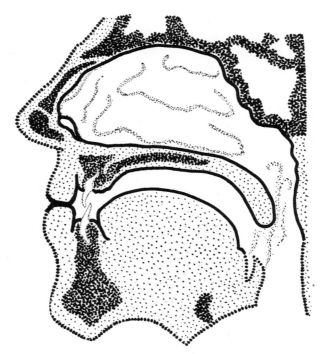

Fig. 65. The position for **m**.

Only three nasal sounds in English can be distinguished from one another. We usually list symbols for two other nasal sounds, but they are for use in close transcription only and each has a close relative among the other three from which it is indistinguishable.

m as in "Mat" mæt (Voiced Bilabial Stop, Nasal Continuant)

Only one modification of the neutral position is necessary in producing the sound **m**, namely, an approximation of the vocal folds, adding the element of voice to the outflowing column of air. The whole articulatory mechanism remains in the neutral position, and the sound is emitted nasally (Fig. 65). This is the most easily produced speech sound in the English language.

In the production of this sound the tongue remains in the

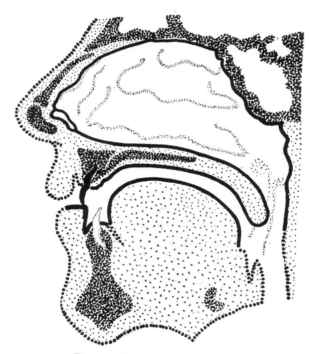

Fig. 66. The position for **ŋ**.

neutral position. However, it may execute a wide variety of movements or assume a number of different positions without altering the essential nature of the sound. Apparently the one factor limiting its movement is that the whole length of the oral cavity must be available as a resonator. Thus if the front of the cavity is blocked off by the tip, or the whole cavity by the back of the tongue, the resulting sounds are recognized as belonging to different phonemes. The position for **m** is the position for the plosive phase of **b** except that the soft palate is open and the sound is emitted nasally.

The symbol **m̩** is sometimes used to represent a labiodental *m* (see Fig. 66). Such a sound sometimes occurs accidentally in such words as *caveman* **keɪvm̩æn**. The nasal sound following the labiodental **v** tends to be made with the same lip-teeth position. **m̩** and **m** cannot be distinguished acoustically.

n as in "None" nʌn (Voiced Lingua-alveolar Stop, Nasal Continuant)

The movements involved in the production of **n** are exactly the same as those for the plosive phase of **d** except that the port into the nasopharynx remains open and the voice is emitted through the nasal cavities (Fig. 67).

The articulatory mechanism must remain in this position throughout the duration of the sound. When the **n** is final the position is maintained until the cessation of voice, i.e., until the drawing apart of the vocal folds, after which the mechanism returns to the neutral position. When the **n** is initial or medial the tongue moves toward the position of the following sound simultaneously with the closure of the palate. All discussion of the movements of the tongue, lips, and jaw during the plosive period of **d** is applicable to **n**. Like the **t** and **d** sounds, *n* can be made dentally **ṇ** or retroflexed **ɳ** but these differences in position are of practically no acoustic significance.

If we look at these nasal sounds from the point of view of their acoustic characteristics, it is clear that they resemble the vowels more than the consonants. The voicing and the continuant nature of the movement are qualities that are shared with the voiced fricatives as well as the vowels but the presence of resonance patterns that are key factors in identification and discrimination make them more closely akin to vowels. If, on the other hand, we consider their behavior in syllable formation, they belong with the consonants, since normally they do not serve as the "peak of sonority" that must be present in every syllable, but rather as a dispensable accompanying sound. However, partly because these sounds do have considerable vowel quality and hence sonority, they do sometimes stand alone in syllables and serve as vowels. This happens frequently with **n** in such words as *mutton* **mʌtn̩**, *bitten* **bɪtn̩**, and *leaden* **lɛdn̩** and occasionally with **m** in combinations such as *cabin boy* **kæbɪnbɔɪ** when by a process of assimilation the **ɪn** changes to **m̩**, thus, **kæbm̩bɔɪ**. Such syllabic nasals are often spoken of as vowels.

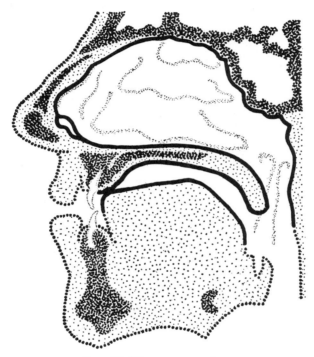

Fig. 67. The position for **n**.

We should note that the only difference between the consonantal *n* in *no* **noʊ** and the vowel *n* in *button* **bʌtn̩** is one of time. The size of the discharging orifice is ordinarily the distinguishing factor between vowels and consonants, since it determines the presence or absence of friction noises. With the nasals, however, the orifice remains constant and the only thing that can vary is the time. If the duration of the nasal sound is short we call it a consonant; if long, a vowel.

ŋ as in "Lung" lʌŋ (Voiced Linguavelar Stop, Nasal Continuant)

This is the **g** sound emitted nasally as a continuant. Its position is the same as that for the plosive phase of **g**, except that the port into the nasopharynx is not closed (Fig. 68).

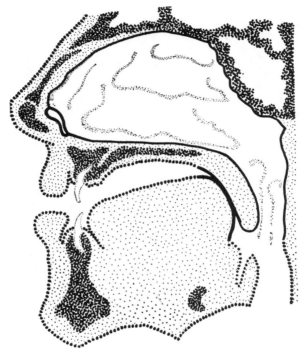

Fig. 68. The position for ŋ.

In a similar fashion the nasal emission of **ʒ** results in another nasal continuant, the symbol for which is **ɲ** (Fig. 69).[2] Strictly speaking, a whole series of nasal sounds lies between **ɲ** and **ŋ**, just as there is a series of voiced plosives between **ʒ** and **g**. They

[2] The symbol **ɲ** is sometimes used to represent the sound of *gn* as in *champagne* (French) and *montagne* (Italian). The sound is a rapid **j** glide beginning from the **ɲ** position and made with the soft palate open. An approximation of the sound is heard in some pronunciations of *signal*, i.e., **sɪgɲjəl**. The IPA, however, lists the symbol **ɲ** simply as a palatal nasal.

are not distinguishable from one another acoustically. ŋ is the symbol used in broad transcription.

Summary of the Nasal Sounds

We have seen that **m** depends upon the use of the whole mouth cavity as a cul-de-sac resonator. **n** depends upon that part of the

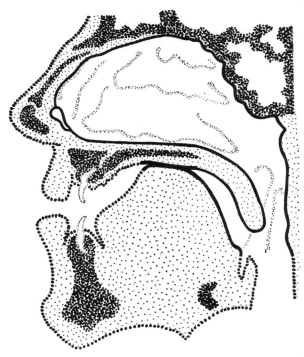

Fig. 69. The position for ɲ.

cavity that lies behind the lingua-alveolar contact made for this sound. For **ŋ**, on the other hand, the mouth cavity is entirely cut off by contact between the back of the tongue and the soft palate, and the only cul-de-sac resonator that remains is the faucial entrance.

There is little point to a discussion as to whether these sounds should be thought of as consonants or vowels. It is simpler to think of them as continuant nasal sounds. They provide one of the methods of initiating, connecting, or terminating vowel sounds.

Summary of the Methods of Initiating, Connecting, and Terminating Vowels

It will be recalled that we began this section with a considera-tion of the neutral position of the speech mechanism and the neutral vowel ʌ. We next described the vowels of English and found that in terms of movement they grouped themselves into front vowels, mid vowels, back vowels, and laterally emitted vowels. We proposed then to view the remaining sounds of speech as ways and means of starting and stopping these basic vowel tones. We began with a consideration of the results of the actions of the vocal folds, including the glottal fricative, the glottal vibratory, and the glottal plosive approach and termination. We next considered the glide movement as a method of connecting one vowel with another. We spoke of receding and approaching glides centering around the five key positions of u, i, ɝ, l̩, and ʌ. This brought us to a study of the consonant sounds under the general heading of oral modifications of vowel tones. These consonants were divided on the basis of movement into continuant fricatives and stop plosives. Finally we discussed under nasal modifications the nasal sounds m, n, and ŋ.

In the following chapter we will consider the nature of the special consonant combinations in which a plosive and a fricative are "fused" and produced together in the same articulatory position.

Chapter 10   Homorganic Plosive and Fricative Combinations

Consonant Combinations

Combinations of two consonants are very common in English and three are not at all unusual but, fortunately for most of us, we are rarely called upon to articulate four consonants one after the other as, for example, in the word *sixths* **sɪksθs**. Some combinations involve two or more fricatives such as those in *fifths* **fɪfθs**, *lives* **laɪvz**, *bathes* **beɪðz**, and others contain two plosives as in *act* **ækt**, *apt* **æpt**, *mobbed* **mɑbd**, etc. Most, however, are two- or three-consonant combinations of plosives and fricatives such as those illustrated in the words *desk* **dɛsk**, *wasps* **wɑsps**, *asks* **æsks**, *sobs* **sɑbz**, *leads* **lidz**, *latch* **lætʃ**, *rushed* **rʌʃt**, *casts* **kæsts**, *best* **bɛst**, and *bets* **bɛts**.

If we look at this last group of words more closely we will note that they can be divided into two general groups: (1) those in which the proper utterance of the consonants requires a change in the articulatory position in going from one to the other, and (2) those in which both the plosive and the fricative are made in the same (homorganic) position and in which there is an actual fusing of the two sounds. The two commonly accepted prototypes of the second category are the **tʃ** and **dʒ** combinations. These two sounds are usually called affricates and described in textbooks of phonetics as a special variety of sounds belonging in the consonant group. They are also regarded as phonemic, a point which will be discussed later in this chapter.

The concept presented in this chapter is that **tʃ** and **dʒ** are in fact only samples of a type of sound combination that is very common in English (as well as in other languages) and illustrative of two important phonetic principles. The first part of this statement means, in effect, that there are many other "affricate" combinations. However, since the word has been so long used to apply only to **tʃ** and **dʒ** and to movements in only one direction (away from the plosive), it seems wiser to suggest a new terminology rather than to attempt to reshape the familiar and somewhat fixed concepts that cluster around the word *affricate*. It is for this reason that we have titled this chapter "Homorganic Plosive and Fricative Combinations" and described the process involved as the "oral plosive approach or termination for continuant consonants." The two phonetic principles referred to above are as follows: (1) these combinations can profitably be viewed as ways of starting and stopping continuant fricatives; and (2) whenever a plosive and a fricative sound which have the same or adjacent articulatory positions occur together, they will tend to be fused into one acoustic unit and made in one position unless there is a syllable break or some other form of hiatus between the two sounds. Just as a stop sound may be used as a method of beginning or ending a vowel, so it can be used to begin or end a continuant consonant. Note the words *best* **bɛst** and *bets* **bɛts**. In the first the continuant fricative **s** is brought to a termination by the stop, **t**; in the second the **s** starts from the **t** position. We have called this the oral plosive approach or termination. We can best illustrate this approach by speaking in detail of the combination **tʃ**.

The Oral Plosive Approach and Termination

We should say in the beginning that **tʃ** and its voiced analogue **dʒ** have been commonly described by phoneticians as separate sound units made by combining **t** and **ʃ** and **d** and **ʒ**, respectively. Such a description is not entirely accurate. Evidence from palatograms indicates that the initial position in the **tʃ** combination is somewhat different from that of the **t** when that sound is pronounced in isolation.

The initial position for **tʃ** is closer to that for **ʃ**, except that the narrow orifice between the flattened tip of the tongue and the anterior hard palate which was noted for ʃ is now completely closed by a slight additional elevation of the tongue tip. Thus the sound has an explosive beginning from what might be called a closed ʃ position. On the other hand, the position might equally well be described as one of a variety of *t* positions.

There is also a difference in the manner of effecting the explosion from this closed position. We have noted that when **t** is sounded in isolation the whole tongue is depressed suddenly to the neutral position, resulting in a sudden release of the dammed-up air stream. In **tʃ**, however, the front of the tongue drops relatively slowly from the closed ʃ position to form momentarily the typical linguapalatal orifice previously described for ʃ. Following this the whole tongue is depressed to the neutral position. The acoustic effects of this series of movements are as follows: (1) With the depression of the tip of the tongue there occurs a modified explosion that is usually less sharp and clear-cut than that for **t**. (2) As the tongue passes through the ʃ position there is a brief period when the friction noises characteristic of that sound are produced. (3) Finally the depression of the whole tongue results in the escape of a puff of air. Put together in rapid succession this all results in the **tʃʰ** as it is pronounced in isolation.

Apparently, then, there are two factors of difference between **tʃ** and **t**: first, the initial tongue position differs slightly; second—and this seems to be by far the more important factor—there is a difference in the nature of the movement that opens the orifice. Starting with the tongue in the closed ʃ position, the sound resulting from the opening movement can be made to resemble either a **t** or a **tʃ** depending upon the way in which the opening is made. The **dʒ** combination may be mentioned in passing as the voiced analogue of **tʃ**.

Homorganic Consonant Combinations

Other combinations are formed according to the same general principles. Thus **ts** as in *cats* **kæts,** **dz** as in *fads* **fædz,** **tθ** as in *eighth* **eɪtθ,** **dθ** as in *width* **wɪdθ,** and **dð** as in *around the* **əraʊndðə** may be noted in this connection. These combinations are similar in nature to **tʃ** and **dʒ**. We are not interested here in a detailed description of each of them. The same working principles described for **tʃ** are applicable in each case. By way of summary, we may say that each of the continuant fricatives **s**, **θ**, and **ʃ**, along with their voiced analogues, may have an explosive or *t* attack; i.e., they may be approached from the closed position of the fricative under consideration. In a similar manner the fricative *r* **ɹ** may have a *t* approach as in *try* **tɹaɪ** and this seems to be in principle an "affricate," though it is not conventionally so regarded.

We have here the practical application of the principle that the positions for two such adjacent sounds will be fused and uttered as one unit. Compare the position for the **t** in *pat*, the **s** in *pass*, and the **ts** in *pats*. In a similar manner compare the **t** in *eight* with the **θ** in *youth* and the **tθ** in *eighth*. In both cases it will probably be found that the positions for the plosive and the fricative differ considerably when they are made separately, that they are made in one position when they are in combination, and that this position is much nearer to the typical position for the fricative sound than it is for that of the plosive.

Each of these fricatives may likewise have a *t* termination; that is, it may end in a closed position. Note for example, **s** in *cast* **kast**, **z** in *razed* **reɪzd**, **ʃ** in *rushed* **rʌʃt**, **ʒ** in *waged* **weɪdʒd**, **θ** in *lathed* **læθt**, **ð** in *bathed* **beɪðd**, and **ɹ** in *heart* **haɹt**. In each of these cases the fricative ends in the closed position of the sound under consideration instead of beginning from it. Note especially the word *waged*, in which the **ʒ** sound has both its beginning and ending in the closed position. These are examples of oral plosive terminations.

Although we have limited our discussion to the linguapalatal and linguadental sounds, the same principles can be applied at any point in the articulatory mechanism *where plosives and fricatives are formed in the same region*. Thus the voiced and voiceless linguavelar plosives **g** and **k** and the voiced and voiceless linguavelar fricatives **ɣ** and **x** can be combined to form **kx**, **xk**, **gɣ**, and **ɣg**. In a similar fashion **p** and **b** may be combined with the voiced and voiceless bilabial fricatives **β** and **φ** to form **bβ**, **βb**, **pφ**, and **φp**. These combinations occur only accidentally in English but they may be common in other languages. Note the German word *pfennig* **φɛnɪç**, often pronounced **pφɛnɪç**.

Summary of Homorganic Positions

We may summarize this discussion of the oral plosive approach or termination by saying again that it may occur at any point in the articulatory mechanism where plosives and fricatives are made by similar adjustments of the articulators. If we divide the **k g** phonemes into front and back sounds there are four such points where clusters of plosives and fricatives occur: the bilabial cluster with **p** and **b** as the plosive sounds; the linguadental cluster with **t** and **d** as the plosives; the **c ɟ** cluster; and the **k g** cluster. These are shown in the accompanying table on the following page with their respective clusters of fricative sounds. The various oral plosive combinations are given on the right. We should mention also that one member of a plosive fricative combination may be voiced and the other unvoiced. Such combinations seldom occur in English except accidentally.

For purposes of broad transcription it is permissible to write these homorganic plosives and fricatives simply as pairs of sounds, **tʃ**, **dʒ**, **st**, **ts**, etc. The oral plosive nature of the combination is assumed. However, in narrow transcription, it is better to use a ligature, thus, **t͡ʃ**, **s͡t**, etc., to indicate the organic union of the two sounds. The ligature is also occasionally necessary to avoid ambiguity. The basic difference between a mere juxtaposition of two sounds and their union in an affricate combination is shown by the classic examples of **baɪ t͡ʃip** vs. **baɪt ʃip**.

Phonemic Considerations

We return now to the question as to whether the **tʃ** and **dʒ** should be considered as separate phonemic units in the English language or simply as two of a number of such oral plosive approaches to continuant fricatives. Two opposing answers can be given, depending upon the basis used for defining a phoneme. The traditional answer that these sounds are phonemic is based on the historical development of the spellings for the sounds in the written language and the fact that we have in our modern spelling the letters *ch* that, when used together, represent consistently the sound **tʃ** and the letters *j* and "soft" *g* representing **dʒ**. The question is, in essence, whether the phonemic structure of a language is conceived as residing in, or being determined by, its

		Oral Plosive Approach	**Oral Plosive Termination**
p — φ, f		pφ pf	φp fp
b — β, v		bβ bv	βb vb
t — θ, s, ʃ, ɹ		tθ ts tʃ tɹ	θt st ʃt ɹt
d — ð, z, ʒ, ɹ		dð dz dʒ dɹ	ðd zd ʒd ɹd
c — ç		cç	çc
ʒ — ɟ		ʒɟ	ɟʒ
k — Я, x		kЯ kx	Яk xk
g — Я, ɣ		gЯ gɣ	Яg ɣg

spoken or its recorded (written) form. From the latter point of view there can be little question but that **tʃ** and **dʒ** should be regarded as phonemic. It is doubtful, however, if the question as to whether or not these sounds are phonemic would ever have arisen if it were not for the special spellings *ch*, *j*, and *g* in the written alphabet. In the absence of such special characters, these two sounds would almost surely be thought of as consonant combinations similar in principle to **ts**, **dz**, etc., and without any particular phonemic significance.

On the other hand, if we disregard the recorded form of the language and approach the question from the point of view that phonemes are essentially auditory phenomena, we can only conclude that **tʃ** and **dʒ** are no more and no less phonemic than **ts**, **dz**, and similar combinations. The same type of acoustic characteristics and the same movement patterns are present in each. If we apply the test of meaningful significance in words we find ourselves saying that **t** is phonemic in *cat*, **ʃ** is phonemic in *cash*, and **tʃ** is phonemic in *catch*, since in each case the meaning changes. We might by this method establish the presence of three phonemes, one of which would be **t**, one **ʃ**, and the third **tʃ**, made up of the two in combination. If this same reasoning is applied to *cat*, *Cass*, and *cats*, we can only conclude that **ts** is also phonemic. This opens the way to declaring phonemic three or four similar combinations **dz**, **tθ**, **dð**, **tɹ** that occur frequently in English, a position that is obviously untenable. The fact that *chew* means something different from either *too* or *shoe* does not establish **tʃ** as a separate phoneme. It only demonstrates the obvious—that **t** and **ʃ** may be used in combination to form a word with a meaning that is different from that of otherwise similar words formed with either of these sounds alone. From this point of view, **tʃ** is not a separate sound (phoneme) but a consonant combination that can be divided into its component parts, each of which has meaningful significance in words. **t** and **ʃ**, on the contrary, are phonemic in part because neither can be broken down into smaller sound units that can be used to form words with different meanings.

Since the approach in this book is essentially phonetic rather than linguistic and oriented to the spoken rather than the written language, **tʃ** and **dʒ** cannot be considered as phonemic within this particular frame of reference.

Chapter 11   A Summary of
Kinesiologic Phonetics

Outline Analysis of Speech Sounds

In developing this classification of speech sounds we have used as a starting point the resting state of the speech mechanism. The vowel ʌ was discussed as resulting from minor changes in this position and the rest of the vowels as further modifications of the position for ʌ. The various ways in which these vowel tones can be initiated, connected, or terminated were then considered, under the headings of laryngeal modifications, glides, oral modifications, and velar modifications. Finally, the special combinations of plosives and fricatives produced in homorganic positions were described as a method of starting and stopping continuant fricatives. This approach is here summarized in outline form (pp. 196–197) in an attempt to show in a single chart the approach used in this section of the book. It should prove useful in reviewing the material covered.

A Reclassification of Speech Sounds from the Placement Approach

The discussion in Section II, developed from a kinesiologic approach, has included a classification of speech sounds as continuants, stops and glides, and descriptive names for the consonants that indicate the positions of the articulatory mechanism. In order to review this material from a slightly different angle, a second classification of speech sounds will now be suggested based *entirely* upon the position of the articulatory mechanism. Upon this basis the sounds already described are divided into nine groups: beta consonants, delta consonants, gamma consonants, glottal sounds, glide sounds, front vowels, mid vowels, back vowels, and laterally emitted vowels. Each of these groups will be discussed in more detail.

Beta consonants.[1] These include those sounds in which the lips are the articulators and the tongue plays only a neutral or passive role. They are **p**, **b**, **m**, **ɸ**, **β**, **f**, **v**, and **ŋ**.

Delta consonants. The delta family includes those in which the tip of the tongue plays against the teeth or the anterior hard palate and in which the lips have only neutral or passive roles. These sounds are **t**, **d**, **n**, **s**, **z**, **θ**, **ð**, **ʃ**, **ʒ**, **ɹ**, **ř**, and **ɾ**.

Gamma consonants. The gamma group is a small one in English, embracing the sounds in which the back of the tongue plays against the roof of the mouth, the tip of the tongue and the lips being out of the physiologic pictures. The important English sounds in this group are **k**, **g**, **ŋ**. However, we should also include here **ʝ**, **ʒ**, **ɲ**, **ç**, **c**, **γ**, and **x**, as well as varieties of the *r* made with the back of the tongue, i.e., **Я**, **Ř**, and **ʁ**.

Glottal sounds. This group includes only **h** and **ʔ**.

Glide sounds. This group includes the approaching and receding glides centered around the **u**, **i**, **ɝ**, **ḷ**, and **ʌ** positions.

Front vowels. The front vowels include those relatively open voiced sounds in which the mouth cavity is used as a unit resonator, the shape and size of which is controlled by modifying the aperture through which the sound is delivered to the outer air. This modification is accomplished by arching the tongue and holding it in various positions with its highest point about opposite the middle of the hard palate, thus forming a transverse weir over which the sound is delivered to the outer air and behind which is formed a single resonating cavity, including as one chamber the cavities of the mouth and pharynx.

---

[1] The student should not gain the impression that, since the term *beta* is used to designate this class of sounds, we mean that all the members of this group have been derived from the sound given by ancient Greeks for the letter *beta*. We have chosen the terms *beta*, *delta*, and *gamma* quite arbitrarily, merely as a helpful mnemonic device.

	Approximation of Vocal Folds	*Elevation of Soft Palate, Dropping of Mandible*	*Modifications of Neutral Vowel Position to Produce Other Vowels Through Orifices Large Enough to Avoid Friction Noises*
Resting State of Speech Mechanism as in Normal Quiet Respiration	Laryngeal tone as in **m**	The neutral vowel ʌ	The front vowels **i, ɪ, (e), ɛ, æ, (a)** The central vowels **ɝ, (ɜ), ʌ, ɑ** The back vowels **u, ʊ, (o), ɔ, (ɒ)** The schwa vowels **ə** The laterally delivered vowels **l̩ to (ɫ̩)**

NOTE: The symbols used in narrow transcription or for the representation of foreign sounds have been placed in parentheses.

Ways of Initiating, Connecting, or Terminating the Vowels	*The Oral Plosive Approach or Termination for Fricative Continuants*

Laryngeal Approach or Release
Glottal fricative   **h**
Glottal plosive   **(ʔ)**
Glottal vibratory   —

Intervowel Glides

Receding	Approaching
eɪ	**jɑ** etc.
aɪ	**wɑ** etc.
ɔɪ	**rɑ** etc.
aʊ	**lɑ** etc.
oʊ	**(əɛ)** etc.
ɛə etc.	
ɑr etc.	
ɑl etc.	

Oral Modifications

Stops (Plosives)		Continuants (Fricatives)	
Voiceless	Voiced	Voiceless	Voiced
p	**b**	**(ɸ)**	**(β)**
t	**d**	**f**	**v**
(c)	**(ɟ)**	**θ**	**ð**
k	**g**	**s**	**z**
		ʃ	**ʒ**
		(ç)	**(ʝ)**
		(x)	**(ɣ)**

Velar Modifications
m-(ɱ)
n
ŋ-(ɲ)

Plosive Approach		Plosive Termination	
Voiceless	Voiced	Voiceless	Voiced
tʃ	**dʒ**	**ʃt**	**ʒd**
ts	**dz**	**st**	**zd**
tθ	**dð**	**θt**	**ðd**
(tɹ)	**(dɹ)**		
(pɸ)	**(bβ)**	**(ɸp)**	**(βp)**
(kx)	**(gɣ)**	**(xk)**	**(ɣg)**
etc.		etc.	

The lowest of the front vowels is **a**. In this sound the arch of the tongue is least and the tongue itself is held the lowest in the mouth of any of the series—the rest of the series having been previously described as running through æ, ɛ, e, and ɪ to i, the highest, which involves a very small front opening for the outward delivery of the sound.

Back vowels. With the back vowels the tongue is arched in the back so as to make a resonator in front of the line of arching. The anterior opening of this front resonator is between the lips. In general, the higher the arching of the tongue the smaller is the orifice between the lips. ɒ, the lowest vowel in this series, is made with the tongue almost flat in the mouth and the lips widely open. The series progresses through ɔ, o, and ʊ, to u, which is the highest of the back vowels and made with the tongue arched nearly to the roof of the mouth and the lips distinctly pursed.

Mid vowels. For the mid vowels the tongue is arched along a line between the lines for the front and back vowels. The lowest vowel in this group is ɑ; [2] next comes ʌ, then ɜ, and finally the highest, ɝ.

Laterally emitted vowels. This group includes only the vowel ḷ, which, as we have noted, is subject to variations in its place of production. It is distinguished from all of the other vowels and consonants by the fact that the air stream is emitted laterally on one or both sides, instead of centrally.

Dynamic Phonetics

The Dynamic Approach

The term *dynamic phonetics* is used here to express the concept underlying the consideration of speech sounds as they actually occur *in situ*, that is to say, in the moving stream of speech. We have endeavored to keep this concept foremost in mind throughout this section on kinesiologic phonetics, but the very process of describing individual speech sounds tends to make us forget that the finished product, like a building, may be quite different from the units with which it is constructed. At this point, therefore, we turn our attention to a consideration of the dynamic pattern of connected speech, beginning by describing a short sample of

[2] In the pronunciation of some people ɑ may be the lowest of the back-vowel series.

English speech according to the terminology and approach used in this section. If complete, such a sample would include an analysis of the movements of the speech mechanism together with the muscles and nerves involved in the production of the sounds.

The phrase chosen for illustrative purposes is *will you come here* **wɪl ju kʌm hɪr**. In terms of the previous discussion, this phrase would be described as follows: The speech mechanism passes from the resting position to approximately that of the vowel **u**. The vocal folds close to the point of phonation, the soft palate closes, and the articulatory mechanism glides to the position of the vowel **ɪ**, thus producing the approaching glide **wɪ**. The glide movement continues in a receding glide from the **ɪ** position to that for **l̩**. There may be a slight pause at this point, but for all practical purposes the glide movement continues to the position of the vowel **i** and passes thence to that of **u**, producing the approaching glide **ju**. Following the completion of this movement, the vocal folds open, and the articulatory mechanism assumes the position for the voiceless stop consonant **k** which is produced in both its implosive and explosive phases. As the explosive phase of the **k** is completed the vocal folds again close to the point of vibration and the articulatory mechanism takes the position of the neutral vowel **ʌ**. This vowel is terminated by the lowering of the soft palate and the assuming by the articulatory mechanism of the position for the continuant nasal **m**. Following the production of **m** the velum is again raised to close off the nasal passages and the articulatory mechanism goes into the position for **ɪ**. Simultaneously the vocal folds open to the whisper position and close again relatively slowly to the point of vibration thus producing a glottal fricative approach to the vowel **ɪ**. The articulatory mechanism glides with continuous voicing to the position for the vowel **ɝ**, producing the receding glide **ɪr**. The vocal folds then return to a wide open position, the soft palate opens, and the articulatory mechanism passes without noticeable acoustic effect to the resting position.

Fig. 70 shows something of the nature of such a complicated sequence of articulatory events in the pronunciation of the word *bed-tick*.

In the mental tie-up between speech and writing—between sound and letter—much stress naturally falls upon the principle of the individuality of the speech sound. As letters are distinctly individual units, so must be the sounds that the letters represent; and since these letters remain the same in any combination in which they appear, the sounds must be static building blocks out of which spoken words are constructed. Even the student of phonetics is likely to get this impression when he is first shown the phonetic alphabet and told that we have one symbol, and only one, for each speech sound. This principle of the fixed individuality of the phoneme is true in part, but only in part. When one

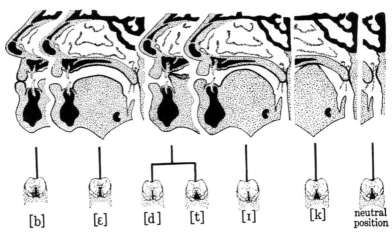

Fig. 70. Articulatory adjustments in the word *bed-tick*.

listens to a speaker and as he speaks transcribes in phonetic symbols the sounds that are uttered, one identifies the sounds to be transcribed partly by noting their individuality and inherent fixed qualities and partly by noting their development from phase to phase and the relationship between successive sounds. A phonetic study emphasizing these developments and relationships may be described as dynamic in point of view.

Many forms of human behavior so largely involve movement patterns that if motion be arrested in mid-phase, or even retarded, the significance of the behavior seems modified or lacking entirely. Still photography reveals this importance of movement when it catches and makes static some posture or expression that is but a phase in a series of bodily or facial movements. The bodily posture may seem grotesque and awkward and the countenance may seem to express stupidity or inanity.

Slow-motion pictures, as well as reversed-motion pictures, again reveal how much we depend upon movement to give us the significance of any behavior pattern. Motion pictures that are out of synchronization with their sound tracks also give us the effect of distorted facial movements. Even the person who could not adequately describe the series of articulatory movements that should accompany a series of acoustic events in the uttering of a given word or phrase will nevertheless be able to detect immediately a lack of synchronization between picture and sound.

Sculptors, painters, and portrait photographers who endeavor to catch the spirit of persons whose likenesses they would preserve must avoid postures and expressions that are parts of movement series and catch those that are naturally, even though briefly, static. In walking, for example, there is one phase in which both feet are planted on the ground, at the instant in which the weight is being shifted from one foot to the other. Here the movement is naturally but momentarily arrested. A still picture of this phase looks "natural." If, on the other hand, the artist should catch the foot on its way to its new position on the ground, the effect would be grotesque.

It is so with speech. Many acoustic events have significance only in their movements or development from sound to sound. In fact there are few speech sounds in which movement does not play a significant part in their phonemic characteristics. These few sounds can be prolonged indefinitely without modifying their character. They would be analogous to the static postures that the artist paints. All other sounds cannot be prolonged, or if prolonged, seem to move out of their phonemes, or may even cease to be speech sounds and become only mechanical noises made by the organs of speech. The English vowels **i**, **a**, **ɑ**, **ɜ**, **ɝ**, **ɔ**, and **u** are prolonged with relatively little perceptual distortion; and **m**, **n**, **s**, **ʃ**, in so far as each has special semantic significance when standing alone,[3] can be prolonged without alteration of their

---

[3] **m** and **n** are employed to convey various social attitudes, such as affirmation, denial, surprise, disapproval, etc. **ʃ** is used to signal for quiet, and **s** means warning or disapproval, depending upon the situation.

perceptual nature. All other sounds must be heard in moving context to seem "natural." [4]

These sounds that involve development by movement may be classed as follows: (1) these vowels whose duration is short; (2) all sounds (both sonants and surds) whose chief characteristics are friction noises, i.e., plosives, affricatives, fricatives, and sibilants, except ʃ and s; (3) all glide vowels; (4) the nasal ŋ; and (5) the aspirate h.

The Short Vowels

If one utters the vowel ɪ as in the word *sit* so that the vowel has the duration of i as in *seat*, the vowel will, if the quality of the ɪ is kept pure throughout its utterance, appear to have changed to the i phoneme. A part of the ɪ characteristic is the shortness of duration of utterance.

Other English vowels whose phonemic values lie partly in the shortness of the time given to their utterance are ɛ, æ, ɒ, ʌ, ʊ, and ḷ. The shortness of utterance is so prominent a part of the perceptual characteristics of these vowels that if "long" vowels in adjacent phonemes be spoken with short duration they will seem to change in phoneme. *Seat* spoken with shortened i seems to be almost sɪt; just as sɪːt resembles sit. Many errors in foreign dialects of English are due to this perceptual confusion of vowel quality with vowel length.

In order to produce the effect of shortness of duration the vowel must be cut off sharply. This is accomplished in English by the succeeding consonant. Thus it happens that none of the "short" vowels appear finally in a stressed syllable of an English word; obversely, "long" vowels are those that may appear as final stressed sounds. Thus we have *pea, pa, paw, pooh, purr* pɜ or pɜ˞, and even *par* pɑ (or pa in Maine and elsewhere in New England).

---

[4] A distinction needs to be made at this point between the question as to whether or not a sound can be produced in isolation and whether or not, if so produced, it will "seem natural." Strictly speaking, there are certain groups of sounds that cannot be produced in isolation because their perceptual pattern becomes evident only when there is a movement to another sound. These are the stop plosives, the intervowel glides, and the glottal sounds. When an attempt is made to produce these sounds in isolation, the distortion is so great that we conclude that it cannot be done. There are other sounds that, because they are continuants, can be produced in isolation but since they are customarily of very short duration they lose their "natural" quality when prolonged.

But we do not have such words as **pɪ, pɛ, pæ, pɒ, pʌ, pʊ**, or **pl̩**, since these sounds would lose a significant part of their individuality without succeeding consonants to cut them off short.

To summarize: If one were to arrange the vowels in a diagram on the basis of their overtone structures and the tongue positions required to produce them, the short vowels would lack definite places in the scheme. Their characteristics are partly dependent upon a thing that can be perceived only when these sounds are uttered in syllables. They have "tongue-placement" and overtone structure, but they have more—characteristics of temporal development and relationships to other sounds.

Friction Sounds

The mechanical noises used in English speech, made at the lips or in the mouth, are blended so closely with preceding or succeeding sounds that when they appear without such sounds they seem merely like meaningless mechanical noises; at least the longer they are prolonged if they are continuants, or the more times they are repeated in a series if they are plosives or affricatives, the less they appear as speech sounds and the more as mere mechanical noises. Probably the chief reason why these mechanical sounds made in isolation seem not to be speech sounds, is that when so made they are pure (not mixed with, or influenced by, other sounds); and in speech we have come to identify these mechanical sounds by the blends they make with other sounds. This can be demonstrated by making a phonographic recording (say on a low fidelity dictating machine with a mechanical cutting head) of isolated friction sounds like **f, θ**, or **p**. On the playback they will be either missing completely or so distorted as to be unidentifiable. Put these sounds in syllables, even in nonsense syllables, and their characteristics appear. Why? Because in our person-to-person speech contacts under adverse conditions we are often unable to hear the friction noises, but we identify the missing elements by the transition sounds that appear between the friction sounds and their preceding or succeeding neighbors.

Compare, for example, **ʃ** and **f** followed by **æ**. Between the **ʃ** and the **æ** is a short glide vowel, partly voiced and partly unvoiced; the **æ** following the **f** is more nearly a pure vowel, not introduced by a glide. This change in the·vowel is an incident of the change from ʃ to f and hence becomes perceptually a part of the difference between the consonants—a part so important that when we can actually hear no other differences we still seem to hear them because of our tendency to reconstruct the whole of a "gestalt" from a significant part of it. Thus we hear the words *shad* and *fad* as significantly different even when spoken under conditions that make the ʃ and f alone impossible to hear. Since the uninitiated is aware of only one essential difference between ʃ and f—the difference in mechanical noises—he thinks he has heard these noises.

Let us take for another example the difference between the syllables **æv** and **æʒ**. Here the identifying differences are partly the off-glides from the vowels that introduce the consonants, which are ordinarily, at least in context, sufficient to engender the perception of the fricative patterns for these sounds.

We may say, then, that the ʃ, or any other friction-sound phoneme, includes not only the friction noise appropriate to it but also the sounds incidental to joining it to other sounds in a syllable. Thus we have as many ʃ sounds as we have ʃ combinations. The element that binds all members of the phoneme together is the friction noise; but, when one has had experience in listening to this sound in varying combinations one learns to identify the ʃ by its various incidental linking sounds. Conversely, we learn to recognize as defective, sounds that seem quite standard standing alone but differ in their linkings with other sounds.

As we have already pointed out, the sound **s** may be made in isolation from other sounds, since it has semantic significance even when standing alone. Many *s*-lisps sound quite regular when so uttered; but when they are made with the tongue or jaws in nonstandard positions the transition or linking sounds are unusual and unexpected, thus rendering the **s** defective in connected speech.

The plosives and affricates also present special kinesiologic phenomena. Let us compare the **k** sounds in the words *keen* and *mock*. They not only differ in place of production in the mouth and in the quality of the aspirated sound that links each with the rest of the word, but also in the portion of the plosive sound that is emphasized. In *mock* the implosion of the sound is the part that is strongly stressed and in *keen* it is the explosion. In fact, in *keen* one usually hears no implosion at all; and it is possible for one to perceive a perfectly convincing *k* in *mock* even though the speaker deliberately masks, subdues, or obscures the sound of the final explosion. We have therefore two *k* sounds that are not only different in fricative elements, but are actual reverses of each other. The *k* in *keen* is an explosive introduction to a vowel sound, while the *k* in *mock* is a sudden termination of a vowel. We have learned to recognize and identify the various linking sounds in these introductions and terminations so that they give us the clue to the plosive sound, even though acoustically the sounds identified may be radically different.

The Glide Vowels

It has been pointed out earlier in this text that the phonemic significance of a glide vowel depends more upon the direction of the glide than upon the positions of beginning and ending of the movement. Two vowel glides, one beginning in the position of **a** and proceeding to about the position of **o**, and the other beginning in the position of **ɒ** and proceeding to about the position of **u**, both fall clearly within the same phoneme, broadly transcribed as **aʊ**. Yet these two glides overlap only slightly in the sections of the vowel gamut that they span. It is clear, therefore, that if the **aʊ** phoneme is to be seen completely, it must be viewed from the kinesiologic point of view as well as from that of vowel qualities and positions. There is, however, another kinesiologic consideration that must be recognized: the vowel glide must not only proceed in a given direction from one approximate position to another but it must also be accomplished with considerable speed. If the **aʊ** glide is made slowly the perceptual experience of the glide will disappear and the auditor will hear only a series of vowels graduated in quality from **a** to **u**. What we have just said applies equally well to both crescendo and diminuendo glides; **ja** and **wɑ** are as much kinesiologic phenomena as are **aɪ** and **aʊ**.

The ŋ Sounds

The *m* and *n* sounds may be perceived as either the initial or the final elements in a syllable; the sound **ŋ**, however, when uttered initially in a syllable, is usually heard as **n**. This auditory illusion is probably due simply to the fact that no English words employ the **ŋ** in the initial position. The **ŋ** is also (and probably for a similar reason) perceived with difficulty if standing alone or following ɜ, r, ḷ, or l. Thus we may say that ŋ depends for its perception more than do other nasals upon its place in a series of acoustic events.

The Aspirate Attack

The sound **h** is sometimes said to be merely a whispered vowel, there being, therefore, as many *h*'s as there are vowels. These aphorisms are only superficially true. If one whispers the vowel **a** and does not join the sound so uttered to any voiced sound, no *h* is produced. If one whispers **a** and then, holding the vowel steady, merely adds voice to the utterance, the *h* appears; but it is not perceived until the precise moment at which voicing begins. Thus the *h* is merely a perceptual phenomenon depending upon the addition of voice to an unvoiced vowel. Strictly speaking, the unvoiced vowel itself is no more an *h* than is the voiced vowel; the *h* is the momentary phenomenon of transition from the one to the other. If the transition be reversed, however, and the movement progresses from the voiced vowel to the unvoiced, no *h* results, although the transition from the voiced vowel to the unvoiced is as definitely sensible as is the reverse. We perceive an *h* in one case and not in the other merely because one transition has been employed as a speech sound while the other has not.

Reversed Speech

Some objects that we view must be seen from certain perspectives to be rightly understood. Such are printed words. A pencil is as easily recognizable from one point of view as from another, but the word *pencil* must be viewed with the *p* at the left and the *l* at the right. Analogously, most sounds must be heard from a standard "perspective"; that is, the acoustic events cannot be reversed without distorting the perception of the sound so reversed. Much can be learned about the kinesiology of speech by playing phonograph recordings backwards. It will be discovered that some sounds are reversible and some are not. All the continuant sibilants and fricatives are reversible with relatively little distortion. The vowels are reversible only if intoned as in song. The spoken vowel, if reversed, suffers a distortion of inflection that so markedly alters the effect as to seem to make a change of phoneme. In addition to this reversal of inflection pattern, a final spoken vowel is further modified on being played backward by an apparent *h*-attack. The unvoicing of the final portion of the vowel is not heard as an *h* when spoken normally, but when reproduced in reverse the *h* is strikingly apparent. Reversal of the glide sounds produces diametric changes of the direction of the glides, the **aʊ** becoming **wa**, the **aɪ** becoming **ja**, etc. Thus *now* in reverse seems very like *wan*. Reversal of voiced plosives changes them very little; but reversal of voiceless plosives produces a marked change. In the usual utterance of the surd plosives, a voiceless glide vowel is produced at the moment of explosion. Since this "off-glide" is so definitely a sound incidental to joining the plosive to the succeeding sound or to bringing the articulatory organs to the neutral position after a final plosive, it is usually unnoticed, at least by the uninitiated hearer. But when the plosive is reversed the sound that now precedes the plosive becomes conspicuous.

In summary, we may say that from the point of view of kinesiology a speech sound has two aspects, production and perception. Its production consists of a series of physical events in which the energy of an air stream is converted into sound waves to be propagated into space in a given pattern of pitch, quality, volume, and duration. Its perception consists of the recognition of this physical pattern, and for this recognition only a portion of the physical pattern need be actually sensible; indeed, a large portion of the pattern may be completely wanting.

Whispered Speech

Whispering is an interesting phonetic phenomenon. One who does not vocalize in speaking is of course hampered in conveying his meanings, because, first, his speech lacks carrying power, and second, the difference between surd and sonant analogues is markedly reduced, since all his sounds are virtually surds.

With respect to the first of these limitations, it should be noted that the reduction of power is in the low-frequency range (see Chapter 14). The high-frequency sounds are not reduced in power; in fact they may actually be increased in power to compensate for low-frequency losses. Thus in whispered speech the pattern of energy distribution is greatly modified. The sounds that are most intense in voiced speech are least intense in whispered speech.

In meeting the second limitation, that of differentiating surds from sonants, the whisperer resorts to certain interesting devices. In unvoiced speech the effect of vocalization is produced by a partial closure of the glottis as the air stream is forced through between the vocal lips. The friction of this passage generates a high-frequency noise capable of activating the resonators of the throat and mouth so as to produce the characteristic tones of the vowels. When the cords are widely separated, this generating noise and its attendant vowel effects cease. In voiced speech the effect of an *h* is produced by attacking the vowel while the glottis is closing to the point of phonation; in whispered speech the *h*-effect is produced by attacking the vowel while the glottis is closing from its most open posture to that point of partial closure that produces a maximum of friction noise without actual vibration of the cords. Thus the "whispered" *h* and the "voiced" *h* are basically different; yet we learn to identify each. The difference between surd and sonant plosive analogues is produced by the device of making the surds more *fortis* than the sonants (see pages 273–275). Thus a whispered *time* may be made distinguishable from *dime*, or *peat* from *beat*, or *curl* from *girl*.

The surd and sonant analogues among the fricative and sibilant continuants cannot usually be distinguished in whispered speech.

Chapter 12 Narrow Transcription

We have indicated previously that the purpose of narrow transcription is to indicate variants within the phonemes of a language. It aims to set down finer shades of difference than can be represented by the relatively gross phonemic symbols presented at the beginning of this book. Consequently narrow transcription employs additional symbols along with various modifying signs to indicate these variants. Most of these symbols and many of the modifying signs have been used and explained in presenting the material of this section. The following table of sounds contains all those that have been used in this book, including those presented in the original *Table of Phonetic Symbols*. The additional symbols that are but refinements of distinction for purposes of close transcription and to aid in a better understanding of the phonetic principles involved are starred; symbols representing foreign sounds are listed separately.

Table of Phonetic Symbols Used in This Book

English Consonants

	Printed Symbol	*Key Word*	*Transcription*
1.	**p**	pay	**peɪ**
2.	**b**	bay	**beɪ**
3.	**m**	may	**meɪ**
4.	**t**	tip	**tɪp**

	Printed Symbol	Key Word	Transcription
5.	**d**[1]	dip	**dɪp**
6.	**n**	nip	**nɪp**
7.	**c***	key	**ci**
8.	**ɟ***	geese	**ɟis**
9.	**ɲ***[2]	sing	**sɪɲ**
10.	**k**	call	**kɔl**
11.	**g**	gone	**gɔn**
12.	**ŋ**	lung	**lʌŋ**
13.	**f**	fat	**fæt**
14.	**v**	vat	**væt**
15.	**ɱ***	caveman	**keɪvɱæn**
16.	**θ**	thin	**θɪn**
17.	**ð**	then	**ðɛn**
18.	**s**	sue	**su**
19.	**z**	zoo	**zu**
20.	**ʃ**	shoe	**ʃu**
21.	**ʒ**	vision	**vɪʒən**

Non-English Consonants[3]

	Printed Symbol	Key Word	Transcription	Description
1.	**ɸ**	Pfennig (German)	**ɸɛnɪç**	voiceless bilabial fricative
2.	**β**	Havana (Spanish)	**aβana**	voiced bilabial fricative
3.	**ç**	ich (German)	**ɪç**	German *ich-laut*, voiceless lingua anterior-palatal fricative

[1] The symbol **d** is sometimes used to represent an affricate **d͜ʒ** combination. It is one of the supplementary IPA symbols.

[2] Also used sometimes to represent an **ɲj** glide.

[3] **F** and **ʋ** are additional symbols used in close transcription to represent lax *f* and lax *v*, respectively.

Printed Symbol	Key Word	Transcription	Description
4. ɹ	fille (French)	fiɹ	voiced lingua anterior-palatal fricative
5. x	ach (German)	ɑx	German *ach-laut*, voiceless lingua posterior-palatal fricative
6. ɣ	rogar (Spanish)	řoɣɑř	voiced lingua posterior-palatal fricative

English Vowels

Printed Symbol	Key Word	Transcription
1. i	eat	it
2. ɪ	it	ɪt
3. e*	vacation	vẹkeɪʃən
4. ɛ	pen	pɛn
5. æ	man	mæn
6. a*⁴	ask	ask as often pronounced in America. Between æ and ɑ
7. ɑ	father	fɑðɚ
8. ɒ*⁴	sorry	sɒrɪ̣ as commonly pronounced in England and frequently in America. Between ɑ and ɔ
9. ɔ	all	ɔl
10. o*	notation	nọteɪʃn̩
11. ɵ*	stone	stɵn New England short *o*

---

⁴ The symbols **a** and **ɒ** and **ɜ** are starred as representing "refinements of distinction" only in terms of general American speech. It is recognized that many Southerners and Easterners will rightfully consider them as broad transcription symbols. They could, in fact, easily be considered as broad symbols needed for the transcription of American English in general, since they represent rather gross variants that occur frequently. They are starred in part because they are not here considered as phonemic for the language as a whole, even though they may be for some individuals in certain sections of the country.

	Printed Symbol	Key Word	Transcription
12.	ʊ	pull	pʊl
13.	u	pool	pul
14.	ʌ	sun	sʌn
15.	ə	sofa	soʊfə used only in unstressed syllables
16.	ɝ* [4]	bird	bɝd as pronounced in Southern England and parts of Eastern and Southern America
17.	ɝ	bird	bɝd
18.	ɚ	better	bɛtɚ as pronounced in general American dialect
19.	l̩ [5]	little	lɪtl̩ vowelized clear *l*
20.	ɫ̩*	buckle	bʌkɫ̩ vowelized dark *l*

Non-English Vowels [6]

	Printed Symbol	Key Word	Transcription	Description
1.	y	pur (French)	pyr	rounded i
2.	ʏ	grün (German)	gʁʏn	rounded ɪ
3.	ø	œufs (French)	ø	rounded e
		Goethe (German)	gøtə	
4.	œ	seul (French)	sœl	rounded ɛ
		können (German)	kœnən	

[5] This symbol is used in broad transcription to represent all varieties of the vowel *l*.

[6] Additional vowel symbols: ɯ a spread **u**, ʊ̵ a spread ʊ, ɤ a spread **o**, i a centralized **i**, ʉ a centralised **u** and ɐ a lightly stressed **a**. With the exception of ɐ, the sounds represented by these symbols do not occur regularly in any of the languages derived from Latin.

Members of the *r* Phoneme [7]

Printed Symbol	Key Word	Transcription	Description
1. ɝ	early	ɝlɪ̣	a high central vowel
ɚ	better (general American)	bɛtɚ	
2. r	bar	bɑr	glides to or from the
	rob	rɑb	ɝ position
3. ř*	hard (Scotch)	hɑřd	rolled or trilled *r*
4. ɾ*	very (British)	vɛɾɪ̣	semirolled or one-tap *r*
5. ɹ*	try	tɹɑɪ	tongue-tip fricative *r*
6. ʁ*	grape (one of the possible pronunciations)	gʁeɪp	back-tongue *r*
7. Ř* [8]	Rote (German)	Řotə	uvular rolled *r*
8. ʁ* [8]	Rath (German)	ʁɑt	velar or uvular fricative *r*

Methods of Initiating or Terminating
Certain Speech Sounds

Printed Symbol	Key Word	Transcription	Description
1. h	hat	hæt	glottal fricative approach or termination, articulatory mechanism stationary

[7] Some phoneticians list also a bilabial trilled *r*. It is not an IPA symbol.

[8] **R** is a one-tap trill. The IPA also gives **χ** as a voiceless form of **ʁ**. All of these *r*'s might be used interchangeably in the illustrative words.

Printed Symbol	Key Word	Transcription	Description
2. ɦ*⁹	tea	tʰi	glottal fricative approach or termination, articulatory mechanism in movement
	what	ɦwɑt	
	huge	ɦjudʒ	
3. ʔ	up, but (as sometimes heard)	ʔʌp	glottal explosive approach or glottal implosive termination
		bʌʔ	
4. t͡ʃ ¹⁰	church	t͡ʃɝt͡ʃ	oral explosive approach or oral implosive termination
d͡ʒ	judge	d͡ʒʌd͡ʒ	
s͡t	stance	stæn͡ts	
z͡d	razed	reɪz͡d	
etc.			

Receding Intervowel Glides

Printed Symbol	Key Word	Transcription	Description
1. eɪ	made	meɪd	diminuendo glide from mid front vowel e to high front key vowel position
2. aɪ	dine	daɪn	diminuendo glide from low front vowel a to high front key vowel position
3. ɔi	point	pɔɪnt	diminuendo glide from low back vowel ɔ to high front key vowel position

⁹ The IPA lists **h** as a voiceless laryngeal fricative and **ɦ** as a voiced laryngeal fricative. The symbol **ħ** is used in the IPA to represent a "pharyngeal fricative," the voiced equivalent of which is **ʕ**.

¹⁰ The ligature is not used in broad transcription.

	Printed Symbol	Key Word	Transcription	Description
4.	**aʊ**	sound	**saʊnd**	diminuendo glide from low front vowel **a** or low central vowel **ɑ** to high back key vowel position
5.	**oʊ**	load	**loʊd**	diminuendo glide from mid back vowel **o** to high back key vowel position
6.	**ɑr** etc.	far	**fɑr**	diminuendo glide from any vowel to high central key vowel position
7.	**ɑl** etc.	doll	**dɑl**	diminuendo glide from any vowel to lateral key vowel position
8.	**ɛə*** etc.	bed	**bɛəd**	receding schwa glides diminuendo glides from any vowel to neutral key vowel position

Approaching Intervowel Glides

	Printed Symbol	Key Word	Transcription	Description
1.	**w**[11]	wait	**weɪt**	crescendo glides from high back key vowel position to any vowel
2.	**j**	yes	**jɛs**	crescendo glides from high front key vowel position to any vowel

[11] The symbol **ɥ** is sometimes used to represent a close **w**.

Printed Symbol	Key Word	Transcription	Description
3. 1^{12} ɫ	lead loop	**lid** **ɫup**	crescendo glides from lateral key vowel position to any vowel
4. r	rob	**rɑb**	crescendo glides from central key vowel position to any vowel
5. əɛ*	bed	**bᵊɛd**	crescendo glides from neutral key vowel position to any vowel

Modifying Signs for Use in Close Transcription[13]

1. ˌ placed beneath **m**, **n**, and **l** indicates that these sounds, usually considered as consonants, have become syllabic. Examples: *cotton* **katn̩**, *captain* **kæpm̩**,[14] and *little* **lɪtl̩**. The IPA uses the same sign under *r* to indicate syllabification. In this book we have followed the American practice of using the vowel symbol **ɚ** to represent the unstressed *r* vowel in words such as *better* **bɛtɚ**.

2. ː placed after a vowel indicates that its sound is long in duration as compared to an unmarked vowel. Example: *park* **pɑːk**.

3. ˈ placed after a vowel indicates intermediate length. Example: *research* **riˈsɝˈtʃ**.

4. ˔ placed after a vowel and slightly above the line indicates a raising of the position for the vowel.

5. ˕ indicates lowering.

---

[12] Other *l* symbols are **l̪** for a very clear *l* and **ʎ** for the **lj** glide.
[13] This is a partial list based upon that given by the International Phonetic Association. It contains the more commonly used signs.
[14] As sometimes heard.

6. ⌐ indicates advancing or fronting.

7. ⌐ indicates retracting.

8. | placed above and to the left of a syllable indicates primary accent.

9. ₁ placed below and to the left of a syllable indicates secondary accent.

10.   placed above two symbols indicates that the sounds represented are not separate and distinct but fused, thus t͡s, z͡d.

11. ₙ placed below a symbol indicates that the sound, not ordinarily made so, is made dentally. Example: dental *t* is t̪.

12. ₒ placed below a symbol indicates the partial or complete unvoicing of a sound that is ordinarily voiced.

13. ᵥ placed below a symbol indicates the partial or complete voicing of a sound that is ordinarily unvoiced.

14. ~ placed over a symbol indicates nasalization of a sound that is ordinarily nonnasal.

15. ţ retroflexing is indicated by a curl added to the right of the symbol for the sound. Thus a retroflex *t*, *d*, *l*, or *r* is written as t̢, ɖ, ļ, or ɽ.

16. ˇ placed over a symbol indicates a trill.

17. ɬ indicates that the sound is "dark" or produced farther back in the oral cavity.

18. ɦ indicates that this sound is made with the articulatory mechanism in motion.

19. æᴵ, ouᵂ, nᵗ, etc., indicates that the sounds written above the line are present but in a weakened or abbreviated form. Examples (as sometimes pronounced): *fad* **fæᴵd**, *toward* **touᵂɚd**, and *defence* **dɪfɛnᵗs**.

20. . placed under a vowel symbol indicates partial unstressing which does not go all of the way to ə. The vowel remains identifiable although considerably unstressed, thus: **æˌdrɛs, ɔfįs**.

Sample Transcriptions

In order to present some of the problems of narrow transcription we have summarized below the uses of some of the symbols and modifying signs. Each part presents a different problem. Possible alternate pronunciations are written vertically below the sound in question. *The following examples are in no way concerned with the question of right and wrong pronunciation.* They are intended to illustrate the representation of different modes of utterance.

Unstressing and Syllabic Consonants

He	added	that	if	the	chasm	had	been	deeper	the
he	**ædẹd**	**ðæt**	**ɪf**	**ðə**	**kæzɪ̣m**	**hæd**	**bɪn**	**dipɚ**	**ði**
ɪ̣	ə				ə	æ	ɪ̣		ə	ɪ
ə					ṃ	ə				ɪ̣

accident	would	have	been	fatal.
æksɪ̣dɛnt	**wʊd**	**hæv**	**bɪn**	**feɪtəl**
ə ɛ̣			æ		l̩
ɪ			ə		
ə					

Duration

Farm	**fɑrm**	opposite	**ɑ·pozɪt**
	fɑːm	this city	**ðɪsːɪtɪ̣**
	fɑᵊm	hot tea	**hɑtːi**

Raising, Lowering, Fronting, and Retracting

cat **kæˑt** lowered toward **a**
   kæˍt raised toward **ɛ**
cop **kɑˬp** retracted tongue position
   kɑˎp fronted tongue position

Accent

dictionary	**ˈdɪk ʃən ˌɛri**	defect	**ˈdi ˌfɛkt**
	ˈdɪk ʃən ə rɪ̣		**dɪ̣ ˈfɛkt**
	ˈdɪk ʃn̩ rɪ̣		

Oral Plosive Approach or Termination

church t͡ʃɝt͡ʃ   bus station bʌs s͡teɪʃən

judge d͡ʒʌd͡ʒ   bʌsːteɪʃən

Partial Voicing or Unvoicing

dog dɔg̊ (dialectal)   satisfy saṭɪsfaɪ

bet b̥ɛt (dialectal)   Betty bɛtɪ

Nasalization

man mæ̃n   on ɑ̃n

Retroflexing

turn t̢ɝn   row ɽoʊ

Use of c, ɟ, and ɲ

Go get the key to the car.

goʊ ɟɛt ðə ci tṳ ðə kɑr

Sing a song of thanksgiving.

sɪɲ ə sɔŋ əv θæɲcsɟɪvɪɲ

Use of ŋ

The caveman emphasized his words.

ðə keɪvmæn ɛmpfəsaɪzd hɪz wɝdz

    ŋ   ɱf

         mpɸ

Use of r, ř, ɹ, and ʀ

Don't gripe, try to be merry.

doʊnt gʀaɪp tɹaɪ tṳ bi mɛrɪ

     r   r   ř

                   ɾ

Use of ɦ

Where the huge house tops the hill

ɦwɛr ðə ɦjudʒ haʊs tʰɑps ðə hɪl

Indication of Drawls, Shortened Glides, and Accidental Glides

Pool **pul**	Cat **kæt**	Please **pliz**
pu^{ə}**l**	**kæ**^{ə}**t**	**p**^{ə}**liz**
pu^{wə}**l**	**kæ**^{ɪjə}**t**	**pəliz**
puwəl	**kæjət**	

SECTION III
Phonetic Metamorphology

Chapter 13   Phonemic Etymology

Linguistics is the science concerned with the study of all forms of arbitrarily coded human communication. Philology is that branch of linguistics whose business is the study of *verbal* communication. Etymology is that branch of philology that is concerned with the histories of individual words, tracing their changes from age to age and from language to language. Phonetic metamorphology is that aspect of etymology in which the scrutiny of the scientist is directed at the changes of *sound* of the spoken word. Since up to recent times there has been no accurate record of the phonology of verbal sounds comparable to the written forms in books and manuscripts, the etymologist who studies phonetic metamorphology must rely more upon speculation and inference than he who scrutinizes the visible records of past verbal forms.

What Is a Word?

In the chapters of this book that are concerned with the changes of phonetic form, the term *word* is employed frequently. Of all the words commonly used, and ostensibly understood, this symbol *word* is itself the most difficult to define. A *word* is a unit in the code of oral and/or written communication. The term has two aspects: the meaning, and the vehicle that carries the meaning. These verbal vehicles are of two sorts: (1) purely arbitrary, coded forms,[1] such as *cat* and *feline*, *dog* and *canine*, *hand* and *manual*, *eye* and *ophthalmic*, *amicable* and *friendly*; and (2) forms that are related to the verbal meanings. These relationships of forms to meanings are of three kinds: (a) forms that are acoustically imitative of the thing named, such as *sizzle*, *tinkle*, *bark*, *pop*, *giggle*, *stutter*, *hiss*, *buzz*, *thunder*, *rumble*; (b) forms that suggest, or imitate, by lips, tongue, or design of letter, the shape or behavior of the thing named, such as *plate*, *flat*, *splash*, *plane*, *nick*, *teeny*, *snout*, *sneer*, *ball*, *roll*; and (c) forms that carry meanings of things discussed by children in the articulatory mode of children, such as *papa*, *mama*, *baby*, *bye-bye*, *bow-wow*, *daddy*, *pooh-pooh*, *doo-doo*, *wee-wee*.

Although a given word may mean many things to a given user, varying from situation to situation, it probably never means exactly the same to two speakers or to a speaker and hearer. If a given word assumes two different phonetic patterns having substantially identical meanings, the two verbalizations constitute two forms of the same word (*either* aɪðə vs. *either* iðə). If a word appears in two written or printed forms with the same pronunciation and the same meanings, the two are one (*labor* and *labour*). But when two oral or two written forms, though traceable to the same parent form, have diverse meanings, they may be regarded as two words. Thus *primer* (a first reader) and *primer* (a first coat of paint) are virtually two words, though pronounced alike in England and in parts of Canada. So also *capital* and *capitol* are different words. Even two codified units of the same ancestry, the same phonetic structure, and the same written form may be thought of as two words if their meanings are divergent. The expressions, "I *lay* down yesterday," and "I will *lay* my hand on the book," involve two different words spelled *lay*, both pronounced leɪ. One of the common causes of the change of the phonetic form of a word is the separation and specialization of its meanings; and one of the common causes of the separation of meanings of a word is its divergent pronunciation. This is more than a hysteron-proteron analysis. It is not the question of which

---

[1] The arbitrary nature of these words is attested by the fact that in each pair parallel meanings are precisely indicated by symbols of radically different phonetic forms and of quite different etymology. The great majority of English words are of this kind, though some of the words may have come originally from nonarbitrary parentage.

always comes first, the chicken or the egg; sometimes one is first, and sometimes the other.

The etymologist who studies the visible word notes the Latin *charta*, a leaf of paper. He notes that the word began to evolve in meaning until it signified not so much the physical thing as the thing drawn or written upon the paper or even an idea or principle exemplified by the writing on the paper, as the *Magna Charta*. He notes that in French the word has two forms *carte* and *charte*, the former having a meaning more nearly like that of the original Latin, and the latter showing a specialized evolution of meaning along two lines, one signifying a document written upon the paper and the other signifying a drawing upon the paper. In English *carte* becomes *card*; while *charte* becomes *chart*, and practically loses one of its meanings in passing from one language to the other. He notes also related words, such as *charter*, and *cartographer*, *cartridge*. He notes, again, the changes of endings from language to language. He studies the modern influence of the surviving parent form upon the meaning and spelling of the modern forms. These and many other studies of the ancestry of these words are the business of the visual etymologist.

The oral etymologist, on the other hand, notes that for the initial sound of the modern words *card* and *chart* we have definitely different sounds **k** and **tʃ**. For the ending sounds we have **d** and **t**. He notes that in the related words *charta, cartographer, cartridge,* **k** is used as a beginning sound in modern pronunciations, and that in charter **tʃ** is employed. It seems safe to assume that at some time in the history of these words *ch* was pronounced in two ways, as a back consonant and as a front one. In every one of the related words except *card*, the sound following the *r* is **t**. The oral etymologist infers from this that the original sound represented by the *t* in *charta* was probably an unvoiced consonant. He guesses further that in changing from *carte* to *card*, a significant number of persons sounded the second consonant with a sufficiently unaspirated effect (see page 270) to suggest a voiced consonant. These inferences are the business of the phonetician. He is concerned with those pronunciations about which he has some reason to be confident. Hence he must overlook in his observations most of the ancient forms whose pronunciations can never be surely known and center his attention upon those forms of whose pronunciation he is sure—usually the modern forms only. Thus he may overlook changes of meaning, changes of spelling, changes of grammatical inflection, and changes of context, except in so far as these changes must be kept in mind in identifying a word, and he must center his attention upon those few members of the evolutionary series whose pronunciation is known. It usually happens in this study that he cannot trace the pronunciation of a word through this evolutionary cycle. *All he can do is to take the few pronunciations that are known* and compare them, whether or not the forms studied are descendents of one another, or are descended from another form about whose pronunciation he can only hazard a guess. The changes involved in this study of phonetic metamorphology are therefore primarily *changes of sound.*

The Biology of Phonetic Changes

In its most fundamental analysis etymology is a study of certain kinds of change in human behavior. If the human machine were made of steel or glass there would probably be, not a hundred or so English dialects, but one. The human machine, however, is made of protoplasm, a substance capable of great variability of form and adjustability of function. Hence ceaseless changing is the rule. That these changes are by no means random variations is attested by the laws of "consonant shifts" as stated by Verner, Grimm, Grassmann, Burgmann, *et al.*; [2] and that these changes are the result of the operation of many causes is attested by the numerous exceptions to the laws. The more powerful the factor that produces a change, the more definitely predictable will be the course of the change, and hence the more nearly universal the law; but the weaker and more conflicting the factors of change, the less predictable the change will be and hence the less easily discernible, will be the etymologic law that expresses the trend of the change.

The phonetic changes from age to age apparently do not evolve any considerable number of new sounds, but make use of sounds once discarded or even of sounds discarded from words in current use. Hence the science of phonetic metamorphology concerns itself quite largely with interchangings among the sounds of speech with which we are already familiar in modern languages.

[2] See Webster's *New International Dictionary,* 2nd ed., G. & C. Merriam Co., 1934, for statements of the laws referred to under the names here listed.

The factors of phonetic metamorphology are the following:

1. The innate variability of response of the peripheral neuro-muscular mechanisms of utterance and of writing.

2. The innate variability of auditory perception of the spoken word and of the visual perception of the written or printed word.

3. The innate variability of inner linguistic functions involved in spelling, grammar, and dialect.

The Significance of Verbal Doublets

Phonetic metamorphology is a function of historic time; and the farther into the past one explores to determine the phonetic structure of the ancestor of a given modern word, the less one may rely upon fact, and the more he must depend upon inference. Inferences as to the pronunciation of a given ancient word must be made with caution. There is, however, one method that may be used with some degree of assurance. This is the device of determining the pronunciation of the ancient word by comparing two or more of its surviving descendants. For example: One reads in classical Latin manuscripts the word MAIOR, with nothing at all to indicate the consonantal value of the middle letter of the word. However in both surviving descendants, *mayor* and *major*, the *a* and the *o* are linked by consonants. From this one fact one may infer that, in classical Latin: (1) The letter I once stood for a pure vowel (classical Latin had no *J*), and that this vowel was, in some contexts, changed to the semivowel **j**, which was at a later date changed to the affricate **dʒ** in certain frames of reference; or (2) the letter I in MAIOR was heard and pronounced by some users of Latin as **j** and by others as **dʒ**, both forms descending in parallel to modern English. Similar inferences may be drawn from the study of many other descendants of the Latin comparative adjectives ending in IOR. Without mechanical phonographic recordings of the speech of classical Romans the comparative validity of these inferences cannot definitely be established. One can be reasonably confident, however, that, if the Latin I stood for a vowel, it was a high front vowel, like **i** or **ɪ**, and that the transition to **j** was but a short step. Several existing forms of similar Latin words support this assumption: *ulterior, exterior, ameliorate,* and so forth. Several modern forms suggest that at some time the vowel **i** or **ɪ** changed to **j**: *mayor, prior, senior*, and others. Only two of the comparatives in IOR have made the transition to **dʒ**, in *majority* and *pejorative*, from the comparative forms of words for *great* and *bad*, respectively. An interesting inconsistency in the metamorphosis of the Latin ɪ occurs in the comparative adjective IVNIOR. The first ɪ in the word became **dʒ** in the modern form, and the second one **j**, to result in the English word *junior*. Incidentally the story of the v in IVNIOR is quite parallel to that of ɪ. The v in Latin was apparently used both as a vowel (probably **u** or **ʊ**) and as a species of **w**, a semivowel.

Inferences similar to those above may be drawn for any families of words that have descended to the present in two or more parallel forms. These forms, called *doublets*, are incontrovertible evidence of phonetic metamorphology, as convincing of phonetic metamorphosis as is that of Darwinian of biologic metamorphosis. One cannot be sure of the exact form of the ancestor, but one can draw some plausible theories as to the skeleton of the "missing link" by comparing the surviving, but differing, descendants. So doublets are solid, concrete evidence of the kinds of phonetic metamorphology involved in their changes from a parent form.

In the doublets cited in this section are many instances of relationships in which the connecting sounds do not appear in the doublets. Frequently the missing sounds are non-English. Between the *v* and the *b* in *Havana—Habana*, for example, the missing link in all probability was (and is) **β**, which has the labial position of the **b** and the fricative quality of the **v**; and between the *c* in *Ricardo* and the *ch* in *Richard* the missing link probably was **χ**. In short the reader must not assume that the change of sound illustrated by each of these English doublets was a direct metamorphosis from one word to the other. The order in which the two words of a given doublet appear could, in many instances, be reversed without changing the significance of the metamorphoses involved.

In the doublets presented as examples in this and the succeeding chapter the factors of the phonetic changes are indicated in the headings of the sections in which they appear. It is not to be assumed, however, that only one factor is involved in each pair of doublets. It may be understood that in each doublet at least the one factor mentioned in the heading is operative, but that in many doublets other factors than the one indicated may be as important. Thus it may be quite proper to cite the same pair of doublets as examples of two or more factors of metamorphology.

In other instances the pairs given are, strictly, not real etymologic relatives, but having somewhat similar pronunciations and overlapping meanings they have been drawn together and have influenced each other's phonetic form. *Fiscal* and *basket*, though real relatives etymologically, have got so far apart in pronunciation and meaning that they no longer influence each other; but *allege* and *allegation*, having similar spelling and related meanings, though they are of quite different descent, have become "adopted" relatives—as close as *defame* and *defamation*—and will doubtless continue to influence each other in phonetic form. So the Latin *populus* (people) and *pubes* (adult), of distinctly different origin, have strongly influenced each other. The first syllables of the two words are closely similar in consonants and, at least politically speaking, *people* are *adults*. Hence, as the words evolved, there eventually appeared in English three classes of derivatives: (1) words regularly descended from *populus*—*people* and *popular*; (2) words that are direct descendants of *pubes*—*pubic* and *puberty*; and (3) words that are the children of the union of these two lines of descent—*public* and *publication*. *Public* has the *u*, the *b*, and the *ic* that it received from one side of the house, and the *l* that it got from the other. Had the Romans used, as a common noun meaning *adult*, a word that was markedly different from *populus*—say, the participle *adultus*—instead of *pubes*, one might today speak of the *popular* (not *public*) policy; and the London "public-house" would be a *pop* (not *pub*).

The doublets cited in the next two chapters are not primarily designed to exhibit etymologic relationships, but rather to illustrate sound changes and the probable phonetic principles operating to cause such changes. Inferences concerning the derivations and relationships of words must not be made simply because they appear in parallel columns. If such relationships are not already known to the student, he should consult some recognized authority in the field of etymology. He will then find that in each case there exists some relationship that warrants the use of these words as illustrations of sound changes. In fine, the reader is cautioned not to force the parallelism between pairs of illustrative words

farther than is intended by the authors in displaying the principles
demonstrated by such illustrations.

The Phonemic Balance of the Language

Any change resulting from the extension and application of a
special trend of pronunciation is likely to cause changes in
sounds other than those directly affected by the trend. In any
language there is a constant rebalancing of phonemes to counter-
act the ambiguity of meaning that may result from the overloading
of a given phoneme. It is to be expected, for example, that when
the "*ar*" words gradually lose their *r* sounds and are pronounced
with the pure vowel ɑ, the phoneme ɑ will become heavily loaded
with ambiguous combinations. This particular unbalancing of the
language is especially likely to take place in parts of the English-
speaking world in which the "short *o* words" are pronounced
with the ɑ sound. In such dialects there are not only words like
father, calm, ah, and words like *nob, cob, lock, Tom,* but also the
very large additional group of words spelled with *ar.* This necessitates the removal of a group of these words to another phoneme,
in order to avoid such ambiguities as *balm* vs. *bomb, barb* vs. *Bob,
part* vs. *pot, tart* vs. *tot.* Consequently, in the resolution of the
ambiguities, the short *o* words may be separated in their pronunciation by being given a vowel quality of a distinctly different
phoneme than that of ɑ. The one usually employed is ɒ.

It is interesting to observe also that the æ phoneme seems now
to be in a state of flux. This flux is evidently a rebalancing of the
phonemes ɑ, a, æ, and ɛ. Note the following variant pronunciations:

catch	kɛtʃ	kætʃ
thresh ⎱ thrash ⎰	θrɛʃ	θræʃ
can	kɛn	kæn
half	haf	hæf
dance	dans	dænts
drama	drɑmə	dræmə
almond	amənd	ælmənd

One influence upsetting the balance of this æ phoneme is doubtless the pull of the stage pronunciation of such words as *chance,*

path, can't, etc. Another may be the accumulation of homophones such as *can't* and *cant, ant* and *aunt, have* and *halve,* etc.

In the conflict of styles, therefore, the direction of evolution is determined not only by the influence of the social, political, financial, and cultural leaders of a given community but also by the internal conflicts within the language itself. Leadership may produce a given change, which may in a succeeding generation produce another change that is quite separate from the style set originally by the leader or leaders who started the evolutionary wheels in motion; each change tends to upset the balance that has been achieved in the dialect. Other changes take place to re-establish the balance and they in turn start still other modifications. Thus a language is constantly in a state of flux and is never static until it ceases to be the language of the people and becomes only the language of the scholar and teacher. The more a language is limited in its use to a group of intellectual initiates, the more static it becomes; and the more a language escapes from the classroom and from the printed page, the more rapidly the processes of balancing and rebalancing take place.

Hence one would expect the unschooled pioneer, whose chief concern is the wresting of an economic security from the forces of nature, to modify his language rapidly, and the Roman Catholic priest or the Hebrew scholar to retard the evolution of the pronunciation of Latin and Hebrew, since they employ these languages with great care to preserve forms that they regard as proper and correct. Such languages achieve a balance that remains more nearly fixed than the living language of the person to whom a language is only a commonplace tool.

Chapter 14 Linguistic Changes of Sound

Inner Linguistic Functions

Some of the factors of phonetic metamorphology are to be found upon examination of the linguistic processes of the highest levels of the central nervous system. In the motor association areas of the cortex of the cerebrum, usually on the left hemisphere, are established the patterns of utterance of word and phrase. The influence of these patterns, or engrams, is, in general, to preserve and to perseverate language forms; but in some contexts the engrams produce striking metamorphoses. For example:

1. Foreign words introduced into English may have sounds foreign to the language. These sounds are gradually recast in the mold of English sounds having similar neural engrams, as *Havana*, in which β has become **v**, or *Miller*, in which ɪ has substituted for **y**, or *Gretchen*, in which t∫ has supplanted ç.

2. Foreign spellings may have pronunciations different from those they would have in English. *Cuba, Mexico, llama, ski, coup de grâce* are recast into the English phonetic system.

3. Foreign words often make use of syllables which, though they may be easily pronounceable, seem alien to English word forms. These, too, are recast to employ syllables having engrams already established in the brain of the English speaker. Thus have developed *dandelion (dent de leon); catchup, ketchup, catsup (kechap); Brooklyn (Bruekelen); bedlam (Bethlehem); chestnut (castana); mushroom (mousseron).*

232

Changes of Sound in Reduplications

One of the aspects of the central mechanism of language is its tendency to repetitions and iterations. This tendency gives rise to what is known grammatically as reduplication. Reduplications stem from motor patterns far more primitive than the most primitive of ideational languages. These patterns are inherent in the very nature of animal life, with its constant cyclical metabolism. When in the evolutionary development of animals it became possible for them to signal to each other, repetitions of short bursts of this signal became the rule of life. The firefly flickers, the cricket chirps, the tree frog croaks. Reduplication is universal among animals with voice. This rhythmic repetition is inherent in the air-blood type of vegetation. Such animals, whether they cheep, whinney, bleat, bark, mew, or caw, produce interrupted voicing.[1] The human being has inherited a reduplicating central nervous system. Even in his sophisticated writings he marshals his utterances in measured beats and recurrent rhythms.

The most primitive of the human being's reduplications are those with which he strives to name the reduplicators around him. He names the animals in accordance with their calls, or his reduplicating perception of their calls. He notes two flycatchers, quite alike except in size, having similar cries: a high-pitched whistle, lasting a half a second or so, followed by a lower note of about the same length. He calls the larger the *phoebe*, and the smaller the *pewee*. Similarly he names the *cuckoo* and the *kiwi*. His children, with some help from their parents, call the dog *bow-wow*, the sheep, *bah-bah*, and the donkey, *he-haw*.

A little less primitive reduplicatives are the homely words, without pride of ancestry, invented expressly as substitutes for more erudite words in communication with or between simple folk in simple situations: *pee-pee*, *wee-wee*, *doo-doo*, *doodad*, *fiddle-faddle*, *flim-flam*, *gew-gaw*, *falderal*, etc.

More sophisticated reduplications come next, in which at least one of the units in the reduplication is a word in its own right, lineally descended from an earlier form, the other of the pair being

---

[1] See the discussion "Rhythm," in C. L. Meader and J. H. Muyskens, *Handbook of Biolinguistics*, Herbert C. Weller, 1950, p. 263.

fashioned to make a suitable mate in the reduplication. *Wishy-washy* is such a pair. The word is really *washy*; *wishy* has been added to amuse the hearer and to facilitate the utterance. So developed *mishmash, teeter-totter, pell-mell*. Whenever, in order to make the reduplication tongue-easy and ear-pleasing, one of the elements of the combination has to be changed, fidelity to the etymology may be sacrificed, and important changes of sound may be introduced.

At this point is may be said that reduplicatives are not mere repetitives. When the Hawaiian girl talks about her dance as the *hula-hula*, she is not simply repeating the word as a sort of an echo; the second part of the phrase is as important as the first. The first is a preparation for the second, and the second is a fulfillment of the first. To her the idea is too big for two syllables; it needs four. As either of the phoebe's notes is meaningless without the other, so is one *hula* quite inadequate.[2] In the word *rococo* (from the French *rocaille*) the second syllable became changed to fit the first in a smooth-running reduplication. The same is true also of *hotchpotch* (from hotchpot). So with *hurly-burly*—the *burly* adds nothing to the denotation of the word, but is an intrinsically empty word added merely to emphasize the meaning of *hurly*, which is a word in its own right. But in *tattoo* (from *taptoe*) it is the first syllable that is altered to make it more definitely reduplicative of the second.

As with *hurly-burly*, reduplicatives are often used by children for intensifiers or emphasizers, as in *wee-wee* house, *long-long* ago, *no-no* mama, *good-good* candy, *very-very* cold, etc. Some of these childish combinations persist into adulthood and are accepted as dignified verbalisms. Children also have various reduplicative series, distinctly ablaut[3] in character, by which they choose a child to play a special part in a game: *tit tat toe, three in a row*; or *eenie meenie minie moe*, etc.

Reduplicative compound words may be divided into three

---

[2] One notes a phenomenon parallel to reduplication in spoonerisms, those distortions of words or phrases in which initial consonants are exchanged, as in *Mangor Baine* for *Bangor Maine*. In the spoonerism the main trunks of the words are never reversed in order, only the consonant approaches. Significantly also, the consonants are always completely, never partially, changed; that is to say, it never would be *Bangor Baine* or *Mangor Maine*.

[3] See the discussion of the *ablaut* on page 255.

classes on the basis of vowel-consonant patterns: (1) Those in which the two elements of the pair are essentially identical in both vowels and consonants, such as *bon bon*,[4] *can can, mama*. (2) Those in which the vowels remain the same and the initial consonants change, as with *pell-mell, helter-skelter, humdrum*. (3) Those in which the consonants are the same (at least those in accented syllables) but the vowels change, as in *seesaw, mishmash, knick-knack*, and *crisscross* (from *Christ's cross*). These alterations of vowels are generally ablaut changes, i.e., the vowel in the second half of each pair is more open and more sonorous than that in the first.

Compare *pell-mell* and *pall-mall*, often pronounced exactly the same **pɛlmɛl**. There is little likelihood that *pall-mall* will ever be **pɛlmɑl** or **palmɛl**. Such forms would not be sufficiently reduplicative to suit the needs of the nervous system. There could be **pɛlpɑl** or **mɛlmɑl**, but not a combination in which both the initial consonant and the vowel change.

When a reduplicative is born such phonemic changes take place as are necessary to fit the coupled vocables into one of the three classes mentioned above.

Linguistic Idioms

Another aspect of the central or cerebral mechanism of language is that involved in the syntax of English. Many phrases or expressions, taking each word in its individual and distinctive meaning, are (or have become) *intrinsically* redundant, meaningless, ambiguous, or illogical. Yet they are learned by the child and made a part of his set of engrams to be combined automatically with intrinsically proper, meaningful, and logical words. Read the following as a foreign tourist in the United States would read it, consulting his travel dictionary to get the meanings word by word:

I am *going* to *remain* here.
By and *large* the new car is inferior to the old.
I *have* to *have* all I can get.
It is lucky for you that *it* is Christmas.
He was slow to *get* up and *get* his mail.

---

[4] The idea carried by this word, imported from the French, seems peculiarly conducive to reduplication. The English synonym is the reduplicative *sweetmeat*.

Then will you *now* do this for me?
He was *intro*duced *into* the club.
There are *here* only four children.
I was not mad *at* him, but I was angry *with* his brother.
He promised *faithfully* (faith lies in the keeping rather than in the
    giving of a promise).
Thank you *kindly* (thank you for your kindness).

With such intrinsically irrational utterances, meanings are tied,
not to the individual words, but to the combinations. As idioms
they are as clear in meaning as though they were individual words.
Indeed, from combinations such as these have evolved such
efficient and useful words as *nevertheless, however, although,
whereas, whereupon, herewith, hereto-fore, wherewith-al,* and *inasmuch.* However, whenever words used in idioms have lost the
distinctive, individual meanings they originally had, phonetic
changes may occur. Examples: *I have to have* **hæftə**, *I would
have gone* **wʊdəv**, *I am going to do it* **gɔɪntə**. The contractions
ain't I and *won't they,* as questions, are obviously survivals of a
quaint syntax, no longer employed in the uncontracted form, viz.,
am not I and *will not they;* the average speaker has so lost the
derivation of the contraction *ain't* that he may employ it in the
third person. A change of syntax thus often results in a change of
sound.

Another kind of idiom resulting in change of sound is the
modification of profane expressions so that one may swear without
feeling guilty about it or offending the hearer. Examples: *for gosh
sakes, gosh almighty, landsakes, gracious, dear me, oh dear, I don't
give a darn,* etc.

The Language of Solemnity

In contrast to these idomatic expressions engendering phonetic
metamorphosis are certain expressions that resist change, viz.,
those connected with poetry and religion. In fact there exists
what amounts to a separate English language for the expression of
religious and poetical thoughts. The nervous engrams for this
language are so firmly fixed that one finds it difficult to mix them
with the general form of English. One will not say, without
conscious effort, *thou are, you art, thou have,* or *you hast* (using
these verbs in the present indicative); but the expressions *thou art*

and *thou hast* say themselves. When one is thinking in biblical concepts, they are as easy to say as *you are* and *you have*, in other contexts. Along with the archaic conjugation of the verbs and the special declension of the pronouns, go dozens of archaic words— *behold, lo, yon,* etc.

This language of solemnity one learns without any formal schooling in its idioms, as the children of Paris learn French. Yet this language is surprisingly complex: in its conjugation the general rule is for the second person, singular, present indicative to end in *est* and the third person to end in *eth.* Yet the verbs most commonly used—*do, be, have, say,* etc.—are irregular in their conjugations. In addition to this conjugation for the present tense, there are special uses for the auxiliary verbs—*be, have, do, shall, will, may,* and *can*—in other tenses and moods.

Examples: present, *thou lovest, dost love, art loving*; imperfect, *thou wast loving*; future, *thou wilt love, shalt love*; perfect, *thou didst love, hast loved*; pluperfect, *thou hadst loved*; future perfect, *thou wilt* (or *shalt*) *have loved,* etc., through the subjunctive and imperative moods, using such forms as *mayst, mightst, canst, couldst, shouldst,* and *wouldst.* Extremely complicated; yet it comes easily to the solemn tongue.

Orthographic Factors of Change

The most conspicuous evidence of the phonetic metamorphology of English is the inconsistency of its spelling. English is obviously a phonographic language, yet many of its words are only roughly phonetic. Words of identical spelling are differently pronounced, *bass* (voice) vs. *bass* (fish); and words of different spelling are identically pronounced, *colonel* (officer) vs. *kernel* (the fruit of the grain). This inconsistency of phonography obtains not only in words of different origin, but even also in relatives: identical in spelling but differently pronounced are *again* əgɛn vs. *again* əgeɪn; different in spelling but identically pronounced are *plain* vs. *plane.* Such words of inconsistent orthography are fossils of earlier spellings or pronunciations or both. Their implication is that at various stages of the growth of the English language people adjusted the spelling of words to their pronunciation. It seems clear, however, that these adjustments have been piecemeal and by no means consistent in phonography from age to age.

English is a fabulous museum of linguistic fossils, not only of Anglo-Saxon and Old English, but also of hundreds of the languages of the world. One can trace the changes of pronunciation of the foreign language from which English words are borrowed by comparing the borrowings of one century with those of another, or by matching the English word borrowed from a given foreign tongue in some past century with that same word in the modern style of the foreign language. When the orthographic forms of these related present-day words are different one may make one or more of the following assumptions:

1. The word has phonetically evolved in the foreign language.

2. The word has changed orthographically in the foreign language, but not phonetically.

3. The word has phonetically evolved in its English history.

4. The word has changed in English only orthographically, not phonetically.

Only by comparison of what has happened to the individual members of large groups of phonetically analogous words can one know which of these four assumptions are valid in the case of a given word.

Alphabetic Changes

Another group of significant English fossils are the letters of the language. Just as the Bells (see page 309) developed a set of symbols accurately descriptive of the sounds they represented, so, apparently, spelling reformers of past eras have attempted to simplify English phonography. To be completely descriptive every phonogram should have some characteristic serif, diacritic, or overall form to show the following information: (1) Is it surd or sonant? (2) Is it nasal or oral in emission? (3) Is it a continuant? (4) Is it fricative? (5) Is it plosive? (6) Is it labial, lingual, guttural, or laryngeal? English literation shows evidences of attempts to display some of these descriptions in the very forms of the letters used to represent sounds.

Obviously it is impossible for us to fathom definitely the mechanization and motivation of changes in letter form. It is entirely possible that the apparently logical systems that obtain in letter forms are the result of unconscious manipulation of these forms, similar to the changes of word form that result from an unconscious attempt to simplify language by making it grammatically systematic—such as *hang, hanged* (instead of *hung*), or *freight, freighted* (instead of *fraught*). Changes in letter form apparently have been as capricious as those in suits, frocks, and hats. They have been most rapid, of course, in the cursive script, wherein each writer exhibits his own idiosyncrasies, probably not knowing whence his peculiarities came. The physician who writes ℞ at the beginning of his prescription may think that he is making the ancient sign for Jupiter, said to have been used by Roman doctors to propitiate the Gods, lest they take offense at his deigning to interfere with the course of fate; or he may think that he is writing a short form of *Rex*, the king of the Gods, Jove; or he may think that all prescriptions by licensed physicians must start with ℞ to make them legal; but most likely he is copying the copies of the copies of the prescriptions of some reputed Roman physician, or his secretary, who was too much in a hurry to write out the clearly understood word RECIPE, and who therefore clumsily telescoped the last five letters of the word into a simple scrawl on the downstroke of the R. In all likelihood there was little realization at that time that an age-long convention was being established. That ℞ is the product of haste and economy of effort on page space is shown by the fact that the same ℞ is used in the prayer book to indicate congregational responses.

So a person may write *viz.* and *ibid.* or *Xmas*, pronouncing them **vɪz, ɪbɪd, ɛksməs**, without knowing the complete form of *viz.* and *ibid.* and without realizing that originally *X* was the Greek letter *chi.*

Any group of workers who need to communicate with each other by writing develop special letter forms. So the proofreader corrupts the letter *d* (for *dele*) to ϑ; the physician writes ₥ for *mix*; āā for *of each*, and c̄ for *with*. Note the various special forms of the capital *P*: ¶ or ℙ for *paragraph*, P for *peso*. *P* as the Greek *rho* appears as ℗, the symbol of the Christ. The Latin *et* has various corruptions, from a mere + to the formal &.

Doubtless most of these changes of the letters were not arrived at by deliberation and formal agreement among writers, but were the result of acceptance of the leadership of persons famous and respected. Out of this changing letter form, the wielders of the stili, quills, chisels, brushes, pencils, and pens have accepted and formalized a set of symbols that is broadly logical in its phonetic symbolization. At what time each part of the alphabet of today was invented is of little moment, for the same genius that invented them is a continuing influence to preserve, adapt, and readjust them to changing pronunciations. The readjustment of the alphabet is one of the forces that effects changes of pronunciation.

Limiting the analysis to the English alphabet, *P* and *B*, *p* and *b*, *S* and *Z*, *s* and *z* appear to be attempts to represent analogous sounds with similar, but significantly different symbols. The special form of the letters *M* and *N*, *m* and *n* appears to represent the nasal element. The letter *w* ("double-*u*") and the letter *y* seem to represent the diphthongal forms of the vowels *u* and *i*, respectively. Their letter forms show the phonetic relationship. As a diphthongal representation the letter evolution may well have been *i* to *j* to *y*. The capital forms *I* and *J* are obvious relatives, the *J* representing the consonant, or diphthongal, analogue of *I*. The labial nature of the sounds *w*, *v*, and *u* is indicated by their similar forms, *W*, *V*, and *U*. The lip-rounding of *O* and *o* is obvious.

As suggested above, these phonographic systems were not necessarily conscious and deliberate inventions. In some cases carelessness, ignorance, laziness, or left-handedness (the ¶ sign of the paragraph is really a left-handed *P*; the *S* is a cursively drawn, left-handed *Z*) originally created new forms which others adopted and adapted to special uses. Considering the lower-case forms of the consonants *b*, *p*, *m*, *d*, *t*, *n*, *g*, *k*, *ng*, one can see either the fossil remains of a definite system or the first stage in the evolution of one. Remarkable agreement obtains between the IPA system and that which evolved as a "natural" growth of the language. Only four of the modern English phonograms, and only three of the IPA symbols, need changing to make the entire set internally consistent and logical, viz., *ng* (or *nk*), *t*, *k*, *g*. See Fig. 71. The substitution of ŋ for *ng* (or *nk*) is even now made in some glossaries and pronouncing dictionaries and may possibly be extended to literary texts. The *g* is very like the related plosives, *b* and *d*. If it were turned upside down it would be completely consistent with them. The *t* and *k* would require a complete change of design to show by their forms that they are plosives like *p*, and that they are voiceless relatives of *d* and *g*, respectively. The similarities and differences in letter form between *q* (*Q*) and *g* (*G*) are interestingly paralleled by the similarities and differences between *qu* (*QU*) and *gu* (*GU*) in such words as *vanquish* and

Bilabial	Linguarugal	Linguavelar	
b	d	g (ƃ)	Sonant
p	t (q)	k (g)	Surd
m	n	ng (ŋ)	Nasal

Fig. 71. Showing related English consonants in related letter forms.

languish. (See the following table.) The *Q* and the *G* in these words apparently show by their similarities that they are articulatory cognates, and by their differences that they are phonatory opposites. The letters **f** and **p** are close physiological relatives, their common ancestor being *φ*, which gave **f** its fricative nature and **b** its bilabial articulation. **v** and **b** are similarly related through **β**. These relationships are intriguingly suggested by the similarities between the capital *F* and *P* and the lower-case *f* and *p*.

The following are examples of similar, but significantly different, representations of surd vs. sonant consonants:

	Sonant			*Surd*
b	(bib)	vs.	p	(peep)
B	(bib)	vs.	P	(peep)
G	(goal)	vs.	C	(coal)
gu	(languish)	vs.	qu	(vanquish)
GU	(languish)	vs.	QU	(vanquish)
gu	(guest)	vs.	qu	(quay)
GU	(guest)	vs.	QU	(quay)
z	(zeal)	vs.	s	(seal)
Z	(zeal)	vs.	S	(seal)

Certain labial sounds vs. their tongue-tip analogues are the
following:

b	(bib)	vs.	d	(did)
B	(bib)	vs.	D	(did)
m	(maim)	vs.	n	(noon)
M	(maim)	vs.	N	(noon)

One labial sound vs. its labiodental analogue is the following:

p	(pipe)	vs.	f	(fife)
P	(pipe)	vs.	F	(fife)

One famous orthographic sound change appears in the pronunciation of the first sound in *you, yours,* and *ye.* These words
are all descendants of old Germanic words introduced by delta
plosives, possibly ţ and/or ḍ, from which also the modern German
du, dir, dich, and *die* are descended. In the Anglo-Saxon variety of
Old German the plosive nature of the initial sounds of these
words became softened to what was virtually a linguadental
fricative. Now the Anglo-Saxons had adopted the Latin alphabet,
but had added to it three runes from their previous letter system
—the thorn, the eth, and the wen. Since the thorn and the eth
(*đ* and *þ*) were often indifferently used to stand for both the θ
and the ð sounds, the second person pronoun and the definite
article were written sometimes with the eth and sometimes with
the thorn. Hence there came to be two more or less standardized
phonograms for the initial linguadental fricative of the article and
of the second person pronoun. Now in the hasty and careless
writing of the scribes the thorn, *þ,* became confused with the *y.*
People began to read *þ* as *y.* So developed two sets of parallel
words signifying the second person pronouns, and the definite
articles as well. These parallel sets have lasted to the present day
in the following forms:

Modern Spelling *Pronunciations*	*Ancient "correct"* *Pronunciations*
you **ju**	thou **ðu**[5]
ye **ji**	thee **ði**
ye (as in *ye editor*) **ji**	the **ði**

---

[5] It seems likely that *thou* has been preserved to modern times largely because
of its connection with religious and classical forms of communication. Were it

A similar spelling confusion involved the wen, þ, which apparently was a kind of a *w* sound. Its form, but not its sound, became confused with the *q* and the *g*, when these letters were followed by *u*. Hence in the thirteenth century (about the time when the eth was replaced by the *th*) the wen was eliminated from the alphabet, and the less ambiguous *w* took its place. At the time of this transition the þ, the *qu*, the *gu*, and the *w* were read with great confusion. To add to this babel growing out of the orthographic idiosyncrasies of the scribes (printing from type was still two centuries away) there was the confusion that had arisen from the introduction into English of certain words originally Teutonic but modified by the Normans, as they had accepted the French language and the Latin alphabet. So English speakers of today find themselves possessed of sets of parallel words reflecting these confusions of orthography:

guard	ward
guerrilla	warrior
guarantee	warrantee
gage	wage
quay	cay (key)

Many centuries before the elimination of the wen a fundamental parallelism brought the **w** and the **kw** into linguistic competition. This parallelism concerned the basic interrogatory words, *who, what, which, where,* etc. Among the speakers of Latin the trend was toward **kw**, but among the Germans it was toward the **w**. That is to say, the Romans emphasized the plosive (or it may have been fricative) sound made at the back of the mouth, while the Teutons emphasized the sound made with the rounding of the lips, both, however, employing both lips and tongue. Thus when the two spellings of the question words were rejoined at the marriage of the Romanic and Germanic languages, as the Normans and the Anglo-Saxons blended their vocabularies, this factor of

---

not for the English Bible and the works of Shakespeare it might have been completely superseded by *you*. Perversely enough, however, the vowel of the religious form was changed during the period when great numbers of the **i** sounds of the language became **aɪ**, and when the **u** more often than not became **aʊ**; but the vowel **u** in the informal word *you* resisted the pressures of change, as did the **i** sounds in the other four words, both formal and informal.

confusion was added to that of the evolution of the wen and its replacement by other letters or letter combinations. At that time the question words from the German still showed the voiceless, fricative beginning (analogous to the Latin *q*), represented by an initial *h*, in the words of interrogation. Compare the Latin and Anglo-Saxon question words:

Latin	*English*	*Anglo-Saxon*
quis	who	hwa
quid	what	hwæt
quod	which	hwilc
quo	where	hwǣr

The change of spelling from *hw* to *wh* is usually explained as follows: It was noted that question words often had rhyming correlative, answering words, like *hwæt* and *thæt*. In the question word the *h* appeared as the first letter, but it was second in the answering word. "Surely," thought the scribes, "something is wrong in this copy." Apparently they did not recognize that in *hæwt* the *h* was a letter in its own right, but that in *thæt* it was a part of a digraph representing a single sound. So, in the interests of logic, consistency, and "correctness," they transposed the *w* and the *h*, resulting in the modern forms of *what*, *which*, *where*, *whence*, *when*, correlated with *that*, *this*, *there*, *thence*, *then*. This metathesis of the *w* and the *h* has prompted English speakers to "omit the *h*" as they pronounce these words, giving **wɒt, wɪtʃ, wɛr, wɛns**, and **wɛn**.

The history of other *wh* words has been generally parallel to that of the question words. Compare *whale*: A.S., *hwal*; L., *squalus*. The pronunciation has followed the *h* spelling except for a few words in which the *wh* is followed by a vowel in which the lips are closely rounded. The **w** requires a definite opening from one lip aperture to a greater. Hence, when *wh* appears before a closely lip-rounded vowel, it is virtually impossible to produce a **w**. The result is an uncomplicated **h** attack in place of the **hw**, in such words as *whoop*, *who*, *whom*, *whose*. By analogy this pattern of elision of the *w* appears even in *whole* and *whore*, words in which the *w* would not complicate the pronunciation. Note *wold*, *wore*, and *whoa*.

Miscellaneous Orthographic Changes

Because lexicographers still preserve the ancient spellings of such words as *often*, *calm*, and *salmon*, including the "silent letters," some speakers insist upon pronouncing them as **ɒftən, kɑlm,** and **sælmən.** These orthographic changes may be quite inconsistent. Traditionally the *er* in *clerk*, *derby*, and *sergeant* is pronounced **ɑ** or **ɑr.** Spelling pronunciation has changed the first two to **ɝ** in America, but *sergeant* remains **sɑrdʒnt** in spite of the spelling.

Again: The *e* in *sure* is silent, and is of the nature of a diacritical sign to indicate the pronunciation of the vowel preceding. But make a noun out of that adjective by adding *ty*, *surety*, and one hears that word frequently so pronounced as to give a vowel value to the silent *e*, thus making a third syllable in the word. Waltham is historically **wɔlthəm,** the syllables being separated between the **t** and the **h**; but, because *th* is often pronounced **θ**, the word has been changed to amalgamate the two letters into a single digraph with a different pronunciation from that of the two taken separately, i.e. **wɔlθəm.** So one sometimes hears *hartshorn* pronounced **hɑrtʃɔrn** because of a similar amalgamation of the *s* and the *h*. It is obvious that *s* and *h* separately have no kinship with the digraph *sh*. Here a spelling pronunciation is responsible for the change of sound.

Chapter 15   Neurophysiologic
Changes of Speech Sounds

The Peripheral Mechanisms of Speech

To the organs of articulation run six pairs of cranial nerves to activate and, in part, to monitor the articulatory movements involved in the production of the consonants, as follows:

The seventh, or facial, nerves carry all the impulses that are involved in the labial activity in the production of **b, p, m, w, f, v.**

The twelfth, or hypoglossal, nerves control in a similar way the articulatory activity of the anterior third of the tongue, in such sounds as **d, t, n, s, z, θ, ð, ʃ, ʒ, l, r.**

The ninth, or glossopharyngeal, nerves control the movements of the posterior two-thirds of the tongue in the production of **k, g, ŋ, j.**

The tenth, or vagus, and the eleventh, or accessory, nerves combine with the ninth to make up a special nasopharyngeal nucleus to control the nasopharyngeal valve, whose activity differentiates nasal from nonnasal sounds. The vagus nerves also control voicing or unvoicing in differentiating the sonant and surd analogues, such as **b** and **p, d** and **t, z** and **s.**

The fifth, or trigeminal, nerves control the movements of the mandible in the production of all sounds, vowels and consonants.

In addition to these six pairs of motor nerves the eighth, or auditory, nerves, are concerned with all of the sounds of speech, in that it is through the functioning of these nerves that they are monitored. A phonemic change may occur when a given sound closely resembles another acoustically, provided change to the second sound does not involve a radical shift of *motor* control.

The production of the vowels is by no means so specialized as that of the consonants. They are the result of the coöperative control of many nerves, which doubtless accounts in part for their instability. When the etymologist is tracing the history of a given word from generation to generation, and from language to language, he keeps his eye on the consonants. The variability of the vowels is so great that he cannot trust them as etymologic identifiers.

A skill involving one peripheral articulatory unit is not readily moved to another. Hence, when, under the pressure of spelling changes or of foreign language influence or of any other factor, a given consonant changes its form, it usually remains under the control of the nervous unit that erstwhile produced it. Thus **b** may change to **v**, since only a slight seventh-nerve change of control is involved; or **p** may change to **b**, since only a change of the control from the vagus is concerned; or **b** may change to **m**, since only the nasopharyngeal nucleus is involved in the change from **b** to its nasal analogue. Seldom, however, will **b**, **p**, or **m** change to **d**, **t**, or **n** (twelfth nerves); and even more seldom will they change to **k**, **g**, or **ŋ** (ninth nerves).

A Neurophysiologic Grouping of Speech Sounds

Sounds may be grouped into classes on the basis of the physiologic processes involved in their production. Sounds of similar production tend to displace each other more readily than do sounds of dissimilar production; that is, sounds that involve the same muscles and nerves are more readily interchanged than sounds that involve disparate neuromuscular units. Listed below are five of these physiologic groups or classes of sounds:[1]

1. The beta consonants, the seventh nerve sounds, include **b**, **p**, **m**, **f**, **v**.

2. The delta consonants, the twelfth nerve sounds, include **d**, **t**, **n**, **s**, **z**, **ʃ**, **ʒ**, **θ**, **ð**.

[1] See Chap. 11 for a more complete classification of sounds.

3. The gamma consonants, the ninth, tenth, and eleventh nerve sounds, are **g**, **k**, **ŋ**.

4. The centrally delivered vowels,[2] which may be divided into three subgroups are the following:

    (a) Front vowels: **a**, **æ**, **ɛ**, **e**, **ɪ**, **i**.

    (b) Back vowels: **ɒ**, **ɔ**, **o**, **ʊ**, **u**.

    (c) Mid vowels: **ɑ**, **ʌ**, **ɜ**, **ɝ**.

5. The laterally delivered vowel **ḷ**.

Special Notes on the Neurophysiology of the Vowels

Front Vowels

These sounds involve the mid-portion of the dorsum of the tongue, measuring from front to back. The adjustments vary, from pressures against palate and dental ridge, with **i**, to mere equipoising of the levator and depressor musculature of the tongue to hold the dorsum in the desired position for **a**. These adjustments—for **i** and for **a**—differ from each other somewhat as do those involved in the playing of the saxophone versus playing the trombone. With the saxophone, valve levers provide the stopping points for the finger muscles. All the player needs to do is to exert sufficient pressure to hold the desired valve open, though this pressure is of no importance in determining the note produced. But with the trombone the player pushes (or pulls) the slide to a desired position. The extensor and flexor muscles of the right arm, operating as antagonists, must be delicately adjusted, one group against another, to produce the right kinesthetic sensation and the correct auditory effect. The utterance of **i** is analogous to the playing of the saxophone, since this sound involves a bracing of the tongue against a firm point of contact; but **a** is like a note on the trombone, requiring a nice balancing between the antagonistic muscles involved. This difference in neuromuscular adjustment is probably responsible for the instability of **a** and the related **æ**. In respect to equipoising versus bracing the front vowels vary in a continuum from **a** to **i**. For the most part the musculature involved in the adjustments here described is innervated by the twelfth nerves.

---

[2] The unstressing of a front or back vowel tends to bring it into the group of mid vowels.

Back Vowels

With the back vowels the posterior dorsum of the tongue is adjusted to provide differing apertures between the tongue and the velum, the aperture being smallest for **u** and greatest for **ɒ**. As with the front vowels, there is greater equipoising and less stability of utterance of the lower vowels—in this case **ɒ** and **ɔ**. In these adjustments the ninth nerves are chiefly involved, with some supplementary innervation from the tenth and eleventh.

In addition to the adjustments of the linguavelar aperture the back vowels require adjustments of the labial aperture—the smaller the one, the smaller the other, the anterior aperture for a given vowel being approximately equal to the posterior opening. Thus, in addition to the equipoising of the lingual muscles there is a corresponding equipoising of the labial group. These muscles are innervated by the seventh nerves.

Mid Vowels

The mid-vowel group involves adjustment of that portion of the dorsum of the tongue that is, generally speaking, between the portions raised to produce, respectively, the front vowels and the back vowels. Of course, since the dorsum of the tongue is one continuous muscular organ, parts of both the front- and the back-vowel surfaces must be carried along with the mid-vowel surface as it is raised. The greatest raising is for the vowel **ɝ**, the least for **ʌ**. The musculature of the articulation of the mid-vowel group is innervated largely by the twelfth nerves.

Laterally Delivered Vowels

The *l* sounds are accomplished by shaping the tongue to permit the lateral discharge of the vowel tone. The musculature involved in this adjustment is innervated by the twelfth and ninth nerves, the former serving to raise the tip, or at least a part of the blade, of the tongue, and the latter serving to depress the posterior portion.

Illustrations

Beta Interchangings

Because the labial sounds involve activity of the lips and no activity of the tongue, they are physiologically so similar that they often become confused with each other. The following doublets [3] are examples of these interchangings. The sounds of the beta group are **b, p, m, f, v.**

b	**v**		fe*b*rile—fe*v*er
b	**v**		Ha*b*ana—Ha*v*ana
b	**f**		*b*rother—*f*raternal
b	**p**		crum*b*le—crum*p*le
f	**p**		*f*ather—*p*aternal
p	**v**	**b**	scri*p*t—scri*v*ener—scri*b*e
f	**b**		*f*iscal—*b*asket
b	**p**		*b*ox—*p*yx
f	**p**		*f*oot—*p*edal
p	**f**		*p*late—*f*lat
b	**f**		*b*reak—*f*racture
f	**p**		*f*ire—*p*yre

Delta Interchangings

The sounds of the delta group are **t, d, n, s, z, θ, ð, ʃ, ʒ.**

t	**d**		stripe*d* **straɪpt**—stripe*d* **straɪpɪd**
s	**ʃ**		*s*cissors—*sh*ears
s	**t**		sen*s*e—sen*t*iment
z	**s**		pal*s*y—paraly*s*is
t	**d**		*t*en—*d*ecimal
t	**s**		me*t*er—men*s*uration
t	**d**		hear*t*—car*d*iac
d	**z**	**st**	re*d*—ro*s*y—ru*st*
θ	**t**		tee*th*—den*t*al
z	**θ**		read*s*—rea*th*eth
t	**d**		quar*t*er—qua*d*
d	**t**		*d*uo—*t*wo
ð	**t**		mo*th*er—ma*t*ernal
ð	**t**		fa*th*er—pa*t*ernal
z	**d**	**ʒ**	ri*s*ible—deri*d*e—deri*s*ion
θ	**t**		McCar*th*y—McCar*t*y
θ	**t**		smi*th*—smi*t*e
z	**d**		*Z*eus—*d*iety
θ	**d**	**t**	*th*rill—*d*rill—nos*t*ril

[3] See note on doublets, page 229.

d θ *d*rum—*th*rum
t ð swar*t*—swar*thy*
t s ʃ transmi*t*—transmi*s*sal—transmi*ss*ion
t ʃ ra*t*e—ra*t*io
ʃ s *Sh*ibboleth—*s*ibboleth
ʃ s *s*ure—*s*ecure
t ʃ preven*t*—preven*t*ion
t z wi*t*—wi*s*e
s ʃ prehen*s*ile—prehen*s*ion

Gamma Interchangings

The sounds of the gamma group are **k, g, ŋ**. There are relatively few interchangings within this group. Factors that induce migrations of gamma sounds to vowel groups or to the delta group are so strong that, if a change of a gamma sound is effected, that sound is likely to escape entirely from the gamma family. The following are illustrations of the sorts of changes that do take place within the family.

g k hag*g*le—ha*ck*—hac*k*le—he*ck*le
g k a*g*nostic—ac*k*nowledge
k g fi*c*tion—fi*g*ment
k g re*x*—re*g*al
g k tin*g*le—tin*k*le

Interchangings Among Front Vowels

The sounds of this group are **ɑ,[4] a, æ, ɛ, e, ɪ, i.**

i ɪ s*ea*t—s*i*t
cr*ee*k (pronounced both **krik** and **krɪk**)
b*ee*n **bin** (Brit.)—b*ee*n **bɪn** (U. S.)
ɪ eɪ s*i*t—s*a*te
ɛ æ s*e*t—s*a*t
ɑ æ a *a*sk **ɑsk, æsk, ask**
c*a*rtridge **kɑrtrɪdʒ** or **kɑːtrɪdʒ**
(sometimes also heard as **kætɹɪdʒ** or **katɹɪdʒ**).
ɛ æ thr*e*sh—thr*a*sh

[4] The vowel **ɑ** really belongs to each of the front, mid, and back series, since it is the vowel toward which all three series converge. If **ɑ** belongs to any of them alone it is to the mid series.

Interchangings Among Back Vowels

The sounds of this group are **u, ʊ, o, ɔ, ɒ, ɑ.**

    u ʊ Note the variant pronunciations of the words, r*oo*f, sp*oo*n, s*oo*t, r*oo*t, and r*oo*m, which sometimes use **u** and sometimes **ʊ.**

    ɔ ou "n*a*w"—n*o*

    ɒ ɔ n*au*ght (pronounced two ways)

u ɒ ɑ r*oo*d—r*o*d

    u aʊ r*ou*te (pronounced two ways)

ʊ ɒ ɑ f*oo*t—p*o*d

ɑ ɒ ɔ God, pronounced variously **gɑd, gɒd, gɔd.** n*o*t, **nɑt** (U. S.), **nɒt** (Brit.)

Interchangings Among Mid Vowels

The sounds of this group are **ɑ, ʌ, ɜ, ɝ**

    ʌ ɝ b*u*st—b*u*rst
          f*i*rst rate (pronounced **fʌst**)
          n*u*ts (pronounced **nɝts**)

    ɑ ɝ f*a*rther and f*u*rther, the variants in the first syllable being **fɑr, fɑː, fʌ, fɜ,** and **fɝ**

    ɑ ʌ m*u*ch **mʌtʃ,** or **mɑtʃ** (as sometimes heard in British speech) w*a*s **wʌz** or **wɑz** (variants heard in the Midwest)

    ɝ ɜ sh*i*rt (pronounced both **ʃɝt** and **ʃɜt**)
          g*i*rls (pronounced **gɜlz, gɝlz,** or **gʌlz**)
          b*i*rd (pronounced **bɝd** and **bɜd**)

Horizontal Interchangings Among the Vowels

The interchangings among vowels that have been discussed above have been along vertical lines, keeping within vowel groups, but making substitutions of one member of the group for another. There are also horizontal interchangings that cut across group lines to substitute a vowel in one group for one in another, the two vowels having approximately analogous positions in their respective groups. Thus a high back vowel may take the place of a high front vowel, or a medium front vowel may take the place of a medium mid vowel. Note the two words *halloo* **hælu** and *holler* **hɒlɝ.** When one changes from the former to the latter word, he changes both the first and the second vowel. The first vowel in the formal word *halloo* is a relatively low front vowel. The first vowel in the colloquial word *holler* is a relatively low back vowel. While these changes in the first vowel are taking place, the last vowel is changed in the opposite direction from the high back vowel **u** to the high mid vowel **ɝ**. Examples are the following:

	Front	*Mid*	*Back*
wish	wɪʃ		wʊʃ
yolk	yɛlk		jolk
what		hwʌt	hwɒt
just (adv.)	dʒɛst	dʒʌst	
such	sɛtʃ	sʌtʃ	
was		wʌz	wɒz
hello ⎫ hollo ⎭	hełou	həlou or	hołou
plat ⎫ plot ⎭	plæt		plɒt
you ⎫ ye ⎭	ji		ju
tight ⎫ taut ⎭	taɪt		tɔt
goose ⎫ geese ⎭	gis		gus
brother ⎫ brethren ⎭	brɛðrɪ̨n	brʌðɚ	
mouse ⎫ mice ⎭	maɪs		maʊs

Interchangings Between Laterally and Centrally Delivered Vowels

Sometimes *l*'s become regular centrally delivered vowels. This is true not only of the pure vowel *l* but also of the glide *l*. On the other hand, centrally delivered vowels often become *l*'s.

As an example of the change from a laterally delivered to a centrally delivered vowel note the word *colonel* in which the second consonant is a definite *r*, in spite of the fact that the word comes down to us from *columna, colonna, colonnello* to its present form. If one takes the position that perhaps the *l*'s in these words were always pronounced as *r*'s, then we have an example of a change from a centrally delivered consonant to a laterally delivered one in the modern word *column*, from the word *columna*. Another example of an interchanging of this sort is the word *almond*, which usually employed the centrally delivered vowel ə in place of the l. In this word we can discern in dialectal pronunciations two complete series of variants: **almənd, aəmənd, amənd** and **ælmənd, æəmənd, æmənd**. This word is evidently now in the state of transition. Other examples: *American* as pronounced by the Cantonese, giving the *r* an *l* value; *plum* and *prune*, both from the same word *prunum*; *milk*, as often spoken by children **mɪək;** *bobble, bobber; spindle, spinner; stopple, stopper; temporary, temporal.*

Phonetic Migrations

In addition to the substitutions of sounds for others in their own groups, there are also substitutions of sounds of one group for those of another. These intergroup substitutions or migrations take place in definite directions through definite physiologic and phonologic causes. Four such phonetic migrations can be described: (1) the tendency of gamma sounds to become vowels or semivowels; (2) the tendency of gamma sounds to become delta sounds; (3) the tendency of less sonorous sounds to become more sonorous; and (4) the tendency toward the palatization of certain crescendo glides.

Gamma-Vowel (or Gamma-Semivowel) Migrations

g	j	le*g*al—lo*y*al
g	ɪ	di*g*nity—da*i*nty
k	j	impre*c*ation—pra*y*er
k	ɪ	pa*x*—pa*y*
k	ɪ	o*c*to—ei*gh*t
k	ɪ	homeli*k*e—homel*y*
k	ɪ	fi*c*tion—fe*i*gn
g	j	*g*arden—*y*ard
g	j	*g*old—*y*olk
g	j	*g*ale—*y*ell

Gamma-Delta Migrations

Three important factors operate to bring gamma sounds into the delta group: (1) the greater visibility of delta sounds as they are made; (2) the greater mobility of the front of the tongue as opposed to the back; (3) the larger number of delta sounds, leading the hearer to perceive a rarer gamma sound as one of the more common and familiar delta sounds. Examples of this migration are as follows:

	k	dʒ	kind—gentle
	k	s	capture—receive
	k	ʃ	skiff—ship
	k	s	vascule—vessel
	k	s	vocal—voice
	k	tʃ	cathedral—chair
	k	dʒ	unction—unguent
	k	tʃ	cadence—chance
	k	ʃ	faction—fashion
k	ʃ	tʃ	candle—chandelier—chandler
	ŋ	n	fishing—fishin'
	ŋ	n	seeing—seein'
	g	dʒ	laryngologist—laryngectomy
	g	z	guitar—zither
	g	dʒ	gargle—jargon
	g	dʒ	purgatory—purge
	g	dʒ	obligate—oblige
	g	dʒ	analogue—analogy
	g	dʒ	regal—regent
	g	dʒ	esophagus—esophageal
	g	dʒ	gardener—jardiniere
	g	dʒ	alga—algae

Migrations from Less Sonorous to More Sonorous Vowels

In many languages of the Indo-Germanic group there is a distinct tendency for verbs to employ root vowels that possess a high degree of sonority; and in cases where the present tense of the verb employs a less open sound there is a marked tendency to change the vowel to a more open one in the preterite or perfect participial forms. Thus the more closed vowels, such as **i**, **ɛ**, and **u**, may be displaced in the root of the verb by such sounds as **ʌ**, **ɑ**, and **æ**. The more closed the mouth opening the more muffled and subdued the sound becomes, and the more open the mouth the more sonorous. The change of vowel is referred to as the "ablaut"; and verbs so modified are called strong verbs.

It is thought by many scholars that this inflection of verb forms is a survival of a pitch change of tense, a system not unthinkable in view of the pitch systems of many modern languages. Thus the "present" form of the verb was spoken at the highest pitch, the "past-continuing" in a lower pitch, and the "past-completed" in the lowest of all. High pitches are more compatible physiologically with vowels made with the tongue held high in the mouth, and low pitches with vowels made with a depressed tongue. If a person is asked to intone as high a note as he can, he will invariably choose either **i** or **u** as the vowel to be sung; and if you ask him to sing a note as low as possible he will shape his mouth for **ɔ** or **ɑ** or **ʌ**. Hence if one tries to make a grammatical discrimination on the basis of pitch he is likely to fall into the habit of altering the vowels as well as the pitch. If this is the explanation of our strong verbs, *sing, sang, sung* is one of the most perfect modern examples of this type of inflection.

It should be remembered that changes in vowel qualities in modern English have erased many of these ancient distinctions and have in some cases apparently reversed the direction of the ablaut. *Come, came, come,* is in modern English a poor example of the ablaut; but it was a much better one when *come* was spelled with the vowel *u*, and *came* was pronounced with the vowel **ɑ**. It is doubtful if today the ablaut would prevail in English were it not for the analogy of so many strong verbs in English and in other languages that touch English closely. Examples of ablaut verbs follow:

Verbs in **i**	*Verbs in* **ɪ**
seek—sought—sought	stick—stuck—stuck
steal—stole—stolen	swim—swam—swum
read—read—read	win—won—won
see—saw—seen	think—thought—thought

Verbs in ɛ	*Verbs in* aɪ
tread—trod—trodden	ride—rode—ridden
sell—sold—sold	fight—fought—fought
tell—told—told	bind—bound—bound
get—got—gotten	shine—shone—shone

Verbs in u	*Verbs in* e [5]
shoot—shot—shot	bear—bore—born
lose—lost—lost	wear—wore—worn
shoe—shod—shod	swear—swore—sworn
choose—chose—chosen	tear—tore—torn

Verbs in eɪ

say—said—said	awake—awoke—awakened
break—broke—broken	(awoke)
take—took—taken	

The Palatization of Certain Glides

When a crescendo vowel glide follows a stop consonant there often takes place what is known as palatization. This phenomenon is characterized by the fricative passage of air through a narrow orifice, the upper boundary of which is the hard palate, or roof of the mouth. This modification of the glide vowel becomes stabilized into what is an unequivocal consonant. *Education* is spoken by many fastidious speakers as ɛdjukeɪʃn̩, though most people say ɛdʒukeɪʃn̩. No doubt the first pronunciation is purer, but it is not necessarily better. The first pronunciation easily degenerates into the second, but the second form would not be corrupted to the first. The explosion of the **d** through the relatively narrow orifice afforded by the **j** position, produces a friction noise very like ʒ. Those who say ɛdjukeɪʃn̩ obviate this friction by a management of the tongue that directs the air blade between the teeth rather than against the palate and dental rugae.

This management requires rather definite care, and is the mark of "propriety." Consistency, however, would require that one go

---

[5] Strictly speaking, these belong with the verbs in ɛ. There are no good examples of **e** ablauts, since **e** is usually the long *a*; before the vowel shift long *a* was undoubtedly pronounced ɑ, and hence could not be ablauted. The words here given, however, are often pronounced dialectally as **er**, though they are marked in the dictionary to be pronounced as ɛr. (See page 322.)

a step farther and pronounce the word **ɛdjukeɪtɪən**, for the palatization in the last syllable was brought about by the same causes as that in the second. But one is not consistent. Compare the two forms *educable* **ɛdʒukəbl** and *educible* **idjusəbl**, from the same Latin root. These two forms are no more inconsistent than their obverses, rarely heard, **ɛdjukəbl** for *educable* and **idʒusəbl** for *educible*.

The following comparisons demonstrate these changes. Here are doublets of related words, the first being palatalized and the second unpalatalized. In some couplets the two forms are merely two pronunciations of the same word. In the last pair the re-pronunciation has resulted in a respelling.

mature	**tj**	mature	**tʃ**
credulity	**dj**	credulous	**dʒ**
don't you	**tj**	don't you	**tʃ**
ratify	**tɪ**	ration	**ʃ**
natal	**tə**	nation	**ʃ**
gradient	**dɪ**	gradual	**dʒ**
tune	**tj**	tune	**tʃ**
duke	**dj**	duke	**dʒ**
diurnal	**daɪ**	journal	**dʒ**

In these alterations what usually happens is that the first element of the glide wholly or nearly disappears and the place is taken by a fricative, either **ʃ** or **ʒ**.

Note also the following words whose present pronunciations, using palatal fricatives, have probably been the result of alterations from some other sounds. In each case the change has apparently been at least partly the result of the presence of a crescendo glide.

	Present Pronunciation	*Possible Original Pronunciation*
so*c*ial	**ʃ**	**kɪ**
na*t*ion	**ʃ**	**tɪ**
an*x*ious	**kʃ**	**ksɪ**
spe*c*ial	**ʃ**	**kɪ**
sche*d*ule	**dʒ**	**dj**
a*s*ia	**ʒ** or **ʃ**	**sɪ**

	Present Pronunciation	Possible Original Pronunciation
hemiple*gia*	**dʒ**	**gɪ**
re*gi*on	**dʒ**	**gɪ**
apha*si*a	**ʒ**	**sɪ**
a*cti*on	**kʃ**	**ktɪ**

Attention should also be called to a long list of words that are spelled in English with a *j* and were undoubtedly originally pronounced with a **j**, but are now pronounced **dʒ**. Apparently what happened was that the **j** was pronounced with so much initial force that it became **dʒ** even in combinations in which it was not preceded by a plosive. This change has taken place in practically every instance in which the modern English word is spelled with a *j*.

Hallelujah still preserves the original pronunciation of the *j*, possibly because of the reverence of the religious person for ancient forms; but *jot* in English is **dʒɒt**, while it is **jɒt** in German. Where the original **j** pronunciation is preserved it is common to employ the spelling *y* as in *yacht*, or *i* as in *dominion*. *Yoke*, derived from a forerunner of the Latin *jungere*, still preserves the original pronunciation of the *j*; but another word has been derived from *jungere*, spelled with a *j* and pronounced **dʒ**, viz., *join*. Similarly the head of the city is called the *mayor* and the head of the battalion is called the *major*. Words like *jury*, *June*, *Jack*, *reject*, and *John*, which have had long histories of pronunciation with the sound **j**, have changed to **dʒ**. Compare *Yiddish* and *Jewish*. As in the case of *yoke*, some words stubbornly refuse to change in pronunciation. In that case the spelling changes to *y*. Note the word *young*, evidently descended as a relative of the Latin *juvenis*, from which has derived a direct synonym of *young*, *juvenile*. Perversely enough, this derivative, though spelled with a *j*, is pronounced with a **dʒ**, in spite of its history and its parallelism in meaning with *young*.

Sound Changes Resulting from Incompatibilities

Many sound combinations are difficult, and some are impossible, to produce. When one of these combinations tends to bring about a phonetic change, due to the influence of one sound upon the other or upon other sounds in the word or phrase, they are called incompatibles. A sound is incompatible with another sound when the utterance of the first of the pair leaves the articulatory organs in a position (1) from which they cannot readily move to the position required for the utterance of the second sound, or (2) from which they can move to the position of the second sound only through positions in which still other sounds are produced. When these incompatibles are brought together in building up words and in their modifications because of sound substitutions and migrations, either one or the other must yield its identity and take on that of a sound more compatible with the sounds with which it is associated, or a third sound must be interposed between them.

The incompatibles are divided into two groups on the basis of the type of adjustment made necessary by their ineptness: (1) those whose utterance in juxtaposition, though possible, is clumsy and accomplished only with a considerable effort and care; (2) those that cannot be juxtaposed except by inserting between them a third linking sound. (Neither class includes combinations that, merely because of their strangeness to the English-trained speaker, seem to be incompatible but are really potentially linkable.)

As an example of the first type of incompatibility note the last three sounds in the phrase *three-sixths* **sɪksθs**. Because of the clumsiness of this linking, the sounds usually resolve themselves into **sɪks**. As an example of the second type of incompatibility note the word *sums* **sʌmz**. To link **m** with **z** is not difficult, but the linking is impossible without introducing a **b** or an **n** between them. In close transcription the linking would be represented as **sʌmⁿz** or as **sʌmᵇz**.

The Table of Incompatibilities (page 261) exhibits the reasons for many sound substitutions. Although only definite consonants are included, it is obvious that all vowels are incompatible with each other: to go from one to another without a stoppage of the breath stream or of the stream of tone is to produce, not the two vowels in question, but a glide. **h** being merely a method of attack on a vowel is not really a sound in and of itself. Only the *voiced* consonants have been included in this table, but linkings between the voiceless analogues of these sounds fall into the same categories as the linkings between the voiced sounds. To illustrate: the last two sounds of *bathes* **ðz** are just as difficult to link as the last two sounds in *sixths* θs, and for the same reason. Again, *Samson* has a linking between the **m** and the **s** that is exactly analogous to that between **m** and **z** in *sums* either **n** or **p** being the linking sound in this case.

TABLE OF INCOMPATIBILITIES [6]

First sound in the pair to be combined

	b	v	m	d	ð	ʒ	z	n	g	ŋ
b								x		x
v										
m				x				x	x	x
d			x							x
ð			x				x	x		x
ʒ			x		x		x	x		x
z			x		x	x				x
n	x		x						x	x
g			x					x		
ŋ	x		x	x	x	x	x	x		

Second sound in the pair

[6] The authors have been careful in constructing this table to include only the most definite incompatibilities; but it should be pointed out that the degree of effort required to produce one of these combinations is no measure of the incompatibility. The combination ðz in a phrase as *with zeal* is clumsy to accomplish, perhaps as difficult as any in the whole table; but its influence upon the sounds involved, to cause intrinsic changes in them, is not as great as that of some easier combinations, as for example ng in the phrase *in God*, or nk in the phrase *in case*. ðz *can* be said, if one is careful enough, but ng and nk absolutely cannot be managed without a linking ŋ. The combinations ng and nk may be regarded as distinctly incompatible, though they seem astonishingly easy combinations to utter. In fact it is the very ease of their utterance that renders them sources of phonetic change wherever these combinations are closely knit, as in *Inca, ingot, inguinal*, and *ink*. Gradually the linking ŋ becomes more and more pronounced until it completely dominates the n and supplants it. Thus *in-caustum* (L.) becomes *ink* ɪŋk, not ɪnk.

A study of this table reveals that **v** and **f** can begin any sound combination. As beginning sounds they have no incompatibles. **ŋ** as an ending sound has at least fourteen incompatibles, counting both voiced and voiceless sounds. This is in spite of the fact that in English **ŋ** is usually a final, never an initial sound, although there are only eight sounds that it cannot precede in combination.

These linkings between consonants often involve pairs having similar mechanical and acoustic characteristics. When this happens, a definite consonantal glide is formed quite analogous to a glide from one vowel to another. Hence, just as we have such glides as **aɪ** and **wɔ**, so we may have **mn**, **nŋ**, **mŋ**, **ðz**, **θs**, **ʃs**, etc.

Often in the creation of new words or new spellings, or in the migrations of sounds for causes other than incompatibility, incompatibles are brought together, one of the commonest causes of this being the building of new syllable combinations in the making of compound words or in the addition of prefixes and suffixes. The following is a sample list of sound changes due to phonological incompatibility:

	Incompatible Combination	*Resolution of the Incompatibility*
nk	han*dk*erchief—hanky	**ŋ**
nb	i*nb*red—imbred	**m**
gn	si*gn*ify—sign	**n**
ðz	clo*thes*—clothes	**z**
bn	a*bn*ormal—anomalous	**n**
gn	di*gn*ity—dainty	**n**
nk	co*nq*uest—conquer	**ŋ**
nk	pa*nc*ake—panicake	**nɪ**
nk	sy*nc*hronic—synchronal	**ŋ**
nm	e*nm*esh—immesh	**m**

An examination of the dictionary will show the powerful effect upon the English language, and the languages from which it borrowed, of the factor of physiologic incompatibility in the metamorphosis of verbal elements. There are many words with prefixes ending in *m* followed by a *b* or *p*, but few words with an *m* followed by a *t* or *d*. Ancient adjustments of the incompatibilities have served to marry the *m*'s with the *p*'s and *b*'s and the *n*'s with the *t*'s and *d*'s. Many of the hundreds of cases of doubled consonants linking the first and second syllables of words derived from the Latin are the result of these adjustments of incompatibles: *connubial, accidental, accommodate, accuse, immaculate*, etc. Most of these words were stabilized before they were borrowed. The Latin *cum* (*with*) had a sibling *con* which was used as a substitute whenever it fitted better than *cum*. So *a* (*away from*) had two alternate forms; *ad* (*to*) had one; *ex* (*out of*) had one; *ob* (*upon*) had one; etc. All of these substitutes were used to make the speaking of Latin easier for the Roman tongue.

These various forms of the prepositions were not, of course, selected consciously, but evolved unconsciously—which is to say, they developed as natural functions of the capricious protoplasmic mechanisms of the humans who spoke the language. Nearly half of the words of modern English are of Latin descent, direct or indirect. One may say, therefore, that English speakers of today not only think in terms of Roman symbols, but they even spell their symbols in the very forms dictated by the biology of Roman organisms that turned to dust more than 2000 years ago. English has now become the *lingua franca* of the world; and so long as English remains a phonetic[7] language the articulatory patterns of the speakers of the world will in large part reflect those of that remarkable strain of human animals who long ago inhabited Latium, a tiny state on the Italian boot.

Sound Changes Due to Economy

In any language innumerable elisions and substitutions take place that may be explained on the basis of a general principle of

[7] The reader may benefit from listening in at this point on a discussion between the two authors concerning this word *phonetic*. Kantner says, in a conference on the manuscript:

"This is not clear to me in this context. I usually call English a very 'unphonetic' language." West replies:

"Yes, it is, when compared to Spanish or German; but what I meant here was that the letters of the English language, in the most part, stand for *sounds*, not *ideas*. The combinations of letters, or phonograms, stand for ideas. Some languages, Chinese for example, are not phonographic, or phonetic, but ideographic. English employs a few interlinguistic symbols, such as those concerned with the concepts of mathematics, music, and science, that are ideographic. Generally, however, when one reads from the printed page he pronounces what is spelled out for him. In that sense English is 'phonetic,' no matter how inconsistent its phonograms may be."

economy of effort. As a language matures, words are constantly being simplified, then built together into new combinations, and then again worn down by simplification and abbreviation. It is obvious that in this erosion many sounds will be dropped. Attention is called here, however, not to the dropped sounds, but to those that are actually changed in order to simplify pronunciation. Examples:

aɪf to **sɪ̣**	housewife—hussy
n to **m**	hanaper—hamper
mp to **n**	comptroller—controller
nkθ to **nθ**	strength—**stɹɛnθ**
θ or **t̪** to **t**	thymus—thyme **taɪm**
fθ to **t**	phthisis **taɪsɪs**
fθ to **pθ**	diphtheria (pronounced **dɪpθ**)
ɪ to **oʊ**	will not—won't
æ to **eɪ**	am not—ain't
ŋ to **m**	something (pronounced **sʌmpm̩**)
mp to **ŋ**	pumpkin—punkin
n to **m**	captain (pronounced **kæpm̩**)
nd to **mŋ**	stop-and-go (pronounced **stɒpm̩ⁿgoʊ**)

It will be noted in the above examples that often the new form of the sound changed is no easier to utter in and of itself than the old form, but it fits into the word or phrase as a whole so as to make it possible to minimize the effort of pronunciation.

Phonetic Time Relations

One of the factors producing phonetic changes in English—a factor partly involved in some of the metamorphoses mentioned above—is that of timing. One can discern four rather independent series of events in the mechanical processes that go on during speech: (1) the bellowslike action of the chest, driving the air column out through the throat; (2) movements of the larynx in opening and closing the glottis; (3) opening and closing of the velum; (4) movements of the articulating structure, tongue, lips, and jaw. Some changes of sound involve no change in these several series of events, but only in the phase relationship that exists between and among them. Series two, three, and four are prone to change time relations with each other and with series one; only series one remains a constant factor or point of reference.

An example of this type of change is the two pronunciations of *humble*, **hʌmbḷ** and **ʌmbḷ**, the former being the commonly accepted form and the latter heard frequently in the formalized address of clergymen. No change takes place in the mechanical movements of the four series described above, but one of them alters its timing, viz., series two, the series taking place in the larynx. For both *'umble* and *humble*, series one, the expiratory movements of the bellows, series three, the closing of the nasal port by the velum, and series four, the shaping of the mouth-mold by the tongue and jaw, all start simultaneously. For *humble*, series two, in this instance the closing of the glottis to the point of phonation, does not start until the others are under way; while in *'umble*, the series of events at the glottis, series two, starts simultaneously with the other three. In **ʌmbḷ** the glottis closes to the point of phonatory vibration at the very beginning of the utterance of the word and remains closed until the end; while in **hʌmbḷ**, although the larynx goes through precisely the same movements, it starts its movements a fraction of a second later than in the utterance of **ʌmbḷ**. During that fraction of a second the other three series have proceeded exactly as they would have in **ʌmbḷ**. Thus the change of pronunciation is said to be due entirely to a phase change of series two.

It may be that some day *humble* and *'umble* may come to have separate meanings and uses, just as *price* and *prize* have separated themselves one from the other. In the former, *price*, series two, the laryngeal series, is speeded up so that it is completed and the glottis is opened, stopping the vibrations, before the other series have been followed out to the end; but in *prize* series two is retarded so that the glottis is not opened until series one, three, and four have been completed. One acoustic effect has come to mean *the value paid* and the other *the value received*, though both were derived from *praetium* (L.).

For an example of a phase change of series three, note the change of the word *handle* from **hændḷ** to **hænḷ**, a change that we may hear in many parts of the South. No change takes place in the mechanical movements of the four series described above, but one of the series alters its timing, viz., the velar mechanism. At one point in the series the closing of the velum is normally slightly ahead of the release of the tongue from its delta position, to produce the plosion of **d** in **hændl̩**. In **hænl̩** the closing is delayed until the exact instant at which the tongue releases to produce the **l̩**. Thus in **hændl̩** the air stream is momentarily arrested by a complete blocking of the mouth and of the nasal port, while in **hænl̩**, when one port is closed, the other outlet is simultaneously opened. But if it were possible for us to watch the movements of the velum in the utterances of these two pronunciations of the word *handle* we would note no difference, the change of timing being so slight and the two movement series being identical otherwise.

Now consider an example of timing in which the sound is altered through a change in the phase relationship of series four, the articulatory series of events, the other three series remaining constant in their timing with respect to each other: take the word *mouse*, derived from an Anglo-Saxon word probably pronounced **mus**. The change of pronunciation in it and many similar diphthongizations is largely due to a change of timing. At the beginning of the word *mouse* the tongue remains in the neutral position **ʌ**; hence, after the **m**, instead of being in the position for **u** the tongue is "caught in the act" of moving toward that position. Since the velum and larynx are ready for vowel production and the tongue is in motion, a "diphthong" results. In **mus** the timing is such that the tongue has moved into the **u** position during the utterance of **m** and hence is ready for a pure vowel at the instant when the lips open at the close of **m**. But it should be noted that the movements made by all of the speech organs are about the same for **mus** as for **mɑus**. In the former case the tongue moves to the **u** position at a time when it will produce no noticeable acoustic effect; in the latter case, the movement of the tongue is delayed·until it produces an actual sound. But the movement has changed chiefly in timing, and only slightly in force and direction. The starting point of this glide is moved from **ʌ** to **ɑ** or in the direction of **ɑ** through the influence of **u**. Since **u** is a back vowel, the neutral position, from which the movement starts, tends to approach the back vowel nearest to the mid vowel **ʌ**. Hence the glide becomes **ɑu** (aʊ in IPA), though with many speakers it is nearer to **ʌu**. As has been observed under the discussion of intervowel glides, the termination of such a sound is difficult to fix. The **u** in the original *mus* may be slightly altered in the direction of **ʊ**.

What has taken place to change **u** and **ʊ** to **ɑu** or **ʌu** has also changed **i** and **ɪ** to **ʌi** or **ɑi** (or **aɪ** in IPA). Through a delay in timing of the tongue, *bindan* **bɪndən** has become *bind* **bɑind**, and *fine* **fine** has become *fine* **fɑin**, while at the same time one still pronounces the adjectival form *finish* **fɪnɪʃ**, employing a high front vowel. Similarly the high mid vowel **ɝ** as in *bird*, *first*, and *Jersey*, becomes diphthongized into something that sounds very like **bə͡ɝd**, **fə͡ɝst**, and **d͡ʒə͡ɝzɪ**. Often the **əɝ** diphthong ends at a point that is closer to **i** or to **ɪ** than to **ɝ**, and sometimes it starts at a point closer to **ɔ** or **ɑ** than to **ʌ**. These variations are particularly frequent in New York City "cockney" and in many Southern dialects. This accounts for the confusion between words like *early* and *oily*, *verse* and *voice*, *adjourn* and *adjoin*.

As an evidence of the strong tendency of an open vowel to interpose itself between an initial consonant and a succeeding high front, back, or mid vowel, because of the tardiness of the tongue to leave a more or less neutral position, note that the "off-glides" for all the consonants but **c** and **ɟ** are best represented by **ə**. That is, if the consonant is sounded alone and the voice (or breath if the consonant be a surd) is continued after the consonant is ended, the sound resulting will be a low mid vowel in the general phoneme of **ə** or its voiceless equivalent. Thus when any consonant but the two mentioned above is used initially, any delay in articulation of the consonant with the vowel will introduce some sort of an **ə** glide.

Because this type of "diphthongization" is so common in English, many other words which had **u** or **i** vowels originally change to **ɑu** and **ɑi** by a process of orthographic analogy. There is no good physiological reason, for example, why *wound*, the injury, should be pronounced **wɑund**. It is true that it was derived from a word using **ʊ** as a vowel, but the **ʊ** in the original word was preceded, as in the modern word, by a **w**. Now, **w** before **ʊ** begins in a position very close to **u**. Hence there was every reason why Anglo-Saxon *wund* should become **wund** or **wʊund**, since to produce the glide would be not only to alter the timing of the movements, but to add others as well. Yet by analogy with *mound, pound, bound, found,* etc., it became changed in the speech of many persons to **waund.**

This diphthongization naturally takes place in other languages as well as in English; and when borrowings are made at different historical periods, inconsistent English derivatives result. A borrowing from old German, through the Dutch, gives *boor* **bur,** while a borrowing from the same German word with a modern pronunciation gives *bower* **bawɚ.** (*Boor,* strangely enough, has refused to diphthongize and to take on the refinement of a modern pronunciation.)

Words in which the initial vowel was originally **i, ɝ,** or **u** have a tendency to diphthongize because of the natural tendency of the tongue and jaw to return to neutral positions after any articulatory adjustment has been completed, and to remain at rest until another articulatory movement is undertaken. At the beginning of a word the tongue and jaw are in the positions taken for the sound **ʌ** (see "Neutral Position," page 63). If, on beginning such a word as *ut* (A.S.), the tongue and jaw are sluggish in leaving the neutral position and assuming that for **u,** the word becomes not **ut** but **ʌut,** and that becomes **əut.** The orderly and synchronous carrying-out of the other three series of movements forces a glide when the tongue and jaw are slow in starting their series of movements.

In the following lists of words the chief difference in pronunciation is in the matter of timing.

Change in Timing of the Laryngeal Series (Series 2)

*w*hite	**hwait**	**wait**
grea*s*e	**gris**	**griz**
rain*s*	**reins**	**reinz**
*h*uman	**hjumən**	**jumən**
blou*s*e	**blaus**	**blauz**

Note also the following close doublets:

> sa*f*e—sa*v*e
> coverle*t*—coverli*d*
> *wh*y (question)—*wh*y (exclamation)
> shea*th*—shea*the*
> loo*s*e—lo*s*e
> hou*s*e—hou*s*e

Change in Timing of the Velar Series (Series 3)

oh, goodness!	**gʊdnɪs**	**gʊnɪs**
singing	**sɪŋɪŋ**	**sɪŋgɪŋk**
Wednesday	**wɛnzdɪ**	**wɛdn̩zdɪ**
singest	**sɪŋɪst**	**sɪŋgɪst**
and	**ændə**	**ænə**
finger	**fɪŋgɚ**	**fɪŋɚ**
brand new	**brændnju**	**brænˌju**
drowning	**drɑʊnɪŋ**	**drɑʊndɪŋ**
Campbell	**kæmbl̩**	**kæml̩**
family	**fæmlɪ**	**fæmblɪ**

Change in Timing of the Articulatory Series (Series 4)

aʊ	**u**
th*ou*	y*ou*
ac*ou*stic	ac*ou*stic
r*ou*te	r*ou*te
d*ou*bt	d*u*bitable
fl*ow*er-de-luce	fl*eu*r-de-lis
sn*ou*t	sn*oo*t
b*ow*er	b*oo*r

aɪ	**i**
p*i*ke	p*i*que
m*y*	m*e*
th*y*	th*ee*
obl*i*que (army)	obl*i*que (general form)
thr*i*ce	thr*ee*
sp*i*re	sp*ea*r
mob*i*le	mob*i*le

Aspiration

A special problem of timing is involved in what is known as *aspirate* and *unaspirate* attacks upon, and releases from, vowels. If the larynx is so managed that whenever the passages through the mouth or nose are open, i.e., when they offer no resistance to the outrushing air stream, the vocal cords are closed to the point of vibration or closer, then one produces *unaspirated* effects; but when the larynx is so managed that there are periods during the utterance of speech when there is an unobstructed passage to the outer air—blocked neither by the vocal folds nor by the articulating organs—then one produces *aspirated* effects.

English, more than many languages, is characterized by these aspirated effects, being much more prodigal of the air in the thoracic reservoir than is a more unaspirate language, such as Chinese. There are two principal situations in which these effects appear in English: (1) following voiceless plosives, and (2) preceding voiceless fricatives. There is also a slight tendency toward aspiration preceding voiceless plosives.

Aspirated and Unaspirated Plosives

Note the word *tap*. There is a distinct interval of time between the explosive release of the tongue from its palatal contact in the production of **t** and the instant at which the glottis closes and the vowel sound **æ** begins. During that interval the air rushes out without resistance. Since the tongue is rapidly assuming the posture for the production of **æ**, the sound produced during that interval might be described as a voiceless glide to the position for **æ** or as an **ɦ**. Now, if one times the movements of the larynx so that the voice begins at the very instant of explosion, i.e., exactly when the tongue is pulled away from the palate, then this *h*-attack on the vowel **æ** does not appear, and one produces a so-called unaspirated *t*. If one times the movements of the larynx so that the glottis closes before the plosion, or during the period of implosion, then he produces not a *t*, but a *d*.

In English there are eight possible combinations of voiced and voiceless sounds introduced, concluded, or connected by plosives. They are here demonstrated by the following descriptive symbols: > represents the period of implosion during which the pressure is building up in the mouth; < represents the period of explosion; the space between, when > < are paired, represents the period of plosion or holding of the impounded air under pressure; x represents a voiced sound; o represents a voiceless sound. Using delta plosives for all eight examples the combinations are:

1. *bad d*ay	x >	< x	5. *tea*		< o
2. ho*t t*ime	o >	< o	6. *day*		< x
3. be*d*-*t*ick	x >	< o	7. *cat*	o >	
4. si*t d*own	o >	< x	8. *cad*	x >	

Example 1 is not aspirated because at no time does the air stream find a free passage to the outer air. It is checked all of the time at the glottis and part of the time by the tongue as well. Example 2 shows two periods of aspiration—when no resistance is offered to the out-rushing air stream—the first being the interval after the cessation of the laryngeal vibrations for the production of the vowel **ɒ** and before the period of complete plosion starts, the second being the interval between the explosion and the beginning of the glide **aɪ**. The aspiration during the second interval is much more prominent than during the first. Example 3 has only one period of aspiration, following the explosion; 4 has only one period of slight aspiration, during the interval between the vowel **ɪ** and the plosion; 5 shows a distinctly aspirate approach to the vowel **i**; 6 has no period of free egress of the air; 7 has only a very brief interval during which the air may rush out unimpeded, and 8 has no such period. (Of course in connected discourse combinations 5, 6, 7, and 8 would often appear as examples of combinations illustrated by 1, 2, 3, and 4; even when standing alone 7 and 8 are pronounced with off-glides, that with 7 being surd and with 8 sonant.) Hence 2 would be the most definitely aspirated, and 1 the most definitely unaspirated. Example 4, though an "accidental," may be described as an unaspirated *t*, because the voicing begins at the moment of explosion, just as is habitual in speech situations in which an unaspirated *t* is standard.

English has few unaspirated plosives with voiceless implosions:

1. Accidentals, as in *sit down, right door, cup-board, thick gum*, etc., in which a voiceless plosive is linked with a following voiced plosive, so that there is virtually only a single consonant, a composite one with the first half of the voiceless plosive joined to the last half of the voiced plosive.

2. Voiceless plosives initiating unstressed syllables as in *city, hopper, heckle*, etc. Usually with a reduction of stress the aspiration of a plosive is diminished.

3. Voiceless plosives directly linked with a preceding **s**, as in *span, stand, school*, etc. *Span* is by no means **pæn** plus an initial **s**. The linking of the **s** and a voiceless plosive in English usually renders it unaspirated.

The accidentals, when they occur in stereotyped unit phrases, do not long remain in English, their place soon being taken by a single voiced plosive. Note what happened to the shelf upon which cups were set. It was a *cup-board*, perhaps at first **kʌpəbord**, then **kʌpbʊrd**, with one implosion and one explosion for the two consonants, the voice starting during the interval of plosion or at the instant of explosion, thus producing a fairly typical unaspirated *p*. Then because the unaspirated plosive with a voiceless implosion is not a part of the language habits of the English speaker, the sound changes to a completely unaspirated plosive, *b*, and today *cupboard* rhymes with *Hubbard*.

Aspirated and Unaspirated Fricatives

In English the transition from a vowel sound to a surd fricative is usually accomplished by opening the glottis at the instant at which the tongue quits the vowel position and begins to move in the direction of the position it will occupy for the fricative. Thus, in the interval between the cessation of the voiced tone and the beginning of the fricative sound air is streaming out without resistance. The sound produced in this interval is a sort of a voiceless glide. This will be heard easily if one speaks slowly the word *ash* **æʃ**, being careful to keep the vowel pure. If the timing at the glottis is altered in such a way that the voice continues until the fricative sound starts, there is a typical unaspirated surd fricative, not standard in English, though occurring in many dialects. The effect is that of a glide that almost merges into the fricative consonant, as **æɪʃ**. If one continues the voice on into the fricative he affects the voiced fricative usual in English, and the word becomes **æɪʒ**. *Azure*, therefore, is not the parallel of *Asher*, because our English pronunciation of the latter is too definitely aspirated. If *Asher* were pronounced with an unaspirated approach to the consonant, it would be a fair analogue of *azure*.

The following are examples of aspirated and unaspirated effects. The changes illustrated are brought about by the juxtaposition of surd and sonant plosives, accidentally producing unaspirated surd plosives.

clapboard	**klæpb̂ord** or **klæbɚd**
sit down	**sɪtd̂aʊn** becomes **sɪdaʊn**
blackguard	**blækĝɑrd** or **blægɚd**

background	bækgra͡ʊnd
make good	meɪkg͡ʊd
scrapbook	skræpb͡ʊk
Campbell	kæmp͡bɛl or kæmbl̩
soapbox	soʊp͡bɒks

The following variations sometimes heard in certain dialects of English illustrate unaspirated fricative effects:

ask	æɪsk	wash	wɒrʃ
flesh	flɛɪʃ	mush	mʌrʃ
dish	dɪɪʃ	class	klæɪs

Fortis and Lenis Effects

Consonants may change their forms in still another way: Those that are *lenis* may become *fortis*, and those that are *fortis* may become *lenis*. These are relative terms, referring to two aspects of the utterance of the consonant: (1) the amount of aspiration and (2) the degree of breath pressure developed between the glottis and the outer air through the impounding of the air stream by the organs of articulation. A consonant made with a considerable release of unvoiced air and/or a vigorous resisting by the articulators of the outrushing air stream is described as *fortis*; one made with little aspiration and/or a lax resistance by the articulators of the air current is *lenis*.

The reader may ask how to describe a consonant made with considerable aspiration and lax articulation, or one with no aspiration and vigorous articulatory resistance. The question is a bit academic, for these combinations are rare, especially in English. The reason these two apparently unrelated aspects are linked as they are is purely mechanical. Consider as an analogue the damming of a stream for the conversion of power from the increased head of water. If two power dams are placed too close together along a stream both can generate power only at high water. At low water the downstream millpond becomes depleted, the head of pressure drops, and the wheel must be stopped until the pond is filled again from the millrace of the upstream plant. If, however, the upper dam is opened and the water is permitted to flood into the lower pond, the pressure builds up against the dam and the downstream wheel may be run more continuously.

In this analogy the upper plant is the glottal mechanism and the downstream, the organs of articulation. If the air stream is stopped at the glottis and its kinetic energy converted there into sound waves, little energy is left to be converted into sound waves at the next dam, the one in the mouth. If, on the other hand, the air stream is permitted to pass through the glottis without resistance, it has adequate energy, when it reaches the mouth, for conversion into sound waves of considerable intensity. Thus, other things being equal, voiceless plosives are always more fortis than voiced ones. Or, to say it another way, if the air stream is arrested at the larynx, the force of the muscles of expiration plays against the resistance offered by the muscles that adduct the vocal cords and hold them approximated; but if the air stream is arrested at the mouth, the muscles of expiration play directly against those of articulation. It is possible by a vigorous expiratory effort to secure a high-water effect and, with both "conversion plants" functioning, to produce intense sound waves even at the second dam; but, since most speakers economize on their phonatory and articulatory efforts, only one power plant operates at a time to convert the energy of the air stream into sound waves of any considerable intensity. Thus with the laryngeal dam functioning, the oral dam must either produce relatively feeble sound waves, or the dam must be held closed through a longer period of time so that pressure may be built up by the accumulation of air that is permitted to pass between the vibrating vocal bands.

An example: The *t* in the word *until* is readily made vigorously, because during the utterance of that sound the glottis is open and the air pressure quickly builds up behind the tongue. Now change the word to *undo*. To get any considerable acoustic effect on the *d* one must either drive much more energy through from the expiratory muscles to the tongue, or he must prolong the period of the plosion of the *d* until the pressure accumulates to a point sufficient to make a vigorous explosion when it is released. The English speaker is too "lazy" to adopt the former course. The latter course alters the English speech pattern and gives a very foreign "accent" to the word *undo*. For example, the word *bravado* **brəvɑdo**, spoken with a definite hold on the *d* and a consequent buildup of pressure, sounds foreign. Spoken exactly the same, except that not sufficient time is allowed for this buildup of pressure, the word has the accustomed English flavor. This method of producing a fortis effect by prolongation of plosion is used in English only when necessary for the meaning, as in the phrases *cab boy, grab bag, red dress, big game, with those, last door*, etc.

English is notoriously a language having alternate stress, with sharp differences in force between accented and unaccented syllables; and since an unaccented syllable is undertaken with less expiratory effort than is a stressed syllable, when a consonant initiates an unstressed syllable that consonant is less vigorously uttered than the same consonant would be at the beginning of a stressed syllable.

Thus there may be arranged in order, from the most fortis to the most lenis, a series of typical English sounds, as follows:

1. Aspirated stressed consonants: *t*ime, ligh*t*, relea*s*e, se*c*ure, cat*t*ail

2. Aspirated unstressed consonants: rea*p*er, bu*ff*er, ta*ck*le, ho*p*ing, *p*erhaps, be*d*-*t*ick

3. Unaspirated stressed consonants: be*g*, re*j*ect, s*t*ick, s*p*an, be*d* *d*own

4. Unaspirated unstressed consonants: s*t*ability, S*p*okane, ru*bb*er, wi*gg*le, fo*dd*er.

Numbers 1 and 4 would undoubtedly be classed respectively as fortis and lenis examples; but 2 and 3 could not be so definitely classified. Thus *fortis* and *lenis* are terms, not of absolute classification, but of descriptive significance when consonants are being compared with one another.

Changes of Attack and Release

Listed below are illustrations of modifications of sounds resulting from change of attack upon or release from fricatives. (See pages 187–193 for a discussion of the principles involved here.)

Change of Attack from Open to Closed and Vice Versa

ga*r*age	**garaʒ** or **gəraʒ gəradʒ**
tin*s*el	**tɪnsəl tɪntsəl**
*ch*antey	**ʃæntɪ tʃæntɪ**
*ch*aps	**ʃæps tʃæps**
cen*s*ure	**sɛnʃɚ sɛntʃɚ**
han*ds*ome	**hændsm̩ hænsm̩**
Ma*tt*hew	**mætθju mæθju**
czar ⎫ tsar ⎭	**zɑr** **tsɑr**
heal*th*	**hɛlθ hɛltθ**
brea*dth*	**brɛdθ brɛəθ** (sometimes)
Wal*th*am	**wɔltθəm wɔlθəm**

Change of Release from Closed to Open and Vice Versa

ha*s*te—ha*s*ten	ne*st*—ne*st*le
ca*st*ellated—ca*st*le	moi*st*—moi*st*en
pi*st*il—pe*st*le	li*st*—li*st*en

Acoustic Changes

Three aspects of speech sounds need to be taken into consideration in trying to understand why one tends to hear one sound for another and hence to make a corresponding substitution: (1) pitch, (2) force, and (3) sonority patterns. Sounds made up of similar sonority patterns are readily confused if the pitch and force are not too dissimilar; and sounds of about the same force will be confused with each other if the other two components are not strikingly different.

Pitch

Three general pitch ranges are of significance in understanding what one says: low frequencies, or fundamental tones; middle frequencies, or resonance tones; high frequencies, or friction sounds.

The low frequencies are those of the fundamental pitch of the laryngeal stream of tone, ranging from about 100 vibrations per second, in the voices of adult males, to nearly 500 in the treble of women and children. The middle frequencies begin at about 400, slightly overlapping the low frequencies, and extend to well above 2400 vibrations per second. The high frequencies begin at this point and extend to somewhere between seven and eight thousand vibrations per second.

A distinction should be made between the high frequencies that are upper harmonics of vowels and those generated as independent vibratory series. Many vowels have as component elements frequency series that in rate are as high as the "noise" components of some of the consonants. Harmonic frequencies differ from "noise" frequencies in two ways: First, harmonic frequencies are dependent upon, and set in motion by, a fundamental tone; the "noise" frequencies are of independent origin and may or may not be the accompaniment of fundamental tones. Second, harmonic frequencies are musical, i.e., the vibrations occur in relatively uniform series, one vibration being of about the same length and intensity as the one before it; while in the "noise" series, though all the vibrations are short, those of varying lengths may indiscriminately follow each other.

Low-frequency sounds may be confused with other low-frequency sounds, middle with other middle frequency, and high with other high-frequency sounds. The following lists of sounds are arranged according to frequencies involved:

High frequency only: **p, f, θ, s, ʃ, t, k, ?**.
Middle frequency only: none.
High and low frequency combined: **b, v, ð, z, ʒ, d, g**.
Middle and low frequency combined: all vowels and glides
     and **m, ·n, ŋ**.

It will be noted that **h** has been omitted from the above classifications. The symbol **h** represents a combination of two elements: (1) the change of adjustment of the glottis from the whisper position to that of voicing, and (2) the experience of the hearer at that critical moment when the whispered vowel becomes voiced. The **h**, therefore, represents an entity that has dynamic significance only. The **h** is recognized, not by its frequencies, but by a specific change of status in its production. Actually, before the change mostly high and middle frequencies are produced and heard, and after the change mostly middle and low frequencies. Before the change only a whispered vowel is produced, not **h**; after the change only the vowel is produced. This change of status has assumed phonemic significance in English and in many other languages. If, however, the changes be reversed, as in playing a tape backwards, so that the voiced vowel suddenly becomes voiceless, the **h** disappears. This reverse change is not usually perceived in English speech, because such a change has no phonemic meaning, with the possible exception of the **h** in such exclamations as *bah* and *ah*.

Force

Sounds are of varying degrees of physical intensity. **ɑ** as usually spoken is hundreds of times as loud as **θ** as usually spoken. Sounds of approximately equal intensity, or force, are sometimes confused, especially if their sonority patterns are similar.

Sounds that are relatively soft: **θ, s, f, ʃ, t, k, p, h, ʔ.**
Sounds that are relatively loud: **ɑ, ɔ, oʊ, z, ʒ, b.**

Sonority Patterns

Syllables, and to some extent individual sounds, have characteristic patterns of loudness. These patterns are as follows:

1. Those in which the sonority suddenly changes from zero order to high intensity, or vice versa, when a plosive or affricate initiates, or terminates, a syllable. The plosives are **b, p, d, t, g, k, ʔ.** The affricates are combinations of plosives with fricatives, such as **tʃ, dʒ, ts, dz.**

2. Those in which the sonority remains relatively constant during the utterance of a sound or syllable, such as the pure vowels, the nasals, the fricatives, and the sibilants. Examples: **ɑ** in *father*, **n̩** in *cotton*, **θ** in *myth*, **s** in *hiss*.

3. Those vowel-like sounds in which the sonority increases or decreases as a function of the change from one resonance to another. Examples: **wɒ, rɑ, lɔ, jæ, ɔɪ, aʊ, ɔl, ɑr.** Since **w, r, l,** and **j**, as attacks on vowels, involve similar patterns of sonority, they may be confused one with another. In like manner, the reverse glides, having similar patterns, may be confused.

CHANGES OF SOUND PROBABLY INFLUENCED PARTLY BY
ACOUSTIC ELEMENTS

1. In the same general range of pitch

High pitch	*s*ure	*s*ecure	ʃ	vs.	s
	*s*ucrose	*s*ugar	s	vs.	ʃ
	bra*c*e	bra*c*ket	s	vs.	k
	the*s*aurus	trea*s*ury	s	vs.	ʒ
	*Ll*oyd	*Fl*oyd	**hl**	vs.	**fl**

Middle pitch	pr*u*ne	p*l*um	**run** vs.	**lʌm**
	fath*er*	fath*er*	ɚ	vs.	ə
	n*er*ve	n*eu*rone	ɝ	vs.	**ɪur**
	c*ir*cular	c*y*clical	ɝ	vs.	**aɪ**
	lett*u*ce	lett*u*ce	ɪ	vs.	ə

2. Approximately equal in force

	*w*ard	*g*uard	**w**	vs.	**g**
	*Ll*ewellen	*Fl*ewellen	**hl**	vs.	**fl**
	pl*a*te	fl*a*t	**eɪ**	vs.	**æ**
	fa*ct*ion	fa*sh*ion	k	vs.	ʃ
	thr*e*sh	thr*a*sh	ε	vs.	**æ**

3. Having similar sonority patterns

Sudden change	ra*b*ies	ra*g*e	**b** . vs.	**dʒ**
	*D*eutch	*T*euton	**d**	vs.	**t**
	*t*wo	*d*uo	**t**	vs.	**d**
	me*d*al	me*tt*le	**d**	vs.	**t**
	wor*d*	ver*b*	**d**	vs.	**b**

Even pattern	d*ee*med	d*oo*med	i	vs.	u
	*s*cissors	*sh*ears	s	vs.	ʃ
	divi*s*ion	divi*s*ible	ʒ	vs.	z
	pal*s*y	paraly*s*is	z	vs.	s
	pri*c*e	pri*z*e	s	vs.	z

Gradual change	*l*lama	*l*lama	**j**	vs.	**l**
	*wh*at	*wh*at	**hw** vs.	**w**
	*hu*mor	*hu*mor	**ju** vs.	**hju**
	q*ui*et	c*oy*	**kw** vs.	**kɔ**
	ni*gh*	n*ear*	**aɪ** vs.	**ɪr**

SECTION IV

English Speech Styles in America

Chapter 16 Speech Style in the United States

In the preceding section the factors responsible for phonetic changes were discussed. Next in order is the matter of the crystallization of those changes when and where they take place. The factor here is that of *style*. Just as in the architecture of houses, design of automobiles, and cut of garments, so in the phonetic clothing of his thoughts one is influenced by what "they" do. "They" are the leaders. In speech those who set the style are the cultured, the traveled, the politically powerful, the educated, the wealthy, the socially influential, and the professional users of speech—preachers, teachers, actors, lecturers, radio and television speakers. This setting of the style is usually not conscious and deliberate, but is accomplished indirectly through the leadership of these influential groups.

Aspects of Style

There are two aspects of any style: the example set by the leader, and the emulation of that example by a significantly large body of followers. Until both of these aspects are manifest, no style has been created. In speech the example, when first brought to the attention of the follower group, may even be regarded as in poor taste—as indeed it often is; yet if the influence of the leader be powerful enough in realms other than speech, the masses may come in time to accept his speech example in spite of their first feeling that he is "incorrect" in his speech forms. When they do accept the example, even though they may not follow it, a style has been set. It often happens, therefore, especially in America, and even also in England, that one comes into a position of speech leadership not through any special inborn ability, training, or interest in diction, but through his skill with the scalpel, or his wife's social leadership, or his father's accumulated fortune. The style of speech that he sets in his community would, if it were not for his social position, remain as it was when he learned it from his mother and father, a purely provincial and homely form, perhaps, not bearing the marks of that thing we call "the mode." Thus a form of speech that in one generation smacks of the rustic and uneducated in another suggests the elite.

An analysis of the mode in any realm reveals that it is not what the masses are doing today, but what the masses may do tomorrow. That is, style is always one step ahead of general practice; it is a body of prevailing or successful influences. One cannot be sure, therefore, whether a given form is in good style until that form has stood the test of time. There are speech fads as well as speech styles.

Another aspect of style is the emphasis that it places upon difference: differences between what those in *this* community do and what those in *that* community do, between what we do *now* and what we did *yesterday*, between what the *cultured* do and what the *uncultured* do. In fact, if any practice becomes absolutely universal in a given area it is no longer a matter of style. Thus a practice that in one region is not stylish, but commonplace, may become a factor of style in an area in which the practice is novel, provided the people of the former area begin to influence strongly those of the latter. No style, then, can be adequately described except in terms of the differences it shows either from some rather general practice or from various provincial, local, or class practices.

Style and the Community

Considered narrowly, there are *general styles* on the one hand, and on the other *local styles* or *dialectal trends*. In the past an isolated community inhabiting a secluded river valley fertile enough to make the community self-supporting, has normally developed styles of its own. Of recent years, however, certain factors have broken down the barriers that separate these communities from the world and have begun to introduce into them more nearly universal styles. So far as speech is concerned these factors are the telephone, radio, television, the automobile, and the motion pictures—they subject the speech of otherwise isolated communities to the influence of distant styles. Whereas once the tendency was for a given language to become more and more broken into dialects, now there is a definite check upon that tendency, and perhaps a reversal of it has set in. However, though these modern influences can break down physical barriers, they are by no means as potent against social and economic barriers— class segregations based on such things as wealth, education, politics, religion, family, occupation, race, or nationality. As a consequence, radio, television, the telephone, and the paved road can scale mountains and span rivers for some, and thus tremendously enlarge their community, while for others these agencies have little if any influence. Hence in a given neighborhood there may dwell persons who are really living in communities of different sizes. The Gullah cotton picker on the South Carolina islands lives in a community no larger than one can traverse on foot, while his foreman's community includes Charleston and the environs, and that of his proprietor may include many states. The broader one's interests and the greater his ability to reach out and touch distant parts of the English-speaking world, the larger his community; and the larger one's community the more cosmopolitan the styles by which he may be influenced.

It follows, therefore, that two persons living in the same area, each following his own community style, may exhibit quite divergent speech uses. This is the way class distinctions in speech forms grow up. In the evolution of these distinctions, greater influence is naturally exerted by those who live in the city, since cities are at the crossing of paths of travel; and city dwellers of a given class get larger and longer vistas into the world around them than do country dwellers of the same class. Thus in speech as in most other matters of style the country mouse is likely to stand humble in the presence of the town mouse.

The most effective physical barrier in setting one group against another, and in the attendant development of divergent styles, is the ocean. Hence the English speech of one continent differs from that of another, and we can discern a general English style for a given continent as different from that of another. A person whose community is the United States of America will be exposed to speech styles which differ in many particulars from those of British South Africa. A statement of the difference of use between these two speakers will be a partial description of the styles of the two continents.

The development of an English style is often influenced by the patterns of speech of another language. While the two languages are spoken side by side we refer to the effect of the foreign tongue upon English as a brogue,[1] or foreign dialect. When, after generations, the foreign language has disappeared and has left its imprint upon English, that form of English is said to have a local or special dialect. The English of an Italian-born Pittsburgh factory hand is a foreign dialect, while that of the Pennsylvania German is an example of foreign dialect changing into a local dialect. The English of the lowland Scotsman is an example of a survival of a foreign influence after the original language has quite disappeared as a native tongue, leaving a local dialect.

We should distinguish between *styles* and *dialects*. Viewed from one helpful point of view, styles are advances, changes from the practices of yesterday, influences that cause persons consciously or unconsciously to adopt speech forms different from those of their parents. Dialects, from this point of view, are survivals of successful styles.

Speech Styles and Cultural Stereotypes

Differences in speech styles often become so linked with social, racial, and national differences that the lay person does not separate the speech style from its associates. Thus in his mind a given set of speech forms connotes a given race, nation, or social culture. If the hearer is a naïve lay person whose speech discriminations are for the most part on a subconscious level, he will like the speech style that connotes the racial, national, and social status that he favors and dislike speech that connotes the conditions of life he dislikes.

Many persons rationalize their likes and dislikes in speech styles

[1] Strictly, and originally, *brogue* refers to the Irish dialect, but the word has assumed more universal significance.

on a basis of what they regard as inherent beauty or ugliness of certain sounds or sound combinations; but it is doubtful if any considerable part of the esthetic value of a vocable is inherently resident within it. It is esthetically attractive when it is employed in a word with a pleasant, comfortable, or inspiring connotation or if it is a vocable used uniquely by a group of speakers whom the hearer admires, respects, or deems socially worthy. A sound or sound combination is regarded as uncouth and ugly when it is employed in a word or phrase that connotes something painful, disgusting, immoral, or cowardly, or if it is commonly used by persons regarded by the hearer as socially unworthy. It thus happens that the same speech forms will arouse quite different reactions from different hearers, depending upon their differing experiences. If one's experience with a given speech style is entirely through his contact with speakers who are haughty, supercilious, insincere, and superficially cultured, that style will seem to the hearer to be intrinsically inferior; but if one's contact with that same style is with people who are kind, tolerant, genuine, and deeply cultured, it will seem intrinsically superior and worthy of emulation. If one's contact with immigrants from a given country is limited to those who are uneducated, immoral, criminal, or uncultured, the dialect that is typical of the language of that country will seem a thing that one should avoid imitating at all costs; but if one's contact with immigrants from that country is limited to those who are educated, traveled, and cultured, that same dialect will be a pleasant one—one that gains for the speaker the hearer's immediate respect.

In England much more than in America class distinctions are marked by differences in dialect or speech style. H. C. Wyld says:

Everyone knows that there is a kind of English which is neither provincial nor vulgar, a type which most people would willingly speak if they could, and desire to speak if they do not. . . . I suggest that this is the best kind of English, not only because it is spoken by those often very properly called "the best people," but because it has two great advantages that make it intrinsically superior to every other type of English speech—the extent to which it is current throughout the country, and the marked distinctiveness and clarity in its sounds.[2]

[2] *The Best English*, S.P.E., Tract No. XXXIX. Oxford University Press (New York).

We question the process of rationalization by which Mr. Wyld arrived at his second "advantage." Since he belongs to that class referred to as the "best people," he is hardly in a position to speak without prejudice about the intrinsic superiority of his own speech. It must be observed, however, that many, perhaps a majority, of those Britishers who do not use the standard forms of speech of the "best people" would gladly endorse Mr. Wyld's opinions. They would heartily disapprove of the use by one of the upper class of local, cockney, or provincial speech forms; in fact they would suspect the genuineness of the claim to breeding of one whose speech was strongly marked by provincialisms. Mr. Wyld says further:

> The "best" speakers do not need to take thought for their utterance; . . . they have perfect confidence in themselves, in their speech, as in their manners. For both bearing and utterance spring from a firm and gracious tradition. "Their fathers have told them"— tha.: suffices.

And Mr. Wyld's inference here is that others, who have not had the advantage of hearing and speaking standard speech from childhood up, cannot master it so as to sound convincingly upper class.

In America class distinctions are less rigid than in England, but to the extent to which class lines are drawn, speech distinctions develop to characterize the classes and distinguish one from another. As the country grows older class distinctions will doubtless increase rather than decrease; at present, however, the only speech distinctions of class that manifest themselves the country over are between the "professional" class and the "laboring" class, and even between these classes the distinctions are perhaps more in grammar and vocabulary than in phonetic diction.

In America distinctions in speech are correlated more with place of rearing and nationality. If one has been brought up in an area of the country generally thought to be inhabited by ignorant and uncultured folk, he will do well—at least in talking to persons outside of his native area—to avoid the more obvious of the localisms of this area, for those localisms will have acquired an inferior social standing. If one has been reared in some colony of foreigners who are generally, even though mistakenly, believed to be uncouth, one should avoid their dialects. If, on the other hand, one has been reared in a community or among a group of people generally noted for their culture and good breeding, one may safely continue to use his native localisms anywhere, since his speech peculiarities will have high social standing.

Travelers from the Midwest are often impressed with the apparent difference in culture between the man-on-the-street in Boston and the man-on-the-street in Chicago. Why? For two reasons: (1) Boston is thought of as the home, not only of baked beans, but of the Cabots, the Lodges and the *Atlantic Monthly*, whereas Chicago is thought of as the center for railroads, gangsters, and the packing industry. (2) The Midwesterner has usually not heard Boston speech except from the lips of the educated and cultured—the other Bostonians have remained in Boston. Hence in the Midwest the Boston accent suggests the elite. When this dialect is imported westward it may be resented—it usually is resented when it is brought back by a Midwesterner who has gone East and then returned to his native state. Nevertheless, it still stands for "culture." The resentment is for affectation on the part of the speaker, not for the speech forms themselves.

North American Speech Styles

On this continent speech style has had an interesting history. The continent was settled by peoples speaking diverse languages. Eventually those who spoke English prevailed, and the country passed through a period of unification of speech uses. When, however, the colonies along the Atlantic seaboard began to send pioneers westward to settle remote and isolated communities, unification of language gave way to divergence and variation. The more self-supporting and independent these isolated communities became, the less intercourse they needed with the other parts of America, and the more definitely local and special their several dialects became. These differences in speech were augmented by the vast numbers of immigrants that poured into the country, who often established themselves in isolated communities of their own kind.

This era of divergence lasted until well into the twentieth century, but its decline began with the development of the railroad systems, which connected river valley with river valley, and seaboard with seaboard. The railroads not only made possible the mixing of speech cultures by transporting citizens from place to place, but they also introduced a new speech influence in the form of traveling dramatic companies who brought to each community, not local styles from other parts, but a more standardized form of speech not typical of any American community, but closely modeled after that of the British stage. Thus local and provincial dialects became widened and fused until the communities that had the greatest amount of intercourse with each other began to develop styles common to all the communities of a given area. So we developed "Eastern" speech, "Southern" speech, and "Midwestern" speech. As the people of each of these areas became conscious of their differences of speech forms, they began to search for the answer to the question, "Which form is correct?"

Then there arose a group of evangelical phoneticians who strove to superimpose upon the speech cultures of America a national speech standard, a "correct" form for North and South, East and West. This movement for a "standard speech" was lost in the rapid speech changes that came with the perfection of the long-distance telephone and the development of the automobile and fast roads, radio, and talking motion pictures. These instruments of communication not only routed the "standard speech" movement, but they, and television, are also now rapidly tearing down the fences between the major speech areas of the country. There is in the making, therefore, a common speech for America, not *the* "standard speech" *superimposed upon* the people, but *a* standard speech *arising spontaneously from* the people.

Although this unifying influence has pervaded the entire continent, there are still sufficient survivals of local styles to enable us to delimit certain speech areas. We must recognize that although in each of these areas the majority of persons today show an influence more definitely general American than local, it is the few characteristic speech forms of this majority that enable us to outline each general area. The speech of small minorities, consisting mostly of elderly persons from native families, exhibiting the local styles of yesterday, provide the data on the basis of which we can describe the special speech forms of each area.

Roughly, allowing for a great deal of overlapping, these areas are: the Eastern area, along the Atlantic seaboard from New Brunswick to Delaware, including a rather narrow strip through New York, New Jersey, and Delaware, and a much deeper section through the New England states; the Southern area, the area of the Confederacy together with Maryland and the southern and mountainous portions of West Virginia; the French Canadian area, the province of Quebec and Eastern Ontario; the British area, Canada west and the north of Ontario. Scattered over the country are also many smaller areas in which the speech forms are so narrowly local or foreign as to deserve distinction from the larger areas in which they are located. Such are the areas of "Cajun" French in Louisiana, the Pennsylvania "Dutch," the Milwaukee German, the Spanish dialect of the Southwest, and others.

This division of the continent into areas does not mean, for example, that all those living in Canada to the west and north of the Ontario borders have a British accent. It means rather that, comparing that area with others on the continent, the characteristic difference, in so far as one exists, lies in the fact that of all the many dialects spoken in this vast Canadian area, one can trace most often the influence of British speech forms. It means that although in the South we may hear Jewish, German, French, or Spanish dialects, these dialects are not the ones that make it possible for us to distinguish the South from the East—the East too has these same dialects. The South has, however, in addition to the dialects mentioned, a dialect that is characteristically different from that of the other areas. This difference is so characteristic that if a person speaking such a dialect is heard in Chicago, one remarks, "There is a Southerner."

The dialect spoken most generally in the area not included in the Eastern, Southern, French Canadian, and British areas may be called a *general American* dialect. It is of course as much a regional dialect as any of the others, but its area is large and increasing while that of the other dialects, with the possible exception of the French Canadian, is decreasing.

Western Ontario provides an interesting example of the competition of dialects. That section has much commerce with the United States that brings with it general American speech influences. French Canadians are crowding in from the East, bringing their dialect. There is much travel to and from England, and on the international border, as well as in urban centers, many government, church, and business executives and clerks are British. They bring with them various British accents. One must not overlook, too, the fact that since Canada is a member of the British Commonwealth of Nations, the British accent has, therefore, the advantage of a strong favoring prejudice. But apparently today the general American influence is stronger.

The general American dialect is geographically the most widely distributed and influences a preponderant and increasing majority of North Americans. One should distinguish between this general American dialect and general American style. The *dialect* is the form of speech actually most typical of a large area of the continent; the *style* is that body of prevailing influences that is modifying the English of the entire continent. Some of these influences are from one dialect area and some from another, a large portion coming from the general American dialect. In the contact of dialect with dialect, the general American dialect is modified, just as are the other dialects, by the general American style.

Now to recapitulate before going on to discuss the characteristics of general American style: Style in speech designates those critical differences in diction between area and area, class and class, generation and generation, that are favored by, are a part of, or are incorporated into the speech of the leaders of their communities and are, or become, habitual speech forms of a significantly large number of followers of these leaders. The speaker's community has both geographical and social boundaries; that is, though persons living side by side are usually to be thought of as in the same speech community, it often happens that they live in quite separate communities, and persons who dwell hundreds of miles apart may be thought of as living in the same community. It is even possible that a person may speak two dialects of English in order to make satisfactory adjustments to the styles of two communities of which he is a member. It is also possible that as a result of the influences of two leaderships, two divergent forms or speech practices may be in good style in a given area—such forms, for example, as **hjumɚ** and **jumə** for *humor*.

The Phonetic Analysis of Style

In discussing style the authors will not concern themselves here with gross differences between speech usages, such as those of grammar and vocabulary; nor will they treat of differences of pronunciations that clearly exhibit two parallel forms, such as the following:

> *apparatus* æpərætəs   æpəreɪtəs
> *either* aɪðə   iðɚ
> *adult* ædʌlt   ædʌlt

The authors are not concerned with words which might be included in a list of "1000 Words Commonly Mispronounced," since in almost every case the words show forms so divergent as to constitute virtually two words for the same idea. The authors prefer to leave to others the dubious question as to whether *again* is əgɛn or əgeɪn. Suppose it is decided that the second vowel should be the so-called short *e*; the phonetician is concerned with (1) analyzing the various pronunciations of those who employ this *e*, and (2) determining, if possible, which of the various forms are in best style. In general American style is the second vowel definitely ɛ? Is it nearer to æ? Is it nearer to ɪ? Is the second vowel nasalized? Is the stress on the second vowel markedly greater than on the first, or is it nearly the same as upon the first vowel? Suppose those who decide matters of pronunciation have determined that the second vowel should be the long *a*; then, in the impact of various dialects, what happens to the utterance of the word? In addition to matters of stress and nasalization, the phonetician must consider here the treatment of the "diphthong." Is the second vowel a definite glide, or is it really an **e** with a slight off-glide? If it is a clear glide, is the first element **e** or **ɛ**? Does the second element have the quality of ɪ or of **i**? What is the preferred general American style for the long *a* pronunciation of this word?

Thus it might be said that phoneticians are concerned not with which of two markedly different forms of a word should be used, but rather with how the chosen form is uttered. As to the use of vowels, this means that the phonetician is concerned, not with which phoneme to use in a given word, but rather with the member of the phoneme used in such a word as spoken in a given dialect or according to a given style. As to the use of stress, it means that the phonetician is concerned, not with which syllable to accent, but rather (1) with the type of stress, force, duration, pause, etc., employed on the stressed syllable, (2) with the degree of stress, and (3) with differences in the vowels caused by differences in syllabic stress.

Certain matters of utterance change more rapidly than others. In general, vowels are more unstable than the consonants. One speaks of the great vowel shift that followed the mixing of French and Anglo-Saxon forms. As a matter of fact the vowels of English are even now constantly shifting. Styles in the pronunciation of the consonants change much more slowly, and trends are more difficult to discern. Consequently, most of what is here said about styles of utterance will concern itself with the pronunciation of the vowels.

Chapter 17 Details of American Style

As has been suggested in the previous chapter, one cannot discuss any style without showing its differences from other styles. Hence, in discussing the general American standard it is necessary to discuss also local and provincial styles as well as the speech of the stage and the speech of other English-speaking countries. Out of the speech forms of the various dialects other than the general American will be selected those that seem to the writers to be used with increasing frequency in the general American area; and out of the forms of the general American dialect will be selected those that seem to be spreading to other dialects and are thus gradually extending the limits of the general American area. Any discussion of style, in speech or any other human conventions, must be of the nature of a prophecy of future uses as well as a survey of present practices. The way of the prophet is hard. After all, he can only record his prophecy and wait for developments. He cannot hope to be right in all details of his prophecy. Since the English language is a living, growing thing, style must be concerned with trends. Only a dead language has a fixed style.

Purity of the Vowels

An almost invariable characteristic of regional and local dialects in America is the tendency to make glides of vowels that are thought of by the speaker as pure vowels. Each area recognizes these characteristics of another region but is unaware of its own "drawls." The man who changes **kæt** to **kæət** does not notice what he is doing, but he does recognize the glides in *ask, camp,* and *tall,* when persons from other regions speak them as **æɪsk, kæəmp,** and **tɔwəl.** If all the regional dialects had the same glides they would pass unnoticed; but since the vowels affected differ so markedly they are brought to the hearer's attention when persons from different regions converse. A common element among the dialects, therefore, is the group of pure vowels. In the contact between dialects this common factor increases, and glides tend to disappear. Thus the general American style is toward purity of vowels. The following list illustrates glides used in various regions in place of the customary pure vowels.

Vowel	*Glide*	*Local Dialect*	*Sample Word* (General American Style) [1]
i	ii	sɪi	si
ɪ	ɪə	sɪət	sɪt
ɛ	eɪ	fleɪʃ	flɛʃ
	ɛə	rɛəd	rɛd
æ	æə	hæət	hæt
a	æɪ	klæɪs	klas
ɑ	ɑə	kɑəm	kɑm
ɔ	ɔu	kɔu	kɔ
ʊ	ʊə	kʊəd	kʊd
u	uu	suun	sun
	ju	tju	tu
ʌ	ʊʌ	mʊʌd	mʌd
ɜ	ɜɪ	dʒɜɪzɪ	dʒɝzɪ
	ɔɪ	θɔɪd	θɝd
ɜ	ʌr	bʌrd	bɝd
l	əl	lɪtəl	lɪtl̩

[1] In some cases other forms are also in good general American style, since there are many alternative forms both of which are in good style.

Standardization of the Glides

As the obverse of the picture of the pure vowels, we find the glides that are recognized as such in general American style to be clear cut and definite in comparison with those heard in many local dialects. These standard glides may be divided into four classes: ᴜ, j, r, and l glides, receding, diminuendo in type. The ᴜ glides are ɑᴜ and oᴜ. ɑᴜ has variant beginning points in American dialects. Thus *house* is heard as hæᴜs, haᴜs, hʌᴜs, hɒᴜs. ɑᴜ seems to be the most used in the general American dialect and seems to be superseding the aᴜ, ʌᴜ, and ɒᴜ glides in the other regional dialects. In many dialects the oᴜ glide appears almost a pure o. Other forms that it takes are oə and ɜᴜ. The latter pronunciation shows a strong stage and British influence. The prevailing trend is toward oᴜ.

The ɪ glides are eɪ, ɑɪ, and ɔɪ. eɪ becomes e in many dialects where foreign influences have been operative, such as Italian, French, and Gaelic. The ɑɪ glide in words like *time, I, my,* etc., in many American dialects, is shortened to what are practically pure vowels ɑ, a, or ʌ. In other dialects, its beginning and ending points vary so markedly that its sonorous initial vowel appears as a, ʌ, ɜ, ɒ, ɔ, or æ, and its less sonorous final vowel as a schwa not possessing a recognizable ɪ resonance. It seems likely that the ɑɪ of Eastern, British, and stage speech will be superseded by the ɑɪ of the general American dialect. Thus in general American style the glides in the words *my house* begin with the same vowel ɑ.

ɔɪ is heard in some parts as ɔɪ and in others as oɪ. A definite ɔɪ seems to be the prevailing trend for this diphthong.

The receding r glides are ir, ɪr, er, ɛr, ær, ɑr, ɒr, ɔr, or, ᴜr, ur, and ʌr. ir and ɪr tend to fuse into one phoneme in general American style, so that *peer* and *pier* are pronounced alike. Probably the place of beginning of this glide is somewhere between i and ɪ. The "diphthong" ɛr is heard in some dialects as a triphthong, so that *care* becomes kɛər or even kejə. In some dialects distinctions are made between the r glides in *Mary, merry,* and *marry,* but in general American style these distinctions are not usually made, ɛr being used in all such words, though sometimes this glide is nearer to er than to ɛr. The glide ɑr varies in its beginning vowel from **a** through **ɑ** and **ɒ** to **ɔ**. **ɑ** is clearly the mode for such words as *hard, dark, sergeant.* **ɒr** as in *borrow* and **ɔr** in *sort* in general American style usually become fused into one phoneme whose place of beginning is quite variant, roving from nearly as low as **ɑ** to nearly as high as **o**. **or**, though usually treated in the general American dialect as a separate glide often becomes confused with **ɔr** or **ɒr**, so that *glory* varies in its beginning vowel from **ɒ**, through **ɔ**, to **o**, or even to **oʊ**. **ʊr** and **ur**, like **ir** and **ɪr**, are fused into one phoneme, which has as its beginning point a sound perhaps half way between **u** and **ʊ**. This is the general American style for the pronunciation of *poor, sure*, and *tour.*

The ending points of these *r* glides vary from **r** to **ə**. Hence we have in some dialects *dear* **dɪə**, *care* **kɛə**, *card* **kɑəd**, *cord* **kɔəd**, *poor* **puə**. In some dialects, also, the schwa endings of the *ar* and *or* glides become so attenuated as practically to disappear, leaving us **kɑːd** for *card* and **kɔːd** for *cord*. The general American dialect favors the **r** endings for these glides.

The **r** glides formed by combining **oʊ** with **r** often lead to triphthongization or to the addition of an unstressed syllable to complete the transition. So *more* becomes **mowər** in some dialects and **mowə** in others, and is thus indistinguishable from *mower.* The trend of general American style seems to be to avoid either of these alternatives by omitting **w** from *or* combinations. Thus *mower* is **mowər**, but *more* is **mor**.

We have the following receding *l* glides: **il, ɪl, el, ɛl, æl, ɒl, ɔl, ol, ʊl, ul, ʌl, əl, ɝl**. In general American style, they are markedly distinct from each other, with little overlapping of phonemes. In many dialects of the East and South, the first five of this list employ a clearer *l* than do the rest, but in the general American dialect the dark *l* is used. In some dialects there is a tendency to interpose a schwa between the vowel and the *l* thus making *wheel* **ʍwiəl**, *bell* **bɛəl**, *furl* **fɝəl**, and *pool* **puəl**.

Just as the ending points of certain *r* glides change from **r** to **ə** and then the **ə** disappears, so with certain **l** glides the **l** changes to **ə**, and then **ə** becomes so softened as to disappear. In fact, this evolution of the *l* glides has gone farther than that of the *r* glides, and has already become the mode in most American dialects for such words as *calm, walk, almond*, and *chalk*. Even *yolk* is pronounced without the *l* by most careful followers of the general

American style. The evolution of the disappearing *l* may be illustrated thus: **wɔlk, wɔək, wɔk.**

l glides made by combining either **eɪ** or **oʊ** with **l** follow the same principle as combinations of **oʊ** with **r**, viz., many regional dialects make triphthongs of the combination, or add a syllable to complete the glide. Thus *pale* becomes **peɪl**, and *pole* becomes **poʊl** or **powəl**. The increasing American trend is toward **pel** and **pol**.

Reduction in the Number of the Vowels

Part of the difference between two nearly similar vowels may be length of utterance (see page 69) as a factor, apart from their absolute acoustic qualities. The words *balm* and *bomb*, as spoken by some, employ the same vowels, acoustically speaking; but such persons usually differentiate them by making the vowel in *balm* longer than that in *bomb*. Thus have grown up sets of vowel couplets, long and short. These couplets are particularly evident in the constellation of open vowels at the lower end of the vowel diagram. With some speakers the distinction between *stalk* and *stock* is made by a difference in the basic vowel resonance, but with others the distinction involves length of utterance of the vowels; with still others the difference is achieved by changing both length and resonance. Similar relatives involving the vowel **æ** are *halve* and *have*; those with **ɒ** are *guard* and *god*; those with **ɑ** are *stark* and *stock*. In England and the deep South the vowel **ʌ** appears as long and short in *bird* and *bud* respectively, with little change of resonance.

In addition to the long and short forms in each vowel couplet there is also a further modification of the vowel when it appears in an unstressed syllable. Thus there are the long **æː** in *France* and the short **æ·** in *sack*, but also the unstressed **æ** in *accrue*.

In this constellation of open vowels here analyzed, counting the unstressed as well as the long and short couplet forms, there are therefore twenty-one possible distinguishable phonemes. That number is not only more than necessary for verbal discrimination, but is not usable by the average speaker or listener. The modern trend seems to be in the direction of simplification of this constellation by reducing the number of phonemes actually used. The sounds of this constellation described by the editors of Webster's

New International Dictionary, 2nd Edition, 1934,[2] as trans-
literated into IPA symbols, are æ, ǽ, ɑ, a, ạ, ɔ, ɒ, ɒ̣, ɒː, ʌ, ʌ̣—
eleven in all. When, however, *The American College Dictionary*
came out in 1947,[3] there were described in this constellation only
æ, ɑ, ɔ, ɒ, ʌ. This reduction of the number of lexicographic
symbols for the sounds of this area of the vowel diagram is a
reflection of the tendency of the present-day speaker of American
English to be less precise than formerly in the production of
narrowly discrete varieties of the sonorous vowels of the language.
It may also be a reflection of a tendency on the part of American
listeners to be less fastidious, or more liberal, than formerly in
their acceptance of vowels heard. It is likely that, because of the
intermixing of Americans, with the breakdown of dialectal
barriers, the hearer is attending less than formerly to the acoustic
phoneme and more to the linguistic. He is learning to hear the
vowel in its context rather than in its resonance pattern.

In this readjustment of the open vowels of this language the
vowel area between ɑ and æ, which in some parts of the country
is divided into three phonemes, æ, a, and ɑ, is now being re-
divided rather generally into two, the phoneme a being eroded by
encroachments from ɑ on one side and from æ on the other. The
same fate is in store for ɒ, between ɑ and ɔ. The present-day
hearer may criticize one's pronunciation of *god*, saying that it
should be **gɑd**, not **gɔd**, or vice versa; but very seldom will he insist on **gɒd**. In fact, if he hears the form **gɒd**, he may understand
it as either **gɔd** or **gɑd**, whichever form he customarily uses.

The standard vowels of American English are being reduced,
therefore, by the dropping out of a and ɒ. The vowel resonances
represented by their phonograms have not disappeared, and
doubtless will never vanish from the language, but they will
probably cease to be the focal points of their own special phonemes.

Individuality of the Unstressed Vowels

The various dialects of English differ in their treatment of
vowels in unaccented syllables. The French-Canadian dialect goes
to the opposite extreme in giving the unaccented vowels distinct

---

[2] G. & C. Merriam Co.
[3] Random House.

individuality. Take *possibility*, for example: in the Midwest it would be **pɑsəbɪlətɪ̦**, while in French-Canadian it would sound like **pɒsɪbilɪtɪ**. In the blending of dialectal influences into a general American style the trend seems to be about halfway between these two practices. The following list gives examples of these various pronunciations:

The Indefinite Schwa Pronunciation	General American Trend	A Level Stress
əvɛnt	i̦vɛnt	ivɛnt
sɛnət	sɛnɪ̦t	sɛneɪt
lɛtəs	lɛtɪ̦s	lɛtʌs
wɒntəd	wɒntɪ̦d	wɒntɛd
drəmætək	drɑ̦mætɪ̦k	dramætɪk
əbɒləʃ	æbɒlɪʃ	æbɑlɪʃ
pəteɪk	pəteɪk	pɑrteɪk
pəteɪta	pəteɪtọ	pouteɪtou
fɑðə	fɑðɚ	fɑðɝ

One of the interesting facts about the schwa as used in America is that the speech styles of different areas vary both in the sound units and in the contexts in which this indefinite vowel may be employed. One group of speakers would always pronounce *menace* as **mɛnɪ̦s**, never as **mɛnəs**, but would pronounce *reader* **ridə**, not **ridɚ**. On the other hand, speakers who say **ridɚ** would be likely to say **mɛnəs**. Others who would pronounce *ability* as **əbɪlɪ̦tɪ̦**, never using a schwa in the third syllable, might pronounce the word *tallow* as **tælə** rather than as **tælọ**. It is this inconsistency of use of the schwa that causes it to be displaced by vowels that have more definite values. Whenever the schwa is used in a given sound unit or context, and is so used in all American areas, such use will remain; but in units and contexts in which the schwa differs from area to area the schwa will be displaced by other unstressed vowels. The use of the schwa in English is widespread, but the purposes for which it is used vary greatly. In the fusing of one dialect into another, one may expect, therefore, a decrease in its use; for, so far as the vowels are concerned, the common factor that binds dialect area with dialect area is not the schwa but the definite forms of the several vowels.

These common uses of the schwa are surprisingly few: in final unstressed syllables spelled *al, ul, ol,* as in *regal, awful, symbol*; in unstressed syllables in which the vowel would, if stressed, be ʌ, as in *caucus, submit, circumstance*; and in word endings spelled *cion, tion, sion, tia, sia, cia, cean, tious,* and *cious,* as in *mission, ocean, vicious.* In all other contexts, and sometimes even in those mentioned above, the schwa uses in one area differ from those in another, so that a syllable pronounced in one area with an undeniably indefinite vowel will in another be pronounced with a resonance that is clearly that of one of the standard vowels. Thus, if modern forces bringing the speech of one region in contact with that of another were not now operative, our language, marked as it is by a vigorous alternation of stress, would evolve so rapidly in such different directions in different areas that one dialect would become unintelligible to the speakers of another. The present forces, however, are tending to reverse this evolution and to reduce the number of schwa uses.

Another factor that is constantly operative to reduce the frequency of the schwa is the rather unintelligent use of the pronouncing dictionary. The reader of the dictionary too often fails to read the introductory remarks about the pronunciations indicated for the words defined. The writer of the dictionary specifies usually that the forms given are for formal, careful, and discriminating utterance. He explains further that in informal situations less careful and less precise pronunciations may be quite acceptable. He may even point out that from area to area there may be acceptable differences of pronunciation. The user of the dictionary, however, is often in too much haste to determine the "correct" pronunciation. The pronouncing dictionary usually represents the unaccented vowels in their most discriminating forms, and hence the user of this dictionary gains the impression that no other forms are acceptable. It is probably impossible to avoid the careless use of dictionaries, and certainly pronouncing dictionaries are necessary. Hence we must recognize that this factor will be an ever present and constant influence in the direction of greater discrimination among the various unstressed vowels.

In summary, the principle to be stated here is that general American style shows two marked tendencies: (1) to give each unaccented vowel some of the quality of one of the standard vowels (though not necessarily the quality of the vowel that would be employed if the syllable in question were to be definitely stressed); and (2) to use the indefinite and nondescript schwa sparingly. It must be said that this principle is a relative one. It means that the use of the schwa is increasing in some areas and decreasing in others. For the great body of inhabitants of the United States of America, however, the pull of style will doubtless be in the direction of greater individuality of the unaccented vowel, since the majority of our speakers employ the schwa so prodigally that it becomes by far their most frequent vowel, perhaps one out of every four vowels in connected speech being schwa.[4]

Discrimination Between Vowels and Voiced Nasal Continuants

One of the characteristics of American speech in general is the assimilation of the vowels with preceding or succeeding **m**, **n**, and **ŋ**. The practice of this type of assimilation is so common in America that it is not recognized by Americans. In fact, when the Englishman characterizes our speech as nasal, the American is inclined to resent the characterization and to think the Englishman speaks from lack of knowledge of American uses. He is inclined to feel that the critic had limited contact with a few Americans whose speech is not typical of the general practice. He may be surprised when he happens upon a phonetic transcription of American speech written by an Englishman for British readers to show how Americans actually talk to note that the author includes a warning that all vowels preceding or succeeding the nasal consonants are to be read as definitely nasal vowels. Whether or not this is an accurate representation of American speech, the fact remains that this nasalization is one outstanding difference between the cultured speech of the British and the cultured speech of Americans.

It is doubtless possible to produce a vowel that is partially delivered by way of the nasal chambers without giving it so-called nasal resonance, but if the passageway into the nasopharynx is greater in size than is afforded by a very slight lowering and

[4] This tendency to employ the schwa is increasingly reflected in modern editions of pronouncing dictionaries. See, for example, the explanation of this principle in the discussion of the pronouncing system of *The American College Dictionary* on page xxii.

retracting of the velum, the vowel so produced will have a nasal quality. Thus, if, while uttering the vowel, one anticipates the articulatory adjustment necessary for the nasal sound that immediately follows, the vowel itself will become nasalized. Or if the velum is not raised definitely so as practically to close the nasopharyngeal port when one makes the transition from a nasal consonant to the succeeding vowel, the vowel will again be nasalized. It is in these ways, doubtless, that the American nasalization is produced and this is why the "Yankee" is said to "talk through his nose." Many "Yankees" carry over this nasalization to other vowels that are not preceded or followed by nasal consonants so that not only do they show this "assimilation" nasality but a general nasal quality on all vowels, due doubtless to the fact that the nasopharyngeal port is allowed to remain markedly open on all sounds that do not actually require the building up of real air pressure in the cavity of the mouth.

In spite of the professed admiration for the sincere Yankee type of speech, the average American has a secret respect for a more cosmopolitan style, and shows his respect by reducing nasalization on the vowels. The nasalized pronunciation of the word *on*, for example, makes for a combination of sounds that is practically a nasal diphthong, so definitely does the first sound blend with the second. *No* becomes a triphthong—the **n** blending into the **o** as smoothly as **o** blends with the final vowel **u**. With increasing frequency, however, Americans are making a sharp distinction between the *n* and the preceding or succeeding vowels so that the place of transition is as definite as though the words were *odd* and *doe*.

Avoidance of Secondary Stress

The English language has developed a definite tendency toward marked differences in stress between syllables of a given word. Among the major languages of the world it stands almost at an extreme in this regard. Yet in various parts of the English-speaking world there is great divergence of practice in the use of this stress. Perhaps nothing so drastically changes the character of an English word as a definite change of stress. Were English not so markedly accented, these differences would be relatively insignificant, but when the person who is used to pronouncing *laboratory* with a stress upon the first syllable hears it pronounced with the primary stress upon the second syllable, he is surprised, and the word becomes to him strikingly conspicuous. The American practice of employing the secondary stress on such words as dic′tion-a′ry, tran′si-to′ry, mis′sion-a′ry, mi′gra-to′ry, sac′ri-fice′, dif′fi-cul′ty, tel′e-gram′, or′gan-i′za′tion, is definitely counter to the British and stage practice of one single stress for each word unit. There are interesting exceptions to this generalization about the difference between British and American accent patterns. The British are quick to notice that Americans pronounce all three syllables of *medicine*, while they elide the second into virtual obscurity. They, however, make three well-defined syllables out of *family*, while Americans treat it as the British do *medicine*, making it **fæmlɪ**.

The American practice of even stress on such words as *program*, *chlorine*, *chaos*, *houseboat*, also runs counter to the principle of stressing these words on one syllable or the other and giving the vowel of the unstressed syllable a schwa value or at least definitely shortening its time of utterance and lowering its intensity. The prevailing and increasing style in matters of stress is in the direction of reducing the number of words in which the secondary stress, or an even stress, is employed.

The avoidance of a secondary stress sometimes necessitates the change of the vowel values in the unstressed portions of the word; so *dictionary* changes its form from **dɪkʃənerɪ** to **dɪkʃənərɪ** and sometimes even to **dɪkʃənrɪ**. The first and third form may be regarded as extremes, for they represent opposing styles. The second form is to be regarded as a compromise, the resultant of the opposition of the first and third forms. So the American who adopts the Britisher's practice of saying **mɪʃənrɪ** is following a style that doubtless is too extreme to be adopted. On the other hand, the American who says **mɪʃənerɪ** or **mɪʃənɛrɪ** is following a local and perhaps provincial style; but the American who says **mɪʃənərɪ** or **mɪʃənərɪ** is adopting a compromise that will be inconspicuous to the ear of the users of either of the extreme styles. It is the inconspicuousness of this compromise that will give it ascendency.

SECTION V
Phonetic Alphabets

Chapter 18 The International Phonetic Alphabet

The Development of the IPA

From the very first, students of the English language have been confronted with the necessity of having some set of symbols to represent speech sounds more accurately than does our puzzling and intricate spelling. There have been many such sets of symbols, but the first to gain any great prominence was Alexander Melville Bell's "Visible Speech" symbols. Bell was interested in the teaching of speech to the deaf and in the course of his investigations worked out a set of visible speech symbols which were published in 1867 in his book *Visible Speech*. This system derived its name from the fact that the symbols were a pictorial representation of the sounds. There were symbols picturing rounded lips, spread lips, a high front tongue position, a high back tongue position, etc. Some of these key symbols picturing vowel positions are listed below:[1]

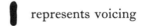 represents voicing

back of tongue high

---

[1] See Alexander Graham Bell, *The Mechanism of Speech*, Funk and Wagnalls Co., 1910, p. 65.

⌋ back of tongue low

T back and front of tongue both high

ℓ back and front of tongue both in mid positions

⊥ back and front of tongue both low

L front of tongue low

ρ front of tongue high

† rounded lip aperture

By using various combinations of these basic symbols, Bell was able to represent any vowel in any language, as well as a number of theoretical vowels not actually existing anywhere. In a similar fashion, the symbol ⟨ⅰ⟩ represented the sound of *m*. This symbol is a combination of **S** meaning open palate, ▬ representing voice, and **Ɔ** representing closed lips. The incomplete circle pictures the oral cavity.

It was Bell's aim to develop a system of symbols so complete that anyone who could understand them could pronounce correctly at sight any language written in these symbols. He succeeded, but his visible speech alphabet was so revolutionary in form and contained so many symbols that few people could understand it. It gradually fell into disuse because its very completeness made it too cumbersome. Nevertheless, it was widely used for several decades, especially in the teaching of the deaf, and remnants of it may still be seen in the literature.

Among those who adopted Bell's Visible Speech symbols in a modified form was Henry Sweet, an English phonetician. He called his simplified version the Organic or Revised Visible Speech. Sweet realized, however, that even his revised form was too complicated for the average reader. He therefore developed a new set of symbols using the characters of the Roman alphabet and called it the Broad Romic system. These symbols were introduced in his *Handbook of Phonetics* published in 1877, given in parallel columns with the Visible Speech signs. Since it was these Broad Romic symbols that later formed the basis of the International Phonetic Alphabet, it is in a very real sense that Henry Sweet is called the father of our phonetic alphabet.

The International Phonetic Association was founded in 1886, and in 1888 it adopted more or less bodily Sweet's Broad Romic symbols as the official International Phonetic Alphabet. At its inception the Association was composed largely of teachers of foreign languages and students of linguistics. It was the purpose of this Association to promulgate an official set of symbols that could be used by scholars all over the world in phonetic and linguistic studies, and especially in the teaching of foreign languages. The alphabet has been modified slightly from time to time since its inception and is now in wide use. *Le Maître Phonétique*,[2] the official publication of the International Phonetic Association, was first issued in 1886. All of its articles are printed in phonetic symbols. Almost every issue contains articles in German, French, and English, as well as several additional languages. It is thus a valuable source not only for information in the field of phonetics but also for the study of foreign languages and of material for practice in the reading of phonetic symbols.

Advantages and Disadvantages of the IPA

The International Phonetic Alphabet has two chief advantages: In the first place, it is the official alphabet of an established body of scholars and thus has behind it the weight of prestige and scholarship. Secondly, it is more widely known than any other system of sound representation except the diacritical markings used in the various dictionaries. It is, as it were, the "Esperanto" of phoneticians—which means that it serves as the best available medium for the exchange of ideas in this professional field.

[2] Presently published at University College, London.

There are, however, several disadvantages inherent in the International Phonetic system. It was originally promulgated largely by European scholars who were concerned chiefly with the phonetic problems of continental European languages rather than English, particularly our American variety of English. Again, it was inevitable, considering the circumstances of its origin, that in many instances accuracy and consistency would be sacrificed to the interests of conflicting views. The present form of the IPA is not to be thought of as the end product of exhaustive research and profound scholarship. It is rather the result of compromise among conflicting groups of scholars and divergent points of view. Like many compromises achieved under democratic conditions, it represents an acceptable and generally workable solution of the problems presented, rather than a consistent and scientific one. Like most fixed institutions, it is conservative and slow to change in the light of more recent phonetic knowledge. An outstanding illustration of this is the fact that the IPA has never had a special symbol to represent the Middle Western vowelized *r* sound.

Of course this conservative resistance to change adds to the value of the IPA as a medium for the exchange and permanent recording of ideas in the field of phonetics; but the very characteristic that is an advantage for one purpose is a handicap when it comes to the teaching of phonetics. A rigid adherence to the IPA means that the present-day teacher of American phonetics must attempt to present a consistent and accurate view of phonetic science with tools that are the results of compromises made many years ago by scholars who were little interested in many of our special problems. Thus it is not at all surprising that writers of textbooks in the general field of speech, as well as in phonetics proper, have frequently modified the IPA in accordance with their needs and views. On the other hand, in writing for professional publication and in recording phonetic studies for future use, there is no adequate substitute for the International Phonetic Alphabet.

Other Systems of Symbolization

Phonetic systems are sometimes divided into two main types: acoustic and physical. Acoustic systems are characterized by their use of the characters of the written alphabet as symbols (augmented when necessary by other symbols and modifying signs) and by their dependence upon key words to indicate the value of the symbols. The IPA and the diacritical markings used in dictionaries are the chief examples of acoustic systems. Any consistent system of pseudo spelling, such as that used in dialect writings for popular consumption, falls also within this type. Stock examples of the use of pseudo spelling to represent sounds are *ah* for α and *aw* for ɔ. We should mention again, in this connection, the Dialect Atlas Alphabet. This alphabet is based upon, and to a large extent overlaps, the IPA, but it contains many additional symbols and modifying signs. These are essentially close transcription symbols made necessary by the work of the Dialect Atlas Association in recording and preserving the various dialects of this country. Strictly speaking, only the IPA and the associated Dialect Atlas Alphabet can be said to be phonetic alphabets. All systems use phonetic symbols, that is, signs representing sounds; but some of them do not qualify as phonetic alphabets under our definition of such alphabets as containing one symbol per sound and one sound per symbol.

The second main type of phonetic systems, the physical systems, is characterized by two features: (1) avoidance of both key words and characters of the written alphabet for symbols, and (2) use of symbols representing positions and movements rather than acoustic values. The two outstanding examples of this type are Bell's Visible Speech symbols discussed above and Jespersen's Analphabetic system.[3]

Differences Between the IPA Symbols and Those Used in This Volume

The present writers have used certain symbols that are not in strict accordance with the IPA. These changes are listed and explained below. Relatively few changes have been made, and most of these are minor modifications for use in narrow transcription. In each case the change was made because the writers felt either that the older symbolization was inaccurate and inconsistent or that a different symbol was needed to express a different point of view.

[3] Otto Jespersen, *Growth and Structure of the English Language*, D. Appleton-Century Company, 1923.

1. *The use of ɝ.* Dr. Kenyon's symbol ɝ [4] is used here to represent the sound of the general American vowel *r.* There is no symbol for this sound in the IPA, although the symbol ɚ which was also introduced by Dr. Kenyon at an earlier date is widely used. The decision to use the symbol ɝ instead of ɚ follows the recommendation made by Dr. Kenyon in the last revision of his *American Pronunciation.* The reasons behind this change are as follows: The generally accepted IPA symbol for the vowel in such words as *bird, heard, fur,* etc., when spoken in standard Southern or Eastern American speech, is ɜ. When Dr. Kenyon was originally searching for a symbol to indicate the general American variety of this vowel he decided to add a retroflexing sign to the schwa, ɚ, and let it represent the "er" sound. The symbol is generally known as the "hooked schwa." Now it is obvious that our general American vowel *r* is by no means a retroflexed schwa; hence the symbol is decidedly misleading. It is much more logical to add the retroflexing sign to the ɜ, thus ɝ, since this is at least partially descriptive of the anatomical relationship between the two sounds. Because the new symbol is more logical and consistent than the old one, and because the present writers believe that its use will spread, it is adopted here.

2. *The use of* **r**, **ř**, *and* **Я**. Strictly speaking, the symbol **r** represents a trilled *r* in the IPA. In accordance with general practice among American phoneticians **r** is used here to represent in broad transcription any of our American consonantal or glide *r*'s, and **ř** is then used in narrow transcription to indicate the trilled *r.* The other symbols for the close transcription of the *r*'s are standard except the **Я**, which the writers have used to help teach the fact that there is a back tongue *r* (which is still not a velar *r*) following back plosives, in the same manner that the front tongue fricative *r* ɹ usually follows front plosives.

3. *The use of dots to indicate partial unstressing.* This is not part of the IPA system, but it is used in the *Century Dictionary.* The writers have adopted it because of the need, even in broad transcription, for a more accurate representation of vowels in unstressed positions than that afforded when the only choice is between some regular vowel symbol and the ə. For a more complete discussion

[4] Actually Dr. Kenyon's symbol uses the "hook" on the bottom stroke of the ɜ.

of this point, see again the description of the schwa vowels on page 92.

4. *The use of* l *and* ɫ. The symbols are standard in the International Phonetic Alphabet but their interpretation is broadened somewhat in this book. It seems obvious that we have in English both a "consonantal" or glide *l* and a vowel *l* just as we have a glide *r* and a vowel *r*. We have separate symbols for the ɝ and its unstressed form ɚ and it seems logical that we should have one for the vowel *l*. Since there is none, the symbol for the so-called syllabic *l* has been used in a broadened sense to represent all of the vowel *l*'s and to symbolize the lateral key vowel position in the discussion of glide sounds.

5. *The use of* ɹ. If **j** is to represent a certain type of glide movement, it is evidently inaccurate to use the same symbol to indicate a continuant sound. In the IPA **j** is made to serve in both categories. Since **j** is used in the present work to indicate glide sounds only, it seemed logical to use a small capital ɹ to stand for the continuant fricative made in approximately the same articulatory position.

6. *The use of* **hw** *and* **hj**. The writers believe that the sounds represented by these symbols are produced by an *h*-approach to approaching *w* and *j* glides, respectively. This is quite different from saying that they symbolize the voiceless counterparts of **w** and **j**. Consequently the IPA symbols ʍ and ç are inaccurate, since they represent voiceless continuants (corresponding to the conception of **w** and **j** as voiced continuants). **hw** and **hj** better represent the actual nature of the two sounds.

7. *The use of* t͡ʃ, ʃ͡t, t͡s, s͡t, *etc.* The ͡ is a modifying sign for purposes of close transcription. It is designed to help teach the nature of these combinations and in certain instances to avoid ambiguity. It is not so used in the IPA, nor are such combinations as ʃ͡t and s͡t usually treated as being in the same category as t͡ʃ and t͡s.

8. *The use of* ɦ. This is also a symbol for narrow transcription designed to aid in teaching the difference between an *h*-approach with the articulatory mechanism stationary and one when it is in movement.

Additional Symbols in the International Phonetic Alphabet

It should be understood that the IPA contains other symbols and modifying signs that have not been presented in this book. No attempt has been made, for example, to describe in detail the sound system for any particular foreign language or to list all possible non-English sounds. The primary purpose has been to present the sound system of English and some of the underlying principles of phonetics. Certain modifying signs and symbols for foreign sounds have been included primarily as adjuncts to the understanding of English phonetics. A number of others have been omitted because they did not seem important in the light of this basic purpose.

Chapter 19   Diacritical Markings

Use of the Pronouncing Dictionary

When one desires to learn what pronunciation of a given word is best in a given area, he must have recourse to a word list that has been prepared by observers situated at strategic points over the area in question, who indicate, with diacritical markings or phonetic symbols or both, the pronunciation of each word as they have heard the "best speakers" utter it. The reliability of such a word list depends, of course, upon both the reader's ability to understand the diacritical markings or phonetic symbols, and the completeness of the phonographic system employed by the compilers of the list. The validity of the information gained by the readers of the list depends not only upon these two factors, but upon the number of observers, their ability to record what they hear, and their discrimination in selecting their exemplars.

Two impediments often stand between observers and readers: (1) The key words given to illustrate a phonogram have such variant pronunciations as to be misleading to some readers. Establishing a table of standard sounds of reference is difficult. (2) The reader of the pronouncing dictionary is usually too easily satisfied with noting the "correct" pronunciation. He does not notice variant pronunciations, nor does he concern himself with a careful study of the author's explanation of the phonographic system used in indicating this "correct" pronunciation. Too often the reader reads into a given phonogram something quite different from what the author intended. A third possible impediment is

317

that the publishers of dictionaries are sometimes obliged for commercial reasons to treat vaguely the pronunciations of words upon which regions differ so markedly as to make for interregional prejudices. Would it be good business, for example, for a dictionary to settle the question as to whether *hard* is **hard**, **haəd**, or **haːd**?

In spite of these limitations, the pronouncing dictionary has its legitimate uses. Few agencies have the resources at their disposal to make so complete an inventory of the speech styles of the country as do the compilers of an unabridged dictionary. To ignore their research in this field, and to substitute for it personal opinions of individuals is of doubtful advantage.

In using the dictionary as a guide to speech uses, one should remember that the dictionary gives the pronunciations that have good standing the country over. One should honor these pronunciations, therefore, in every instance, and deviate from them only when the form given is conspicuously different from that of his community. The person whose speech community is the entire nation would do well to follow the dictionary without deviation from its recommended form. The books selected by the writers as American authorities are *The American College Dictionary* (ACD), Random House, 1947; and *Webster's New International Dictionary*, 2nd ed., G. & C. Merriam Co., 1934.

A Comparison of Three Systems of Symbolization

To assist the student in translating the phonographic system of the dictionary into that employed in this book the following tables are given:

TABLE I.   CONSONANTS AND CRESCENDO GLIDES

Key Words	Phonetic Symbols	Webster Symbols	ACD Symbols
1. *p*in	**p**	p	p
2. *b*oat	**b**	b	b
3. *m*an	**m**	m	m
4. *f*an	**f**	f	f
5. *v*at	**v**	v	v
6. *t*o	**t**	t	t

TABLE I (*Continued*)

Key Words	Phonetic Symbols	Webster Symbols	ACD Symbols
7. *do*	**d**	d	d
8. *no*	**n**	n	n
9. *say*	**s**	s	s
10. *zero*	**z**	z	z
11. *sugar*	**ʃ**	sh	sh
12. *measure*	**ʒ**	zh	zh
13. *thin*	**θ**	th	th
14. *those*	**ð**	~~th~~	~~th~~
15. *chose*	**tʃ**[1]	ch	ch
16. *joy*	**dʒ**[1]	j	j
17. *king*	**k**	k	k
18. *go*	**g**	g	g
19. *sing*	**ŋ**	{ ng ŋ	ng
20. *hot*	**h**	h	h
21. *run*	**r**	r	r
22. *lady*	**l**	l	l
23. *win*	**w**	w	w
24. *you*	**j**[2]	y	y
25. *huge*	**ħ**	h	h

TABLE II. VOWELS AND DIMINUENDO GLIDES

Key Words	Phonetic Symbols	Webster Symbols	ACD Symbols
1. *see*	**i**	ē	ē
2. *recede*, *city*[3]	**i̠**	ė	none[4]

[1] Other combinations of this sort could be included here, such as **ts** in *cats* and *hence*, **st** in *stand* and *paste*, **zd** as in *bruised* and *hazed*, **ʃt** as in *washed* and *dished*, and **ʒd** as in *rouged*. The two listed above were chosen merely because of convention.

[2] This should be distinguished in IPA from the **ɪ**. *Dew* is **dɪu**, but *you* is **ju**. **j** is used only at the beginning of a syllable.

[3] The final sound in *city*, as spoken in most of the "general American" area, is a good example of the sound **i̠**. In England and in many parts of eastern United States *city* is pronounced **sɪtɪ**.

[4] In the ACD column of vowel symbols the word "none" occurs thirteen

TABLE II (*Continued*)

Key Words	Phonetic Symbols	Webster Symbols	ACD Symbols
3. s*i*t	ɪ	ĭ	ĭ
4. Apr*i*l	ɪ̣	ĭ̵	none
5. s*ay*	eɪ	ā	ā
6. ch*a*os	e	å	none
7. s*e*t	ɛ	ĕ	ĕ
8. mom*e*nt	ɛ̣	ĕ̵	none
9. s*a*t	æ	ă	ă
10. *a*ccount	æ̣	ă̵	none
11. h*a*lf	a	ȧ	none
12. tr*a*nslate	ạ	none	none
13. c*a*lm, f*a*r	ɑ	ä	ä
14. *a*rtistic	ɑ̣	none	none
15. f*o*x, sw*a*p	ɒ	ŏ	ŏ
16. c*o*nnect	ɒ̣	ŏ̵	none
17. s*o*rt, *a*ll	ɔ	ô	ô
18. f*o*rget	ɔ̣	none	none
19. n*o*	ou	ō	ō
20. *o*bey	o	ȯ	none
21. c*ou*ld	ʊ	o͝o	o͝o
22. f*u*lfill	ʊ̣	none	none
23. b*oo*t	u	o͞o	o͞o
24. rh*eu*matic	u̞	none	none
25. c*u*t	ʌ	ŭ	ŭ
26. circ*u*s	ʌ̣	ŭ̵	none
27. b*i*rd (Eastern)	ɜ	û	ûr
28. p*er*fuse (Eastern)	ɜ̣	ẽ	ər
29. b*i*rd (General American)	ɝ	û	ûr

times. This does not mean, of course, that the ACD has no representation of the sounds indicated. It means only that there are no *special* phonograms that are equivalent to those in the column of phonetic symbols or to those in the Webster column. In six cases in which "none" occurs in the ACD column the *general* symbol ə is employed in place of more discriminating symbols.

TABLE II (*Continued*)

Key Words	Phonetic Symbols	Webster Symbols	ACD Symbols
30. per*f*use (General American)	ɚ	ẽ	ər
31. bott*l*e	ļ	l	l
32. sof*a*	ə	*a*	ə
33. t*i*me	aɪ	ī	ī
34. s*ou*nd	aʊ	ou	ou
35. b*oi*l	ɔɪ	oi	oi

Special Notes on the Webster System

It will be noted that the phonetic symbolization generally used in this book and the diacritical system of Webster do not meet squarely at all points. Some sounds that Webster discriminates are not listed in our charts of phonetic symbols; and certain sounds listed in the phonetic charts are not represented in Webster's system.

Webster divides the ɒ phoneme into two families of *o*'s, marked ŏ and ô, and differentiates in this way the vowels in the words *cloth* and *odd*. Other words he marks ŏ are *forest*, *torrid*, and *not*; and others he marks ô are *soft*, *dog*, *loss*, and *cost*. The pronunciation of the vowels of these words is so variable from region to region that it seems hardly practicable to follow this microscopic division in phonetic symbolization.

In spite of the fact that Webster does not list as speech elements such obvious combination consonants as *ts*, *dz*, *sht*, etc., he does list the following combinations: *gz* as in *exist*, *hw* as in *white*, *ks* as in *box*, and *kw* as in *queer*. In phonetic representation these combinations are not listed as such, but are made up as needed by combining symbols given to represent the separate units.

The system used in Webster makes no distinctions between l and ļ, h and ɦ, ɝ and ɜ, and between and among the various glide *r*'s. The Webster system provides (as many systems do not) for the symbolization of the unstressed vowels æ, ị, ɛ, ɚ, ị, ɒ, and ʌ, but does not provide for the unstressed vowels ạ, ọ, ʊ, ụ, ɑ̣.

Webster provides alternative representation for the combination **ju**; the single symbol ū may be used, or the sound may be broken up into its elements and written yōo. The choice apparently depends not upon the sound of the word to be pronounced, but upon its spelling, so *youth* is marked yōoth and *use* is ūz. Webster provides even an unstressed form for the phonetic combination **ju**, his representation being u̇, as in *unite*.

Webster also recognizes as a single sound unit **ɛr**, represented in the dictionary as â. It is not clear (perhaps the authors of the dictionary were not anxious to make it so) whether this sign, â, is intended to represent only the **ɛ**, as heard in *care, bear, mare*, or represents also the *r*. At least the only examples of this given by Webster are those in which the vowel is followed by the *r*. **ɪr** is treated similarly by Webster, being given a separate symbol ệ to represent the vowel in such words as *bier, dear, fear*.

Special Notes on the ACD System

In the tables on pages 318–321, the Webster symbols are placed first (i.e., to the left on the page) because historically the Webster system was first; indubitably it influenced the editors of the ACD in the selection of their symbols.

As in the Webster system, ACD makes no differentiation between **h** and **ɦ**, **ɝ** and **ɜ**, **o** and **oʊ**, **e** and **eɪ**. Whereas Webster discriminates between the two vowels in *recede* by diacritics that represent them as relatives, ACD has recourse to what is virtually an "ɪ schwa," merely adopting the symbol ĭ for this purpose, thus giving this character double duty.

ACD makes broad use of the symbol ə, letting it stand for the unstressed forms of any standard vowels. Hence the unstressed vowels in *mountain, system, gallop,* and *porpoise*, are represented by the same symbol ə.

In ACD the distinction between the consonant *l* and the unstressed vowel *l* is made by adding the ə. Thus *little* is spelled litəl, in spite of the fact that most speakers explode the **t** directly into the ḷ without an intervening, centrally delivered vowel—even without ə.

As Webster does it, the combination **ju** is represented in ACD by one symbol, ū; but, unlike Webster, ACD is consistent in this use, even spelling *you* as ū, no yōo; though *your* is spelled yō͝or, since ACD has no single symbol for **ju**.

ACD uses Webster's representation of the **ɛr** in *dare, chair, prayer,* viz., â. But ACD does not follow Webster's parallel representation of **ɪr**, as ē, for such words as *bier* and *fear*.

In the main, ACD is liberal and permissive in its representation of the sounds of English, as compared with Webster's diacritical system, which is strict and directive, except where, probably for business reasons, the "front office" has dictated otherwise.

SECTION VI
Applied Phonetics

Chapter 20   Speech for Those

Impaired in Hearing

The Deaf

Those impaired in hearing may be divided into two main classes: those who have some usable hearing, and those who have none. The former are called the hard of hearing. The latter may be divided into two subclasses, the deaf and the deafened. The deaf are those who were congenitally defective or who lost their hearing before they learned to use it in speech reception; the deafened are those who lost audition at a later date. The therapeutic and educational principles discussed in this chapter are variously applicable to these three kinds of impairment.

An important application of phonetics is in the teaching of speech to those who are deaf. If one is unable to hear the speech of his associates, he cannot follow acoustic models in learning it. He must perforce learn to produce his speech sounds by learning to imitate the positions and movements of the speech organs, letting his mentor check, by hearing, the accuracy of the articulatory and phonatory adjustments. The problem is markedly different from that of learning speech by ear. When the hearing person learns speech, he usually is quite unaware of what movements he makes to produce the various sounds of speech; but when the deaf person learns it he must become aware of every movement necessary for each sound. The hearing person may be as unconscious of the movements of speech as of those of swallowing; he learns by focusing his attention upon the acoustic end result of his movements. The deaf person, however, must focus his attention upon the movements themselves. In order that he may produce the proper acoustic effect, his teacher must be able to show him definitely all the necessary adjustments of the speech organs. This ability on the part of the teacher is based upon a minute and accurate knowledge of kinesiologic phonetics.

General Procedures

The procedure in teaching the deaf child to speak begins with teaching him to produce at will a stream of tone of suitable pitch, intensity, and quality. Since he lacks hearing he must rely for the control of what he is doing with his voice box upon the kinesthetic and cutaneous sensory equipment of the throat. To supplement these sensory controls many mechanical and electrical aids have been found useful. Any means that will make the pupil-patient's vocal tone palpable or visible to him may be employed. He must be able not only to produce an effective vocal tone but also to start it and stop it precisely, so as to meet the requirements of continuous speech, in which voiced and unvoiced sounds follow each other in rapid succession.

The next step is training the control of the muscles that open and close the nasopharyngeal port—the muscles of the velum and the superior constrictors of the pharynx. These muscles must come under direct, voluntary, conscious control, a type of adjustment that is usually wanting in the hearing person, whose control, though voluntary, is unconscious and indirect. The deaf child must learn by feeling to be aware of the positions of the velum, and in that learning process mechanical and electrical aids are often successfully employed to make the movements of the velum and the pharyngeal wall palpable and visible. These aids for the control of the nasopharyngeal sphincter must take the place of the acoustic effects by which the hearing child accomplishes the same results.

After the control of this sphincter has been achieved, the child is ready for lessons in articulation and enunciation. The first lessons should concern themselves with labial and front-tongue sounds, the movements for which the child can see made. After these have been learned, the sounds that are not visible should be developed. With these sounds, again, visual aids through mechanical and electrical means are employed, so that the child may guide by sight what he is unable to guide by hearing.

One of the most difficult problems in teaching speech to the deaf, and a problem usually attacked last, is that of inflections. The deaf child may have good voice, accurate control of nasalization, clear-cut consonants, and well-placed vowels, and his speech may still seem uncouth and mechanical because of his lack of inflection or his use of nonstandard inflections. For the person who is completely deaf the problem of developing normal inflections is insoluble, though some improvement may be expected from assiduous training and industrious practice. In developing these inflections the pupil must learn the "feel" of the muscles of the throat that is associated with the rise and fall of pitch and force. Again, the teacher may aid the learner not only by reporting to him when the inflection seems to the teacher's ears to be satisfactory, but also by showing him instrumentally[1] a picture of the rise and fall of the pupil's inflections.

No matter how intelligent the deaf person is or how well trained, he will need frequent periods of retraining. Such is the tendency for his speech to relapse because of his inability to check it and compare it with the speech of others, that, at least during the first twenty years of his life, he will need the aid of the speech teacher trained in phonetics.

Speech Reading

The deaf and the deafened are in need of the trained phonetician to help in learning not only the *production* of good speech but also

---

[1] References have been made in this section to the use of instruments for teaching speech to the deaf. The scope of this text does not permit a technical discussion of these instruments and their uses. We can pause only to name them and specify their functions in teaching: manometric flame, for training of vocalization, and for rendering inflections visible to the pupil; tonoscope, for teaching the proper pitch, and for teaching pitch inflections; oscilloscope, for teaching vocalization and the control of inflections of pitch and force; and the visible speech apparatus, a special kind of electronic oscilloscope that instantaneously analyzes the speaker's acoustic output into its components in one or more of several frequencies. With this apparatus, for example, the difference between **s** and **z** is clearly visualized, as well as that between **ð** and **n**, or between **z** and **ŋ**, or between **r** and **ʒ**, and many other pairs of sounds troublesome to the deaf. In addition to these instruments there are many simpler devices for teaching the control of nasalization, something that is very difficult for the deaf to learn.

the *perception* of speech. Those who are only partially deficient in hearing and those who lost their hearing in childhood, as well as those who have been deaf from birth, are in need of aid in the perception of speech.

The first method of increasing the ability of these hearing-defectives to comprehend speech is lip reading, or, as it is more properly called, speech reading. The pupil is taught to recognize the sounds of speech by noting the accompanying movements of the visible organs of articulation. If he were able to see all the movements involved in articulation and phonation, he would have a means of perceiving all the sounds of speech, but seeing only the lips, jaw, and tongue-tip, he gets only a fragmentary picture of what is said—the rest he must supply by inference. It becomes important, therefore, that the fragment he can see is observed accurately.

Many sounds which are dissimilar acoustically are similar in the visible picture they present. The pupil must learn to group these similar sounds into sharply differentiated classes. All the members of a given class are called *homophenes*. The hearing person is occasionally confused by *homophones*[2] such as *to, two, too*. Fortunately, words with such similar sounds are rare, hence the confusion resulting from homophones is negligible. But there are many homophenes, and hence the possibility of confusion is thus correspondingly greater in speech reading than in speech hearing. Since the speech reader cannot see the back of the tongue, the velum, and the larynx, such words as *bend, bent, bed, bet, meant, mend, pen, pet, penned*, etc., look alike to him. To this list might also be added other words that have such similar visible movements that the differences can be observed only by the most skillful reader, and then only when the speaker's face is in the best of light: viz., *bait, bayed, made, main, mate, paid, pave, paint, pained*, etc. *Pate* and *men*, to the hearing person seem radically dissimilar, but they are closely homophenous.

Another problem of speech reading is to distinguish incidental and transition movements from movements that are the direct accompaniments of standard speech sounds. For example: *too well* and *to hell* are homophenous, because the speech reader cannot tell

[2] *Homophene* and *homophone*, derived from the Greek, mean, respectively, *of like appearance* and *of like sound*.

the difference between two factors: (1) an incidental movement of the articulators while they are moving from the position **u** in *to* to that of **ɛ** in *hell*, and (2) the directly significant movement involved in the **w** of *well*. In one phrase the movement is to be ignored as only an incident of the transition from one sound to another, while in the other it is a meaning-carrying adjustment of the articulators.

He who would guide the student of lip reading must, therefore, have a detailed knowledge of kinesiologic phonetics.

The second method of aiding the person who is defective in hearing to attain greater efficiency in the perception of speech is the fitting of a hearing aid.

Hearing Aids

Some hard-of-hearing persons suffer only a "level" loss, i.e., an equal reduction of acuity throughout the gamut of speech sounds. In compensating for his loss such a person needs only to have the sounds of speech made more intense for him than for the others in his conversational group. If he could always place himself nearer the speaker than the other auditors, or if he could persuade speakers always to talk to him as though he were much farther away than he actually is,[3] he would not need a hearing aid. The problem of fitting such a person with a hearing aid is not a difficult one. What he needs is the equal amplification of all the sounds of speech. If some of the sounds are more amplified than others the stronger sounds will mask the weaker, so that the person so fitted may not be able to understand speech any better with the aid than without it; he will merely be able to hear it farther.

With those whose hard-of-hearing condition is not that of a simple reduction of acuity, but rather of a disparity of acuities, some frequencies being heard with normal or even supernormal acuity and others with reduced acuity, the problem of fitting the

[3] Both of these contingencies are provided for by a hearing aid. A good aid provides for moving the hearer closer to the speaker, just as one who is sitting in the gallery of the theatre moves forward visually by the use of binoculars. With an audicle the hearer receives the benefit of sound waves as intense as though he stepped closer to the speaker. The second contingency, that of persuading the speaker to speak more loudly, is met by any hearing aid, good or bad, provided only that it is conspicuous enough to remind the speaker that he should speak loudly for the benefit of the hard-of-hearing listener.

hearing aid is much more complex. One may explain the difficulty here by an analogue from the realm of vision. Some children who are deficient in vision need only to have their word more brightly illuminated while others need corrective lenses. The former are analogous to the hard of hearing who need only amplification of all speech sounds; the latter are analogous to those who need hearing aids that rebalance the relative intensities of the sounds of speech. This rebalancing requires the building of a hearing aid with selective amplification.

In prescribing for the hearing aid one must first secure a chart of the patient's hearing, showing which frequencies he hears normally and those in which he is deficient. With this chart one who knows what frequencies are involved in each of the sounds of speech can learn which sounds the hard-of-hearing person is unable to hear, which ones he can hear with difficulty, and which he can hear normally. The problem, then, is to select an aid and adapt it so that it will compensate for the lost frequencies without making other sounds of speech intolerably loud. For such a hard-of-hearing person an "honest amplifier"—one that would admirably suit the person with "level" loss of acuity—may be inadequate, since, even if it amplified the sounds that he cannot hear, it would also amplify the sounds that he can hear, to a point at which they may mask all others. The proper fitting of a hearing aid is therefore a highly technical problem in applied phonetics.

Chapter 21   The Phonetics of
Foreign Accent

.

An Approach to the Problem

Two applications of English phonetics concern themselves with foreign languages: (1) the elimination of foreign accent from the English speech of those who were reared under the influence of a foreign language, (2) the simulation of a foreign accent for dramatic purposes. These two applications involve much the same phonetic principles—in both cases an analysis must be made of the phonetic differences between English and the particular foreign language in question. This analysis concerns itself with the following considerations:

1. Consonants (nasals, fricatives, plosives, affricates, and sibilants) of English that are wanting in the foreign language.

2. Consonants of the foreign language that are wanting in English.

3. Consonants common to the two languages.

4. Consonants of the foreign language that are the nearest substitutes for the sounds peculiar to English.

5. Consonants represented by the same letter in the two languages and those represented by different letters.

6. Inflection patterns and habits of vocal attack and release of the foreign language.

7. Overlapping of the vowel systems of the two languages, i.e., which vowel phonemes are exactly coincident, which ones are

similar but narrower in one language than the other, and which phonemes of one language include parts of two or more phonemes of the other.

A Sample Analysis of English and German

Let us take German as an example (but *merely* as an example) for such an analysis, remembering that this study of the language must be made, not *in vacuo*—in terms of the German grammar book—but in a working situation, in terms of the actual speech of one or more German-speaking persons. If one is to produce an imitation of the German dialect that sounds authentic, he must know the German phoneme system of a particular dialect. Suppose a German were to imitate American attempts to talk his language and were to incorporate into his American speech some southernisms, some eastern American tricks, and some Midwestern speech forms—the result would be an unconvincing burlesque of American speech. Thus in dramatic and interpretative work the dialect must be based upon the speech of actual Germans, preferably those whose brand of German is typical. On the other hand, if one wishes to help a German speak English acceptably, he must know the sound system of that particular German, not the typical German or Germans in general. The following analysis is made on the basis of the speech of a person whose native dialect is that of the cultured resident of Berlin.

1. The consonants θ and ð of English are lacking in German.

2. The consonants χ and ç are lacking in English and usually also ḍ and ṭ.

3. All other consonants of the two languages are common to both. It should be noted that German and English emphasize different combinations of consonants. The combination ʃt, for example, is rare in English and common in German, but the opposite is true of tʃ. The sound ʒ appears in German only as an importation from other languages, but the same is true in English, except that there are more such importations. The importation of dʒ is very rare in German. It is a common sound in English, being a modification of the ʒ importation from French and also an Anglicization of the j sounds of continental languages.

4. The dental *d* d̪ and the dental *t* t̪ are the nearest substitutes in German for the English ð and θ.

5. As to representation of sound by letters one can cite only the outstanding differences between the two languages, such as the following:

Letter	German Sound	English Sound
J	j	dʒ
s	z	s
v	f	v
w	v	w
z	ts	z

6. The inflection pattern of German is less smoothly modulated than that of English and changes are more abrupt. One of the characteristic vocal habits of the language is, in all cases in which a word begins with a stressed vowel, to introduce the vowel with an ʔ, and to unvoice the final sounds of all words except those ending in vowels, vowel glides, or nasal sounds.[1] This habit gives to German speech, as heard by the American, a clipped, explosive effect.

7. To illustrate the overlapping of vowels we need only mention the outstanding differences in phonemes between German and English. The vowels i, ɪ, ɛ, ɑ, u, ʊ, ḷ, ə, are about the same in German as in English. German employs the pure, undiphthongized o and e more than does English. German has an approximation of eɪ in its "long umlaut *a*." German also has a complete set of true umlauts, represented phonetically as y, ө, and œ. German lacks the English vowels æ, a, ʌ, ɒ, ɔ, ɜ, ɝ; and since these vowels are lacking, adjacent phonemes are likely to be much broader than the corresponding phonemes of English. For example, since there are no German phonemes near ɑ, this sound

---

[1] This habit of unvoicing final sounds is so universal that German school children are taught to spell using plurals and other inflected forms so that they may know whether the root form ends in a surd or a sonant. Thus the child is first asked to spell *Hunden*, not *Hund*, because in *Hunden*, the *d* not being final is voiced, whereas in the singular form, *Hund*, it is indistinguishable from a *t*. So, if a child spells the word as *Hunt*, his attention is called to the plural form.

may in various speakers become ʌ, ɒ, or a. German has no approaching or crescendo *w*-glide. Now, what will the German-reared person be likely to do with English?

1. He will substitute some German sounds for ð and θ—usually ḏ and ṯ, but sometimes z and s.

2. Words like *book* and *milk*, that have close German cognates in the final consonant—English using k and c, German using χ and ç—will be pronounced with a fricative termination rather than the English plosive ending.

3. Most consonants will be standard English sounds.

4. The English *d*'s and *t*'s will be dentalized, so that *pet* will be pɛṯ and *tip* will be ṯɪp.

5. Common words, especially those similar in spelling to German words of the same meaning, will be pronounced with German values given to the letters, such as *Jesus* **jesṵs**, *so* **zo**, *very* **fɛЯɪ**, *will* **vɪl**, *zero* **tsɪЯo̤**.

6. The phrasing will be explosive, and voicing will begin and end abruptly. Words like *eyes*, *awes*, *of*, and *all*, will be ʔaɪs, ʔɔs, ʔaf, and ʔɔl.

7. Words such as *pane* and *bone* are likely to be pronounced **pen** and **bon**. Umlauts may often be substituted for ɝ, ɜ, and sometimes for ʌ, in such words as *bird*, *girl*, *mud*. When w as in *wind* is mispronounced, it will usually be uttered as v.

In the correction of any foreign accent or in the development in English speech of a foreign dialect it is usually possible to find accidental sounds that will closely approximate the sound desired. For example, to take German again, suppose one is trying to develop the dental *d* ḏ. Let him take some combination like *with Dot*. As the words are spoken rapidly, blending one with the other in articulation, the phrase becomes easily **wɪðd͡ɒt**. Then the **wɪð** can be deleted, and a good German *d* remains as an initial consonant. Or, to take an opposite case, suppose we are attempting to correct a German undiphthongized *o* as in *don't*, pronounced by the German ḏont. Let him pronounce the German words *wo und wann*, assimilating these words into one vocable. Then let him leave off the *nd wann*, leaving something close to **vou**. Or, again, if the problem is to teach him the approaching *w*-glide, let him take the German phrase *du isst* and, after assimilating them, delete the *d*, leaving **wɪst**.

In this manner[2] any language may be studied, making phonetic comparisons with English.

---

[2] It should be said here that the foregoing is but an example of an analysis for the specific purposes mentioned above and is not to be thought of as a thoroughgoing phonetic study of German in all its varying dialects. Even as an example, it is intended to illustrate the *manner* of the analysis, not the *facts* to be found.

Chapter 22   The Use of Phonetics
in Speech Correction

Phonetics, the Clinician, and the Patient

A thorough knowledge of phonetics is almost indispensable to the clinician who would diagnose and treat defects of speech. Without it his work is narrowed in scope and effectiveness, if not at times actually ill advised. The science of phonetics has its most immediate application to the general type of speech defects called *dyslalias*—the articulatory defects. Such defects may arise from varied causes and they may show quite different speech pictures, but they are all characterized by defective use or utterance of some of the sounds of speech.

From the standpoint of the speech symptom there are four main types of articulatory defects: (1) Sound omissions—certain sounds may be omitted, either because of negligence in articulation or because the speaker is unable to produce them, as in **fɪŋɚ** for **fɪŋɡɚ** in infantile speech. (2) Sound substitutions—the replacing of one standard speech sound by another, as in infantile speech **mʌvɚ** for **mʌðɚ**. (3) Defectively produced sounds—sounds that resemble the intended sound but are not standard in their manner of production or in their acoustic nature, as a lateral *s*. (4) Sounds that are ill fitted to the moving stream of speech, i.e., slurred sounds, unusual linking sounds, overprecise or staccato speech sounds, etc. It is obvious that a complete understanding of any of these types is dependent upon a thorough knowledge of phonetics.

Since these articulatory defects make up from 50 to 75 percent of the cases usually dealt with in the speech clinic, there can be little question as to the value of phonetic training to the speech clinician. He must be familiar with the mechanism for speech and with the acoustic nature, method of production, and inter-relationships of the various sounds of speech—in fact, with most of the body of phonetic knowledge. Lacking such knowledge, his understanding of the case before him will often be superficial, and the same lack of insight may show itself in his course of treatment.

The question as to the value of phonetic knowledge to the speech defective himself is less easily settled. When this question is raised most people think only in terms of whether or not the clinic patient should be taught the phonetic symbols. As we shall see later, the answer depends upon individual circumstances. The teaching of symbols, however, is only a small part of the field of phonetics. On closer examination of the problem, we find that the treatment of almost any articulatory case involves the teaching of phonetics more or less intensively, regardless of whether or not the symbols as such are taught. It is usually necessary to show the subject that certain of his sounds are defective, to tell him why and how they are defective, to teach him the correct sounds by one method or another, and to show him when these sounds should be used in speech. All of this amounts to teaching phonetics on a small scale. It may be quite inaccurate teaching and, if the clinician is not versed in the field, the results may be unfavorable; but it is none the less an attempt to teach the patient something about speech sounds.

Consciously or unconsciously, we follow the practice of teaching the patient as much phonetics as we think he needs to know in order to overcome his defect. How much this will be depends upon the nature and cause of the defect, the age of the patient, his previous training and many other factors. We need to remember, however, that speech correction differs from the normal process of acquiring speech in that the latter involves essentially the formation of new habit patterns, whereas speech correction inevitably means the breaking down of incorrect habits already formed and the formation of new correct habits. This difference is sometimes expressed by the phrases "education versus reeducation" and "training versus retraining." [1] The significance of this difference lies in the fact that, whereas the normal acquisition of speech may take place without much conscious effort and without much attention to details, the reeducative process requires a conscious attention to specific details of the old habits that are to be broken down and the new ones to be formed. Since the habits here involved are those concerned with the production of speech sounds, this means that the very nature of the speech correction process makes it necessary to teach the patient phonetics.

While the conclusion seems inescapable that the correction of an articulatory defect will always involve the teaching of a considerable amount of phonetics, it is less certain that it will always be necessary to teach the patient the phonetic symbols. We need to recall at this point the nature and purpose of these symbols: They are tools in the study of phonetics, and as such they are convenient, efficient, and time-saving. From this standpoint we can say that the patient should be taught the phonetic symbols whenever their value as tools in the administration of therapy will justify their use. Teaching the patient symbols for sounds does not, of course, correct his defect. Such teaching can become mere busywork, yielding no profit in increased progress by the patient. Oftentimes, however, progress can be speeded up materially once the symbols are learned, since they provide the means for an interchange of ideas between clinician and patient. Anyone who has tried to correct the articulatory defects of a clinic patient who knows the phonetic symbols can testify to the saving of time and the increase in effectiveness of teaching.

Obviously the decision as to whether or not the patient is to be taught the symbols must be made on the basis of the best judgment of the clinician as he surveys the possibilities of the case. In general, adults with average or better intelligence, whose articulatory problems are widespread and deepseated, will profit by learning the phonetic symbols. Oftentimes it will prove advantageous to teach only the symbols for those sounds that give difficulty. Another factor to be considered is the length of time that the patient will probably receive training. Other things being equal, the longer the period of training the more profitable it will

[1] See Robert West, Merle Ansberry, and Anna Carr, *The Rehabilitation of Speech*, 3rd ed., Harper & Brothers, 1957, p. 64.

be to teach the phonetic symbols. A knowledge of symbols is of special value to foreign dialect cases with their multiple problems and their constant confusion of foreign and English sounds.

Phonetic Analysis as an Instrument of Diagnosis

A thorough knowledge of phonetics on the part of the clinician will often enable him to make shrewd deductions as to the nature of the speech defect under observation, and thus serve as a short cut to the final diagnosis. In most instances the articulatory syndome is to be regarded as pointing to, or suggesting, a given type of defect arising from a given cause, rather than proving definitely the nature of the case. This is because there are many factors influencing specific articulatory defects that arise from a given cause, and because there is much overlapping in the articulatory symptoms arising from different causes. Nevertheless, such speech defects as those arising from infantile perseveration, tongue-tie, foreign dialect, sectional dialect, lingual paralysis, malformation of the teeth, hard-of-hearing conditions, etc., do show characteristic articulatory pictures that distinguish each from the others. So true is this that not only can foreign dialect be distinguished from baby talk or paralytic speech on the basis of the articulatory lapses, but the expert can also detect whether the foreign dialect case is himself an immigrant or the child of an immigrant, and can usually name the foreign language from which the dialect originated. The broken English of an Italian immigrant differs materially from that of a Norwegian, and these differences often remain observable even unto the third and fourth generations.

It is not the purpose of this chapter to catalog the articulatory syndromes that arise from various types of speech defects. Such material is difficult to reduce to lists and even if so arranged can scarcely be mastered through memorization. Furthermore, it must be borne in mind that such listings of defects can be quite misleading if interpreted from an insufficient background. For example, to say categorically that infantile speech is characterized by the substitution of **w** for **r** is something less than half the truth. Lingual paralysis might likewise be so characterized, as might certain types of hearing deficiencies or even tongue-tie. We can lay down a general principle that individual articulatory lapses are of little significance in differentiating one type of speech defect from another—it is the complete articulatory picture that furnishes the clue to the type and cause of the defect. This picture must be seen by the clinician in its entirety and with all of its implications. He must make mental comparisons with known articulatory lapses in other cases and look for similarities and differences.

This leads us to the second principle in the use of phonetics as a diagnostic device—namely, that diagnosis based on phonetic lapses is essentially a reasoning, not a cataloging, process. As such it is an ability grounded on a thorough knowledge of phonetics on the one hand and of speech correction on the other. It is not to be learned through lists or recipes.

The following analysis will serve to illustrate this method of diagnosis.[2] It is not intended as an illustration of either a complete case history or of all of the steps in the diagnosis of a hypothetical case, but is intended only to indicate the manner in which the clinician can coördinate his knowledge of phonetics and of speech correction in the *preliminary* analysis of a case. For a simple illustration, we may assume a typical case of infantile perseveration in which a boy of ten shows the following articulatory lapses: **w** is substituted for **r** rather consistently; **θ** is used for **s** in many words, especially simple ones, although **s** can be, and often is, made correctly in more recently learned words; **v** is substituted for **ð** medially in words like *mother* and *brother*, but **t** is often used for initial **θ** as in *throw, through, thimble*, etc.; **d** is sometimes used for **ð** in such words as *then* and *those*; **j** is substituted for initial **l** in such words as *lady, lay*, and *little*, but **l** is often made correctly when it occurs medially and is sometimes omitted entirely when it occurs in certain one-syllable words such as *milk, help*, and *twelve*; **d** is used occasionally for initial **g**, but the medial and final sound is usually correct, unless omitted; **t** is likewise substituted for initial **k**; **h** or **ç** is sometimes used for **ʃ**, but **ʃ** is sometimes substituted for **tʃ**; **n** is substituted for **ŋ** in many words, but *finger* is pronounced **fɪŋɚ**.

Assuming that we have no knowledge of this case save for the articulatory syndrome described above, let us proceed to examine

[2] For a similar analysis from a somewhat different point of view, see West, Ansberry, and Carr, *The Rehabilitation of Speech*, 3rd ed., p. 302.

it from the diagnostic point of view, considering in turn the possibility that these symptoms might be caused by tongue-tie, foreign dialect, a hearing deficiency, and paralysis. The possibility of a tongue-tie can be dismissed rather quickly. We know that when the lingual fraenum is overshort the upward movements of the tip of the tongue are restricted. This restriction must result either in the defective production of the high tongue-tip sounds or in the production of these sounds with the jaws closely approximated. The latter symptom is not present, and the first one is eliminated by the fact that in several instances high tongue-tip sounds are actually used in place of sounds in which the tip of the tongue is lower or in which the back of the tongue is active. Thus **t** is substituted for **θ** and **k**, **d** is used for **ð**. These observations can be checked quickly by testing the patient's ability to elevate the tip of the tongue.

When we consider the possibility that a foreign dialect might operate to produce these symptoms we note first that certain of the substitutions, i.e., **v** for **ð**, **t** for **θ**, **d** for **ð**, and **ʃ** for **tʃ**, are typical of many dialects. But other substitutions are decidedly not typical of foreign dialects. Outstanding among these is the use of **θ** for **s**, a substitution that practically never occurs in any commonly known foreign dialect. In fact, the **θ** is missing in most of the languages from which these dialects stem, and some other sound —often **s** itself—is substituted for it. Likewise **w** is seldom substituted for **r** in dialectal speech, since nearly all languages have some variety of **r** which, although it may differ from the English **r**, is used in speaking our language. Nonstandard *l*'s are often heard in foreign dialect, but the use of **j** for **l** is not typical. The substitutions of **t** and **d** for **k** and **g** are also not typical for foreign dialect. Practically all languages contain a back tongue plosive of some type, and corresponding dialectal English will show a nonstandard **k** or **g** rather than the substitution of **t** and **d** for these sounds. Another highly significant clue in this connection is the absence of vowel errors. To the foreigner learning English, the vowels usually present more difficulties than the consonants. It is extremely unlikely that any case of foreign dialect would show errors only on consonant and glide sounds and not on vowels. For these reasons, we can feel reasonably safe in dismissing the possibility of foreign dialect, although we might want

to keep in mind the possibility that a few of the errors may be
influenced by this cause.

We turn our attention now to the possibility of a hearing
deficiency. We note at least six instances in which more visible
front sounds are used instead of less visible sounds made farther
back in the mouth. These are **w** for **r**, **θ** for **s**, **d** for **g**, **t** for **k**, **ʃ**
and **t** for **tʃ**, and **n** for **ŋ**. However, there are four instances in
which less visible sounds are actually used in place of more
visible ones: **j** for **l**, **t** for **θ**, **d** for **ð**, and **h** or **ç** for **ʃ**. We can
scarcely postulate a generalized deafness because there are too
many nondefective sounds. If we assume a general deafness sufficient to cause the defects noted, we must ask why there are so few
defective glide sounds and no defective vowels, and why certain
consonants **b**, **p**, **m**, **f**, **v**, **t**, **d**, etc., are not also occasionally
defective, as they logically should be. We note also that if there
were a generalized deafness we should expect many more sound
omissions than seem to be present, and we should likewise expect
some of the sounds to be produced defectively.

There is, of course, the possibility that we are dealing with a
specialized range deafness. In this case we would have to assume
a deficiency in both middle-frequency and high-frequency ranges.
However, the possibility of a middle-frequency-range deafness is
slight, since there are only two errors in this range, **w** for **r** and **j**
for **l**, and the latter occurs infrequently. There is a stronger
possibility of a high-frequency deafness, since there are many
substitutions of sounds within this range and of such a nature that
they could be explained by a specialized hearing deficiency. We
note again, however, the small number of sound omissions and
the absence of defectively produced sounds, both of which would
normally be expected in high-frequency deafness. We should also
expect interchangings within the pairs **b-d**, **p-t**, **f-θ**, **v-ð**, **s-ʃ**, etc.,
and these are not present. In the sound substitutions that are
present there is a clear tendency to substitute more easily produced sounds for less easily produced ones. This is not necessarily
characteristic of a hearing deficiency. Lastly, we remember that
there is a marked inconsistency in the appearance of the substitutions, whereas if the difficulty lay in the hearing mechanism, we
should expect more stereotyping of the errors. We conclude,
therefore, that a general deafness or a middle-frequency deafness

is quite improbable, and that while there is some evidence pointing toward a high-frequency deafness it is by no means conclusive. We continue our analysis bearing in mind the possibility that the case may be complicated by a partial high-frequency deafness.

The observation made previously that in almost every instance the substitution is of an easier sound for a more difficult one points strongly to the possibility of a paralysis. The fact that only the tongue sounds are affected would indicate a lingual paralysis. Since both front and back sounds are defective, we would have to assume a rather widespread paralysis of the tongue. There are, however, contrary observations. Chief among these is the fact that the errors are more frequent on short and relatively simple words than on longer and more complicated ones. This is in direct contrast to the situation that usually prevails in paralytic speech, in which the patient is often able to produce sounds correctly in isolation or in simple combinations, but has much difficulty with the same sounds when they occur in longer sequences calling for more complicated and rapid coordinations. We note again the absence of defectively produced sounds—a characteristic we would certainly expect in paralytic speech—and the absence of errors among the vowels. We would also expect more consistency in the errors in a case of paralytic speech; that is, we would expect the same type of error to appear more or less regularly. In our hypothetical case, the reverse is true, and sounds are produced correctly more often than incorrectly. With the possible exception of **r**, all sounds are made correctly in one situation or another, and no sound is ever produced defectively. The errors are always substitutions or omissions. This argues strongly against a paralysis. In addition, we have no report of any tension accompanying speech —a characteristic that would be inevitable in paralytic speech. On these grounds, the presence of a paralysis seems to be ruled out.

Finally, we observe that all of the symptoms noted can be explained adequately on the basis of infantile perseveration. The substitutions are all characteristic of this type of speech. The inconsistency of the errors and the tendency to substitute easier sounds for harder ones are both typical symptoms of infantile speech. Every defect noted can be explained upon the basis of the assumption that we are dealing with a person who has learned to produce all of the sounds of English except **r**, and whose speech shows the results of a struggle between old, incorrect habit patterns formed before certain sounds were acquired and newer, less stable patterns that are largely correct. We might wish to safeguard ourselves by testing for high-frequency deafness in order to eliminate any possibility that a hearing deficiency might be a contributing factor.

It should be emphasized again that this analysis is not intended to illustrate a complete diagnostic procedure. No attempt has been made to include all of the possible symptoms of infantile speech or to exhaust all of the possible causes of the symptoms noted. This example merely illustrates the use of phonetic knowledge in making a preliminary diagnosis of articulatory cases. Although the analysis may have seemed long when reduced to writing, it should be remembered that the experienced clinician will make these observations almost intuitively and will arrive quickly at a conclusion as to the probable nature of the case. When this is done he can proceed without waste effort to further examinations designed to eliminate other likely possibilities and verify or disprove his tentative conclusions. The clinician must hold himself in readiness at all times to modify his original inferences in the light of additional information. In the hands of an inexperienced worker who lacks a solid foundation in the fields of phonetics and speech correction this type of phonetic diagnosis can be quite inaccurate and misleading.

Phonetic Training as a Therapeutic Technique

We have commented previously upon the value of a knowledge of phonetics to both the clinician and the patient. It is our purpose here to particularize somewhat upon the uses of phonetics in the actual administration of clinical therapy. It is obvious that phonetic training is not applicable to all types of speech defects. However, such training does play an important part in the treatment of all articulatory defects, with the possible exception of those arising directly from emotional disorders. In general we may say that phonetic training plays an important part in the following processes, any or all of which may be used in the correction of defective articulation: teaching new sounds, teaching proper compensatory movements where these are made necessary by structural abnormalities, correcting sound substitutions and omissions, giving ear training exercises, strengthening new sounds by association, stereotyping the motor patterns of new sounds by repetition, teaching the peculiarities of the English language. Frequently the clinic patient has to be taught a sound that he has been unable to make or has for some reason failed to acquire. Among the various methods for teaching such new sounds,[3] three rely heavily upon the science of phonetics.

1. The simplest of these methods is based upon ear training, followed by trial-and-error attempts to produce the sound. The correct sound is repeated many times for the patient until he is thoroughly familiar with it. He is then asked to make a sound like the one heard, his efforts are criticized, additional ear training is given, and the process is repeated until the correct sound is produced. Once the correct form has been secured, attempts are made to bring about its repetition until it can be made easily. It is then ready for stereotyping into the pattern of everyday speech.

2. If this ear training method fails, the desired sound may be produced by the modification of related sounds. Thus **s** may be taught by approaching the sound from the position for dental *t*. The dental *t* serves to place the tongue in the approximate position for **s**. The sound **s**, or one closely resembling it, can then be secured by showing the patient how to make a fricative rather than a plosive from this position. The **ɹ**, **r**, and **ɝ** sounds may likewise be taught from the position for an alveolar *t* by means of a series of drills working from **tʰ** to **tɹ** to **tɹaɪ** to **ɹaɪ** to **raɪ** to **r-aɪ** to **ɝraɪ** to **ɝ** to **ɝlɪ̩**. Similarly **w** can be taught by means of a glide movement from **u** to **ɑ**, and **ŋ** by asking the patient to prepare to pronounce **g** and direct the air through the nasal chambers by opening the soft palate. The above examples illustrate only a few of the many possibilities. The alert student will discover almost countless ways of using his knowledge of phonetics to lead the patient to produce a new sound through the avenue of one already mastered.

3. The third method of teaching a new sound is sometimes called the "placement method." The patient is shown by means of charts, models, diagrams, and by direct observation of himself

[3] See Charles Van Riper, *Speech Correction*, 3rd ed., Prentice-Hall, Inc., 1954, p. 234.

and other people just how the sound is made, i.e., the *placement* of the articulatory mechanism for the sound. He is then directed to place his articulatory mechanism in a similar position and produce a sound. After repeated trials under direction, a sound approaching the one desired may be obtained. It is obvious that all three of these methods for teaching a new sound are grounded in phonetics.

In still other cases the primary problem is to teach the patient to compensate for some physical defect in the articulatory mechanism that prevents the correct production of certain sounds in the typical manner. Here again phonetic training is of paramount importance in assaying the structural defect, determining its relation to the defective sound, deciding whether, in view of the structural conditions, it will be possible to teach the patient to make the sound in the normal manner, and, if not, selecting the compensatory movements to be taught. Such compensation involves teaching the patient to make certain movements not ordinarily typical of the sound, in order to make allowances for the structural defect and to produce an acoustically acceptable sound. The clinician must synthesize his knowledge of the articulatory mechanism with his knowledge of the minimum essentials for any given speech sound, the manner in which it is normally produced, its acoustic characteristics, and especially the problems involved in effecting smooth transitions from this sound to others in a normal speech situation.

To put this in the form of an example, the clinician may decide that a certain patient has a defective *s* of the "spread" type, because of a wide space on the midline between the two upper incisors. He may further decide that this structural deficiency precludes the making of a normal *s* in the typical manner. A further survey of the situation leads him to decide that the patient could best produce an acoustically acceptable *s* by making it far to the side, perhaps over one of the premolars that seems to be well located for the purpose. This possibility is discarded, however, on the grounds that the movements accompanying the sound attract unfavorable attention, and because transitions to certain other sounds are awkward. The clinician finally decides that the best procedure will be to teach the patient a somewhat lateral *s* made over one of the canines. The result is a sound far superior to the original defective *s*, but not so good as the one that could have been made farther laterally. However, it is not accompanied by con-spicuous movements, and it blends easily with other sounds.

Another problem that confronts the speech clinician even more frequently is that of correcting sound substitutions and omissions. In such cases there are often no structural defects and no sounds that the patient is incapable of making. Instead, certain correctly made sounds are substituted for one another, used in nonstandard positions, or omitted. The problem here is basically one of breaking down certain incorrect habits of sound usage and establishing correct ones. This is the major problem in correcting foreign dialect, and the phonetic principles involved have already been presented in Chapter 22. The techniques of ear training, association, and strengthening described in the following pages are especially applicable to this type of defect.

However, regardless of whether the problem is one of teaching an entirely new sound, teaching compensatory movements, or correcting sound substitutions, the techniques of ear training play an important part. By ear training we mean the process of teaching an individual to *isolate*, *recognize*, and *discriminate* speech sounds. Isolation involves the ability to separate words and syllables into sound units; recognition, the ability to identify a sound properly; and discrimination, the ability to distinguish a sound from closely related sounds or from defective versions of the sound. Van Riper[4] presents specific techniques for such ear training. We need only note here that this training is the direct equivalent of teaching certain phases of phonetics to the patient, and that the clinician who wishes to give such training must be grounded in phonetic science.

A process closely allied to ear training is that of association, by which we mean the establishing of proper connections between the sound and other aspects of language in such a way as to fix the sound firmly in the associative process. This may be accom-plished by associating it with its phonetic symbol or its various orthographic representations, or by tying it up with a picture, a name or a sound made by some animal or machine, etc. For example the sound of *s* might be associated with its symbol **s**, its various spellings, *s*, *ss*, *c*, etc., with a picture of a snake, and with the traditional hissing sound made by a snake. Such associative

---

[4] *Speech Correction*, 3rd ed., pp. 221–234.

techniques help to establish the sound firmly in mind so that it can be recalled instantly when needed for speech.

In addition to the processes of ear training and association there still remains the problem of strengthening or stereotyping the motor patterns of new sounds and new combinations of sound. This involves the repetition of the correct form of the sound, both in and out of speech context, until the motor pattern for it is firmly fixed and the sound is produced automatically when it occurs in speech. This is, as it were, the capstone of the corrective process. Unless the correct sounds can be so stereotyped in their production the original defects will continually recur. The selection of adequate drill material for this purpose, the supervision of the drill to the end that the correct form and not the error is practiced, and the decision as to when the stereotyping process is completed, are all matters that require training in phonetics.

In concluding this discussion of the place of phonetics in speech correction, we should mention that each language has certain peculiarities and characteristics that must be mastered if the speaker is to be fluent and free from error. Ordinarily these are mastered automatically by the maturing child; but some types of defective speech, particularly sectional and foreign dialect, are characterized in part by the failure to master these peculiarities of the language. We may list the following characteristics of English speech: peculiarities of unstressing, including the use of the schwa, of strong and weak forms, of accent, of sound duration, and of tense and lax sounds; the widespread use of glide sounds; unusual patterns of aspiration and unaspiration and fortis and lenis effects; and the intonation pattern. If any of these characteristics must be taught the best approach is from the standpoint of phonetics. In fact, problems arising out of the first three characteristics can be handled adequately only by one who is trained in this field.

In this chapter we have tried to show the general relationship between training in phonetics and the work of the clinician with the patient. We have discussed the application of phonetics to the diagnosis of articulatory defects and the uses of phonetic training in certain remedial techniques. The science of phonetics has many important and immediate applications, and one of the greatest of these is in the field of speech correction.

Chapter 23   Phonetics and the
Teaching of Speech

General Considerations

The first few years of a child's public school education are
devoted mainly to acquiring a mastery of his native language.
Language study continues to play an important part in his education throughout his stay in the public schools and occupies a
considerable portion of his time at the college level. Omitting the
appreciative and artistic aspects, mastery of a language involves
four basic skills—speaking, listening, reading, and writing. Underlying all four of these skills is a large group of customs, conventions,
and precedents established by previous users of the language and
embodied in the rules of grammar, orthoëpy, orthography, and
social and cultural patterns.

It is worth noting that the average child comes to the public
school with some six years of practice in listening to the language,
four in speaking it, and a like amount of unwitting practice in
grammatical usage. On the other hand, the teacher, for all practical
purposes, starts from the beginning in the teaching of reading,
writing, and spelling. It seems self-evident that the most basic of
these language skills is the ability to speak the language, yet this
skill receives only haphazard attention—and often no attention at
all—in the formal education of the child. Back of this neglect is
the assumption, implied or direct, that the child learns to speak
"naturally" and therefore that little or no attention need be paid
to this phase of his language development.

It can scarcely be said, however, that it is any more natural for a child to learn to talk and to understand spoken language than it is for him to learn to read and write. All four processes are highly artificial and must be learned. Speaking and listening are set apart from reading and writing, not by any basic difference in the learning process, but by the fact that speaking and listening are ordinarily learned in early childhood under the tutelage of all of those who speak to the child, whereas reading and writing are learned from the age of six onward, primarily under the tutelage of the classroom teacher. To argue that four years of preschool practice in speaking makes further specific efforts to master this skill unnecessary is as bootless as to argue that this same four years of practice in the use of grammar makes further teaching in this field unnecessary. As a matter of fact, these years of preschool practice frequently impose an additional handicap upon the teacher, inasmuch as he must first overcome the incorrect habits set up during this period. The teaching of reading, writing, and spelling is facilitated by the fact that the teacher has an opportunity to inculcate correct habits at the beginning of training.

It is the purpose of this chapter to evaluate the place of the science of phonetics in the process of improving the pupil's mastery of his native language in its spoken form. It is obvious that there are many facets to this problem and that phonetics cannot be thought of as a panacea for all speech ills. It should, however, be a useful tool in that phase of the mastery of oral language that has to do with the correct utterance of speech sounds and with the combination of these sounds into words and continuous speech.

It should be clear at the outset that the issue is not whether phonetics shall be taught in the public schools, but rather whether phonetic principles are of sufficient value as *a tool in education* to warrant their use. Since many schools are again making use of phonetics as a tool in teaching (usually under the name of phonics), the issues will be further clarified if we consider them as being, basically as follows: (1) How much phonetic science can be used profitably in the teaching of speech in the public schools? (2) At what age levels can phonetic training be introduced most advantageously? (3) Should the phonetic symbols be taught?

Before considering these questions let us note for a moment

some of the conditions that have served to handicap the use of phonetics as an instrument of instruction in the public schools. The first of these has already been mentioned—the erroneous though widespread view that since speech is learned early it does not require any special training to bring it to perfection. It should not require much observation of the speech of typical school children to prove the falsity of this assumption, yet for various reasons this philosophy is prevalent enough to be an effective bar to speech training of any kind in many communities. In the second place, there is a lack of teachers adequately trained to use phonetics effectively as a tool in classroom teaching. A semester of college training in a phonetics course designed to meet the immediate practical needs of the public school situation would be of considerable value to any public school teacher, yet surprisingly few have had such a course.

The third drawback to a more widespread use of phonetics in the public schools has been the lack of suitable material adapted to the lower levels of education. Teachers who desired to teach "phonics" were dependent largely upon their own resources for teaching techniques, aids, and materials. This situation has been greatly improved in recent years,[1] and it is certain that increasing demand will bring additional valuable materials to publication.

[1] The Expression Company (Magnolia, Massachusetts) has taken the lead in the publication of such materials. A booklet called *Speech Aids* which can be obtained from the publishers lists some 30 drillbooks, games, and speech tests designed especially for children. Other publications of a similar nature are as follows: .

Bryngelson, Bryng, and Glaspey, E., *Speech Improvement Cards*, Chicago, Scott, Foresman and Company, 1951.

Daniels, Fannie F., *Good Speech Primer*, New York, E. P. Dutton & Co., 1935.

King, Hilda E., *Speech Training for Infants*, New York, Thomas Nelson & Sons, 1936.

Pray, Sophie, and others, *Graded Objectives for Teaching Good American Speech*, New York, E. P. Dutton & Co., 1934.

Starkey, Mary F., Callery, Julia N., and Slattery, Lucy E., *Speech Training*, Vol. I (first year), Vol. II (second year), and *Teacher's Manual*, New York, Thomas Nelson & Sons, 1935.

Van Riper, Charles, and Butler, Katharine, *Speech in the Elementary Classroom*, New York, Harper & Brothers, 1955.

Wood, Alice L., *The Jingle Book for Speech Correction*, New York, E. P. Dutton & Co., 1934.

Until very recently the fourth and probably greatest deterrent to the use of phonetics—particularly of phonetic symbols—has been the lack of dictionaries giving pronunciation in phonetic symbols and adapted to grade and high school pupils. Although most dictionaries now use some phonetic symbols, there are four that rely more or less completely upon some version of the phonetic alphabet. In 1926, Palmer, Martin, and Blandford [2] published a phonetic dictionary that shows the pronunciation of some 9000 words in British English with the typical variations heard among educated Americans noted in a second column. *An English Pronouncing Dictionary*,[3] by the well-known English phonetician, Daniel Jones, has long been a standard reference on the pronunciation of British English. More recently, a similar dictionary was published for American English.[4] It represents the "colloquial" pronunciation of the three major speech areas of the country—general American, Eastern, and Southern. These three dictionaries are all at the adult level and they give pronunciations only, not meaning.

Finally, there is now available for children in grades four through six a dictionary[5] that uses what is for all practical purposes a phonetic alphabet. Although many of the symbols, and particularly those for the vowels, do not conform to the International Phonetic Alphabet, it does meet the general rule of one symbol per sound and no more than one sound for each symbol. In all, thirty-nine symbols are used. Some are single letters that correspond to IPA symbols as, for example, **b**, **d**, **f**, etc. Others are double letters like the *ch* which is used for **tʃ**, the *zh* which is used for **ʒ**, and the *sh* which is used for **ʃ**. Some are vowel letters

---

Some of the companies that distribute games and toys that are especially designed for, or easily adaptable to, speech training for children are

Creative Playthings, 5 University Place, New York, New York.
The Judy Company, 310 North Second Street, Minneapolis 1, Minnesota.
Children's Music Center, 2858 Pico Boulevard, Los Angeles, California.
Go-Mo Products, Box 143, Waterloo, Iowa.

[2] *A Dictionary of English Pronunciation with American Variants*, W. Heffer and Sons (Cambridge), 1926.

[3] 4th ed., E. P. Dutton & Co., 1934.

[4] John S. Kenyon and Thomas A. Knott, *A Pronouncing Dictionary of American English*, G. & C. Merriam Co., 1953.

[5] *Webster's Elementary Dictionary* (copyright by G. & C. Merriam Co.), American Book Company, 1956.

used with modifying signs. Thus *a* stands for **æ**, *ā* for **eɪ**, *ä* for **ɑ**, and *ȧ* for **a**. However, only four such modifiers are used and the usual key words at the bottom of the page have been eliminated. Meanings are given. Although the student of phonetics will find a number of things to criticize in those "pronunciation symbols" (they are not called phonetic symbols) they have obviously been simplified and adapted for children, are easily learned either with or without a knowledge of phonetics, and do represent a step in the right direction.

Goals in Phonetic Training

The question as to how much phonetic training should be given in the public schools can best be answered in terms of the goals of such training and the relationship of phonetic science to the achievement of these goals. The primary goal is obviously an increased ability to speak the language. This means that phonetic training should aid in the elimination of speech defects and in the normal development of skill in speech. Phonetic study will likewise yield valuable by-products in an increased appreciation and understanding of one's native language, but these are incidental to the main purpose.

The study of phonetics occupies the same relationship to skill in speaking that the study of music does to piano playing or the study of form and techniques to golfing. It is of course possible to play the piano "by ear" or to learn to play golf by trial and error, and some individuals achieve reasonably satisfactory results by these methods. It is commonly recognized, however, that in any activity demanding muscular skill—boxing, swimming, dancing, running, singing, playing golf, tennis, football, or any similar sport—the peak of perfection is reached by those who analyze and study consciously the component parts of the activity until they have found the most effective techniques, and then practice these techniques diligently until their performance becomes automatic.

The articulatory aspects of speech represent, from one point of view, a muscular skill similar in basic principles to any of the activities listed above. It follows that the most efficient way to correct speech defects in school children or to increase their normal speech skill is to approach the articulatory aspects of speech training as if it were a muscular skill. This is the essence of the phonetic approach to speech training. If we accept this purely utilitarian goal as primary and the phonetic approach as the most efficient, we can say that as a minimum there should be enough phonetic training to give the public school pupil a knowledge of the individual sound units of his native language, ability to produce these sound units accurately, ability to recognize these sound units when they are produced correctly and to recognize deviations from these sounds in his own speech and in that of others, ability to produce the various sound combinations common to English and to use these sounds and sound combinations easily and automatically in words and continuous speech, knowledge of the relationship of the spoken and written forms of the language, criteria and standards for making decisions as to "correct" pronunciation and acceptable forms of speech, and a tool for self-help.

Age Level for the Introduction of Phonetic Training

The question as to the age level at which phonetic training should be introduced is easily answered—the earlier the better. The longer a golfer plays by trial and error, the more difficult is the task of learning to play the game right. Similarly, the longer a school child uses incorrect forms of speech, the more difficult it is for him to overcome his defects and the more he is slowed down in his normal speech development. Furthermore, children seem more adept than adults at grasping phonetic concepts, particularly the idea of separate speech sounds. It is as if the more ingrained and automatic speech becomes the more difficult it is for the individual to think of it in terms of its component parts and to revamp habits of speaking.

Under ideal conditions specific training should begin in the first grade. Such training is no more difficult than reading. Children enjoy the work when it is presented in the form of games and play with techniques appropriate to their age. Certainly for the maximum benefit to speech phonetic training should be introduced sometime within the first four years. If such training can be given along with reading, writing, and spelling, these disciplines supplement each other and some of the confusion that normally develops because of the gap between spelling and pronunciation is avoided. Assuming that phonetic training can be started in the first grade, the objectives of the work in articulation and pronunciation during the first four years might be outlined as follows:

First and Second Grades

1. Knowledge of the sound units of English.
2. Ability to recognize these sounds when made correctly.
3. Ability to recognize deviations from these sounds, particularly undesirable deviations.
4. Ability to produce each sound correctly in isolation.
5. Elimination so far as possible of common errors in pronunciation.

Third Grade

1. Finish the task of eliminating articulatory defects so far as these are remediable.
2. Mastery of sound combinations common to English.
3. Study of the relationship between spelling and pronunciation.

Fourth Grade

1. Further study of the rules of pronunciation and of the relationship between pronunciation and spelling.
2. Classification of speech sounds and study of the relationships between sounds.
3. Ability to use strong and weak forms correctly in speaking and reading.
4. Ability to use the dictionary for self-help through study of the diacritic markings.
5. Formulation of criteria for determining questions of correctness and good form in speech.

Beyond the fourth grade, the pupil will be primarily concerned with other aspects of speech, and his work in articulation and pronunciation will continue along the lines laid down in the first four years.

Unfortunately school situations are often far from ideal, and the teacher in the upper grades or high school must often decide whether or not it would be profitable to give phonetic training to pupils who have had no previous work in the subject. Phonetic training at any age level can be well worth while, but the decision as to whether or not it should be given must be made in terms of specific situations. Generally speaking, if there are extensive problems of articulation and pronunciation, and if there is sufficient time to be devoted to them, the phonetic approach will save time and give better results.

Use of Phonetic Symbols

The question is frequently raised as to whether or not it is necessary to teach the phonetic symbols. It is entirely possible to use the phonetic approach to speech training without making use of a phonetic alphabet, and in some instances this may be the logical procedure. However, such training is greatly facilitated if the symbols are taught and used. The same reasons advanced for the use of phonetic symbols in speech corrective work (Chapter 22) apply equally well here. It is apparently no more difficult for a child to learn the phonetic alphabet than it is for him to learn the written alphabet or the numerical system. He learns that certain signs stand for sounds and are used to represent speech as it is spoken, and that these are distinct from the letters of the alphabet used in reading. He learns thus an ear alphabet and an eye alphabet. Instead of confusing the child this actually adds to his understanding of, and ability in, both reading and spelling. If the symbols are to be taught, better results will be obtained if the concept of a given sound and a feeling of the need for a symbol to represent it are developed before the symbol itself is presented. Whenever it is possible for teachers in two or more consecutive grades to coöperate in the use of the symbols, it will probably be worthwhile to teach them in the lower grade. However, if they are to be used for only a short time and then discarded, the advantages gained by their use may not compensate for the time spent in teaching them.

Phonetics at the College Level

While this chapter is concerned primarily with the use of phonetics in the public schools, it will not be amiss to comment briefly on the possible applications of phonetic training at the college level. We have already had occasion to point out the place of phonetics in speech correction, in the treatment of foreign dialect, and in the learning of foreign languages. Phonetics is likewise a valuable aid in fundamental courses in speech, in public speaking, and in voice training courses—in fact in any situation where speech improvement involves matters of articulation and pronunciation. A somewhat different application of the science is found in drama and interpretation work, in which a knowledge of phonetics may be put to use in preparing a dialect reading or in training the actor for a dialect part in a play. The college student will find that a knowledge of phonetics will greatly increase his understanding of speech problems and his ability to improve his own speech. Certainly phonetic training should be an integral part of the preparation of every college student who plans to teach in the field of speech.

APPENDIXES

Appendix A Words and Phrases for
Transcription Practice

The best way to learn the phonetic alphabet is to use the symbols frequently in transcription. The following lists of words and phrases are intended as practice material. They are arranged to exemplify certain sounds or groups of related sounds in the order in which these sounds are discussed in the text. *It should not be taken for granted that every word in a given list necessarily contains the sound that is being illustrated.* Such is often not the case. These lists are not intended to show how words should be pronounced. Their primary purpose is to provide material for practice in transcription which will at the same time stimulate the student's thinking in problems within the field of phonetics.

There are other secondary values to be derived from this material: The word lists are designed in part to show some of the various spellings of the sounds illustrated. They are also intended to raise problems in pronunciation and to indicate some of the variations that exist in the use of sounds. Within a given list, consequently, some of the words may be included because they represent the typical spelling and pronunciation of the sound under consideration. Others may be included because they represent unusual spellings, and others because they present problems in variant pronunciations and raise questions of "correctness."

The instructor will find that the benefits to be derived from such transcription practice can be increased by varying the nature of the assignments. For the most part the student will transcribe the words in his own natural pronunciation. Occasionally, however, he should be asked to transcribe a list in accordance with the pronunciation given in some standard dictionary, or in what he considers to be "standard" speech for his section of the country. Still other variations can be made by asking the student to transcribe the words in what he considers to be "substandard" speech for his section of the country, to transcribe someone else's pronunciations, or to transcribe in stage speech, Southern speech, Eastern speech, etc.

If such transcription practice is introduced early in the course, as it should be, the student may not yet be familiar with the symbols for some of the sounds. The authors believe, however, that if the words were so selected as to include only the sounds already studied plus those for which the phonetic symbol is the same as the usual spelling, the lists would be simplified to the point where they would lose much of their illustrative value. Consequently no attempt has been made to exclude words requiring symbols not yet familiar to the student. It is suggested, rather, that at the beginning of the course the student concentrate on transcribing the illustrative portion of the word and write in the spelling of those sounds for which he does not know the symbols. The student should study each word carefully before transcribing it. Many of the words raise interesting problems in pronunciation, while others illustrate basic concepts in the science of phonetics. The instructor will find it worth while to compare occasionally the student's pronunciation with his transcription in order to help sensitize him to his own speech patterns.

ʌ

tub	doth	among	bomb
come	double	along	ruddy
brusque	blood	buck	above
rough	frontier	hiccough	ultra
does	constable	unction	plover

a

sergeant	from	bazaar	quality
hearth	posterior	onward	knowledge

wash	guard	amen	almond
holiday	flock	psalm	salaam
was	rajah	loll	object

æ

mad	rank	plaid	arrow
ant	crack	anxious	sparrow
draught	baggage	can't	absolute
shaft	casual	hand	agate
plank	character	stand	bag

æ a ɑ

laugh	can't	demand	ghastly
aunt	craft	grass	chance
task	dance	staff	answer
class	France	after	advantage
calf	half	past	telegraph

ɛ

pep	leopard	cleanly
head	Leopold	carry
knell	many	many
egg	said	merry
says	again	many
Thames	leg	pair
friend	primary	pear
fiend	air	pare
element	bear	vary
genuine	bare	bury

e eɪ

abate	maintain
chaotic	locate
chaos	location
fatal	designate
fatality	designation

ɪ

mint	business	ready	prepare
since	sieve	Monday	biscuit
tryst	English	holiday	women
hear	hymn	character	empty
hearty	city	minute	built

i

deceive	receipt	atheist	cereal
least	recipe	monkey	repeat
feet	tepid	Caesar	penalize
retell	creek	eon	leisure
praline	people	serious	breeches

ɔ

fraught	office	dawn	daub
talk	bought	stalk	fare
soft	for	pause	wasp
broad	more	are	swamp
war	log	or	water

ɑ ɒ ɔ

not	orange	laundry
odd	coffee	Washington
mock	off	posse
what	often	daughter
soft	cloth	pa and ma
hospital	stock	Oregon
sorry	hog	wash
watch	bog	gone
possible	frog	horrible
foreign	warrant	what

o oʊ

veto	connotation	oratory	potato
vetoed	bowl	denote	console
rotate	bowling	denotation	consolation
rotation	orate	annotate	motto
rote	oration	hobo	flotilla

ʊ

coop	bosom
could	forsook
full	look
wolf	rook
cupful	stood

u

two	shoe	fruit	Andrew
school	group	noon	Sioux
Louise	Sault St. Marie	tattoo	movie
true	Sauk City ⁻	ghoul	duty
voodoo	coupon	tomb	student

ʊ u

soot	spoon	cooper	coop
room	woof	roof	your
broom	poor	hoof	hoop
soon	root	rooster	sure

ɜ ɝ

church	myrtle	stirring	thorough
heard	joŭrney	hurry	guerdon
pretty	colonel	worry	virulent
shirt	America	courage	fur
pert	purr	current	furry

ə ɚ

betterment	prefer	history	perjury
flattery	preference	perverse	perjure
better	perspire	songster	furrier
altar	prescribe	anger	courtier
mirror	umbrella	singer	periphery

l̩ əl

sample	snarled	tooled	troubling
cradle	missile	schooling	swivel
crackle	tabled	curling	trifle
battled	jostled	bubble	nasalize
chortled	preamble	bubbling	whittling

ə

basket	quality	adage
batted	specimen	furnace
integral	ability	tennis
doorman	difficult	baited
ultimatum	vanilla	civil
betrayal	appeal	civility
peripatetic	agree	approachable
breakfast	soda	apply
gentleman	cinema	applicant
judgment	sycamore	fistula
quiet	considerable	tomato
notable	analysis	basis
potation	gradation	
account	suffocate	

h

annihilate	ahoy	human	unhook
humble	likelihood	whoop	anyhow
herb	lighthouse	pothole	behind
behead	high house	mishap	big horse
ahem	shepherd	perhaps	toe-hold

ʔ

little	wouldn't	we entered	I said *out* not *in*
bottle	gentle	two hours	he *always* fails
cackle	utmost	three eagles	where *are* you?
sentence	alacrity	two eyes	Oh! Oh!
couldn't	black hole	too wise	no onions

eɪ

able	Seine	height	crane
blame	player	sleigh	aid
cake	wane	amen	amiable
later	heinous	aged	agency
painful	Wayne	ague	trainable

aɪ

ideal	Mayan	idolize	dyne
blythe	mayor	diameter	diamond
pied	fire	diaper	Carlisle
mighty	nigh	aerie	briny
lichen	waif	eyesight	briar

ɔɪ

noise	thyroid	join	boiling
boycott	Detroit	disappoint	foible
toil	royal	destroy	poison
oyster	buoy	deploy	soiled
joint	ointment	boisterous	foist

aʊ

profound	howl	sour	brown
allow	bough	power	dowry
town	tough	gouge	doubt
loud	rowdy	laud	pronoun
plowed	house	Faust	frown

oʊ

boat	roar	throw	so
note	sore	brow	soap
bone	sour	though	lobe
flown	yeoman	sew	mow
roll	hose	sow	hoe

w

weak	were	quit	owing
woo	wool	sword	hoeing
trowel	twinkle	sward	wooing
will	quick	toward	throwing
nitwit	twirl	shadowing	doing

hw

whoa	watt	erstwhile	quick
whirl	who	somewhat	why
which	whose	wharf	tu-whit, tu-whoo
witch	where	quite	Whig
what	wear	Dwight	whom

j

yesterday	alien	volume	amuse
yawl	value	Europe	beauty
bayonet	union	view	pure
Mayan	ambient	tube	stupid
mayor	nature	lieu	tune
yellow	Yale	imbue	student
loyal	joist	cue	
million	ewe	future	

hj

huge	tube	suite	hewed
humor	cupid	Hugh	exhume
hue	putrid	Hubert	humble
human	humiliate	hum	cute
humid	suit	humility	hula

r

rare	chord	hard	tire
rear	rural	farm	your
rue	rhubarb	form	ear
roar	railroad	tear	sure
yearly	very	bare	more

l

lolling	milk	lemon	play
lily	bulk	lea	boil
mail	balk	learn	wall
lark	label	loup	bold
walk	allow	alight	chilled

f   v

Stephen	phonate	caveman	laugh
diphthong	vivid	valve	fifth
very	diffuse	prophet	half full
nephew	halve	soften	If have to go
fluff	rough	of the people	I have it

θ ð

tithe	worth	strength	clothe
wither	thorn	these	method
theme	mouths	lengthen	breathe
youths	Southern	thimble	worthy
worthy	loathe	thither	paths

s z

zigzag	houses	explosion	muscle
absurd	bases	raise	corps
absolve	essence	pansies	scissors
exit	fence	sure	discern
mass	hose	scent	exhibit

ʃ ʒ

beige	vision	sagacious	machine
garage	mission	seizure	bijou
hosier	Charlotte	cushion	issue
precious	sugar	rouge	vicious
ration	treasure	azure	special

p b

hobby	raspberry	grandpa
thumb	comb	captain
table	glimpse	cap and gown
purple	cupboard	cabman
proper	warmth	cap full
hiccough	hop toad	capture
pumpkin	rub down	Bob will come
empty	tub brush	cab very full
lap five	lampwick	cabin by a lake
campfire	thimble	thump Bob

t d

dreadful	postman	nutcracker
dawdle	handful	pitfall
traded	sadder	bid high
asked	satisfy	slit open
hasten	little	slip down

tempted	kitty	slick trick
Christmas	acted	slim dog
handsome	rinse	fine deal
friendship	since	good deal
thyme	tenth	great deal

k c g ʒ

chromium	eke	bookcase
pick	morgue	egg cup
concede	thicken	dog leg
goggle	pickle	flag pole
tie	awkward	bragging
ghost	extinct	rugby
luxury	exact	black house
exist	quick	exquisite
success	acquire	big goose
Bach	length	sick cow

ɹ r Я

trust	rip	berry	shrive
drape	treed	her own	throne
very	greed	ever and ever	prairie
drip	growl	purring	diary
grip	gruel	bread	cork

m ɱ n̪ n ɲ ŋ

sickness	wringer	income
think	augment	ember
cotton	signal	England
canst	single	last night
eggnog	angle	last man
sample	younger	bottom
turpentine	humdrum	among my
inkling	ninepin	black night
omnibus	hymnal	come near
symbol	ingrate	laugh more
strangle	camphor	above me
mangle	man made	finger
drinker	grandma	ninny

tʃ dʒ, etc.

eighth	poached	paged
tenth	blazed	jousts
latch	blest	that thimble
hatchet	blushed	sister
stitch	fudge	called them
hatched	trade	don't they
ninth	drain	not these
witches	tests	with Tom
riches	pushed	bath towel
Natchitoches	dazed	used to

Appendix B Practice Material for
Nonsense Dictation

Ear training, which has as its aim the developing of a keen sense of discrimination between sounds, is an important part of the study of phonetics. Practice in transcribing the speech of other people, as well as one's own speech, is a valuable exercise. However, one of the best ways to develop a sense of discrimination between sounds is through the use of nonsense material. It is almost inevitable that a listener will sometimes hear in another's pronunciation of familiar words his own stereotyped pronunciation of the same words. Consequently, when real words are used for dictation there is always a danger that the student will transcribe the words as he himself would have pronounced them. This defeats the purpose of the drill. Practice in the transcription of meaningful speech should come after the student has developed the ability to discriminate between sounds, and after he has acquired the ability to listen to speech sounds objectively, divorcing the auditory stimulus from his own motor habits of pronunciation. These abilities are best developed by frequent practice in transcribing nonsense dictation. The merit of nonsense material lies in the fact that since the combinations of sounds are for the most part unfamiliar, they call for keener discriminations and they do not come in conflict with previously stereotyped motor speech patterns.

The nonsense material below is included to facilitate this training. It is graded in a general way from easy to more difficult exercises, and from nonsense syllables to nonsense words and phrases and finally nonsense sentences. It should be noted that when nonsense syllables are formed by combining three or four sounds, it is difficult to avoid completely combinations that resemble words. However, there are usually slight differences. This material can be used by the instructor as the basis for class practice in transcribing from dictation, or two or more students can drill each other by alternately dictating and transcribing. The usual procedure is for the person dictating to pronounce each unit distinctly two or three times, while the listener without further help writes in phonetic symbols what he thinks was said. Obviously, the success of this drill depends in large part upon the ability of the one doing the dictating to pronounce in exact accordance with the symbolization and to pronounce the same unit without deviation two or three times in succession. Incidentally, the value to be derived from learning to pronounce this material fluently is almost as great as that gained by learning to transcribe it accurately. Thus these exercises can be made to serve a double purpose.

1. *Vowel Drills*

A	B	C	D
1. mib	1. sɜn	1. tad	1. juf
2. nʌs	2. met	2. rɝk	2. lɪb
3. kug	3. tad	3. tug	3. zif
4. bɪp	4. vɔl	4. dan	4. lʊv
5. tɛk	5. mɝb	5. wɑs	5. kɝn
6. zɝf	6. dɑn	6. rʌz	6. kit
7. kʊt	7. lɛp	7. næs	7. vuf
8. tæl	8. gɝb	8. wɔr	8. zʊk
9. fov	9. wʊk	9. had	9. gɝk
10. bæz	10. pʌm	10. sɛz	10. dɑs

E	F	G	H
1. leɪp	1. jɔk	1. kɔp	1. tɒv
2. tuk	2. dɝb	2. pig	2. pak
3. vɑk	3. lɝs	3. dæg	3. rɔz
4. pɑb	4. zʌm	4. gup	4. zɝk
5. mek	5. sɝg	5. sɔv	5. pʌv

1. *Vowel Drills* (Continued)

E	F	G	H
6. nɜ·k	6. bæf	6. zʌt	6. lʊd
7. kif	7. fɑt	7. sʊk	7. mɔg
8. zɪv	8. vʌd	8. vis	8. dʊv
9. duz	9. sæf	9. zɔt	9. kɜ·z
10. sʊd	10. sɔd	10. kɑv	10. gɛv

I	J	K	L
1. kod	1. pɒb	1. lʌf	1. ṽeg
2. laz	2. zam	2. haf	2. tyd
3. mɒb	3. meg	3. klɛp	3. sɔf
4. spo	4. mɜb	4. guz	4. soep
5. hɜ·k	5. zʌd	5. byt	5. hɒt
6. pep	6. dɜv	6. puz	6. byt
7. kot	7. baz	7. fẽv	7. pɪd
8. fɒv	8. teg	8. tɸb	8. vɸb
9. bl̩k	9. ml̩g	9. fɣd	9. jʌg
10. zʊn	10. kɒf	10. zɑd	10. sæl

M	O	P	Q
1. bɪme	1. ẹpoʊk	1. vɪlæ	1. fɛta
2. tækɜ·	2. kupɚ	2. hibu	2. situ
3. tʌmɚ	3. zeɪl	3. bɜ·kl̩	3. pɪkʌ
4. bɪtɑ	4. tadə	4. batọ	4. pəkɔ
5. kalɔ	5. rɒbɪ	5. sl̩kə	5. tæpɑ
6. fɜ·zu	6. bɜ·sɔ	6. tɜki	6. vɛlọ
7. bɛsu	7. l̩dʌk	7. sʌpọ	7. kəsɑ
8. əlɔk	8. nɔvə	8. zɒtɚ	8. bʌpʊ
9. bʌlə	9. vənɛl	9. fɔvi	9. dʊbɜ·
10. kɛpɪ	10. wɔtʊ	10. dʊlẹ	10. jækɚ

R	S	T	U
1. tɪpɪ̣d	1. ætup	1. ɑbətʊ	1. zæbədɑ
2. ọbɔd	2. əkit	2. ɪpəteɪ	2. sotɪ̣pɔ
3. fɑdɚ	3. bəsɛ	3. ʌfɪ̣tæ	3. ịtabo
4. dẹtæ	4. ɜ·pak	4. ɔpɜ·tɪ̣	4. əkɪpʌ
5. zɛpị	5. ɛvəf	5. badəti	5. sɪzdɔl
6. səzʌ	6. ætuk	6. tizusị	6. fɪtəpɑ

1. *Vowel Drills* (Continued)

R	S	T	U
7. ɑkʊp	7. tibu	7. ẹdəzɔ	7. ikætə
8. əzak	8. kɜzə	8. ætɪbɝ	8. æpikə
9. bɪzɔ	9. ọpʊk	9. gɜbutə	9. ətɝkɪ̣
10. pɜbə	10. dafɚ	10. kətæpɛ	10. ɛstɔbə

V	W	X	Y
1. bɤtə	1. fœvõ	1. tidɪ	1. sœpɪ̣
2. sɪ̣bɔ̃	2. tɜbʊ̣	2. tɤdị̣	2. zubœ̃
3. bụtu	3. vɤtə	3. dụvʌ	3. dɒtə
4. fœtɐ	4. fɪ̣bɑ̃	4. dœk	4. bɜtẹ
5. dɣfɛ̃	5. dɸvọ	5. jḷk	5. bɤtɑ
6. tɒg	6. pɝfɪ̣	6. sɜfɔ	6. sɝtæ
7. fytə	7. sɛt	7. fitɛ	7. dɑ̃bɔ
8. bys	8. nɜd	8. dɪbɔ̃	8. vɸtə
9. zɑ̃bõ	9. fʊvɛ̃	9. ọbyt	9. bydə
10. bɸsə	10. bæbɐ	10. ætʌp	10. loz

2. *Drills on Laryngeal Modifications of the Vowels*

A	B	C	D
1. ɑpɑ	1. kɒtn̩	1. lɪhḷ	1. kɔtə
2. ɑpɑʔ	2. kɒʔn̩	2. bɑhn̩	2. hɔʔə
3. hɑpɑ	3. kɒhn̩	3. ʔɑkɑ	3. ʔɔʔən
4. ʔɑʔɑ	4. kɒtən	4. həhɑ	4. ɔhən
5. hɑʔɑ	5. kɒn	5. ʔoʔo	5. pɑʔə
6. ʔɑhɑ	6. lɪʔḷ	6. kʌpm̩	6. ʔʌʔm̩ʔæʔm̩
7. pɑhɑ	7. bækḷ	7. hæʔu	7. hupæ
8. pɑtɑ	8. lɑtəl	8. kʌʔm̩	8. hutɑl
9. pɑʔɑ	9. lɑtḷ	9. hʌpəm	9. ʔuthɑl
10. pɑtɑʔ	10. lɑtə	10. hiʔi	10. ʔuʔɑl

3. *Drills on Intervowel Glides*

A	B	C	D
1. wɑ	1. ɔr	1. aʊ	1. ʌr
2. aɪ	2. ɛʊ	2. ær	2. ʊl
3. aʊ	3. ɪr	3. il	3. oʊl
4. rɑ	4. or	4. aɪ	4. ɛɪ

3. Drills on Intervowel Glides (Continued)

A	B	C	D
5. aɪ	5. oʊ	5. ɜʊ	5. aɪ
6. ar	6. ɛr	6. ɪl	6. æə
7. la	7. ʊr	7. æʊ	7. ɪə
8. ʌʊ	8. ɔo	8. ɪʊ	8. jɔ
9. la	9. æl	9. ul	9. ɛə
10. ir	10. ul	10. ji	10. wɜ

E	F	G	H
1. oʊə	1. lɔɪjɚ	1. aɪljə	1. weɪrɪ
2. ɔlaɪ	2. wɜɪl	2. lɔrə	2. teil
3. eɪr	3. ɛloʊ	3. wærɪ	3. reɪwaɪ
4. aɪwu	4. jilə	4. weɪl	4. ruəl
5. ɛjul	5. aʊr	5. jɜril	5. eɪlijə
6. waloʊ	6. jaljə	6. jarɪl	6. aʊwɛə
7. ɔɪlɪ	7. poʊɚ	7. lɛrɪ	7. ælarə
8. wʌɪl	8. wʌrɪ	8. loʊeɪl	8. wɔrlɪ
9. pɜɪb	9. wəreɪl	9. laʊɚ	9. lɪə
10. jɔwl	10. wɜrɪ	10. walə	10. wɜleɪju

4. Drills on Consonants and Nasal Sounds

A	B	C	I
1. θɪmp	1. hʌkt	1. ðampɚ	1. ɛŋkθ
2. bəðɔɪd	2. zɪld	2. miç	2. natsi
3. tʃɛnts	3. ðarʃ	3. tsɔl	3. βadʒ
4. vɜʃ	4. naʊðə	4. βɔrp	4. tʃɔrd
5. ʒadʒ	5. stɪmpəl	5. apətʃ	5. lax
6. hwɛlθ	6. θufɛtʃ	6. ɔpɸə	6. ɔftæz
7. ʒuks	7. hrɔɪd	7. dzaʊvɪ	7. uʃtə
8. faɪʒ	8. dʒælb	8. axnɪg	8. dθaɪk
9. ðæŋ	9. fɜθ	9. ɪçnal	9. pɸaʊt
10. ʊŋgə	10. ziðɚ	10. tsaɪtnɪŋ	10. zdæŋks

5. Drills in the Attack and Release of Fricatives

A	B	C
1. ants	1. howlzsʌm	1. mʌtʃ
2. ans	2. howlsəm	2. mʌʔʃ

5. *Drills in the Attack and Release of Fricatives* (Continued)

	A	B	C
3.	hɛndz	3. howltsəm	3. mʌʃ
4.	hɛnz	4. jʌŋkstɚ	4. bɒtlɪn̩
5.	risn̩	5. jaŋstɚ	5. bɒklɪn̩
6.	ristn̩	6. jʌŋztə	6. mɪst
7.	ristən	7. si	7. ʃuʃt
8.	harlθ	8. tsi	8. skæsk
9.	harldθ	9. dzu	9. bɔtsən
10.	harltθ	10. ist	10. bɔsən

6. *Nonsense Words*

1. ɔpɪŋ	1. wʊmbə	1. janvɔɪ
2. kɛnɪg	2. havɪl	2. ludʒən
3. oʊlweɪ	3. loʊfɪ	3. rʌdn̩
4. ratsæn	4. kugət	4. tsɝgə
5. ʃʌbladʒ	5. eɪθraɪb	5. avbɔɪŋ
6. ʊdwɛŋ	6. ʒətʃu	6. ʃædl̩ŋ
7. dræn	7. hwavæn	7. dugɔl
8. hɒdaʊ	8. bɝwɪg	8. juʒim
9. zævnɪtʃ	9. rɔzdib	9. hɒspɪl
10. sɔɪgɚ	10. raʊdɪm	10. ærɪŋgə

D	E	F
1. fugl̩paɪ	1. baɪdoʊnə	1. dæsnisɚk
2. θɔsbrɔɪp	2. ruwɔrbz	2. zaɪləvu
3. azdɛntə	3. fɔɪdæp	3. ribəvɪtʃ
4. faðtwɔr	4. tsɪdɚ	4. hwɪzəlɪ
5. fɛmblaɪ	5. wʊdʒɝg	5. vɚlaŋk
6. iʒɛmpɚ	6. oʊzimætəs	6. ðɪzwʊdə
7. zipulə	7. foʊbridə	7. sapdoʊnɚ
8. juwanə	8. abənɪtʃ	8. hjaʒə
9. ðɪbətʃi	9. zæksɪg	9. slɝʒ
10. fʊnɚlaɪ	10. ɪdʒnɔɪk	10. ʃɪnfupra

G	H	I
1. ɔpmaɪl	1. apɸɪk	1. bʌɪgəmən
2. keɪrukəl	2. kœnəg	2. lɔɪnakx

6. *Nonsense Words (Continued)*

G	H	I
3. lɪŋəweɪ	3. Rɔvbax	3. tʃɔbul
4. nɚkulə	4. vɸbimə	4. dɔnəvɪ
5. vɔɪʒid	5. bravɪj	5. kuʔn̩
6. tʃɪbzɚ	6. tynl̩	6. aβor
7. hjɛrbə	7. dzupf	7. lɪçki
8. ʃubmɪl	8. namp	8. gɣdɪn
9. jæðdɔɪŋ	9. flaʔl̩	9. βambə
10. wibɚveɪs	10. ɪkstɜɪm	10. rɛmbaʊnɚ

7. *Nonsense Sentences*

1. vɪl zɔɪ ʃtadan zu bɚpɚ ʒɪk
2. ɔɪ ʃa ʃrɛ zɪks ə sælbun deɪ
3. hrap ni θə zrɪp ɛŋ vaɪ ʊbə ɪkʌtnɪk mwaʊ
4. ulbə jɪrd zu skædʒ ðɪŋgɔɪn
5. pɔnrouz ðiʒ hwɪr likl̩
6. ʃtalz nɛl aɪn əmæbəlɔɪ
7. hɪθ wu ɔbɚ zɪn ə brɛn bɔkɪŋ
8. hɛ ðul na dʒub naɪgə tumbəla
9. rɛts voʊ du ifɔk paʃ zɪmbɔɪŋ
10. ɪ ʔɪzn̩t neɪn zə naɪmbɚ paʊl dɔz
11. ɪtʃ woʊbɔd dæljəpaɪdə
12. zəθɪŋ bə mɜt ɛŋ dʊdl̩ gneɪʃ
13. flɪz dɪltɚ jaɪs ʒɔf hwævɚ lɪŋ
14. frə tʃɛk ðæk oʊn ɚ pampfɚ krɔɪ
15. zə skuŋ ʒat zə skum jɛr eɪ baʊnaɪk
16. jæn ɪkəl undʒən feɪðən ɔl æzoʊm
17. rʌkɪ rɚdl̩ lɛŋk du pɛɪŋ
18. ʒæf wu nɪmpɪ hwapoʊk tu
19. hrɛks sɚ kɔgɚn geɪʃ nu jaʊl
20. hɚg du paʃ æmbəlinə tɔɪŋk
21. æt meɪbɚli foʊbɪŋ ibeɪ ɪs dɔlk zɛt bluʃ
22. matu nu dʒɛp fa paɪ kə zoʊl
23. vɔɪ ʃæ gə lʌnt taʊ du kæsant skoʊ
24. pa tu kəmgæ deɪ dugɪn nɛr wɚb bilaʊtʃ
25. fi ðivə saɪ zændɚ snædʒ
26. ʃa munə eɪ tʃɛp zi lun kɔmɪ aʊ wɔɪsɛt

7. *Nonsense Sentences* (Continued)

27. bʌnɪ kæ nɑ sɔɪ sə pɛltu
28. ʃæp hə θɑ gaʊ vifæ aɪlun
29. dɚ gɔɪ næ tʃɛpɚ jeɪ lu eidə
30. ɛl zoʊ laɪd rə naʊtʃ ɛpi jə hɑlɪg
31. ʃɛp unə zɔɪ mɛtə ladʒeɪ ɛp tɪg kʊf
32. fɔɪg zæp nu lʌm ni sæstoʊ
33. mʌp ʃʌtnɪ saɪlə dʒæf vən jimɚ gɔbə mæf
34. rɑpɚd sæknɪ taɪkọ ðoʊk dəpwi dɔtmɚ mæs
35. ʃæn lʌpsu kɚb ə grubɪŋ
36. eɪ laɪkə mɔtnɪk ɚ zuf di væz
37. tʃʌsu dɚklə ni kɑt lɪmɚn
38. sɪnəp lu ɪp fɚd θɑŋgoʊ snæf
39. præk dəpɚlɪ nʌk kutʃi
40. seɪ dʒup dəsɛn goʊfɚ krɪd niz
41. lɛŋ mægəlfrɑ frɛp ɔf joʊvɛ dʒeɪl
42. hwaɪkən dɚ smɛŋ kæp ʃædə zɪk toʊsɪ
43. veɪnɚ kwil daʊzim bifən θrɛk wɚdæp
44. sɛknɪ dʒɚb lɪstʊp aɪ doʊsɛf
45. teɪfəs snɪl kɪsnɛk maɪ dʒɚnɛg
46. lɪkʃʊp dukɚ aɪzneɪ dʒɛt dansɛp tɔlgə pæf roʊfɛl
47. ʃɑn lʌsu kɚp ə θraɪn kjubɚ mɔtnɪk aɪ ʃɚp
48. mə ʃʊtnɪ saɪkəl dʒæf jumə gɔbɚ loʊ
49. rɪbɚd sɑgnɚ taɪkoʊ ðoʊk kwɔl hwɪvnɪst
50. kɑt lɪmɚn ni ʃɪnəp lu snæf prɛm hwaɪkən

8. *Nonsense Verse* [1]

twəz brɪlɪg ænd ðə slaɪðɪ toʊvz
dɪd dʒaɪr ænd dʒɪmbəl ɪn ðə weɪb
ɔl mɪmzɪ wɚ ðə boʊrọgoʊvz
ænd ðə moʊm ræðz aʊtgreɪb

bɪwɛr ðə dʒæbɚwɔk maɪ sʌn
ðə dʒɔz ðæt baɪt ðə klɔz ðæt skrætʃ
bɪwɛr ðə dʒub dʒub bɚd ænd ʃʌn
ðə frumiəs bændɚsnætʃ

[1] This most delightful piece of nonsense is from Lewis Carroll's *Through the Looking Glass.*

8. *Nonsense Verse* (Continued)

hi tʊk hɪz vɔrpəl sɔrd ɪn hænd
lɔŋ taɪm ðə mæŋksəm foʊ hi sɔt
soʊ rɛstəd hi baɪ ðə tʌm tʌm tri
ænd stʊd əhwaɪl ɪn θɔt

ænd æz ɪn ʌfɪʃ θɔt hi stʊd
ðə dʒæbɚwɔk wɪð aɪz əv fleɪm
keɪm hwɪflɪŋ θru ðə tʌldʒɪ wʊd
ænd bɚbəld æz ɪt keɪm

wʌn tu wʌn tu ænd θru ænd θru
ðə vɔrpəl bleɪd wɛnt snɪkɚsnæk
hi lɛft ɪt dɛd ænd wɪð ɪts hɛd
hi wɛnt gəlʌmpfɪŋ bæk

ænd hæst ðaʊ sleɪn ðə dʒæbɚwɔk
kʌm tu maɪ ɑrmz maɪ bimɪʃ bɔɪ
oʊ fræbdʒəs deɪ kæ̣lu kæ̣leɪ
hi tʃɔrtl̩d ɪn hɪz dʒɔɪ

1. ʃup wɔl noʊgɚd ɪk zaləp [2]
   ʃup wɔl əbrɛkst hɑ tɪg
   aɪ vʊz əgrɪŋ pɑl mænəp
   bəgru ɑvbɛp pɔr slɪg

2. kɪtʃəroʊ taɪvəpɛd
   tigpədu bɪf
   prɪtʃdəstɪk ɪpədɑt
   kæpɚoʊ kɪf

3. juwɑr ɔlu wɑnʊlɪŋ
   rɪljɔl mɑnu ɑlərɔm
   wɑn mɑrʊl mənɑrɪŋ
   lu wɔmlə ɔi aɪlɔrm

4. mɪg eɪ puf
   pɑt ɛmp mə guf
   ɑ krɛg mɚ paʊ dɛg
   mɪtoʊ
   mɪg tʃɛp brɪt
   eɪ laʊ sɑg θrɪt
   eɪ puf ðɪn dʒɝgələp nɪʃoʊ

---

[2] The remaining nonsense poems in this section were composed by students enrolled in classes in phonetics.

8. Nonsense Verse (Continued)

5. minə luʃə vɑlɪ ʒɔr
   beɪtə frʌŋɡə lɪstəmɔr
   əŋktɛlɪ ʃæbɚ dutɪs plaɪ
   steɪ nɛlərɑɪn vjuθ ɡɑrlə saɪ
   hwɪ kɑpə tʃɪzɚ mɑrlə veɪn
   kɚrɑndə ɪmpaɪ ɡæzɚ dʒeɪn
   plaɪoupə fikəs tərɑmə lu
   ʃeɪk dɪvɚ næɡəl ɪnmɪs nru

6. ɪtsɪ ɡɪtsɪ ɡu
   sisɪ lisɪ tu
   oujə sɪkəl
   mɔɪlə pɪpəl
   ɪtsɪ ɡɪtsɪ ɡu

7. ʃul rɔɪʃənu i lɑnou
   kwaɪ ʃwɑm li nɛs
   ʃul pɑfəhwɑn i dɑvou
   bwi ðwɔŋ mi sɛs

8. jumi kumi
   iki u
   kihɑ diɑ
   audɪ du

9. ikəl bʌz ikəl bʌz
   ikəl ɡɚ ku ðeɪ
   mɔr ki ɔz du kɪdəheɪ
   æðɚ auzɪ ɡeɪ

10. hwɪŋkəl jɔlz hwɪŋkəl jɔlz
    hwɪŋkəl mɔl də jeɪ
    tou sɔt pʌn dəbɪztə haɪd
    bɛnə tʌn wɔrs lukən beɪ

11. asǫ tibį kæŋkəm tiði
    neɪnək teɪbɚ i fifi
    tæŋki afi zɑbədu
    ilaɪ mɑtɑ i lɑ mu

12. ɪlunə rɪbʌfəl əgli
    rəlɔrdḷ ɪmɔrdɚ fəsi
    fɪɡaɡəl əʃʌp
    uzʌkəl ɪðʌp
    bɪlunə ðɪkunə tɚli

13. dævəlpɔʃ ɪɡəfu
    pɛdəɡouʃ fɪɡəru
    kɑpəpɛl ribəweɪ
    doupəθɛl θɪvəpeɪ

14. riθɚ diθɚ lɪkɚ lɑ
    nɑkɪ sɑkɪ dʒu
    sælɪ wælɪ pɑdɪstɑ
    zʊkə θʊkə tʃu

15. ɪʃbukəwa dʒʌmdįkɑ pɪʃ-
    kətulaɪ
    fɔstɚpə di sɛmbəku lɪstə-
    pətaɪ

16. kɛbdəʃi ʃafətɑ ɡɛvɚdə-
    ɡeɪ
    hulsəbɑ zɑbəki tʌbənəveɪ

17. wɪminə kætʃɚlə ʃɛlɪstɑ
    pəvu
    ɪkaɪtə θəɡidə mɑtou
    kəpɛpɪ pəlɪlɪ bəɡuʃə rəku
    dərɪvə təwusi ʃaɪlou

18. pɪŋɡəl pɛŋɡəl pæŋɡəl pu
    ʃufɚ loutɚ ampɔr
    kɛkəm jɔrfɚ dɔrpən tu
    dʒæmpɚ beɪtə fantɔr

8. *Nonsense Verse* (Continued)

19. ʃɪndɚ fɪnsə rʊs
    fɔnsu malənʊs
    tʃoʊdn̩ dʒɛdɚ kru
    beɪnə vænəlu

20. meɪgəl slaɪbz binɚ slɑt
    ri nɝs də bin ə roʊ
    meɪ rubə daɪ ki meɪgəl
    saɪ
    ðoʊ buk nɚ ri ə soʊ

21. rivə dɚ rubəs neɪtɚ kə
    tuvəs
    matn̩ di flɑtsn̩ əmoʊ
    əbɪgəl si gaɪdɚ ən spatn̩ li
    kaɪdɚ
    tʃoʊkən zə doʊtʃn̩ əgoʊ

22. ɪpsən ʃeɪn doʊ fɝlɪ geɪm
    an gugən froʊ diloʊ
    laɪtn̩ greɪ foʊ dulɪ peɪ
    di baɪgən tru bivoʊ

23. beɪlɪ reɪlɪ ʃeɪlɪ deɪ
    maɪdǫ slaɪdǫ paɪdǫ bei
    ʌpsən dʌtsən mʌtsən reɪ
    bakən lakən dakən geɪ

24. bəlaktɪ ɔs marlɪn
    rivɪθ æpəlstaɪn tənɔɪ
    pɪŋkar tarnɪŋ lə dɪlfɪn
    ʌn rimɚskɔl də æpɚsɔɪ

25. lufapi soʊteɪ anəkaɪ
    hi jupə foʊdi karsənoʊ
    lufapi mɛkleɪ santɪlaɪ
    hi pɛlə noʊni parsənoʊ

26. forəs mileɪ aʒɛt ʃnoʊ
    lɪmɚɔ kæpʊs natɪŋ watʃ
    toʊpəs bʊlɔɪ stapɛt ðoʊ
    ɝməli vaʊpəl frʌŋgə
    mætʃ

27. æbə kæbə strublman
    dʒɛt dʒɛt ɪmpəl kan
    unənægəl ðisəmɪn
    mæpə ræpə kigəsan

28. mimə ɛs ə lukatʃə
    kabulə guvə nɔɪl
    kæntʊndə sǫlatʃə
    ləlɪndǫ ɛpsǫ pɔɪl

29. lə zoʊ tu fu si pɑ
    mə pak dɑ mu fi wɑ
    al hoʊ wi dɑ
    ɛl koʊ ʃi vɑ
    lə ʒoʊ tu fu si pɑ

30. hɚtædə pɚkæbə tʃɛb ʊŋ
    rəbaf
    roʊlb ɛf bɪnt ə proʊst
    pəntsi
    frʊsk oʊb ɛnt ɚb eɪbz
    foʊl sɔkədaθ
    əlatə pʊlwatə hʊf si

8. *Nonsense Verse* (Continued)

31. lubɪʃə tubɪʃə froʊ
zɚ klætʃ vɔm hɛpf zɚ kloʊ
sɚ kloʊ strump saɪm
wɪb fʊm ɚ naɪn
lubɪʃə tubɪʃə froʊ

32. jɚ doʊ wæf vəbeɪdə kaɪ
tʃal mɛθ hin sloʊ
pɑg dʒʊf brikt vrɑ lɪbidɚ
zaɪ
kwɛn uθə sroʊ

33. ẹbæʃki frɑntaɪlə bɛθɛɪ
pəwiski əntɑlə ɔrdeɪ
lɚp ʃulɚ wʊmf hɛdọ
tʊl kɑmbə ðɔk dʒɛbọ
frəmbjuləs kɑroʊbrən
mʊlkeɪ

34. dʒɚ hætə ðɑl punwʊdɪ
fri ɚ rudeɪ
hwɛθ ʃivrədor doʊkəl
ɑndru
wəl mæfləvɪk tʃæ jɔkitsəl
θrubeɪ
mɛn ɚ jʌbəl sludɪ ɪbkru

35. sækəl frɑnd kaɪm eɪmbʊʃ
rɔl
dʊp stiθ nɪf tʃub æb dri
æŋ kælɪkoʊn datʃ sækəl
gɪŋ
feɪb rɔl pləb jɛg æf bri
sækək frɑnd kaɪm eɪmbʊʃ
rɔl
eɪmbʊʃ rɔl eɪmbʊʃ rɔl
saɪkəl frɑnd kaɪm eɪmbʊʃ
rɔl
dʊp stiθ nɪf tʃub æb dri

36. kwi tɔɪtʃ læt
bru maʊtɪ ʃæt
krɑ plutɪ ɑnɑ kæt
nɑn buz aʊg
raʊt ʃikə baʊt
wʌg ukə ʃaʊt
ʊŋgə piʃə faʊt
kraʊ plaʊ hwaʊ

37. rə kɔɪbi lə kɑbə
ʃə tubə tal kruθɚ
hwæp waʊgz sə brʌn kə
bub
lə kup tə bɑnə brunə fɔɪ
kwə bujə fɑgə tub

38. læt lə fruðəm kə brupəl
gævən
aʊmə ðrupst keɪ tutɪ
læt brupəl gævən lɛk ḷ
kruðən
ɛkbɔɪ aʊ luʃən rutɪ

39. hjɔwi gæbɚ blæbɚ kraʊ
præt aʊ krudɚ truk wu ðaʊ
ɛg ɪ puvwɛ slug nə gaʊ
lɔrdɪ kraʊnɪt ɪŋgə graʊ

40. ʃɪlɪ ʃɛlɪ ʃalɪ tʃoʊb
ɪk tʃɪp ʊkɔb tʃæk
ʃɪkɪ ʃɛkɪ ʃakɪ tʃoʊb
ɪʃ tʃɪk ɔbʊk tʃæk

8. *Nonsense Verse* (Continued)

41. zɪgətou zɛnəbar tʃɪnəka 42. hatʃ ʌŋgəl rɛdʒɔ klaust
    sɛkɪ   lun ɝsɔɪŋ wæʃɛ stɪlk
    tɛnəpɚ sɪkəbeɪ dɪnɚgɔɪ   jædʒ əmʌl routʃɛ glaust
    dʒɛkɪ   rim ɚzeɪn weʒæ tsɪlk
    ʌpsɪpǫ dousidou utətu
    pɝmə
    dʒʌtəmɚ sʌdəmɚ tʃʌbəmɚ
    fɝmə

43. sun ɪkan ɪ kɛpzɪnz   44. ʌn ʌŋgə ʌŋgəl wi
    ɪpugu rɛgɪtrɔɪ   umli umli um
    frou ņ kwʊntɪ krɪbɚgz   ɔrtə akəl ɪkəl ti
    pugɛp utə krɔɪ   dʒɝbə dʒi dʒɝbə fi
    punən gwaʊ ɔɪn ɔtɛnd   umli umli um
    i barts tigwan kwəʃɔn   wɝkə tikɪŋ ɔltə gri
    jɔs θɛp ɪ pugəlgɔʃ   umli umli um
    kju pran əvɔɪ ədɔŋ   wɝkə bæzɚ tumə pri
                                   tumə fræbə ʌŋgəl di
                                   umli umli um
                                   kwɝbə makəl ɪbə zi
                                   umli umli um
                                   tʃɝlə bræzə ɪmlə gi
                                   dʒɝmə klɛgə apə ni
                                   umli umli um

45. daʊn əmɔŋ ðə wɔlrɪŋz   46. ou ma sǫ teɪ meɪ la ǫfeɪ
    talu   kəratəm lɛvǫ ʃurəfeɪ
    lɪvd ə figəlu kəbalu   ʃǫpɛl əzumeɪ di ǫmeɪ
    tsal hi waz ənd ou sou   nə seɪ ənubə dubəleɪ
    lʌʃnu
    hwɛn hi ʃaʊtəd ugan
    kʌʃnu

47. ʃlɛrɪmp hi sɛd ənd bɔldəd 48. pumɚ tɔtʃau kaug
    flɪmlɪ   binɚ dɛdʒæf geɪg
    pəpɛlərɪŋ ǫmɛl kədɛrɪŋ   mumɔ zeɪʃæf staug
    gərɔɪŋ wɪl du hi jɔldəd   wɪnɔ soʒav dzeɪk
    glɪmlɪ
    aɪdoulə rɪŋ ləbɛl dɪspɛrɪŋ

8. *Nonsense Verse* (Continued)

49. tɪf ɑlu aɪn raɪlɪf soʊmbru
 joʊfaɪ θrænlæps zʊk ɪn
 mɔrlu
 ɑlə zɛmpɚə kig ɪn kwan-
 tiəs
 tʃɔglən oʊ daʃzɛnɪk θoʊ
 dakəbi da blɛmp aɪ sæpəg
 sæpəg aɪ dʒɚlɛmp foʊ

50. ɚbloʊk tɪmaʒ ɪk zɑgusi
 in suf təlakɪ san tʃu bi
 in tʃu dʒak ʃufli piŋ ʊz
 θrɛk
 ɪpæst vəbroʊnst vɪs lɛflu
 trɛk

Appendix C   Exercises

The following exercises are arranged under main subdivisions taken from the text. They are intended in part to serve as the basis for formal class assignments to be turned in by students in written form. Others may well be used as subjects of oral reports in class. Still others are designed to stimulate the student's thinking and to open avenues for personal observation and investigation, or perhaps to serve as subjects for term papers. The exercises described here will suggest others of a similar nature. Instructor and student should feel free to delete and supplement this material in accordance with individual interests and the scope and purpose of the class.

I. The Phonetic Alphabet

1. Read a paragraph of prose carefully. Note each sound unit and draw dividing lines between the letters of the alphabet in such a way as to mark off the separate speech sounds. Consult the *Table of Phonetic Symbols* and write the proper symbols above the line, thus:

ð iz wi meɪ prɑpɚlɪ kɔl spi tʃ saʊndz
Th|e|se| w|e| m|ay| p|r|o|p|er|l|y| c|a|ll| s|p|ee|ch| s|ou|n|d|s

Do you find some sounds that are not represented in the spelling? Do you find letters that have no sound? Are there times when two letters have only one sound, or one letter has two sounds? What evidence of the value of, or the need for, a phonetic alphabet do you see in this exercise?

2. Observe a child eighteen months to three years of age, and try to transcribe his repertory of sounds. Do you notice some that are not standard sounds in English speech? How do you account for the eventual disappearance of these sounds from the child's sound system and for the difficulty of relearning them at a later date?

3. Invent new sound units for use in American speech. Make up symbols for these sounds. Do these symbols meet the requirements set down in the text? Give reasons why these sounds should or should not be added to the English sound system.

4. Explain the pronunciation of the letter *e* (or *a* or *i*, etc.). The introductory material in a large dictionary will be your best source of information. Write out the explanation once using phonetic symbols and again without the aid of such symbols.

5. Have a friend (preferably a foreigner) read slowly a page or two of a foreign language with which you are unfamiliar. Try to pick out the sound units of the language. Use the symbols you have already learned for sounds that are familiar and devise new symbols for those that are not. If possible, check your findings with someone who knows the sound system of the language. Watch for sounds that vary slightly from the corresponding English phonemes.

2. Basic Principles of Phonetics

1. Choose one or two of the following sounds for observation: ɑʊ, ɑɪ, ɔ, ɑ, or ɛ. Make a list of ten or more words containing the sound. Select ten people who were born and reared in the same state and study the differences in their pronunciations of the sound under observation. If you find variations, try to account for their presence. Does the pronunciation of the sound seem to be influenced by neighboring sounds?

2. Repeat Exercise 1 above, this time studying individuals from various states or sections of the country. Discuss your findings.

3. Select a group of about ten people. These individuals may be drawn from the same section of the country and represent a homogeneous speech environment; they may be selected from different sections of the country in such a way as to give a sampling of different speech environments; or they may be made up of representatives of various foreign dialects. Study the way in which they pronounce the *r* sounds in the following sentence: "Early one

winter morning, he left his farm and wandered far and wide in search of fur-bearing animals, particularly deer and bear." What variations do you observe? How do you account for them?

4. Study the way in which ten or more individuals make the *s* sound. You will probably find variations. How do you account for them? Compare the causes for variation in the *s* sound with the causes for any variations you may have observed in Exercises 1, 2, and 3 above.

5. Using the phonetic alphabet given in the early pages of this text, determine by observing a friend, or by watching your own articulation in a mirror, the sounds that are capable of analysis by direct observation. List each of the sounds of English speech under one of the following groups: (a) easily observable, (b) partially observable, and (c) practically unobservable. Be sure to keep your pronunciation normal.

6. Practice making the various speech sounds paying special attention to the sensations arising from contacts made within the articulatory mechanism and from movements of the mechanism. Place each sound in one of two groups: (a) sounds accompanied by rather definite sensations, and (b) sounds lacking such specific sensations. What conclusions would you draw about the relative stability of the sounds in these two groups? Are these inferences borne out in fact? What is the bearing of this exercise on the teaching of the deaf? What implications does it have for the speech clinician who is teaching new sounds to speech defectives?

7. If time and materials are available, several students should make, or have made by a dentist, artificial plates for the hard palate and practice making palatograms and linguagrams. Note the points of contact for the various sounds and the variations in two palatograms of the same sound. Study the effect of the preceding and following vowels. Make a list of the sounds that cannot be studied from palatograms. Drawings or photographs of typical palatograms and linguagrams of all of the sounds analyzable by this method would make excellent material for a term paper in phonetics.

3. The Speech Mechanism

1. Study models and charts of the speech mechanism until you are familiar with the structures and with their functions in speech.

Time spent in acquiring a detailed knowledge of the speech mechanism will yield rich dividends in the study of phonetics.

2. If possible, arrange a demonstration laryngoscopic examination. Have the patient demonstrate the positions of the glottis for ordinary breathing, whispering, the *h*-approach, the glottal stop approach, and the glottal vibratory approach. Write up your observations.

3. Observe the effects of emotional conditions upon speech. What aspects of speech are most affected? What emotions or feelings disturb articulation the most? Observe an actor's simulation of some of these emotions. Does his speech reflect a true-to-life reaction to the emotion?

4. If an artificial larynx and a bellows are available, practice speaking with it until you become reasonably adept. What sounds are difficult to produce with the artificial larynx? Why? What sounds are easy? What sounds or approximations of sounds could you make without the aid of any artificial appliance if there were no moving column of air to be used for speech?

5. If a recording machine and a contact microphone are available, make a recording of continuous speech with the microphone placed successively upon the subject's chest, larynx, mandible, maxilla, nose, forehead, top of the head, and back of the neck. Write up your observations, noting especially the effect of the position of the microphone on resonance and understandability. With the contact microphone on the thyroid cartilage, record such sound combinations as **pa**, **ta**, **ka**, **sa**, **fa**, **ʃa**, etc. Could you identify the consonants when the record was played? Why?

6. Examine the articulatory mechanisms of five people, observing similarities and differences. Devise simple tests for speed of tongue, lip, and jaw movement and try them out on your subjects. Do you find differences in their ability to make such movements? If so, how do you account for them?

4. Kinesiologic Phonetics

1. Practice making such sounds as **s**, **ʒ**, **ʊ**, **a**, **b**, **eɪ**, **ra**, etc., until you have developed an accurate sense of feeling of the nature of the sounds, i.e., continuant, stop-plosive, or glide.

2. With a stethoscope or a contact microphone or with the

fingers placed on the thyroid cartilage, compare voiced and voice-less pairs of sounds until you can distinguish them easily.

3. Arrange all of the sounds of English in order from the least sonorous to the most sonorous. What use could you make of this list in speech correction? In public speaking or interpretation?

4. Arrange all of the vowels, English and foreign, according to their nearness to each other acoustically. How many of these vowels could be used as phonemes in one language without giving rise to confusion? Are there any vowels that could be added to the English sound system? Are there any vowels in English that should be discarded to avoid confusion? Construct an "ideal" vowel system for a language.

5. Select three or more of the vowel sounds of English for study. List as many as possible of the ways in which each of these vowels is spelled.

6. Prepare a list of ten words containing two or more un-accented syllables. Analyze the pronunciation of this list of words by ten or more individuals, with particular reference to their handling of the vowels in the unstressed syllables. If possible, include subjects from different sections of the country. Tabulate your results.

7. Make your own measurements of the distance of the jaw opening in the production of the various vowels. Do you observe much variation? Did you notice any differences between good and bad speakers in this respect?

8. Find ten examples of the use of the glottal stop ʔ in normal speech. If you have an opportunity to observe speech defectives, note the types of defects characterized by use of the glottal stop. If such observation is not possible, what types of speech defects would you expect to be characterized by use of the glottal stop?

9. Arrange all of the consonant sounds, English and foreign, in the order of their nearness to each other acoustically. Cross out those that could not be used as phonemes in one language without confusion. Are there any consonants that could be used as pho-nemes in English in addition to those already in the language? Are there any now used in English that should be discarded to avoid confusion? Construct an "ideal" consonant system for a language.

10. List words and phrases showing as many different forms of

the explosive phase of **t** (or any other plosive) as possible. Examples: *cat-tail, catnip, ketchup.*

11. The various members of the *r* phoneme do not at present have separate phonemic significance. Arrange these various *r*'s in order according to their tongue position and circle those you think could be used as separate phonemes. Test your judgment by making nonsense words that are alike except for the type of *r* used. If other people can readily distinguish one such nonsense word from another, it may be assumed that each word could carry a different meaning and that the respective *r*'s could serve as separate phonemes. Do not let the listener watch your pronunciation of the test words. If you find that some of these *r*'s could serve as separate phonemes why are they not so used at present? Or are they?

12. Pronounce in random order the combinations **mɑ, mɑ, nɑ, ŋɑ, ṇɑ, ɲɑ,** and **ŋɑ** to various subjects and study their ability to discriminate the nasal sounds. Draw such conclusions as the evidence warrants.

13. List one word or phrase, if possible, exemplifying each of the affricate combinations.

14. Let the members of the class transcribe separately or in pairs the same selection of recorded speech. Play the record as often as necessary for accurate hearing of the sounds. Compare the transcriptions in class, keeping the record available for use in clearing up disputed transcriptions. This exercise can be repeated profitably a number of times using recordings of increasing difficulty and of different types of speech. Students will find it profitable to study carefully commercial or homemade records of various types of speech. If these are not available, study the speech of radio announcers and performers or of public speakers. The habit of jotting down in phonetic symbols unusual pronunciations wherever they are heard can become an interesting pastime.

5. The Phenomena of Dynamic Phonetics

1. Find twenty examples of transition sounds such as those occurring in *fence* and *something.*

2. Read a short paragraph and count the number of full stops in articulation, the number of pauses in position and the number of

glides. What is the relative frequency of these three aspects of articulation?

3. With a stop watch determine the time it takes to speak normally a short passage of prose. Compute the number of speech sounds produced per second. How many gross movements did the tongue make? How many times did the articulatory mechanism come to a full stop? How often did the vocal folds open and close? How many times did the soft palate open and close? Comment on your findings.

4. Make a study of the carryover of nasality from nasal sounds to preceding or following vowels. Explain why this happens and how it is to be avoided.

5. Prepare words and short phrases for recording. Write in phonetic symbols how you think these phrases will sound when heard in reverse. Check your judgment by playing the record backwards. Try to work out some combinations for recording that will sound the same whether the record is played forward or backward.

6. Pronounce the following isolated sounds: ɪ, ɛ, æ, ʊ, eɪ, ɑʊ, b, p, ʒ, and ʃ. Now pronounce the same sounds in words. What differences do you observe?

7. Describe what happens to the separate sounds in the phrase, *up and at them* ʌpændætðɛm when these words are pronounced rapidly. A four-year-old child recognized immediately ʌʔæʔæʔm̩ as the above phrase. Write in phonetic symbols the degree of slurring you would consider permissible in good speech. What problems arise in making such a decision.

8. Learn to say sɛːt, hæːp, bɒːks, buːk, bļːk, tʌːk. Using a shortened vowel, say **sit, but, kæt, klæk, tɝk, sup.** Pronounce the following words, then repeat them omitting the final sound but preserving the incidental connecting sounds: **hæv, hæz, lig, liv, bɪg, bɪd, ræŋ, ræn, bɪŋ, bɪm.** Pronounce the following words, omitting the "off-glide" following the final plosive: *bag, head, cob, leak, bet, peep.* Which pronunciations are most altered from that usually given them? Pronounce in the same manner *seep, seek, seat.* Do these words sound alike? Could a hearer distinguish one from another? How? Utter a slow glide beginning with **i** and ending with **ɑ.** Time it with a watch having a second hand. How short an utterance can you manage without producing the effect of **jɑ**? Try this experiment also with a glide from **u** to **ɑ,** comparing such a

glide with **wa**. Pronounce **ŋɑ** to a friend not phonetically trained and ask him to spell it. Explain his spelling. Try also **alŋ**, **ɜŋ**, and **ŋi**.

9. Pronounce in reverse *house, cautious, saying, when, wen*. What happens to the **h** in *house*? What is difficult about the reversal of the *c* in *cautious*? Why is it difficult to distinguish in reverse between *when* and *wen*? Whisper **aʊ** and **haʊ**. How do you produce the distinguishing characteristics of these two whispered words?

6. Phonetic Metamorphology

1. Find ten examples of interchangings of sounds of the beta group. It is not necessary that the interchangings be between the same pairs of sounds and in the same direction, as in the illustrations given in the text. Find ten examples of delta interchangings and ten of gamma interchangings.

2. Find ten examples of interchangings among front vowels, ten among back vowels, and ten among mid vowels.

3. Find five examples of horizontal interchangings among the vowels and five of interchangings between centrally delivered and laterally delivered vowels.

4. Find ten examples of gamma-to-delta migration of sounds.

5. Find ten examples of ablaut verbs, employing at least five different vowels in their present tense forms. Find five reduplicative, ablaut, vocables, and also five reduplicatives that have consonant changes only.

6. Find pairs of words in which strong, definite, stressed vowels are compared with parallel schwa forms. Find one pair like each of the samples given in the text.

7. Find five pairs of words in each of which a **tj** combination is palatalized in one word and not in the other. The words of each pair need not necessarily be related philologically but should exhibit similar approaches to and releases from the **tʃ** and the **tj**. Find also five similar pairs illustrative of the palatalization of **dj**. Find also five pairs of words in which **j** has changed to **dʒ**, or in which we have two parallel forms one pronounced **j** and one **dʒ**, as *yoke* and *joint*.

8. Find ten examples of sound changes due to combinations of word units that bring into juxtaposition incompatible sounds.

9. Find ten examples of sound changes (not merely omissions) that are due to the operation of the principle of articulatory economy.

10. Find ten examples of word pairs in each of which a vowel appears as a glide in one word and as a pure vowel in the other because of a difference in the consonants that follow the vowels. The words of a given pair need not be related philologically but should have similar approaches to the vowel and similar releases from the consonant. Find ten examples of a change from a glide vowel to a pure one through a change in stress.

11. Find ten examples illustrative of changes of timing of the laryngeal movements. Find also ten examples showing changes of timing of the velar movements. Find also ten examples of changes of timing of the articulatory series.

12. Find ten examples of "accidental" unaspirated plosives with voiceless implosion. Find also ten examples of unaspirated, voiceless plosives initiating unstressed syllables. Find also ten examples of unaspirated, voiceless plosives initiated by **s**. Find ten examples of definite aspiration preceding voiceless fricatives.[1]

13. Find five examples each for the following categories of fortis and lenis effects: (a) aspirated stressed consonants; (b) aspirated unstressed consonants; (c) unaspirated stressed consonants; (d) unaspirated unstressed consonants.

14. Find five examples of change of attack upon fricatives, from "open" to "closed" or from "closed" to "open."

7. American Speech Styles

1. Find five words, using as many different vowels, that are pronounced in your locality with vowel glides, in spite of the fact that they are marked in the dictionary to be pronounced with pure vowels. Indicate the glide that is used.

2. Find ten examples of unstable diphthongs like that in *Mary*, which may be **ɛr, ær, er,** or **eɪr**.

3. List the five words in which you consider the use of the compromise **a** is most justifiable. Make similar lists for **ɒ** and **ɜ**.

---

[1] In working out Exercises 12 and 13 the following procedure is helpful: Take a piece of rubber tubing of small diameter, about 12 inches long. Hold one end of the tubing in the opening of the meatus of the ear and the other in front of the lips. One will thus be able to note clearly the periods of aspiration.

4. Do you use schwas for the italicized vowels in the words that follow: inf*a*nt, nov*e*l, c*o*ntrol, ev*i*l, cab*i*n? Write phonetically your ordinary pronunciation of each. Compare your pronunciations with those given in your favorite pronouncing dictionary. If your use differs from that given in the dictionary, how do you reconcile the difference? Or don't you?

5. Take the tubi*ng* you used i*n* Exercises twelve and thirtee*n* above. This ti*m*e put o*n*e e*n*d i*n* your ear a*n*d the other just i*n* the e*n*tra*n*ce of the *n*ostril. Read orally the directio*n*s for this exercise. You should hear a clear to*n*e through the tubi*ng* o*n* all the italicized sou*n*ds. If you hear clear to*n*es o*n* other sou*n*ds, you are "*n*asalizi*ng*." Practice the readi*ng* u*n*til you ca*n* avoid such *n*asalizatio*n* or u*n*til you have deter*m*i*n*ed that such avoida*n*ce is i*m*possible for you.

6. Compare your habitual pronunciation of the following words with that given in your favorite dictionary, paying special attention to the stress marks: *prisoner, capillary, secondary, government, memory, wondering, preference, ice cream, cowboy.* Justify your own usage, if possible.

7. If you could by fiat fix a style of pronunciation of English for all cultured Americans, indicate what changes you would make from the form illustrated by the transcription on page 11 of Chapter 1. Justify your changes.

8. The Pronouncing Dictionary

1. Construct a table of equivalent phonetic values, taking your own pronouncing dictionary as a basis. Make your table in three columns: the dictionary symbol, the key word or words, the phonetic symbol. Such a table will constitute the opposite aspect of the table given on page 318 in Chapter 19. There is displayed the dictionary equivalents of phonetic symbols. What you are to do is to display the phonetic equivalents of dictionary symbols.

9. Applied Phonetics

1. If you could hear only the fundamental tones of the human voice—not the harmonics and the friction noises—what would you hear when one asked you, "How far is it to Chicago?" Write it phonetically. Now write what you would hear if you could hear

all but the friction noises of speech. What are the homophenes of *bat, come,* and *red*?

2. Analyze the speech of some person whose first language was not English. Write a few sentences of the dialect in phonograms. Judging from the phonetic lapses in the dialect, construct the sound system of the subject's native or childhood language; then check your guesses by having him give you samples from that language.

3. Show how you might teach an individual each of the following sounds by making certain modifications of sounds present in the English sound system: **hw, ɪ, ɝ, ç,** and **ʁ.**

4. Describe the methods you would use in teaching a deaf person the following sounds: **d, p, ɑ, k,** and **w.** How would you teach the same sounds to a blind person?

5. Describe the placement and manner of production of the following sounds in enough detail so that someone who does not speak English might read your description and produce the sounds with reasonable accuracy: **hj, u, f, tʃ,** and **ŋ.**

6. Plan the procedure and prepare the materials for teaching the sounds **θ, ð, r, l,** and **s** to a first grade class.[2]

7. Plan the procedure and prepare the materials for correcting the following sound substitutions in small children: **θ** for **s, w** for **r,** and **f** for **θ.**

Appendix D Phonetic Transcriptions
for Reading Practice

The following transcriptions are included primarily for use as practice material in the reading of phonetic symbols. The student should develop the ability to read phonetic transcription easily and accurately. This ability is based upon a thorough knowledge of the sound values of the phonetic symbols and the various modifying signs. Fluency in the reading of transcription is gained only by constant practice. Additional material for practice may be found in certain of the books presented in the bibliography. The reader should take care to note each symbol and give it its exact value. He is cautioned to avoid the error of pronouncing in his own habitual manner after having grasped just enough of a word to recognize it. The many varieties of speech represented below make such procedure especially inaccurate.

With the exception of the first nine sections, these transcriptions are not intended as typical samples of a particular local, regional, or foreign dialect, or yet of "correct" speech. The first nine are transcribed in what is called general American speech. The style represented is colloquial, that is, reasonably careful but casual pronunciation as it occurs in connected conversational speech among educated people—not in the somewhat more formal and precise manner that is sometimes used in platform speaking.

Questions of pronunciation or symbolization in this group were usually resolved in accordance with Kenyon and Knott's

Pronouncing Dictionary. Only broad transcription symbols are used and variant pronunciations have been avoided. Even so, it was necessary to make some rather arbitrary choices. The glide **our** is usually shortened to **or**, whereas **oul** has been written out in full. Thus the word *poured* is transcribed as **pord** with the **u** part of the glide, which is present with varying degrees of prominence in different words of this type, taken for granted. Again in these first sections the symbol **t** has been omitted in such words as *since, fence, sense,* etc. It is, however, to be assumed that a **t** sound, which may vary from barely perceptible to fully emphasized, will almost always appear when **n** is followed by **s** in rapid succession and without any hiatus between the two.

A word of explanation is also needed about the use of the use of one bar | to indicate a pause and a double bar ‖ to represent a period or full stop. Anyone who has read Washington Irving's still delightful story will realize at once that two punctuation marks will never suffice to guide the reader through his long, devious, and complicated sentences. The double bar has been placed wherever Irving indicated the official end of a sentence, but the location of the single bars has virtually no relation to correct punctuation. They have been used, rather, to mark some of the points where it is particularly important for the reader to pause and regroup his forces if he wishes to follow the twists and turns of the author's meanings.

Sections 10 through 20 are still, broadly speaking, transcribed in general American speech. However, close transcription symbols and modifying signs are used occasionally, variant pronunciations are introduced, and some of the elisions and linkages that occur in more rapid speech are illustrated. Accent marks are included on occasion to exemplify their use. Not all of this is intended to represent "good" speech. In fact some of the transcriptions will seem to some to represent undue carelessness of articulation or incorrect pronunciation.

The student is also warned not to expect consistency, which was not one of the important purposes of these transcriptions. Accent marks, the dot under vowels, and other modifying signs are used sporadically, not regularly. The same words may be transcribed in one way one time and in a different way another. This lack of consistency could be justified by pointing out that

such differences do occur in actual speech; but its real purpose is
to force students to read symbols—to pronounce the words as
they are written and not to rely upon his own habits of pronunciation or his preconceived ideas as to how words ought to be
pronounced.

From sections 21 on, the transcriptions introduce various
deviations of defective and dialectal speech with increasing use of
modifying signs, close transcription symbols and symbols for
foreign sounds. There are still occasional passages that are for all
practical purposes in general American speech. Although most of
the passages in this group were originally transcribed from actual
recordings, they have been so modified for the purposes of reading
practice that they can no longer be said to be either transcriptions
of the speech of an individual or samples of a native or foreign
dialect. Most of the modifications were in the direction of simplification, that is, elimination of some of the deviations in order to
enable the reader to concentrate on fewer problems of symbol
recognition and pronunciation at a time.

rɪp væn wɪŋkl̩

baɪ waʃɪŋtən ɝvɪŋ

1. hu ɛvɚ hæz meɪd ə vɔɪdʒ ʌp ðə hʌdsən mʌst rɪm ɛmbɚ
ðə kætskɪl mauntn̩z‖ ðeɪ ɑr ə dɪsm ɛmbɚd bræntʃ əv ðə greɪt
æpəleɪtʃɪən fæmlɪ ænd ɑr sin əweɪ tu ðə wɛst əv ðə rɪvɚ|
swɛlɪŋ ʌp tu ə noubəl haɪt æn lɔrdɪŋ ɪt ouvɚ ðə səraundɪŋ
kʌntrɪ‖ ɛvrɪ tʃeɪndʒ əv sizən| ɛvrɪ tʃeɪndʒ əv wɛðɚ|
ɪndid ɛvrɪ aur əv ðə deɪ prədjusɪz sʌm tʃeɪndʒ ɪn ðə mæd-
ʒəkəl hjuz ænd ʃeɪps əv ðiz mauntənz| ænd ðeɪ ɑr rɪgɑrdɪd
baɪ ɔl əv ðə gud waɪvz fɑr ænd nɪr æz pɚfɪk bərɑmətɚz‖
hwɛn ðə wɛðɚ ɪz fɛr ænd sɛtl̩d| ðeɪ ɑr kloudd ɪn blu ænd
pɚpəl æn prɪnt ðɛr bould autlaɪnz ɑn ðə klɪr ivnɪŋ skaɪ| bʌt
sʌmtaɪmz hwɛn ðə rɛst əv ðə lændskeɪp ɪz klaudlɪs| ðeɪ wɪl
gæðɚ ə hud əv veɪpɚz əbaut ðɛr sʌmɪt| hwɪtʃ ɪn ðə læst
reɪz əv ðə sɛtɪŋ sʌn wɪl glou ænd laɪt ʌp laɪk ə kraun əv
glorɪ‖

2. æt ðə fut əv ðiz fɛrɪ mauntn̩z| ðə vɔɪədʒɚ meɪ hæv
dɪskraɪd ðə laɪt smouk kɚlɪŋ ʌp frʌm ə vɪlɪdʒ huz ʃɪŋgəl rufs

glim əmʌŋ ðə triz dʒʌst hwɛr ðə nɪrɚ lændskeɪp mɛlts əweɪ
ɪntu ðə ʌplændz‖ ɪt ɪz ə lɪtl̩ vɪlɪdʒ| hævɪŋ bɪn faʊndəd baɪ
sʌm əv ðə dʌtʃ kalənɪsts ɪn ðə taɪmz əv ðə pravɪns dʒʌst
əbaʊt ðə bɪgɪnɪŋ əv ðə gʌvɚnmənt əv ðə gʊd pitɚ staɪvəsənt|
meɪ hi rɛst ɪn pis| and ðɛr wɚ sʌm əv ðə haʊzɪz əv ðɪ
ərɪdʒənəl sɛtlɚz stændɪŋ wɪðɪn ə fju jɪrz| bɪlt frʌm smɔl
jɛlo brɪks brɔt frəm halņd| hævɪŋ lætɪst wɪndoz æn geɪbəl
frʌnts| sɚmaʊntəd wɪð wɛðɚ kaks‖

3. ɪn ðæt seɪm vɪlɪdʒ ænd ɪn wʌn əv ðiz vɛrɪ haʊzɪs hwɪtʃ|
tʊ tɛl ðə prəsaɪs truθ| wəz sædlɪ taɪmworn ænd wɛðɚ bitņ|
ðɛr lɪvd mɛnɪ jɪrz sɪns| hwɛn ðə kʌntrɪ wəz stɪl ə pravɪns
əv greɪt brɪtən| ə sɪmpəl gʊd neɪtʃɚd fɛlo əv ðə neɪm əv rɪp
væn wɪŋkəl‖ hi wəz ə dɪsɛndənt əv ðə rɪp væn wɪŋkəl hu
fɪgjɚd soʊ gæləntlɪ ɪn ðə ʃɪvəlrəs deɪz əv pitɚ staɪvəsənt ænd
əkʌmpnɪd hɪm tʊ ðə sidʒ əv fort krɪstinə‖ hi ɪnhɛrətɪd haʊɛvɚ
bʌt lɪtl̩ əv ðə marʃəl kærɪktɚ əv hɪz ænsɛstɚz‖ aɪ hæv əbzɚvd
ðæt hi wəz ə sɪmpəl gʊd neɪtʃɚd mæn| hi waz moroʊvɚ ə
kaɪnd neɪbɚ ænd æn obidiənt hɛnpɛkt hʌzbənd‖ ɪndid tu
ðə lætɚ sɚkəmstæns maɪt bi owɪŋ ðæt mɪknəs əv spɪrɪt hwɪtʃ
geɪnd hɪm sʌtʃ junəvɚsəl papjulɛrətɪ| for ðoʊz mɛn ar
moʊst æpt tʊ bi absikwiəs ænd kənsɪlieɪtɪŋ əbrɔd hu ar ʌndɚ
ðə dɪsəplɪn əv ʃruz æt hoʊm‖

4. ðɛr tɛmpɚz daʊtləs ar rɛndɚd plaɪənt ænd mæljəbəl ɪn
ðə faɪrɪ fɚnəs əv domɛstɪk trɪbjuleɪʃən ænd ə kɚtņ lɛktʃɚ
ɪz wɚθ ɔl ðə sɚmənz ɪn ðə wɚld fɔr tɪtʃɪŋ ðə vɚtʃuz əv
peɪʃəns ænd lɔŋ sʌfrɪŋ‖ ə tɚməgənt waɪf meɪ ðɛrfor ɪn sʌm
rɪspɛkts bi kənsɪdɚd ə talɚəbəl blɛsɪŋ ænd ɪf soʊ rɪp væn
wɪnkl̩ wəz θraɪs blɛst‖ sɚtņ ɪt ɪz ðæt hi wəz ə greɪt feɪvɚət
əmʌŋ ɔl ðə gʊd waɪvz əv ðə vɪlɪdʒ hu| æz juʒjuəl wɪð ðə
mor eɪmiəbəl sɛks| tʊk hɪz part ɪn ɔl fæmlɪ skwabəlz ænd
nɛvɚ feɪld| hwɛnɛvɚ ðeɪ tɔkt ðoʊz mætɚz oʊvɚ ɪn ðɛr
ivnɪŋ gasɪp| tʊ leɪ ɔl əv ðə bleɪm an deɪm væn wɪŋkl̩‖ ðə
tʃɪldrən əv ðə vɪlɪdʒ tu wʊd ʃaʊt wɪð dʒɔɪ hwɛnɛvɚ hi
əproʊtʃt‖

5. hi əsɪstəd æt ðɛr sports| meɪd ðɛr pleɪθɪŋz| tɔt ðəm tʊ
flaɪ kaɪts ænd ʃut marbəlz ænd toʊld ðɛm lɔŋ storiz əv
goʊsts wɪtʃɪz ænd ɪndiənz‖ hwɛrɛvɚ hi wɛnt dadʒɪŋ əbaʊt

ðə vılıdʒ| hi wəz səraundəd baı ə trup əv ðəm| hæŋıŋ an
hız skɜ˞ts| klaımıŋ an hız bæk ænd pleı:ŋ ə θauzənd trıks an
hım wıð ımpjunətı| ænd nat ə dɔg wud bark æt hım ðruaut
ðə neıbə˞hud‖ ðə ɛrə˞ in rıps kampəzıʃən wəz ən ınsʌfə˞əbul
əvɜ˞ʒən tu ɔl kaındz əv prafətəbul leıbə˞‖ ıt kud nat bi frəm
want əv æsədjuətı ə˞ pɜ˞səvırəns for hi wud sıt an ə wɛt rak
wıð ə rad æz hɛvı æz ə tartə˞z lænts ænd fıʃ ɔl deı wıðaut ə
mɜ˞mə˞| ivən ðou hi ʃud nat bi ınkɜ˞rıdʒd baı ə sıŋɡəl
nıbəl‖

6. hi wud kærı ə faulıŋ pis an hız ʃouldə˞ fə˞ aurz təɡɛðə˞|
trʌdʒıŋ θru ðə wudz ən swamps ænd ʌp hıl ænd daun deıl
tu ʃut ə fju skwɜ˞lz ə˞ waıld pıdʒənz| hi wud nɛvə˞ rıfjuz tu
əsıst ə neıbə˞ ivən ın ðə rʌfıst tɔıl ænd waz ə formoust mæn
æt ɔl kʌntrı fralıks fə˞ hʌskıŋ ındıən kɔrn ə˞ bıldıŋ stoun
fɛnsız‖ ðə wımən əv ðə vılıdʒ tu justu ımplɔı hım tu rʌn
ðɛr ɛrəndz ænd tu du sʌtʃ lıtḷ ad dʒabz æz ðɛr lɛs əblaıdʒıŋ
hʌzbəndz wud nat du fɔr ðɛm‖ ın ə wɜ˞d rıp wəz rɛdı tu
ətɛnd tu enıbadız bıznıs bʌt hız oun| bʌt æz tu duıŋ fæmlı
djutı ænd kipıŋ hız farm ın ɔrdə˞| hi faund ıt ımpasəbəl‖

7. ın fækt hi dıklɛrd| ıt wəz əv nou jus tu wɜ˞k an hıs farm|
ıt waz ðə moust pɛstılənt pis əv graund ın ðə houl kʌntrı|
ɛvrıθıŋ əbaut ıt wɛnt rɔŋ ænd wud gou rɔŋ ın spaıt əv
hım‖ hız fɛnsız wɜ˞ kəntınjuəlı fɔlıŋ tu pisız| hız kau wud
iðə˞ gou əstreı ə˞ ɡɛt əmʌŋ ðə neıbə˞z kæbıdʒız| wıdz wɜ˞ ʃur
tu grou kwıkə˞ ın hız fıldz ðən ɛnıhwɛr ɛls| ðə reın ɔlwız
meıd ə pɔınt əv sɛtıŋ ın dʒʌst hwɛn hi hæd sʌm autdor wɜ˞k
tu du| sou ðæt ðou hız pætrəmouniəl əsteıt hæd dwındḷd
əweı ʌndə˞ hız mænıdʒmənt eıkə˞ baı eıkə˞ ʌntıl ðɛr wəz
lıtḷ mor lɛft ðən ə mır pætʃ əv ındıən kɔrn ænd poteıtoz| jɛt
ıt wəz ðə wɜ˞st kəndıʃənd farm ın ðə neıbə˞hud‖

8. hız tʃıldrən tu wɜ˞ rægəd ænd waıld| æz ıf bılɔŋıŋ tu
noubadı‖ hız sʌn rıp| ən ɜ˞tʃən bıgatṇ ın hız oun laıknəs|
pramıst tu ınhɛrıt ðə hæbıts əlɔŋ wıð ðə ould klouðz əv hız
faðə˞‖ hi wəz dʒɛnə˞əlı sin trupıŋ laık ə koult ət hız mʌðə˞z
hılz| ıkwıpt ın ə pɛr əv hız faðə˞z kæst ɔf ɡæləɡæskənz hwıtʃ
hi hæd mʌtʃ ədu tu hould ʌp wıθ wʌn hænd æz ə faın leıdı
dʌz hɜ˞ treın ın bæd wɛðə˞‖ rıp væn wıŋkḷ hauɛvə˞ wəz wʌn

əv ðouz hæpɪ mɔrtl̩z əv fulɪʃ‖ wɛl ɔɪld dɪspəzɪʃən hu teɪk ðə
wɜld izɪ‖ it hwaɪt brɛd ɚ braun‖ hwɪtʃɛvɚ hi kən gɛt wɪð
list trʌbəl ænd wud ræðɚ starv an ə pɛnɪ ðən wɜk fɚ ə
paund‖ ɪf lɛft tu hɪmsɛlf‖ hi wud əv hwɪsl̩d laɪf əweɪ ɪn
pɚfɪkt kəntɛntmənt bʌt hɪz waɪf kɛpt kəntɪnjuəlɪ dɪnɪŋ ɪn
hɪz irz əbaut hɪz aɪdl̩nəs‖ hɪz kɛrləsnəs ænd ðə ruɪn hi wəz
brɪŋɪŋ an hɪz fæmlɪ‖

9. mɔrnɪŋ nun n̩ naɪt hɚ tʌŋ wəz ɪnsɛsəntlɪ gowɪŋ n̩
ɛvrɪθɪŋ i sɛd ɚ dɪd wəz ʃur tu prədjus ə tɔrənt əv haushould
ɛləkwənts‖ rɪp əd bʌt wʌn weɪ əv rɪplaɪːŋ tu ɔl lɛktʃɚz əv
ðə kaɪnd ænðæt baɪ frikwənt jus həd groun ɪntu ə hæbɪt‖ hi
ʃrʌgd hɪz ʃouldɚz‖ ʃuk ɪz hɛd‖ kæst ʌp ɪz aɪz bʌt sɛd nʌθɪŋ‖
ðɪs ɔlwɪz provoukt ə frɛʃ valɪ frəm hɪz waɪf sou ðæt i wəz
feɪn tə drɔːf ɪz forsɪz n̩ teɪk tu ðə autsaɪd əv ðə haus‖ ðə
ounlɪ saɪd hwɪtʃ ɪn truθ bɪlɔŋz tu ə hɛnpɛkt hʌzbənd‖ rɪps
soul domɛstɪk ædhɪrənt wəz hɪz dɔg wulf hu wəz æz mʌtʃ
hɛnpɛkt əz ɪz mæstɚ‖ fɔr deɪm væn wɪnkl̩ rɪgardəd ðɛm æz
kəmpænjənz n̩ aɪdl̩nəs ændivən lukt əpan wulf wɪð ən ivəl
aɪ æz ðə kɔz əv ɪz mæstɚz gowɪŋ əstreɪ‖

10. tru ɪt ɪz ðæt ɪn ɔl pɔɪnts əv spɪrɪt bifɪtɪŋ ən anɚəbəl
dɔg‖ hi wəz æz kɚeɪdʒəs ən ænəməl əz ɛvɚ skaurd ðə
wudz‖ bət hwat kɜɪdʒ kæn wɪθstænd ði ɛvɚ ɪndjurɪŋ n̩d ɔl
bɪsɛtɪŋ tɛrɚz əv ə wumənz tʌŋ‖ ðə moumənt wulf ɛntɚd
ðə haus hɪz krɛst fɛl‖ hɪz teɪl drupt tu ðə graund ɚ kɜld
bɪtwin ɪz lɛgz‖ hi snikt əbaut wiθ ə gæloz ɛr‖ kæstɪŋ mɛnɪ ə
saɪdlɔŋ glæns ət deɪm væn wɪŋkəl‖ ænd æt ðə list flɜɪʃ əv ə
brumstɪk ɚ ə leɪdl̩‖ hi wud flaɪ tu ðə dor wɪð jɛlpɪŋ prisɪpə-
teɪʃən‖ taɪmz gru wɜs ən wɜs wɪð rɪp væn wɪŋkəl æz jɪrz
əv mætrəmounɪ rould an‖ ə tartːʌŋ nɛvɚ mɛloz wɪð eɪdʒ
ænd ə ʃarp tʌŋ ɪz ðə ounlɪ wɛpən ðæt grouz kinɚ wɪθ
kanstənt jus‖

11. fɔr ə lɔŋ hwaɪl hi just tu kənsoul hɪmsɛlf hwɛn drɪvən
frəm houm baɪ frikwəntɪŋ ə kaɪnd əv pəpɛtʃuəl klʌb əv ðə
seɪdʒɪz‖ fɪlasəfɚz n̩d ʌðɚ aɪdl̩ pɚsənədʒɪz əv ðə vɪlɪdʒ hwɪtʃ
hɛld ɪts sɛʃənz an ə bɛntʃ bəfor ə smɔl ɪn dɛzɪgneɪtəd baɪ ə
ˈrubəˌkʌnd pɔrtreɪt əv hɪz mædʒɪstɪ dʒɔrdʒ ðə θɜd‖ hɪr

ðeɪ justʊ sɪt ɪn ðə ʃeɪd θru ə lɔŋ sʌmɚz deɪ| tɔkɪŋ lɪstləslɪ
oʊvɚ vɪlɪdʒ gɑsɪp ɚ tɛlɪŋ ɛndləs slipɪ storɪz əbaʊt nʌθɪŋ‖
bʌt ɪt wʊd əv bɪn wɜˑθ ɛnɪ steɪtsmənz mʌnɪ tuæv hɜˑd ðə
profaʊnd dɪskʌʃənz ðæt sʌmtaɪmz tʊk pleɪs wɛn baɪ tʃæns n̩
oʊld njuzpeɪpɚ fɛl ɪntu ðɛr hændz frəm sʌm pæsɪŋ trævələ‖
haʊ sɒləmlɪ ðeɪ wʊd lɪsn̩ tʊ ðə kɑntɛnts əz drɔld aʊt baɪ
dɛrɪk væn brʌməl| ðə skulmæstɚ| ə dæpɚ lɜˑnəd lɪtl̩ mæn|
hi wəz nɑt dɔntəd baɪ ðə moʊst dʒaɪgæntɪk wɜˑd ɪn ðə
ˈdɪkʃən|ɛrɪ n̩d haʊ seɪdʒlɪ ðeɪ wʊd dɪlɪbɚeɪt əpɑn pʌblɪk
ɪvɛnts mʌnθs aftɚ ðeɪ həd teɪkən pleɪs‖

12. ði ɒpɪnjənz əv ðɪs dʒʌnto wɜˑ kəmplitlɪ kəntroʊld baɪ
nɪkɒləs vɛdɚ| ə peɪtriɑrk əv ðə vɪlɪdʒ ænd lændlɔrd əv ðə
ɪn| æt ðə dorz əv hwɪtʃ hi sæt frəm mɔrnɪŋ tɪl naɪt dʒʌst
muvɪŋ səfɪʃəntlɪ tʊ əvɔɪd ðə sʌn ænd kip ðə ʃeɪd əv ə lɑrdʒ
tri| soʊ ðæt ðə neɪbɚz kʊd tɛl ðə aʊr baɪ hɪz muvmənts æz
ækjərɪtlɪ æz baɪ ə sʌndaɪl‖ ɪt ɪz tru ðæt hi wəz rɛrlɪ hɜˑd tʊ
spik bʌt smoʊkt ɪz paɪp n̩sɛsəntlɪ‖ hɪz æ̩dhɪrənts haʊɛvɚ|
for ɛvrɪ greɪt mæn hæz ɪz æ̩dhɪrənts| pɚfɪktlɪ ʌndɚstʊd hɪm
ænd nju haʊ tʊ gæðɚ hɪz ɒpɪnjənz‖ hwɛn ɛnɪθɪŋ wəz rɛd or
rɪleɪtəd ðæt dɪsplizd hɪm| hi wəz əbzɜˑvd tə smoʊk hɪz paɪp
vɪəmʌntlɪ æn tu sɛnd forθ frikwənt ænd æŋgri pʌfs‖

13. hwɛn plizd hi wʊd ɪnheɪl ðə smoʊk sloʊlɪ ænd
trænkwɪlɪ ænd ɪmɪt ɪt ɪn laɪt ænd plɛsənt klaʊdz| ænd
sʌmtaɪmz| teɪkɪŋ ðə paɪp frʌm ɪz maʊθ| ænd lɛtɪŋ ðə
freɪgrənt veɪpɚ kɜˑl əbaʊt hɪz noʊz| wʊd greɪvlɪ nɑd ɪz hɛd
ɪn toʊkən əf pɚfɪkt ˈæprɒ|beɪʃən‖ frʌm ivən ðɪs strɒŋhoʊld
ðə ʌnlʌkɪ rɪp wəz æt lɛŋkθ raʊtəd baɪ hɪz tɜˑməgʌnt waɪf hu
wʊd sʌdn̩lɪ breɪk ɪn əpɑn ðə trænkwɪlətɪ əv ðə æsɛmblɪdʒ ænd
kɔl ðə mɛmbɚz ɔl tʊ nɒt| nor wəz ðæt ɔgʌst pɚsn̩ɪdʒ vɛdɚ
hɪmsɛlf seɪkrəd frʌm ðə dɛrɪŋ tʌŋ əv ðɪs tɛrɪbəl vərɑgɒ| hu
tʃɑrdʒd hɪm aʊtraɪt wɪð ɪnkɜˑədʒɪŋ ɪm ɪn hæbɪts əv aɪdl̩nəs‖

14. pʊr rɪp wəz ət læst rɪdjust ɔlmoʊst tʊ dɪspɛr ænd hɪz
oʊnlɪ |ɔlˈtɜˑnətɪv tu ɛskeɪp frəm ðə leɪbɚ əv ðə fɑrm ænd ðə
klæmɚ əv ɪz waɪf wʌz tə teɪk ə gʌn n̩ hænd ən stroʊl əweɪ
ɪntu ðə wʊdz‖ hɪr hi wʊd sʌmtaɪmz sit hɪmsɛlf æt ðə fʊt əv
ə tri æn ʃær ðə kɑntɛnts əv hɪz wɑlət wɪð wʊlf| wɪθ hum hi

sımpəθaızd az ə fɛlǫ sʌfɚʒ ɪn pɚsəkjuʃən‖ pʊr wʊlf| hi wʊd
seɪ| ðaɪ mɪstrəs lidz ði ə dɔgz laɪf əv ɪt bʌt nɛvɚ maɪnd
maɪlæd| hwaɪlst aɪ lɪv ðaʊ ʃælt nɛvɚ wɑnt ə frɛnd tʊ stænd
baɪ ði‖ wʊlf wʊd wæg hɪz teɪl| lʊk wɪstfʊlɪ ɪnɪz mastɚz aɪz|
ænd ɪf dɔgz kən fil pɪtɪ̩| aɪ vɛrəlɪ bɪliv ri̩'sɪprǫ'keɪtəd ðə
sɛntəmənt wɪð ɔl ɪz hɑrt‖ ɪn ə lɔŋ ræmbəl əv ðə kaɪnd ɑn ə
faɪn ˌɔ'tʌmnəl deɪ rɪp hæd ˌʌn'kɑnʃəslɪ skræmbəld tʊ wʌn
əv ðə haɪəst pɑrts əv ðə maʊntənz‖

15. hi wəz æftɚ hɪz feɪvɚət sport əv skwɚl ʃutɪŋ ænd ðə
stɪl saɪləns hæd ɛkǫd ænd riɛkǫd wɪðːə rɪports əv hɪz gʌn‖
pæntɪŋ æn fətigd hi θru hɪmsɛlf leɪt ɪnðə æftɚnun ɔn ə grin
noʊl kʌvɚd wɪð maʊntn̩ hɚbɪdʒ ðæt kraʊnd ðə braʊ əv ə
prɛsəpəs‖ frʌm ən oʊpənɪŋ bɪtwin ðə triz| hi kʊd oʊvɚlʊk
ðə loʊɚ kʌntrɪ fɚ mɛnɪ ə maɪl əv rɪtʃ wʊdlænd‖ hi sɔ æt ə
dɪstəns ðə lɔrdlɪ hʌdsən| muvɪŋ ɑn ɪts saɪlənt bʌt mædʒɛstɪk
kors wɪðːə rɪflɛkʃən əv ə pɚpəl klaʊd or ðə seɪlz əv ə lægɪŋ
bark hɪr ænd ðɛr slipɪŋ ɑn ɪts glæsɪ buzəm| æn æt læst luzɪŋ
ɪtsɛlf ɪn ðə haɪlændz‖ ɑn ðə ʌðɚ said hi lʊkt daʊn ɪntu ə dip
maʊntən glɛn| waɪld ænd loʊnlɪ| ðə batəm fɪld wɪð fræg-
mənts frʌm ðə ɪmpɛndɪŋ klɪfs ænd skærslɪ laɪtəd baɪ ðə
rəflɛktəd reɪz əv ðə sɛtɪŋ sʌn‖

16. fɔr sʌm taɪm rɪp leɪ mjuzɪŋ ðɪs sin| ivnɪŋ wəz græd-
ʒuəlɪ ædvænsɪŋ| ðə maʊntn̩z bɪgæn tə θroʊ ðɛr lɔŋ blu
ʃædǫz oʊvɚ ðə vælɪ| hi sɔ ðət ɪt wʊd bi dark lɔŋ bɪfor hi kʊd
rɪtʃ ðə vælɪ ænd hi hivd ə saɪ wɛn hi θɔt əv ɪnkaʊntɚɪŋ ðə
tɛrɚz əv deɪm væn wɪŋkəl‖ æz hi wəz əbaʊt tə dɪsɛnd| hi
hɚd ə vɔɪs frʌm ðə dɪstəns hæluɪŋ| rɪp væn wɪŋkəl| rɪp væn
wɪŋkəl‖ hi lʊkt əraʊnd bʌt kʊd si nʌθɪŋ bʌt ə kroʊ wɪŋɪŋ ɪts
ˌsǫlə'tɛrɪ flaɪt əkrɔs ðə maʊntn̩‖ hi θɔt hɪz fænsɪ mʌst əv
dɪsivd ɪm ænd tɚnd əgɛn tʊ dɪsɛnd| wɛn hi hɚd ðə seɪm
kraɪ rɪŋ θru ðə stɪl ivnɪŋ ɛr| rɪp væn wɪŋkəl| rɪp væn wɪŋkəl‖
æt ðə seɪm taɪm wʊlf brɪsl̩d ʌp hɪz bæk ænd gɪvɪŋ ə loʊ graʊl
skʌlkt oʊvɚ tʊ hɪz mæstɚz said lʊkɪŋ fɪrfʊli daʊn ɪntu ðə
glɛn‖

17. rɪp naʊ fɛlt ə veɪg ˌæprɪ̩'hɛnʃən stɪlɪŋ oʊvɚ hɪm| hi
lʊkt æŋkʃəslɪ ɪn ðə seɪm dərɛkʃən æn pɚsivd ə streɪndʒ

fɪgjɚ sloʊlɪ tɔɪlɪŋ ʌp ðə rɒks bɛndɪŋ ʌndɚ ðə weɪt əv sʌmθɪŋ
hi kærɪd ən ɪz bæk‖ hi wəz səpraɪzd tə si ɛnɪ hjumən biɪŋ ɪn
ðɪs loʊnlɪ æn ʌnfrikwəntəd pleɪs| bʌt səpoʊzɪŋ ɪt tə bi
sʌmwʌn əv ðə neɪbɚhʊd ɪn nid əv əsɪstəns| hi heɪsn̩d daʊn
tu jild ɪt‖ ən nɪrɚ æproʊtʃ i wəz səpraɪzd æt ðə sɪŋgjulɛrəti
əv ðə streɪndʒɚz æpɪrəns‖ hi wɑz ə ʃɔrt skwɛr fɛlọ wɪθ:ɪk
bʊʃɪ hɛr ænd ə grɪzl̩d bɪrd‖ hɪz drɛs wəz əv ðə æntik dʌtʃ
fæʃən| ə klɔθ dʒɚkən stræpt əraʊnd ðə weɪst| sɛvrəl pɛrz əv
brɪtʃɪz| ðə aʊtɚ wʌn əv æmpəl vɑljəm| dɛkəreɪtəd wɪð roʊz
əv bʌtənz daʊn ðə saɪdz æn bʌntʃəz æt ðə niz‖

18. hi bor ɔn hɪz ʃouldɚ ə staʊt kɛg ðæt simd tə bi fʊl əv
lɪkɚ ænd meɪd saɪnz fɔrːɪp tu əproʊtʃ æn əsɪst hɪm wɪð:ə
loʊd‖ ðoʊ raðɚ ʃaɪ n̩ dɪstrʌstfʊl əv ɪz nu ækweɪntəns rɪp
kəmplaɪd wɪðɪz juʒuəl əlækrətɪ ænd mjutʃuəlɪ rɪlivɪŋ wʌn
ənʌðɚ ðeɪ klaɪmd ʌp ðə nærọ gʌlɪ| əpærəntlɪ ðə draɪ bɛd əv
ə maʊntən tɔrənt‖ æz ðeɪ əsɛndəd| rɪp ɛvrɪ naʊ n̩ ðɛn hɚd
lɔŋ roʊlɪŋ pilz laɪk dɪstənt θʌndɚ ðæt simd tu ɪʃɪu aʊt əv ə
dip rəvin| or ræðɚ klɛft bɪtwin ðə rɒks tord wɪtʃ ðɛr rʌgəd
paθ kəndʌktəd‖ hi pɔzd fɚ n̩ ɪnstənt bʌt səpoʊzɪŋ ɪt tə bi
wʌn əv ðoʊz trænʃənt θʌndɚ ʃaʊɚz hwɪtʃ ɔfən teɪk ples ɪn
maʊntən haɪts| hi prọsidəd‖

19. pasɪŋ θru ðə rəvin| ðeɪ keɪm tu ə halọ laɪk ə smɔl
ˈæmfəˌðiətɚ| sɚraʊndəd baɪ ˌpɚpənˈdɪkjulɚ ˈprɛsəpɪsɪz|
oʊvɚ ðə brɪŋks əv hwɪtʃ ɪmpɛndɪŋ triz ʃat ðɛr bræntʃɪz soʊ
ðæt ju oʊnlɪ kɒt glɪmpsəz əv æʒɚ skaɪ ænðə braɪt ɪvnɪŋ
klaʊd‖ djurɪŋ ðə hoʊl taɪm| rɪp ænd hɪz kəmpænjən həd
leɪbɚd ɑn ɪn saɪləns| fɔr hwaɪl ðə fɔrmɚ marvəld greɪtlɪ
hwɑt kʊd bi ðə pɚpəs əv kærɪːŋ ə kɛg əv lɪkɚ ʌp ðɪs waɪld
maʊntn̩| jɛt ðɛr wəz sʌmθɪŋ streɪndʒ ænd ɪnˈkamprɪ-
ˌhɛnsəbəl əbaʊt ðə ʌnːoʊn ðæt ɪnspaɪrd ɔː æn tʃɛkt fəmɪli-
ɛrəti‖ ɑn ɛntəːɪŋ ðə æmfəθiətɚ| nu abdʒɛkts əv wʌndɚ
prɪsɛntəd ðɛ̣msɛlvz‖ ɑn ə lɛvəl spat ɪn ðə sɛntɚ wʌ̣z ə
kʌmpənɪ əv ɒd lʊkɪŋ pɚsənɪdʒɪz pleɪːŋ æt naɪnpɪnz‖ ðeɪ wɚ
drɛst ɪn ə kweɪnt aʊtlændɪʃ fæʃən| sʌm wor ʃɔrt dʌbləts|
ʌðɚz dʒɚkɪnz wɪð lɔŋ naɪvz ɪn ðɛr bɛlts| ænd moʊst əv
ðəm hæd ɪn̩ɔrməs brɪtʃɪz əv sɪmələ staɪl wɪð:æt əv ðɛr
gaɪd‖

20. ðɪr vɪzɪdʒəz tu wɝ pəkjulɚ| wʌn hæd ə lardʒ bɪrd|
brɔd feɪs ænd smɔl pɪgɪʃ aɪz| ðə feɪs əv ənʌðɚ simd tə
kənsɪst ɪntaɪrlɪ əv nouz| ænd wəs səraundəd baɪ ə hwaɪt
ʃugɚ louf hæt| sɛt ɔf wɪð ə lɪtl̩ rɛd kaksteɪl‖ ðeɪ ɔl hæd birdz
əv væriəs ʃeɪps ən kʌlɚz‖ ðɛr wəz wʌn hu simd tə bi ðə
kəmændɚ‖ hi wəz ə staʊt oʊld dʒɛntl̩mən wɪθ ə wɛðɚ bitn̩
kantənəns| hi wor ə leɪst dʌblət| brɔd bɛlt ænd hæŋgɚ|
haɪ kraʊnd hæt ənd fɛðɚ| rɛd stakɪŋz n̩d haɪ hild ʃuz wɪð
rouzɪz ɪn ðəm‖ ðə hoʊl grup rɪmaɪndəd hɪm əv ðə fɪgjɚz ɪn
ən oʊld flɛmɪʃ peɪntɪŋ ɪn ðə parlɚ əv daмəni̩ væn ʃaɪk| ðə
vɪlɪdʒ parsən| ænd wɪtʃ hæd bɪn brɔt oʊvɚ frəm hɒlənd æt
ðə taɪm əv ðə læst sɛtl̩mənt‖

21. wat simd pɚtɪkjələ˞lɪ ad tə rɪp wəz ð̩t ðoʊ ðɪz foʊks
wɝ ɛvədənlɪ əmjuzɪŋ ðəmsɛlvz| jɪt ðeɪ meɪteɪnd ðə greɪvəst
feɪsɪz| ðə moʊst mɪstɪriəs saɪləns æn wɝ wɪðɔl ðə moʊst
mɛlənkalɪ partɪ əv plɛʒɚ hi həd ɛvɚ wɪtnəst‖ nʌθɪŋ ɪn-
tɚʌptəd ðə stɪlnəs əv ðə sin bʌt ðə nɔɪz əv ðə bɔlz hwɪtʃ|
wɛnɛvɚ ðeɪ wɝ roʊld| ɛkoʊd əlɒŋ ðə mæʊntn̩z laɪk
rʌmblɪŋ pilz əv θʌndɚ‖ æz rɪp n̩ ɪz kəmpænjən əproʊtʃt
ðəm| ðeɪ sʌdn̩lɪ dɪsɪstəd frʌm ð̩ɚ pleɪ n̩d stɛrd ət ðəm wɪθ
sʌtʃ fɪkst stætʃulaɪk geɪz ænd sʌtʃ streɪndʒ ʌnkuθ læklʌstɚ
kantənənsəz ðæt ɪz hart tɝnd wɪðɪn hɪm ənd ɪz niz smoʊt
təgɛðɚ‖ hɪz kəmpænjən naʊ ɛmᵖtɪd ðə kantɪnts əv ðə keɪg
ɪntu lardʒ flægənz ænd meɪd saɪnz tu ɪm tə weɪt əpɒn ðə
kʌmpəni̩‖ hi əbeɪd wɪθ fɪr n̩ trɪmblɪŋ| ðeɪ kwaft ðə lɪkɚ ɪn
pɚfaʊnd saɪlənᵗs æn ðɛn rətɝnd tu ðɛr geɪm‖

22. baɪ dɪgriz rɪps ɔ° æn æprɪhɪnᵗʃən səbsa.dəd‖ hiːvən
vɛntʃəd hwɪn noʊwən wəz lukɪŋ tə teɪst ðə bɛˑvərɪdʒ|
hwɪtʃ hi fæund hæd mʌtʃ ðə fleɪvərəv ɛksələnt haləndz‖ hi
wəz nætʃərəlɪ ə θ3stɪ soʊl æn wəz sun tɪmᵖtɪ̩d tə rɪpit ðə
dræft‖ wʌn teɪst prv̩oʊkt ənʌðə| hi rɪpitɪd ɪz vɪzɪts tu ðə
flægən soʊ ɔfən tæt ət lɛŋθ hɪz sɪnsəz w3 ovəpaːd| hɪz aɪz
swæm n̩ ɪz hɛd| hɪs hɛd grædjuəlɪ dɪklaˈnd ænd hi fɛl ɪntu ə
dip slɪp‖ ɔn weɪkɪn hi fæund hɪmsɛlf əpɒn ðə grin noʊl wɛr
i həd fɜst sin ðə oʊld mæn əv ðə glɪn‖ hi rʌbd ɪz aˈz| ɪt wəz
ə braɪt sʌnʃaˈnɪ mɔːnɪŋ‖ ðə bɜdz w3 twɪtərɪŋ əmʌŋ ðə buʃɪz
ænd ðɪ igəl wəz wɪlɪŋ əlɒft| brɛstɪŋ ðə pjuᵊ mæuntən briz‖

23. ʃɜlɪ θɔt rɪp| aɪv nɒt slɛpt ɔl naɪt‖ hi rikɒld ðə streɪndʒ
əkɜrənˈsəz bɪfɔᵊ hi fɛl əslip‖ ðə streɪndʒ man wɪðə kɛg əv
lɪkə| ðə maʊntən ˈrəvin| ðə waɪld rɪtrit əmʌŋ ðə rɒks| ðə
woʊbɪgɔn paːti æt naɪnpɪnz| ðə flægən| oʊ ðæt wɪkɪd flægən|
θɔt rɪp| hwɒt ɛkskjus ʃæl aɪ meɪk tu deɪm væn wɪŋkəl‖

24. hi lʊkt raʊnd fɔr hɪz gʌn| bʌt ɪn pleɪs əv ðə klin
wɛlɔɪld faʊlɪŋ pis| hi faʊnd æn oʊld faɪrlak laɪːŋ baɪ hɪm| ðə
bɛrl ɪnkrʌstɪd wɪθ rʌst| ðə lak fɔlɪŋ ɔf ænðə stak wɜrmɪtŋ‖ hi
naʊ səspɛktəd ðæt ðə greɪv rɔɪtəʒz əv ðə maʊntən hæd pʊt
ə trɪk əpɔn hɪm ænd| hævɪŋ doʊst hɪm wɪθ lɪkɚ| hæd rʌbd
hɪm əv hɪz gʌn‖ wʊlf tu hæd dɪsəpɪrd| bʌt hi maɪt hæv
streɪd əweɪ æftɚ ə skɜrl ɔr ə partrɪdʒ‖ hi hwɪsl̩d æftɚ hɪm
ænd ʃaʊtəd hɪz neɪm| bʌt ɔl ɪn veɪn| ði ɛkoʊz rɪpitəd hɪz
hwɪsl̩ ən ʃaʊt| bʌt noʊ dɔg wəz tu bi sin‖ hi dɪtɚmɪnd tu
rɪvɪzɪt ðə sin əvðə læst ivnɪŋz gæmbəl ænd| ɪf hi mɛt wɪθ ɛnɪ
əv ðə partɪ| dɪmænd hɪz dɔg ænd gʌn‖ æz hi roʊz tu wɔk|
hi faʊnd hɪmsɛlf stɪf ɪn ðə dʒɔɪnts| ænd wantɪŋ ɪn hɪz juʒuəl
æktɪvətɪ‖ ðiz maʊntŋ bɛdz du nat əgri wɪθ mi| θɔt rɪp æn ɪf
ðɪs fralɪk ʃʊd leɪ mi ʌp wɪθ ə fɪt əv ðə rumətɪzəm| aɪ ʃæl hæv
ə blɛsəd taɪm wɪθ deɪm væn wɪŋkəl‖ wɪθ sʌm dɪfəkʌltɪ hi
gat daʊn ɪntu ðə glɛn| hi faʊnd ðə gʌlɪ ʌp hwɪtʃ hi ænd hɪz
kəmpænjən hæd əsɛndəd bʌt| tu hɪz æstanɪʃmənt ə maʊntən
strim wəz naʊ foʊmɪŋ daʊn ɪt| lipɪŋ frəm rak tu rak ænd
fɪlɪŋ ðə glɛn wɪθ bæblɪŋ mɜrmɚz‖

25. hi haᵂɛvɚ meɪd ʃɪft tu skræmbəl ʌp ɪts saɪdz| wɜrkɪŋ
hɪz tɔɪlsəm weɪ θru θɪkəts əv bɜrtʃ sæsəfræs æn wɪtʃ heɪzəl|
ən sʌtaɪmz trɪpt ʌp ɔr ɛntæŋgl̩d baɪ ðə waɪld greɪp vaᵊnz
ðæt twɪstəd ðɛə kɔɪlz ɔᵊ tɪndrɪlz frəm tri tu tri| æn sprɛd ə
kaᵊnd əv nɛtwɜrk ɪn ɪz pæθ‖ æt lɛnθ hi rɪtʃt tu wɛᵊ ðə
rəvin hæd oʊpᵊnd θru ðə klɪfs tu ðə æmfəθiətə| bʌt noʊ
treɪsɪz əv sʌtʃ ən oʊpənɪŋ rɪmeɪnd‖ ðə raks prɪsɛntəd ə haɪ
ɪmpɛnətrəbəl wɔl oʊvə wɪtʃ ðə tɔɪənt keɪm tʌmblɪŋ ɪn ə ʃit
əv foʊm| æn fɛl ɪntu ə brɔd dip beɪsɪn blæk frəm ðə ʃædǫz əv
ðə səraʊndɪŋ fɔˈɪst‖ hɪə ðɛn poᵁə rɪp wəz brɔt tu ə stæn‖ hi
əgɛn wɪsl̩d ən kɔld æftə hɪz dɔg| hi wəz oʊnlɪ ænsəd
baˈɪ ðə kɔɪŋ əv ə flak əv aˈɪdl̩ kroʊz| spoətɪŋ haɪːn ðə ɛə
əbʌv ə draᵊ tri ðæt oʊvəhʌŋ ə sʌnɪ prɛsəpɪs æn hu|

səkjuə ɪn ðɛə ɛləveɪʃən simd tʊ lʊk daʊn æt ðə poʊə mænz
pəplɛksətɪz‖

26. wat wəz tə bi dʌn | ðə mɔːnɪŋ wəz pæsɪŋ əweɪ æn rɪp
fɛlt fæmɪʃt fɔ̩ wʌnt əv ɪz brɛkfəst | hi grivd tʊ gɪv ʌp ɪz dɔg
æn gʌn | hi drɛdɪ̩d tʊ mit ɪz waɪf bʌt ɪt wʊd nat du tu staːv
əmʌŋ ðə maʊntn̩z‖ hi ʃʊk hɪz hɛd | ʃʊldəd ðə rʌstɪ faɪr
lak ænd‖ wɪθ haːt fʊl əv trʌbəl ən æŋᵏzaɪtɪ tɝnd ɪz stɛps
hoʊmwəd‖ æz hi æproʊtʃt ðə vɪlɪdʒ | hi mɛt ə nʌmbəəv
pipəl bət nʌn hi nu | wɪtʃ sʌ̩mwat səpraɪzd ɪ̩m fɔr hi θɔt
hɪmsɛlf əkweɪntəd wɪð ɛvrɪwʌn ɪn ðə kʌntrɪ raʊnd‖ θɛə
drɛs tu wəz əv ə dɪfrənt fæʃən frəm ðæt tu wɪtʃ i̩ wəz
əkʌstəmd‖ ðeɪ ɔl stɛəd ət hɪm wɪθ ikwəl maːks əv səpraɪz
ænd wɛnɛvə ðeɪ kæst aɪz əpɔn hɪm ɪnvɛrəblɪ stroʊkt ðɛə
tʃɪnz‖

27. d̩i kanstəns (constant) rɪ̩kjurənts əv d̩ɪs jɛst̩ə ɪnd̩ust rɪp
ɪnvɔləntɛrəlɪ t̩u d̩u d̩i seɪm | wɛn t̩u hɪs ˌæsˈt̩anɪʃmənt | hi
faʊn hɪz̩ bɛrd (beard) hæt̩ groʊn t̩u bi e̩ fʊt laŋ‖ hi naʊ ɛntəd
d̩i ɛskɝts (outskirts) əv d̩i βɪlɪʒ‖ e̩ t̩rup əv ɛst̩reɪnʒ ʃɪldrən
ræn æt hɪz̩ hilz̩ | hutɪŋ æftə hɪm ænd pɔɪntɪŋ æt hɪs greɪ
bɛrd‖ d̩i d̩aks tu | nat wʌn əv hwɪʃ hi rɛkəgnaɪzd | fɔr æn
oʊld ˌækwəˈtænts (acquaintance) bɛrkəd (barked) æt hɪm æs hi
pæst‖ d̩i βɛrɪ βɪlɪʒ (village) wəz æltəd | it wəs laʒɝ æn mor
papjuləs‖ θɛr wɝ roʊz̩ əv haʊz̩ɪz̩ hwɪʃ hi hɛd nɛvə sin
bɪfor | æn doʊz̩ hwɪʃ hɛd bɪn fæmɪljə haʊnts (haunts) hæ̩d
dɪsæpɪˈrd‖ ɛstreɪnʒ neɪms wɝ oʊvə d̩i d̩ors | ɛstreɪnʒ feɪsɪs
æt di wɪndos‖ ɛvrɪsɪŋ was ɛstreɪnʒ‖ hɪs maɪn naʊ mɪs-
geɪv hɪm | hi bɪgan t̩u d̩aʊt wɛd̩ə bot hi æn d̩i worl (world)
æraʊn hɪm wɝ nat biwɪʃt‖

28. ʃɝlɪ ðɪs wəz hɪz neɪtɪv vɪlɪdʒ hwɪtʃ hi hæd lɛft ðə deɪ
bəfor‖ ðɛr stʊd ðə kætskɪl maʊntn̩z‖ ðɛrːæn ðə sɪlvə hʌdsən
æt ə dɪstəns | ðɛr wəz ɛvrɪ hɪl æn deɪl prɪsaɪslɪ æz ɪt hæd bɪn |
rɪp wəz sorlɪ pəplɛkst | ðæt flægən læst naɪt | θɔt hi | hæz
ædl̩d maɪ pʊr hɛd sædlɪ‖ ɪt wəz wɪθ sʌm dɪfɪ̩kʌltɪ ðɛ̩t hi
faʊnd ðə weɪ tu ɪz oʊn haʊs | hwɪtʃ hi əproʊtʃt wɪθ saɪlənt
ɔ | ɪkspɛktɪŋ ɛvrɪ mɪnət tu hɪr ðə ʃrɪl vɔɪs əv deɪm væn
wɪŋkəl‖ hi faʊnd ðə haʊs gɔn tu d̩ɪkeɪ | ðə ruf fɔlən ɪn | ðə

wɪndǫz ʃætɚd æn ðə dorz ɔf ðə hɪndʒez‖ ə hæf stɑrvd dɔg ðæt
lʊkt laɪk wʊlf wəz skʌlkɪŋ əbaʊt ɪt‖ rɪp kɔld ɪm baɪ neɪm | bʌt
ðə kɝ snɑrld | ʃʊd hɪz tiθ ænd pæst ɔn‖ θɪs wəz ən ʌnkaɪnd
kʌt ɪndid | maɪ vɛrɪ dɔg | sɛd pʊr rɪp | hæz fɔrgatən mi‖

29. hi ɛnt̪əd ðə haʊs wɪtʃ t̪u t̪ɛl ðə t̪rut̪ (all *t*'s and *d*'s are
dental in this selection) deɪm ɣæn ɣɪŋkəl hæd ɔlɣəz kɛpt ɪn nit
ɔdə‖ ɪt ɣʌʐ ɛmᵖtɪ | fɔlɔᵊn (forlorn) ænd æpæʁəntlɪ æbandənd‖
dɪs dɛsǫleɪtnɪs ouvɚkeɪm ɔl hɪz kənʌbiəl firs | hi kɔld
laʊdlɪ fɔr hɪz waɪf ænd tʃɪldrɛn | ði loʊnlɪ tʃeɪmbɚz Ʀæŋ
fɔ ə moʊmənt wɪð hɪz vɔɪs ænd ɔl əgɛn wʌz saɪləns‖ hi naʊ
hʌrɪd fort ænd heɪsn̪d tu hɪz oʊld Řisɔrt | ðə vɪlɪdʒ ɪn | bʌt ɪt
tu wʌz gɔn‖ e laːdʒ Ʀɪkɪd̪i wʊdn̪ bɪldɪŋ stʊd ɪn ɪts pleɪs wɪð
gʁeɪt geɪpɪŋ wɪndǫz | sʌm əv ðɛm bʁoʊkən ænd mɛndəd
wɪθ oʊld hæts ænd pɛtikoʊts | ænd ouvɚ ðə dɔr peɪntəd | ðə
junjən hoʊtɛl | baɪ dʒanəθən dulɪtl̪‖ ɪnstɛd əv ðə gʁeɪt tʁi
ᵈðæt just tu ʃɛltə ðə kwaɪt lɪtl̪ dʌtʃ ɪn əv jor | ðɛr wʌz naʊ
Ʀɪʁd ə tɔl neɪkəd poʊl wɪð sʌmtɪŋ an tap ðæt lʊkt laɪk ə
 Řɛd naɪtkap ænd fʁɒm ɪt wəz flʌtəʁɪŋ ə flæg ɒn wɪtʃ wʌz
ə sɪŋgulə əsɛmblɛdʒ əv starz n̪d stʁaɪps | ɔl ᵈðɪs wəz
stʁeɪndʒ ænd ɪŋkɒmprih̩ɛnsəbəl‖

30. hi rɛkəgnaɪzd ɒn ði saɪn haʊɛvɚ ðə rubɪ feɪs af kɪŋ
dʒɔdʒ ʌndə wɪtʃ hi hɛt smoʊkt tsoʊ mɛnɪ ə pisfʊl paɪp bʌt
ivən ðɪs wʌs sɪŋgjulɛrlɪ mɛtəmɔrfoʊst‖ ði rɛt kot wʌs
tʃeɪnʃt fɔr wʌn əf blu ænd baf (buff) | e sɔrd wʌs hɛlt ɪn ðə
hant ɪnstɛd əf ę̇ sɛptɚ | ðə hɛt wʌs dɛkǫreɪtəd wɪs ə kakt
hæt ænd andɚnit wʌs peɪntəd ɪn laːtʃ kɛrɛktɚz | dʒɛnɚrəl
wɔʃɪŋtən‖ ðɛr was æz juʒʊl ə kraʊd əbaʊt ðə dɔr | bʌt nan
ðæt rɪp rɪkəlɛktɪd‖ ðə vɛrɪ kɛrɛktɚ af ðə pipəl simd tʃeɪnʃt‖
ðɛr wɔʐ ə bɪʐɪ bʌslɪŋ toʊn əbaʊt ɪt | ɪnstɛd af ði əkastəmd
flɛm ænd draʊsɪ trænkwɪlɪtɪ | hi lʊkt ɪn veɪn fɔr ðə seɪtʃ
nɪkləs ɣedɚ wɪθ hɪs broᵊd feɪs | daḅəl tʃɪn ænd fɛr lɔŋ paɪp
ʌtɚrɪŋ klaʊts əf tǫbakǫ smok ɪnstɛd əf spitʃəz | ɔr væn
brʌməl ðə skuɫmæstɚ doʊlɪŋ fɔːθ ði kɒntɛnts af æn eɪnʃənt
njuspepɚ‖

31. ɪn pleɪs əv ðiz ę̇ liən biljus lʊkɪŋ fɛlǫ waz həræŋɪŋ
viəmɛntlɪ əbaʊt raɪts əv sitəzɛnz | ilɛkʃənz | bʌŋkɚz hɪl |

hiroz əv sɛvn̩tisɪks ænd ɑðə wɛrdz| wɪtʃ wɛr pəfɛkt
bæbəloʊnɪʃ ʒɑrgan tu ði bɪwɪldəd væn wɪŋkəl‖ ði æpiræns
əv rɪp| wɪð ɪz lɑ̃ŋ grɪzl̩d bird| hɪz rʌstɪ faʊlɪŋ pis| hɪz ɑnkuθ
drɛs ænd æn ɑrmɪ əv wɪmən ænd tʃɪldrn̩ æt hɪz hilz sun
æ̩træktəd ði æ̩tænʃən əv ði tævrən palətɪʃənz‖ ðe krɑʊdɪd
əraʊnd hɪm| arːŋ hɪm frɑm hɛd tu fut wɪð greɪt kjʊriasətɪ‖
ði ɔrətə bʌsl̩d ʌp tu hɪm ænd drɔɪŋ hɪm pɑrtlɪ əsaɪd ɪŋkwaɪrd
ɑn wɪtʃ saɪd i votəd‖ rɪp stɛrd ɪn veɪkənt strʊpɪdətɪ‖ ənɑðə
ʃɔːt bət bɪzɪ lɪtl̩ fɛlo̩ pʊld hɪm baɪ ðə ɑrm ænd raɪzɪŋ ɑn
tɪpto ɪŋkwaɪrd ɪn ɪz ir wɛðə i waz fɛdrəl ɔr dɛmo̩kræt‖

32. rɪp wɔz ikwɔlɪ at ə lɔs tu kɒmprihɛnd θi kwastʃən|
hwɛn e̩ nowɪŋ sɛlf ɪmpɔrtant oʊld dʒɛntl̩mɛn ɪn e̩ ʃɑrp
kɒkt hæt meɪd hɪz weɪ θru θi kraʊd| pʊtɪŋ θɛm tu Ɓaɪt n̩
lɛft az hi past and plantɪŋ hɪmsɛlf bifɔr βan wɪŋkəl wɪθ
wɔn ɑrm akɪmbo̩| ði ɔðə rɛstɪŋ ɔn hɪs keɪn| hɪs kin aɪs n̩d
ʃɑrp hat pɛnɪtreɪtɪŋ as ɪt wɛr intu hɪs vɛrɪ soʊl| dɪmandɪd
ɪn an ɔstir toʊn| hwɒt bƁɔt hɪm tu ði ilɛkʃən wɪθ e̩ gan an
hɪs ʃoʊldɚ and e̩ mɒb at hɪs hilz and hwɛðə hi mɛnt tu
bƁid e̩ Ɓaɪət ɪn ði βɪlɪdʒ‖ alas kraɪd Ɓip aːm e̩ puʷə kwaɪt
man| e̩ neɪtɪv əv ðɪs pleɪs and ə lɔjəl sabdʒɛkt əv ði kɪŋ‖
gad blɛs hɪm‖ hɪə e̩ dʒɛnɛ̩ral ʃaʊt bɜst frɔm ði baɪstandəz|
e̩ tɔrɪ| e̩ tɔrɪ| e̩ spaɪ| e̩ Ɓɛfjudʒi| hʌsl̩ him| e̩weɪ wɪθ
him‖

33. ɪt waz wɪð greɪt dɪfəkʌlti ðæt ðə sɛlf ɪmpɔrtənt mæn
ɪn ðə kakt hæt rɪstoʊrd ɔrdɚ| æn hævɪŋ e̩sjumd ə tɛnfoʊld
ɔstɪrətɪ əv braʊ| dɪmændəd əgɛn əv ðə ənfɔrtʃənət kʌlprɪt
hwɑt hi keɪm fɔr ænd hum hi wəz sikɪŋ‖ ðə por mæn
hʌmblɪ æ̩ʃʊrd hɪm ðæt hi mɛnt noʊ harm bʌt mirlɪ keɪm
ðɛr ɪn sɜtʃ əv sʌm əv hɪz neɪbɚz hu just tu kip abaʊt ðə
tævən‖ wɛl hu ar ðeɪ| neɪm ðəm‖ rɪp bɪθɔt hɪmsɛlf ə
moʊmənt ænd ɪnkwaɪrd| hwɛrz nɪkələs vɛdɚ‖ ðɛr wəz
saɪləns fɔr ə lɪtl̩ hwaɪl hwɛn æn oʊld mæn rɪplaɪd ɪn ə θɪn
paɪpɪŋ vɔɪs| nɪkələs vɛdɚ| waɪ hiz dɛd n̩ gon ðiz eɪtːin jɪrz‖
ðɛr wəz ə wʊdn̩ tumstoʊn ɪn ðə tʃɜtʃjard ðət just tu tɛl ɔl
əbaʊt hɪm| bʌt ðæts ratn̩ æn gon tu‖ hwɛrz bram dʌtʃɚ‖ oʊ
hi wɛnt ɔf æt ðə bəgɪnɪŋ əv ðə wɔr| sʌm seɪ hi wəz kɪld æt

ðə stɔrmɪŋ əv stounɪ pɔɪnt | ʌðɚz seɪ i̦ wəz draʊnd ɪn ə skwɔl
æt ðə fut əv æntəniz nouz‖ aɪ dount nou | hi nɛvɚ keɪm
bæk əgæn‖

34. hwɛəz væn brʌməl ðə skulmæstə‖ hi wɛnt ɔf tu ðə
wɔːz tu | waz ə greɪt məlɪʃə dʒɛnrəl æn ɪz nau ɪn kangrəs‖
rɪps haːt daːd əweɪ ət hɪrɪŋ əv ðiz sæd tʒeɪndʒəz ɪn hɪz houm
æn frɛnz æn faɪnɪŋ hɪmsɛəf ðʌs əloun ɪn ðə wɜld‖ ɛvrɪ
ænsə pʌzəld hɪm tu | baɪ tritɪŋ əv sʌtʃ i̦nɔːməs læpsɪz əv
taəm æn əv mætəz hwɪtʃ hi kud nat əndəstænd | wɔː |
kangrəs | stounɪ pɔɪnt | hi hæd nou kɜɪdʒ tu æsk aftə morəv
ɪz frɛnz | bʌt kraɪd aut ɪn dɪspɛə | dʌz noubadɪ hɪr nou rɪp
væn wɪŋkəl‖ ou rɪp væn wɪŋkəl | ɛksleɪmd tu ɔr θri | ou tu bi
ʃuə | ðæts rɪp væn wɪŋkəl jandə | linɪŋ əgænst ə tri‖ rɪp lukt
æn bɪhɛld ə prɪsaəs kæntəpaːt əv hɪmsɛəf æz hi wɛnt ʌp ðə
mæuntn̦z | əpɛrənʔlɪ æz leɪzɪ æn sɜtənlɪ æz rægəd‖

35. ðə pur fɛlo̦ wəz nɛu kɒmplitlɪ kɒnfɛundɪd‖ hi dɛutɪd
hɪz ɛun aɪdantɪtɪ and hwɛðə hi wɒz hɪmsɛlf ɔɹ ɛnaðə man‖
ɛn θi mɪdst ɒv hɪz biwɪldəmənt | ðə man ɪn ði kɒkt hat
dɪmandɪd hu hi wɒz and hwɒt wɒs hɪz neim‖ gɒd nɛuz |
ɛksleɪmd hi | at hɪz wɪts ɛnd | aɪm nɒt maɪsɛlf | aɪm sʌmbɒdɪ
ɛls | ðats mi jɒndə | nɛu ðats sʌbɒdɪ ɛls gɒt ɪntu maɪ ʃuz |
aɪ wɒz maɪsɛlf last naɪt hwɛn aɪ fɛl əslip ɒn ði mauntɪn and
ðeɪv tʃeɪndʒd maɪ gan | and ɛvrɪθɪŋ tʃeɪndʒd | and aɪm
tʃeɪndʒd and aɪ kantːɛl hwɒts maɪ neɪm ɔr hu aɪ æm‖ ðə
beɪstandəz bigan nɛu tu luk at ɪtʃ ʌðə | nɒd | wɪŋk sɪgnɪfɪ-
kəntlɪ and tɛp ðɛə fɪngəz ̦ageɪnst ðɛə foəhɛdz‖ ðɛə wɒz
e̦ hwɪspə ɔlso̦ əbɛut sɪkjurɪŋ ði gan and kipɪŋ ði ɛuld fɛlo̦
frɒm durɪŋ mɪstʃɪf | at ðə vɛr̆ɪ səgdʒɛstʃən ɒv hwɪtʃ ði sɛlf
impɔːtn̦t man ɪn ði kakt hat ritaɪəd wɪð səm prisɪpɪteɪʃən‖

36. æt ðɪs krɪtəkəl moumənt ə frɛʃ kamlɪ wumən prɛst
θru ðə θrɔŋ tu gɛt ə pip ət ðə greɪ bɪrdəd mæn‖ ʃi hæd ə
tʃʌbɪ tʃaɪld ɪn hɚ armz hwɪtʃ | fraɪtn̦d baɪ hɪz luks bəgæn tu
kraɪ‖ hʌʃ rɪp | kraɪd ʃi | hʌʃ ju lɪtl̦ ful | ðə ould mæn wount
hɜt ju‖ ðə neɪm əv ðə tʃaɪd | ðə ɛr əv ðə mʌðɚ | ðə toun əv
hɜ vɔɪs | ɔl əweɪkəŋd ə treɪn əv rɛkɒlɛktʃənz ɪn ɪz maɪnd‖

hwɑt ɪz jʊr neɪm| maɪ gʊd wʊmən| æskt rɪp‖ dʒudɪθ
gɑrdnɚ‖ ænd jʊr fɑðəz neɪm‖ ɑː pʊr mæn| rɪp væn wɪŋkəl
wɑz hɪz neɪm| bʌt ɪt ɪz twɛntɪ jɪrz sɪnˈs hi wɛnt əweɪ wɪθ
hɪz dɔg ṇd gʌn ænd hæz nɛvə bɪn hɜrd əv sɪnˈs| hɪz dɔg
keɪm hoʊm wɪðaʊt hɪm| bʌt hwɛðɚ hi ʃɑt hɪmsɛlf| ɔr wəz
kærɪd əweɪ baɪ ðə ɪndiənz| noʊbɑdɪ kæn tɛl‖ aɪ wəz ðɛn
bʌt ə lɪtḷ gɜrl‖

37. rɪp hæḍ bʌt wʌn mor kwɛstʃən tu æsk bʌt hi pʊt ɪt ɪn ə
fɔltɚɪŋ vɔɪs‖ hwɛrz jor mʌḍə| oʊ ʃi had daɪd bʌt ẹ ʃɔrt taɪm
sɪnts| ʃi broʊk ə blʌd vɛsəl ɪn ẹ fɪt əv pæʃən æt ẹ nju
ɪŋglənd pɛdlɚ‖ ðɛr waz ẹ drɑp əv kʌmfort æt list ɪn ðɪs
ɪntɛlədʒənts‖ ði hanẹst man kʊd kənteɪn hɪmsɛlf noʊ
lɔŋgɚ| hi kɒt hɪẓ dɔtɚ ɪn hɪs ɑrmz‖ aɪ æm jur fɑðɚ| kraɪd hi|
oʊld rɪp væn wɪŋkəl naʊ‖ dʌẓ noʊbɑdɪ noʊ por rɪp væn wɪŋ-
kəl‖ ɔl stʊd æmeɪzd ʌntɪl æn oʊld wʊmən| tɑtɚɪŋ aʊt frəm
əmʌŋ ðə kraʊd| pʊt hɚ hænd tu hɚ braʊ æn| pɪrɪŋ ʌndɚ ɪt
æt hɪẓ feɪs for ẹ moʊmənt| ɛkskleɪmd| ʃor ẹnʌf ɪt ɪẓ rɪp
væn wɪŋkəl| ɪt ɪẓ hɪmsɛlf‖ wɛlkəm hoʊm əgɛn oʊld neɪbɚ‖
hwɛr hæv ju bɪn ðɪs twɛntɪ lɔŋ yɪrz‖

38. rɪps stɔrɪ wəz sun toʊld fɚ ðə hoʊl twɛntɪ jɪrz hæd bɛn
tu hɪm æz bʌt wʌn naɪt‖ ðə neɪbɚz stɜrd hwɛn ðeɪ hɜrd ɪt|
sʌm wɜr sin tu wɪŋk æt ɪtʃ ʌðɚ æn pʊt ðɛr tʌŋz ɪn ðɛr tʃiks| ṇ
ðə sɛlf ɪmpɔrtənt mæn ɪn ðə kɑkt hæt hu| hwɛn ðə əlɑrm
wəz oʊvɚ| hæd rɪtɜrnd tu ðə fild| skrud daʊn ðə kɔrnɚz əv
ɪz maʊθ æn ʃʊk ɪz hɛd| əpan hwɪtʃ ðɛr wəz ə dʒɛnɚəl ʃeɪkɪŋ
əv hɛdz θruaʊt ðə əsɛmblɪdʒ‖ ɪt wəz dịtɜrmṇd haʊɛvɚ tu
teɪk ðə ọpɪnjən əv oʊl pitɚ vændɚdɔŋk hu wəz sin sloʊlɪ
ædvænsɪŋ ʌp ðə roʊd‖ hi wəz ə dɪsɛndənt əv ðə hɪstɔrịən
əv ðæt neɪm| hu rout wʌn əv ðə ɜrlịəst ækaunts əv ðə prɑ-
vɪnˈs‖ pitɚ wəz ðə moʊst eɪntʃənt ɪnhæbətənt əv ðə vɪlɪdʒ
ænd wɛl vɜrst ɪn ɔl əv ðə wʌndɚful ịvɛnts ṇ trədɪʃənz əv ðə
neɪbɚhʊd‖

39. hi rɛkəlɛktɪd rɪp æt wʌnts ən kərabəreɪtịd hɪz stɔrɪ ɪn
ðə moʊst sætịsfæktɚɪ mænɚ‖ hi əʃord ðə kʌmpənị ðæt ɪt
wəz ə fækt hændɪd daʊn frəm ɪz ænsɛstɚ| ðə hɪstɔrịən|

ðæt ðə kætskɪl mauntənz hæd ɔlwɪz bɪn hɔntəd baɪ streɪndʒ
biɪŋz‖ ðæt ɪt wəz əfɜmd ðæt ðə greɪt hɛnrɪk hʌdsən| ðə
fɜst dɪskʌvə̣ə əv ðə rɪvə æn kʌntrɪ kɛpt ə kaɪnd əv vɪdʒəl
ɛvrɪ twɛntɪ jɪrz wɪθ hɪz kru əv ðə hæf mun| bɪŋ pəmɪṭɪd ɪn
ðɪs weɪ tu rɪvɪzɪt ðə sin əv hɪz ɛntəpraɪz æn kip ə gɑrdiən
aɪ əpɑn ðə rɪvə æn ðə greɪt sɪtɪ kɔld baɪ ɪz neɪm‖ ðæt hɪz
fɑdə həd wʌnts sin ðɛm ɪn ðɛr ould dʌtʃ drɛsɪz pleɪ:ŋ æt
naɪnpɪnz ɪn ə hɑlọ əv ðə mauntṇz æn ðæt hi hɪmsɛlf hæd
hɜd| wʌn sʌmə æftənun| ðə saund əv ðɛr bɔlz laɪk dɪstənt
pilz əv θʌndə‖

40. tu meɪk ə lɔŋ storɪ ʃɔ:t| ðə kʌmpənɪ brouk ʌp æn
rɪtɜɪnd tu ðə mor ɪmpɔ:tənt kənsɜɪnz əv ðə i̦lɛkʃənz‖ rɪps
dɔtə tuk hɪm tu lɪv wɪθ hɜ| ʃi hæd ə snʌg wɛlfɜnɪʃt haus æn
ə staut tʃɪrɪ fɔ:mə fɔrə hʌzbənd hum rɪp rɛkəlɛktɪd fọ wʌn
əv ðə ʌɪtʃənz ðæt just tu klaɪm əpɔn hɪz bæk‖ æz tu rɪps
sʌn æn ɛr| hi wəz ɪmplɔɪd tə wʌɪk əpɔn ðə fɔªm| bʌt
ivɪnst ən hərɛdɪtɛrɪ dɪspọzɪʃən tu ætɛn tu ɛnɪθɪŋ ɛls bʌt ɪz
bɪznəs‖ rɪp nau rɪzumd ɪz oul wɔks ṇ hæbɪts| hi sun faund
mɛnɪ əv hɪz fɔ:mə krouniz| ðou ɔl rædə wɜɪs fọ ðə wɛr æn
tɛr əv taɪm æn pəfɜɪd meɪkɪŋ frɛnz əmʌŋ ðə raɪzɪŋ dʒɛnə-
reɪʃən| wɪθ hum hi sun gru ɪntu greɪt feɪvə‖ hævɪŋ nʌθɪŋ
tu du æt houm| æn biɪŋ əraɪvd æt ðæt hæpɪ eɪdʒ hwɛn ə mæn
kən bi aɪdḷ wɪθ ɪmpjunətɪ| hi tuk hɪz pleɪs wʌnts mor æt ðə
bɛntʃ æt ðə ɪn doª| æn wəz rɛvərənst æz wʌn əv ðə peɪ-
triɑ:ks əv ðə vɪlɪdʒ æn ə krɑnəkələ əv ðə oul taɪmz bifoª
ðə wɔ:‖

4I. ɪt wəz sʌm taɪm bɪfor hi kud gɪt ɪntə də rɛgələ træk
əv gɑsəp ə kud bi meɪd tə kʌmprəhɪnd də streɪndʒ əvɪnts
ðət həd teɪkən pleɪs dɜɪŋ ɪz tɔrpə‖ hau ðæt dɛr həd bɪn ə
rɛvəluʃənɛrɪ wɔr| ðæt də kʌntrɪ həd troun ɔf də jouk əv
ɪŋlən æn dæt ɪnstɪd əv biɪŋ ə sʌbdʒɪk əv ɪz mædʒəstɪ dʒɔrdʒ
də θɜd| hi wəz nau ə fri sɪtəzən əv ðə junaɪtəd steɪts‖ rɪp ɪn
fæk wəz nou pɑlətɪʃən| də tʃeɪndʒəz ɪn steɪt ṇ ɛmpairz
meɪd bət lɪtḷ ɪmprɛʃən ɔn ɪm| bʌt ðɛr wəz wʌn spiʃiz əv
dɛspətɪzəm ʌndə wɪtʃ hi əd ground æn dæt wəz pɛtəkout

gʌvmənt‖ hæpəlɪ dæt wəz æt ən ɛn| hi əd gɑt ɪz nɛk aʊt əv
də joʊk əv mætrəmoʊni æn kʊd goʊ ɪn n̩ aʊt wɛnɛvɚ hi
plizd wɪðaʊt drɛdɪŋ də tɪrənɪ əv deɪm væn wɪŋkəl‖ wɛnɛvɚ
hɝ neɪm wəz mɪntʃənd haʊɛvɚ| hi ʃʊk ɪz hɛd| ʃrʌgd ɪz
ʃoʊldɚ æn kæst ʌp ɪz aɪz wɪtʃ maɪt pæs ɪðɚ æz ən ɛksprɛʃən
əv rɛzɪgneɪʃən æt hɪz feɪt ɚ dʒɔɪ æt hɪz dɪlɪvɚənᵗs‖

Appendix E   Selected Bibliography

Bender, James F., and Fields, Victor A., *Phonetic Readings in American Speech*, New York, Pitman Publishing Corp., 1939.

Block, Bernard, and Trager, George L., *Outline of Linguistic Analysis*, Baltimore, Linguistic Society of America, 1942.

Bloomfield, Leonard, *Language*, New York, Henry Holt and Company, 1933.

Fairbanks, Grant, *Voice and Articulation Drillbook*, 2nd ed., New York, Harper & Brothers, 1960.

Fletcher, Harvey, *Speech and Hearing in Communication*, New York, D. Van Nostrand Co., 1953.

Gleason, H. A., *An Introduction to Descriptive Linguistics*, New York, Henry Holt and Company, 1955.

Heffner, R. M., *General Phonetics*, Madison, University of Wisconsin Press, 1949.

James, Lloyd A., *Historical Introduction to French Phonetics*, London, University of London Press, 1929.

Jespersen, Otto, *Growth and Structure of the English Language*, New York, D. Appleton-Century Company, 1923.

Jones, Daniel, *An English Pronouncing Dictionary*, 4th ed., New York, E. P. Dutton & Co., 1937.

Jones, Daniel, *An Outline of English Phonetics*, 6th ed., New York, E. P. Dutton & Co., 1940.

Jones, Daniel, *Phonetic Transcriptions of English Prose*, 2nd ed., Oxford, The Clarendon Press, 1927.

Jones, Daniel, *The Pronunciation of English*, 3rd ed., Cambridge, Cambridge University Press, 1950.

Joos, Martin, *Acoustic Phonetics* (*Language Monographs* No. 23, Vol. 24, No. 2), Baltimore, Linguistic Society of America, 1948.

Kaiser, L. (ed.), *Manual of Phonetics*, Amsterdam, North Holland Publishing Co., 1957.

Kenyon, John S., *American Pronunciation*, 10th ed., rev., Ann Arbor, George Wahr, 1950.

Kenyon, John S., and Knott, Thomas A., *A Pronouncing Dictionary of American English*, Springfield (Mass.), G. & C. Merriam Co., 1953.

Meader, C. L., and Muyskens, J. H., *Handbook of Biolinguistics*, Part I, Toledo, Herbert C. Weller, 1950.

Noel-Armfield, G., *General Phonetics*, Cambridge (England), W. Heffer and Sons, 1931.

Pike, Kenneth, *Phonemics*, Ann Arbor, University of Michigan Press, 1947.

Pike, Kenneth, *Phonetics*, Ann Arbor, University of Michigan Press, 1943.

Potter, Ralph K., Kopp, George A., and Green, Harriett C., *Visible Speech*, New York, D. Van Nostrand Co., 1947.

Russell, G. Oscar, *Speech and Voice*, New York, The Macmillan Company, 1931.

Stetson, Raymond H., *Bases of Phonology*, Oberlin, Oberlin College Press, 1945.

Stetson, Raymond H., *Motor Phonetics, A Study of Speech Movements in Action*, Amsterdam, North Holland Publishing Co., 1951.

Sweet, Henry, *A Primer of Phonetics*, 3rd ed., London, Oxford University Press, 1906.

Sweet, Henry, *The Sounds of English*, Oxford, The Clarendon Press, 1908.

Thomas, Charles K., *An Introduction to the Phonetics of American English*, New York, Ronald Press, 1947.

Van Riper, Charles, and Irwin, John V., *Voice and Articulation*, Englewood Cliffs (N.J.), Prentice-Hall, Inc., 1958.

Van Riper, Charles, and Smith, Dorothy E., *Introduction to General American Phonetics*, New York, Harper & Brothers, 1954.

Ward, Ida C., *The Phonetics of English*, New York, D. Appleton-Century Company, 1929.

Wise, Claude Merton, *Applied Phonetics*, Englewood Cliffs (N.J.), Prentice-Hall Inc., 1957.

Zipf, George K., *The Psycho-Biology of Language*, Boston, Houghton Mifflin Company, 1935.

INDEXES

Index

Phonetic symbols are indexed separately at the end of this section.
See Index to Phonetic Symbols.

Index to Phonetic Symbols

Since there are as yet no conventions governing the indexing of phonetic symbols it was necessary to adopt an arbitrary method. Phonetic symbols are listed below under the same headings and in the same order in which they appear in the complete Table of Phonetic Symbols on page 209. The numbering of the symbols in the index corresponds with that in the table. All symbols used in the text are listed below with appropriate page references. Certain symbols that are used infrequently do not appear in the Table of Phonetic Symbols. These are listed in this index following the sound to which they are most closely related. They are not numbered.

431